D0908813

PARK MANAGEMENT

PARK MANAGEMENT

Grant W. Sharpe
Professor, College of Forest Resources
University of Washington
Seattle, Washington

Charles H. Odegaard
Deputy Regional Director, Northwest Region
National Park Service
Seattle, Washington

Wenonah Finch Sharpe
Contributing Editor
Seattle, Washington

JOHN WILEY & SONS
New York • Chichester • Brisbane • Toronto • Singapore

Library of Congress Cataloging in Publication Data:

Sharpe, Grant William.
   Park management

   Includes index.
   1. Parks—Mangement. I. Odegaard, Charles H.
  II. Sharpe, Wenonah, III. Title.
SB481.S5 1983   333.78'3'068   82-23860
ISBN 0-471-02153-9

Printed in the United States of America

10 9 8 7 6 5 4 3 2 1

FOREWORD

The decade of the 1980s is already requiring renewed understanding and fresh approaches as we strive to serve a most dynamic and challenging society. These challenges are particularly felt by park and outdoor recreation professionals and volunteers. We are all faced with a rapidly changing social environment: the age level of visitors, two working parents, single-parent families, and the marked changes in general life-style—these factors affect not only park visitors but also park employees.

This textbook, after glancing at the past, addresses the present and the future. It provides the most up-to-date and practical methods for dealing with a number of situations existing in resource-oriented park and recreation management at all levels.

Park Management brings to us the collective knowledge and experience of a professor at a major university (who, together with his wife, has published widely in the resource field) and a nationally recognized park administrator. I recommend it both to students (as a great learning opportunity) and to present practitioners (as a refresher with new approaches and ideas).

Russell E. Dickenson
Director
National Park Service
U.S. Department of the Interior
Washington, DC

PREFACE

This book is intended for individuals who want to continue to learn about park management, whether they are university students or park professionals. Although parks are managed by all levels of government as well as by private and commercial interests, this book generally uses the midlevel of governmental service—the state or province—as the example of a managing agency. It explores the various responsibilities of managers, regardless of the identity of the managing agency, and outlines inherent problems. Practical suggestions for alleviating certain difficulties are offered. The general structure of agencies and their place in the governmental framework, along with the relationship of the manager to the agency, are dealt with in various ways. The nettle of politics is firmly grasped and examined.

The Introduction opens Part One, providing a historical overview of the resource parks movement and the genesis of park management.

Part Two pertains to the administration of parks, mainly at the agency level. "What does a manager need to know about this?" has been the criterion.

Part Three deals with the resource, from planning and acquisition, facilities, and maintenance, to the environmental impacts of use on an already established park.

Problems arising in the course of controlling use while protecting the resource are dealt with in Part Four. The information and interpretation required to encourage intelligent use, and a review of the precautions and provisions necessary to keep visitors safe and reasonably content, make up the remaining chapters of this section.

Finally, "A day in the life of a park manager" is presented in an effort to give students a realistic look at life on the job. The trials, challenges, and rewards of this job; what it can mean in terms of lifestyle; and the joys and problems of living in a park setting are discussed in Part Five.

We hope our diverse and recent practical experience, guided by research findings and joined with the experience and counsel of others in the field, will prove valuable to all individuals who are responsible for park visitors, lands, and facilities.

GRANT W. SHARPE
CHARLES H. ODEGAARD
WENONAH FINCH SHARPE

ACKNOWLEDGMENTS

We appreciate the information, chapter review, or other assistance provided by the following individuals: James Agee, Richard Ambrose, Joseph J. Bannon, Kay Boulter, Gordon A. Bradley, Patty Brown, Sandy Bryson, Philip J. Burke, James Butler, Steve Butterworth, Rosemary L. Cameron, Don Campbell, Peter Celms, William Dakken, Dave DeFoer, Russell E. Dickenson, Gaylord Donnelley, Harold J. Dyer, Robert O. Espeseth, Yvonne Ferrell, William Fessel, Mark Forbes, W. E. Foster, Donald M. Fuquay, Gail Gensler, Gaston Germain, Stanley Gessel, Joe W. Gillings, John Greg, Terry Hall, Nixon Handy, James Harris, Ted Heart, Norman Johnson, Richard K. Johnston, Kerry R. Joy, Robert Kline, R. J. Lampard, Paul Larson, Robert C. Lee, D. W. Lowell, Elaine Lowlor, Joe Massett, James G. McCurdy, Alan Mebane, John B. Morrell, Malachy Murphy, Peter Murphy, Gordon Nelson, Mike Nickerson, Bernard L. Orell, J. T. Page, Brian Patton, Stewart Pickford, Robert A. Pike, John Pinkerton, Russell Plaeger, Jim Presser, David W. Reynolds, Richard Rollins, B. H. Rucker, Alan Runte, Sharon Saare, J. M. Sands, Alan Schmierer, H. Douglas Sessoms, P. E. Skydt, Ezra Stotland, Ange Taylor, Robert F. Toalson, Ben Twight, Richard A. Vickers, Mary Vocelka, J. B. L. Walter, James Webster, Charles W. Wendt, Helen White, Wilfred Woods, James J. Yamashiro, Robert J. Zasoski, and Marsha Zlotolow.

We should also like to thank the many agencies in Canada and the United States who responded to our call for black-and-white photographs. These agencies are recognized under each photo used. We also thank Lynn J. Mills for the use of her tree hazard illustration in Chapter 4.

We are very grateful to the many men and women in our park management courses who read various drafts of these chapters. Their written comments contributed greatly to this book.

We owe special recognition to David C. Martin who served as a reviewer of the entire manuscript and offered many valuable suggestions.

We express our gratitude to those who have graciously allowed us to use quotations from their pages and publications.

G.W.S.
C.H.O.
W.F.S.

CONTENTS

PART ONE

INTRODUCTION

CHAPTER ONE

AN OVERVIEW OF PARK MANAGEMENT

The demand on outdoor recreation areas of every kind has been increasing faster than the supply of lands and facilities needed to accommodate the demand. Budgets are perennially inadequate and recreation land acquisition invariably falls short of projected needs. Because of the tremendous visitation since World War II there has also been severe impact on existing park facilities and lands. As these lands deteriorate and visitor numbers multiply, the role of the park manager becomes more complicated and challenging. This chapter, after outlining the purview of this text, discusses the issues and events that created and still affect parks and their management.

CATEGORIES OF RECREATION

At the outset, a delineation of the management area addressed by this text is essential in order to avoid confusion. There are many ways of defining the various types of park-based recreation found in the United States and Canada today. The two categories found most useful for the purpose of this text are as follows.

Activity-Oriented, Structured Recreation

Usually restricted to urban or suburban parks, this type of recreation depends on certain constructed features or facilities such as playfields, courts, and swimming pools. Activities here, in-cluding the various sports, games, arts and crafts, generally require the supervisory or instructional services of park personnel. Even where they do not, there is an organized formal structure imposed by the facility and shored up by rules that characterize this kind of recreation. Tennis and pitching horseshoes are two examples. Some spectator sports like baseball and soccer at the amateur level may also be accommodated in these park areas.

Resource-oriented, Nonstructured Recreation

Here the dependence is on a particular natural resource or a combination of natural resources that may include lakes, rivers, seashores, meadows, deserts, forests, hills, and mountains. These land or water resources shape the type of activities pursued, and park personnel function primarily as safety-conscious hosts and guardian of the resources. The term *outdoor recreation* is commonly used to describe this category also. In contrast to the urban or suburban location of game- or activity-oriented recreation, this sort of recreation is most often found at some distance from population concentrations. There are exceptions. Some cities are fortunate in having large, relatively unmodified areas in which resource-oriented recreation can be enjoyed, and in recent years resource-oriented areas such as small wood lots or linear parks along streams have become available at short distances from population concentrations. These may contain a mix of structured and nonstructured recreation.

Of course there are "activities" connected with resource-oriented outdoor recreation. The word "activity" is confusing in this sense, so careful note should be made of the above classification.

Having stated these qualifications then, this text is concerned with nonstructured resource-oriented outdoor recreation management. The lands that support these pursuits are usually managed by some government agency—metropolitan, county, provincial, state, or federal. The areas dealt with here may be known as beaches, reserves, scenic areas, forests, refuges, natural areas, parks, cultural sites, or recreation areas. Although the management objectives of these areas will vary with the designation and with the agency, our treatment of objectives will be general enough to be applicable to most areas with little translation of details. We hope, however, that the discussions will be specific enough to engender both interest and recognition of the reader's own situation in the examples.

Figure 1-1 shows the various U.S. agencies that manage lands supporting recreation. The Areas, Facilities, and Activities categories furnish a useful breakdown of recreation providers for the student new to the maze. Recreation opportunities supplied by the private sector are also included here.[15]

WHAT IS A PARK?

The word *park* eludes precise definition since it has so many uses. Perhaps this is just as well, since the intent here is to use it as a generic term for all recreational lands. Historically a park has meant such diverse things as a place to bathe, a hunting preserve, formal gardens, places decorated with statuary, tournament grounds, estates of the nobility, exhibition sites for theaters and other entertainment, a common space for tethering livestock prior to bartering, and, in some countries, places for exercising, walking, and na-

ture viewing. Today we even hear the word used in connection with nonrecreation uses. A cluster of industrial buildings may be called an industrial park, or a cemetery may be referred to as a mortuary park. For our purposes here we will think of parks as *tracts of tax-supported land and water, established primarily for the benefit and enjoyment of people and maintained essentially for outdoor recreation activities.* As noted above, these recreation activities may take place on a refuge, a forest, or on land classified in some other way, but for purposes of this text all these lands will be termed *parks.*

Parks per se come in all shapes and sizes and may have a variety of names. What is known as a park in one area may be known as a recreation area in another. Other names include the more formal designations of parkways, monuments, and historic sites. There are also designations for parks indicating the governmental level administering the area, such as neighborhood and community parks, metropolitan parks, county parks, regional parks, state and provincial parks, interstate parks, national-capital parks, national parks, and international parks.

Sometimes the names of parks indicate their predominant purpose, feature, or activity, such as wildlife parks, forest parks, motorcycle parks, tree farm parks, boat parks, ball parks, and museum parks.

The use of the word park can also be a policy matter. The Forest Service, in the U.S. Department of Agriculture, administers over 186 million acres of land and annually provides over 170 million visitors with recreational opportunities, but it does not use the word *park.* It uses terms such as *forest campgrounds* and *natural areas,* but these areas could also be defined as parks, and indeed, this is what they are frequently called by visitors.

The focus of this text will be on the middle level—state (United States) or provincial (Canada) parks—as representative of the spectrum from national to local. *Visitors* and *users* are the terms we will use for the people who come to

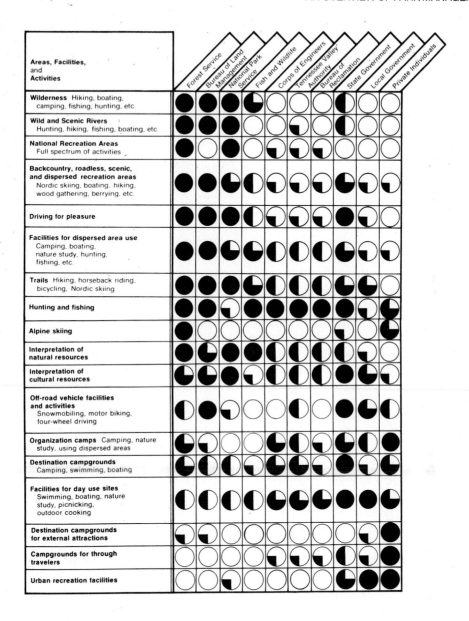

Key:

Very high　High　Medium　Low　Very low

Fig. 1-1. This Forest Service chart provides a handy reference for recreation involvement by federal agencies, state and local government, and the private sector, across the spectrum of recreation offerings.[15] (Courtesy USDA Forest Service.)

parks, who own them, love them, and who if not carefully directed, might well destroy them. To avoid confusion, throughout this book we will use the term *manager* to represent the person in charge of the park, thus making it synonymous with *superintendent, supervisor, chief, director, ranger, warden,* or *park attendant,* any of which might be the title of the person managing the area.

Parks, especially national parks, might have begun as a means of preventing private exploitation, or as a way of showing our European critics that we in North America had a sense of national identity, or in order to lure tourists. But the rationale behind the creation and maintenance of parks represents more than the sum of these now. Parks, especially if the entire spectrum of resource-oriented park lands is considered, have become the focus of even more complicated desires and emotions. Yet we cannot exactly define these desires and emotions. People have to define the word "park" for themselves. Some might say "parks are everybody's place in the country." Others might say "parks are everybody's inheritance of unspoiled frontier land," or "they're a place to get away from it all." Playgrounds, sanctuaries, historical repositories—the evolving park idea encompasses and exceeds all of these definitions. Of course the definition depends on the size and location of the park too. Local picnicking grounds evoke a different response than does Yellowstone or Banff. On the other hand if a family lives near a national park they regard it as a "local park" no matter what its claim to fame.

Sometimes harassed park managers feel the whole country is spending its leisure in their over-burdened parks. Fortunately, this is not true. Many individuals enjoy their leisure hours in city landscapes or pursuing indoor hobbies, at back-yard cookouts, or on weekends at the family cabin. Some spend a week at camp or recreate by driving in the family car, or participate in sports events. Many people travel, either here or abroad, without ever stopping at a park.

Many others are involved in recreation programs on private land or in some vehicle-oriented activity that does not involve public lands. Fortunately for our outdoor recreation lands, not everyone is interested in utilizing them for leisure pursuits. Enough people do, however, to cause a general sense of swamping.

WHAT IS PARK MANAGEMENT?

Management of a resource-oriented park means, among other things, providing safe access for visitors while protecting the resource. Of course complete protection would necessitate a no-entry policy, while unrestricted entry would render protection virtually impossible. Are we then forced to view the park manager's responsibilities as impossible to fulfill? Not impossible, but always difficult. The manager's job tends to focus on conflict and to become an arena for the testing of limits by users. Driving a pair of spirited horses pulling in opposite directions might describe the task. As a matter of fact, the word "manager" comes to us from the Italian for "hand," and originally referred to the training and handling of horses.

The manager must be able to drive this fractious team of access and protection with a firm hand. Some visitors will occasionally want to use parks in a way that depreciates values, others will sometimes urge protection to a degree that preempts legitimate use. Policies on use and protection may be formulated at agency headquarters, but the manager is on site, and must interpret and enforce the policies to the sometimes puzzled, frequently indignant, owners of the area— the taxpaying public.

Origins Of Park Management—The Yosemite Grant

Resource-oriented park management in North America may be said to be well over 100 years old, if we equate its genesis with the establishment of the Yosemite Grant in California in

Fig. 1-2. A horse stage on the Wawona Road, with Yosemite Valley in the background. (Photo courtesy Yosemite National Park Research Library.)

1864. This grant included two separate areas in the Sierra: Yosemite Valley with its spectacular granite walls and waterfalls (Fig. 1-2) and the nearby Mariposa Grove of Big Trees. The grant was the first extensive area of spectacular wild land to be set aside primarily for the nonutilitarian purpose of public recreation.[1,3] Although the land initially was in federal ownership, the federal government had no policy on outdoor recreation matters. Protection of the land was transferred to the state of California and it thus became the first state park in the United States.

Senator John Conness of California secured passage of a bill that gave these areas federal recognition "and charged the State of California with the responsibility of preserving and presenting the natural wonders of Yosemite."[12]

Frederick Law Olmsted, of Central Park fame, who was working at the time near the Valley, was made chairman of the board of commissioners of the Yosemite Grant. He also acted as the grant's first administrative officer.[12]

Yosemite's primary difficulty was with inholdings. Although the settlers fought the issue all the way to the federal Supreme Court, the actions of the commissioners were upheld, and a precedent was set of precluding inholdings wherever possible. The task of dealing with inholders was given to Galen Clark, who had immigrated from eastern Canada. After a variety of jobs (farmer, storekeeper, cabinet maker, miner, hunter, hotel keeper, and surveyor), he homesteaded in Yosemite Valley in 1856 at the age of 42. Clark was an early champion of preservation of the Valley and was appointed first Guardian of the Yosemite Grant in 1866 (Fig. 1-3).[13]

All did not go smoothly however. The twin problems of inadequate funds and ill-defined policy made intelligent management of the two units impossible. The California state legislature voted little money for facilities, and often neglected to appropriate Galen Clark's $500 per year salary.[13] When in 1890 a larger encompassing area was set aside as Yosemite National Park, local communities complained bitterly as many new inholdings were created.

In 1891 the U.S. Cavalry was dispatched to protect the newly established Yosemite National

Fig. 1-3. Galen Clark became the first civilian Guardian of the Yosemite Grant, in 1866. Note the Yosemite Falls in the background. (Photo courtesy Yosemite National Park Research Library.)

Park lands and also the two units of Yosemite Grant (Fig. 1-4).* The troopers left each year in November and returned in May, and were replaced during the winter by civilian rangers, such as Galen Clark. By 1914, with the permanent withdrawal of the cavalry, the park rangers or guardians carried on the work of protection.

The State of California did not relinquish the grant lands until 1906, at which time they reverted to federal ownership and were incorporated into the surrounding Yosemite National Park.

Yellowstone National Park

The first direct federal involvement in the management of a park in the United States came about after the establishment of Yellowstone National Park in 1872. Starting around 1800 and continuing over a period of 70 years, fur traders and other parties noted the unusual beauties of the Yellowstone region. Before a bill could be passed, however, Congress had to be convinced that this area of public domain did *not* have economic potential (mineral wealth), and therefore could be set aside as a "public park or pleasuring ground" because of its geysers, waterfalls, and canyons. There was no state to turn the land over to in this instance, since the area was in Wyoming Territory. The chief proponents of the park were for the most part residents of the territory of Montana, who wanted legislation formed along the lines of the Yosemite Grant. Unfortunately for them, the land lay in Wyoming Territory rather than in Montana Territory and was thus politically out of reach. Also, since California was having difficulty administering the Yosemite Grant, Congress was convinced federal ownership was best for Yellowstone. The bill was similar in many respects to the bill establishing the Yosemite Grant. Beyond the fact of setting the land aside, the legislation left much to be desired.

The area was reserved "from settlement, occupance, or sale under the laws of the United States, and dedicated and set apart as a public

---

*Early park management problems included dealing with the ranchers outside the park. Cavalry troopers sought to keep livestock out of the new park. Ranchers had been running cattle and sheep there since pioneer days, but the park was now off limits to them. When the first intruders were taken into custody it was found there were no penalties for the infraction of park rules. The herder was escorted to a remote section of the park and released; his sheep at the same time were driven out of the park in the opposite direction. By the time the herder located his animals the losses were as great or greater than if a fine had been imposed. After several years of this practice the ranchers learned to keep their stock out of the park.[12]

Fig. 1-4.   In 1899, F Troop, U.S. Cavalry, posed on and in front of the Fallen Monarch, in Mariposa Grove. (Photo courtesy Yosemite National Park Research Library.)

park or pleasuring-ground for the benefit and enjoyment of the people.'' The regulations provided ''for the preservation from injury or spoilation of all timber, mineral deposits, natural curiosities, or wonders within the said park, and their retention in their natural condition'' (S. 392 42nd Congress). What more was needed to protect this area? Money for management and enforcement was completely lacking. Unfortunately, in order to get the park established, a promise had to be made not to ask Congress for an appropriation for several years.[3] Thus the park was established without funds to protect it (a dilemma that was to become familiar in parks throughout all agency levels); but at least a *beginning had been made*. Despite its shortcomings, the Yellowstone act would one day become a matter of great pride for Americans and would, in time, bring international acclaim and respect to the United States for its leadership in establishing the world's first national park.

In order for Yellowstone to gain recognition as an area worthy of park status at a time when ex-

ploitation was unquestioned on frontier lands, its splendors were well-publicized in newspapers and magazines. Consequently, soon after it was established, tourists began to arrive. Trappers and hunters, who had been using the area for some time, continued their activities since no management restraints were possible. Hide hunters, in one spring, killed an estimated 4000 elk in the vicinity of Mammoth Hot Springs[3] (Fig.1-5). Bison heads, selling for $300 each, were being collected in the park. Early park visitors, not able to bring all their supplies with them, were living off the land by shooting wildlife.[14] Stagecoaches were held up by robbers. Cattle were driven into the park for grazing. Hostile native Americans were encountered by visitors. Squatters moved into the park to stake claims and take up residence. Soap was poured into the thermal springs to induce eruptions. Anything loose was thrown into the geysers to see how high it would be ejected during the next eruption. Specimens of encrustations from the hot springs and geysers were collected for souve-

Fig. 1-5. Hide hunters are seen here skinning out elk in Yellowstone National Park, about 1897. The activity was legal at that time. (Photo courtesy Yellowstone National Park.)

nirs. As the Suttons point out, an entire geyser cone was removed and placed on display at the Smithsonian Institution in Washington, D.C.[14] This recital of some early problems points up the fact that management problems have been with us from the very beginning.

The first superintendent of Yellowstone, Nathaniel P. Langford, was expected to work without a salary. Without funds there was no staff, and without a staff, no law enforcement. Mr. Langford was forced to be an absentee administrator, visiting the park only twice during his five years as superintendent.[3] In any case, what could one man do to oversee and protect a mountainous area three times the size of the state of Rhode Island?

Visitors came from the start, although there was no official provision made for them. The scenic wonders and the chance to bathe in the hot mineral springs (then thought medically effective for a variety of ailments) drew as many as 500 people a year between 1873 and 1877 (Fig. 1-6).

Private enterprise, never lacking, provided rough transportation and spartan quarters, but Langford refused to grant road or concession rights until Congress could be induced to establish concession and entry policies. Vandalism in the hot springs areas, as well as the slaughter of game, drew comment. The publicity thus generated exerted pressure on Congress.

An appropriation of $10,000 was made in 1877, but to do what? Park personnel had no authority to make an arrest, to punish, or to evict anyone from the park.[14] The Interior Department eventually asked the Wyoming Territory to administer the area, but this arrangement was short lived. Pressures to build a railroad across the park and to open the park to mining increased. Wildlife and timber were still being removed illegally from the park. Later superintendents abused their office by attempting to obtain land within the park for their own use. The funds that were appropriated could not begin to solve the problems of distance, isolation,

Fig. 1-6. The women seem to be thoroughly enjoying the opportunity to wade in the pool of Great Fountain Geyser, while the man seems more conscious of the camera. 1908. (Photo courtesy Yellowstone National Park.)

and established use. In desperation the Secretary of the Interior turned to the Secretary of War for assistance.

The park was finally placed under the protection of the U.S. Army, whose cavalrymen and engineers successfully managed it from 1885 to 1918, putting an end to the illegal uses of the park.[6] The soldiers were able to enforce the regulations and alter the habits of those who felt free to take what they wanted. "They removed squatters, captured lawbreakers, hunted down poachers, burned illegal dwellings, and confiscated guns and traps."[14] As noted earlier, Yosemite's problems with illegal grazing and poaching were cured in the same manner. It took "armed intervention" to establish park management in our first national parks.

We have seen that Yellowstone did indeed become the first national park. Before leaving the subject, however, we should make one thing clear. It is now generally accepted that the Yosemite Grant played a very strong role in the establishment of Yellowstone National Park. Yosemite's publicity and fame paved the way for public acceptance for later setting aside large ar-

eas of federal land for public recreation. We see this in the following account by Russell. Although Yellowstone became the first national park by name, the "... concept that there are places of beauty and of scientific interest which individuals or private interests have no right to appropriate onto themselves, began with the establishment of the Yosemite Grant."[11]

Huth echoed these sentiments when he wrote: "Contrary to the usual assumption, it was not the establishment of Yellowstone but rather the setting apart of Yosemite which was preeminent in the basic conditioning of opinion. Yosemite is the point of departure from which a new idea began to gain momentum."[4]

The Canadian Experience

Following the reservation of Yosemite as a state Park and Yellowstone as a national park the movement spread rapidly. In 1887 Canada established a 10 square mile reserve around the hot springs at Banff in Alberta, and named it Rocky Mountain National Park (later renamed Banff National Park).

The creation of a scenic recreational area and a wildlife sanctuary at Banff was not envisioned by the Canadian government at that time. Parliament and party leaders saw the hot mineral springs of Banff as a source of revenue, a way to bring passengers onto the Canadian Pacific Railway (CPR). The CPR was deeply involved with the Canadian government in attempting to tie the western lands to the rest of Canada and there was a strong desire to make the mountain section "pay." The prospect of a drawing card rivaling the Hot Springs Reserve in Arkansas was welcome in both quarters. The Banff mineral springs, discovered by railway employees, was envisioned as a national sanitorium, of "sanitary advantage" to the public for treatment of rheumatism and other ailments. Traveling to spas was an occupation of the wealthy in North America and Europe, and this area seemed a good location for a CPR hotel. Like the United States, Canada sought a way to keep tourist dollars at home and perhaps to attract some from the United States and abroad.

Although during the debates some mention was made of the spectacular scenery surrounding Banff townsite, the original reserve was only 10 acres, and even this acreage had to be wrested away from railway employees who had already set up a bath business. The early bathhouse facilities (Fig. 1-7) were soon upgraded; hotels were built at several of the hot springs. Unlike the Yellowstone experience, where the concentration of natural wonders and scenery stimulated Congress to set aside a large area to make sure nothing was overlooked, the Banff reserve was originally conceived of as a whistle-stop spa, with the surrounding ranges left out because they might well contain valuable mineral resources. Yellowstone had the advantage of an aura of mystery. Banff was not as remote as Yellowstone; railway survey and construction had already taken place.

In time, as people and governments began to realize what riches the area's scenic and recreational resources represented, most of the Rocky Mountains' upper reaches were designated as Dominion Parks, becoming Jasper, Yoho, Glacier, Mount Revelstoke, Kootenay, and Waterton Lakes. To this day, as in the Rocky Mountain parks of the United States, the absence of supporting lowlands is sorely felt, and the discontin-

Fig. 1-7. Souvenir tent and bath facilities in 1888 at the Upper Hot Springs in Rocky Mountain National Park, Alberta. The park's name was changed to Banff National Park in 1930. (Photo by Boorne and May, courtesy Archives of the Canadian Rockies, Peter and Catharine Whyte Foundation.)

Fig. 1-8. The town of Banff in 1887, with Cascade Mountain beyond. (Photo courtesy Archives of the Canadian Rockies, Peter and Catharine Whyte Foundation.)

uity of ecological areas presents many management problems, especially with wildlife.

Townsites within the parks were provided for from the start, thus launching the federal government on an endless sea of troubles as it attempted to regulate the activities of the inhabitants (Fig. 1-8).

Hunting, mining, grazing, and logging (Fig. 1-9) were accepted uses well into the twentieth century. Canadian officials closely watched the contest in the United States between utilitarian conservationists, represented by Gifford Pinchot, and the aesthetic preservationists, represented by John Muir. Those in power saw Pinchot's ideas as closer to their own. No Canadian equivalent of Muir rose up, no northern transcendentalism nurtured possessive feelings about wild lands at this time. The small numbers of people and the vastness of the land must have seemed protection enough.

Park Expansion Continues

By the turn of the century, there were five national parks in the United States: Yellowstone, Sequoia, General Grant (later incorporated into Kings Canyon), Yosemite (which surrounded the

Fig. 1-9. An 1890 log run just above Bow Falls, in what today is known as Banff National Park. Presently, natural resource exploitation is not permitted in Canada's national parks. (Photo by John Woodruff, courtesy Archives of the Canadian Rockies, Peter and Catharine Whyte Foundation.)

state-controlled Yosemite Grant), and Mount Rainier. Reserves were also being established throughout the world in South America, Africa, and Australia. Most had problems like those encountered in Yellowstone; indeed, some areas of the world still encounter similar difficulties in park establishment and subsequent management.

In the early years of this century park expansion continued at the federal level in both the United States and Canada. The areas being set aside were, for the most part, large nationally significant areas possessing features that, it was felt, held interest for people nationwide, and perhaps even internationally.

Canada was the first to set up a government organization devoted solely to the management and development of parks through the institution of its Parks Branch in 1911.[2] The U.S. National Park Service was established in 1916. These bureaus helped establish federal area standards and began the encoding of park management guidelines.

Although several states had begun state park systems by the early part of the present century, only wealthier states could participate. Thus park expansion at the national level continued to be important. Soon after the establishment of the U.S. National Park Service in 1916 there was a flurry of park proposals. States not represented wanted their potential park lands to receive national recognition. Most did not possess the outstanding attractions required for national park status, and to have included them would have lessened the value of the total system. On the other hand, many of the areas did contain features worthy of protection, or suitable for inclusion in a state park system. Unfortunately, not every state had such a park system. To stimulate interest in preserving these areas and other areas at the state level, Stephen T. Mather, the first director of the National Park Service, convened a group in 1921, known as the National Conference on State Parks, to discuss state park system expansion. The idea was well received, and today

all 50 states have state park systems under many kinds of administrative structures. In all there are approximately 4000 individual state parks in the United States, plus many types of state areas in categories such as state forests, wildlife refuges, and historical sites administered by other state agencies.

In Canada provincial cooperation with federal authorities in the matter of national parks was not fully achieved until 1930. Provinces were jealous of their considerable powers and did not wish to see mineral and water resources within national park boundaries denied them. Many of the original national parks were created prior to the western territories being granted provincial status. However, until 1930, the federal government retained jurisdiction over the natural resources of the railway belt extending from Manitoba through British Columbia, and thus was free to create national parks within this area even after provincial status was established.[9] Just as in the United States, the eastern part of the country where most of the population was concentrated lacked proportional national park acreage.

Canadians cannot be accused of being unmindful of the claims of extractive industries, utilities, or business enterprises on their natural resources. Yet lands for provincial parks, admittedly not always well protected from entry for certain national or provincial purposes, were set aside.

Ontario was the first province to develop its own park system with the establishment of Niagara Falls Provincial Park in 1888, and Algonquin Provincial Park in 1893. The rationale for this latter reserve stressed maintenance of water supply, the desirability of government-regulated logging, wildlife protection, and the potential for hotel and cottage-style vacationing. In 1894 Rondeau Provincial Park was established—a comparatively small area—close to population centers.[7] Until the 1950s, provincial parks were viewed as financial liabilities and few were established.[8] In 1980, Ontario had 127 operational parks, a considerable growth over 25 years.[10]

EARLY PARK MANAGERS

A problem facing early park management was a lack of qualified personnel. There were no college-trained people in the beginning years of park management.The early rangers or wardens were adventurous types who were often products of the local mining or logging camp, and who could survive in isolated areas. Many of these men worked winters in the parks during the years the Army was still in charge, as the troops were not always kept there at that season. From this group there developed a cadre of very dedicated, capable people who undertook the job of protecting the resource from outside exploitation.

Later rangers, wardens, and managers obtained their positions by various means, including political appointments made by local congressmen and other politicians. "Who do you know?" was sometimes more important than "what do you know?" In some agencies, every time there was a change of political administration, there was a change of park personnel from the director down to the stable boy. In time park employees were hired from civil service rosters and this aspect of the political spoils system came to a halt, or was at least alleviated. On the other hand, present civil service standards are such that people with no natural resources background can often qualify.

In the Canadian parks, the regulations as amended in 1909 made provision for the appointment of game guardians. This was the genesis of the Park Warden Service.[5]

The university graduate entering park work today comes into a system that has gone through many years of adjustment. When the first college-trained people vied for park jobs and were successful in landing them, they were looked on with suspicion as "babes-in-the-woods," and had to prove themselves capable of handling the challenge.

Persons today attempting to rise within the park organization will find it difficult if not impossible to compete with university-trained park managers. The complexities of the job require a thorough understanding of the principles of managing *people having fun*. It is no longer enough to simply protect the resource. Today's managers must also provide visitors the opportunity to enjoy themselves without undue hazard and without serious annoyance to other visitors.

REFERENCES

General References

Chubb, Michael and Holly R. Chubb. 1981. *One Third of Our Time? An Introduction to Recreation Behavior and Resources*. Wiley. New York.

Ise, John. 1961. *Our National Park Policy: A Critical History*. Johns Hopkins University Press. Baltimore, MD.

Nelson, J. G. and R. C. Scace, Eds. 1968. *The Canadian National Parks: Today and Tomorrow*. Proceedings of a conference organized by the National and Provincial Parks Association of Canada and the University of Calgary.

Righter, Robert W. 1979. *The National Parks of the American West*. The Forum Press. St. Louis, MO.

Runte, Alfred. 1979. *National Parks: The American Experience*. University of Nebraska. Lincoln.

Wirth, Conrad L. 1980. *Parks, Politics, and the People*. University of Oklahoma Press. Norman.

References Cited

1. Brockman, C. Frank and Lawrence C. Merriam, Jr. 1979. *Recreational Use of Wild Lands* (3rd ed.). McGraw-Hill, New York.
2. Foster, Janet. 1978. *Working For Wildlife; The Beginning of Preservation in Canada*. University of Toronto Press.
3. Haines, Aubrey L. 1977. *The Yellowstone Story. A History of Our First National*

Park. Volumes One and Two. Yellowstone Library and Museum Association in Cooperation with Colorado Associated University Press.

4. Huth, Hans. 1948. *Yosemite: The Story of an Idea*. Sierra Club Bulletin. San Francisco, CA.
5. Lothian, W. F. 1977. *A History of Canada's National Parks*. Volume II. Parks Canada. Department of Indian and Northern Affairs. Ottawa.
6. McCall, Joseph R. and Virginia N. McCall. 1977. *Outdoor Recreation: Forest, Park and Wilderness*. Bruce. Beverly Hills, CA.
7. Morrison, Ken. 1979. "The Evolution of the Ontario Provincial Park System," *Park News*. National and Provincial Park Association of Canada. Toronto.
8. Nash, Roderick. 1968. "Wilderness and Man in North America." From J. G. Nelson and R. C. Scace (eds.), *The Canadian National Parks: Today and Tomorrow*. The University of Calgary Press. Alberta.
9. Nicol, J. I. 1968. "The National Parks Movement in Canada." From J. G. Nelson and R. C. Scace (eds.), *The Canadian National Parks: Today and Tomorrow*. The University of Calgary Press. Alberta.
10. Rollins, Richard. Personal communication. Lakehead University, Thunder Bay, Ontario.
11. Russell, Carl P. 1964. "Birth of the National Park Idea." From *Yosemite: Saga of a Century*. Yosemite Natural History Association.
12. Russell, Carl Parcher. 1947. *One Hundred Years in Yosemite*. University of California Press. Berkeley.
13. Sargent, Shirley. 1964. "Galen Clark—Mr. Yosemite." From *Yosemite: Saga of a Century*. Yosemite Natural History Association.
14. Sutton, Ann and Myron. 1972. *Yellowstone, A Century of the Wilderness Idea*. The Macmillan Company. New York.
15. USDA Forest Service. 1978. *The Forest Service Roles in Outdoor Recreation*. Program Aid 1205.

PART
TWO

ADMINISTRATION

CHAPTER TWO

STRUCTURE

The seven chapters in this section deal with the various facets of park management and agency operation as seen from the head office, for the most part.

How do park agencies set themselves up to deal with visitors and their diversified activities? How do park agencies best organize to provide their traditional public service while staying on top of changes, conflicts, new demands, budget strictures, and resource deterioration? How does the agency organize to serve individual parks? This chapter will point out some guidelines for effective park agency structures, as well as attempt to locate the park agency within other governmental structures.

It is important to be aware of the total organizational structure within which an agency is located and also of the variety of structural forms agencies can assume. Such knowledge enables one to see how an agency relates to other agencies within government, and also gives a clearer picture of how and why government agencies operate the way they do. This overview should assist newcomers to gear themselves to the pace of agency operations.

Most individual parks within a given agency are too small to have an elaborate organizational hierarchy. They are usually limited to a manager, an assistant manager, and a few seasonal park aides. For this reason, they will not have organizational line charts, or exhaustive areas-of-responsibility lists. Yet at some level of park management, be it state or provincial, or federal, the more complex structures are to be found. To clar-

ify the sometimes confusing subject, it will be dealt with under two basic headings: the park agency among others in government, and the organization of the park agency itself.

THE PARK AGENCY AMONG THE OTHERS IN GOVERNMENT

The purposes of most governmental agencies are commonly categorized into *service* and *regulatory*. *Service* denotes an agency that provides assistance to others, as for instance, a park agency, which offers many services to the recreating public, such as operating a swimming beach or picnic area, or providing interpretation. The term *regulatory* implies that judgments are passed or permits issued, such as, in the case of some parks, for the operation of a ski lift. Therefore, all parks come under the category of service agencies, with some having certain regulatory powers also.

Additionally, all levels of government—local, provincial or state, and federal—have legislative, judicial, and executive functions. The executive branch, and the park agency within it, will be regularly and directly affected by the legislative branch, which probably will have a *parks committee*. It will be the business of that parks committee to know a considerable amount about the controlling agency. This same parks committee will want to personally view areas, facilities, and programs. They will want to know the park director, and to be informed on the agency's long-range plans.

The legislator who chairs the parks committee will play a vital role in the consideration of ordinances and legislation affecting the agency, its operations, holdings and employees. The chair will also have contact either directly or indirectly with the powerful legislative finance committee. Your agency will probably have a person whose responsibilities include working with that parks committee. This liaison is crucial to the success of an agency, so the person must be carefully chosen for depth of knowledge in both park and legislative matters and for an ability to communicate.

The chances are that the judicial aspect of your agency's governmental level will have little relationship to your agency. There might be occasional communications concerning the employment of offenders who will have the opportunity to complete some work time in a park. Generally speaking, however, direct park agency involvement with the judicial branch of government is rare.

Typical Executive Structure

The executive branch needs much greater discussion, as it is under its aegis that park agencies usually are found. Most park agencies are structured in one of the four following ways. These examples of park agency structure come from the county level. If the municipal level were used, the term "county executive" would be replaced by "mayor"; if state, by "governor"; if provincial, by "premier." The four examples include *self-taxing,* and a county executive operating under an *agency, superagency,* or *commission* form of structure.

1. *Self-taxing.* A board, consisting of 3 to 11 persons is elected by the voters, and possesses the legal authority to tax the property owners of the district. The board will be responsible directly to the voters who elect it. Normally the board will have some legislative authority and might even have some judicial responsibility. Usually the board will be nonpartisan. This body will engage a chief administrator whose title will be Director of Parks, or something similar.

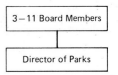

2. *County executive—agency.* The county executive appoints the Director of Parks for a specific term or perhaps for an unspecified term, which means this person serves until replaced. This agency administrator reports directly to the county executive. Generally speaking, under this set-up the agency will be more susceptible to partisan politics than in any other type of structure.

3. *County executive—superagency.* The county executive appoints the administrator of a superagency who appoints division

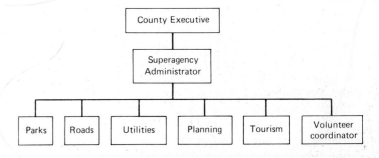

heads, probably with the approval of the county executive. In such instances the park organization is a division within a much larger agency and is at the same level as roads, utilities, and similar departments.

4. *County executive—commission.* The county executive appoints a commission of 3 to 11 members, usually for staggered terms. The commission hires an administrator whose term lasts as long as this person's actions meet with the approval of a majority of the commission members.

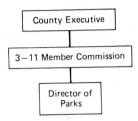

There are variations of these four basic structures, such as the incorporation of advisory committees, for instance. However, most county-level park agencies will fit into one of the above four hierarchies.

THE ORGANIZATION OF THE PARK AGENCY ITSELF

There are almost as many varieties of agency structures as there are agencies. Although there is no such thing as one best system, we consider certain factors vital to proper agency development: separation of the various fiscal functions in order to provide adequate controls, determining which activities need close daily supervision and which need only general guidelines, and the grouping of similar functions.

Internally, each agency groups its personnel into administration and operation. Many agencies also have a planning office. *Administration* (or administrative services) describes those functions that provide for the workings of the agency per se, such as payroll, personnel, or clerical; *op-*

erations is the name given to those actions necessary to fulfill the purpose of the agency for the park visitors, such as park management or ranger patrol; the planning division is usually placed in *resources development*, which covers those internal services necessary to chart a course of development, be it in land acquisition, area or facility planning, design and engineering, or determining future needs.

Organizational Style

Many park organizations still function on a traditional structured concept of administration. Large business organizations function very efficiently under these rather rigid approaches to administration. However, there has been an increasing trend within governmental organizations, particularly in public service and social agency programs, to adopt a personal, humanistic approach to administration by moving toward more casual superior-subordinate relationships. Within any organization there needs to be an awareness of the advantage of both the "formal" and "informal" structure.

The *formal* structure reflects the organizational chart and the subsequent policies and procedures while the *informal* recognizes that employees are better workers when they don't feel totally confined to small boxes and narrow lines on a chart. The chances are there will be elements of both approaches used at different times and modified versions of each at the same time. One must learn through observation what the mix is. Immediate subordinates, at any level of park administration, do not want to be bypassed on the chain of command when orders are given, nor do employees further down the line appreciate reprimands from those not listed as their superiors. Judgment in these matters is part of that complex of talents called "supervisory skills."

As a newcomer to an agency it would be best to show respectful deference to superiors and pleasant civility to subordinates until the tone of the organization can be sensed. It is preferable to err on the side of formality than to immediately assume a casual attitude.

Organizational Structure Development

The sequence of charts illustrated here relates directly to the size of an agency and the complexity of its responsibilities. When an agency is very small or limited in its scope, it is highly probable that all of the permanent full-time staff—two to four persons—will report to the chief administrator as in Figure 2-1(a).

As an organization grows, it is probable that the number of persons directly responsible to the administrator will increase until their daily supervision is too time consuming. Administrators will not be able to do a competent job if they have no time for public relations or for creative, holistic thinking. When this point of overload is reached, whether in an agency or in one of its larger units, a more complex model is needed, allowing for

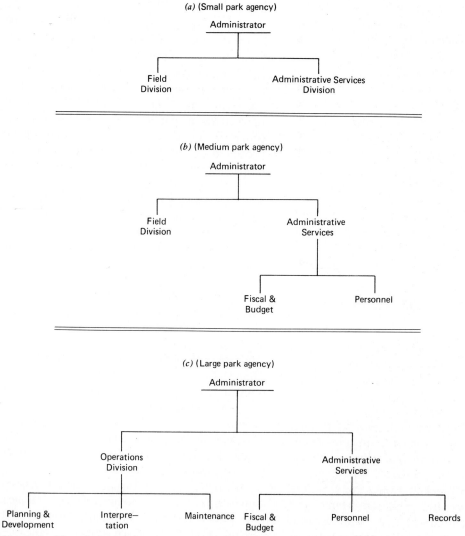

Fig. 2-1. The administrative structure for three different sizes of park agencies: (*a, b,* and *c*).

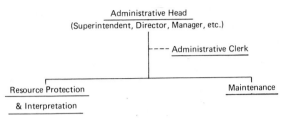

Fig. 2-2a. Examples of an organizational structure of a small park.

delegation of authority as in Figure 2-1 (b and c). This issue, often called *span of control*, will be covered more thoroughly later in this chapter.

The examples in Figure 2-1 are for a total agency and are therefore geared for top-level management, but the same concepts are true for an individual park. Although the park manager frequently will be the only year-round employee in a park and will fulfill all functions, in larger or more complex parks the staff will be increased and the division of authority will probably take place in a similar manner to the three parks illustrated in Figure 2-2 (a, b, and c).

Lines of Authority. It is important that there be clear lines of authority so all employees know not only for whom they work and who works for them, but who has the authority to make decisions and to discipline. An up-to-date organization line chart must be accessible to all, and a copy should be given new employees during orientation.

Organizational theory makes note of two types of job functions: staff and line (Fig. 2-3). *Staff functions* imply an advisory position to an executive, while *line functions* imply that employees have authority of command and carry out the tasks of the organization. Within the organizational structure, staff persons usually function in areas related to research, planning, and budgeting, and normally work directly with executives—as their "staff." They do not give orders or deal directly with personnel in lower line positions. Staff positions customarily branch horizontally on an organizational chart. Line positions are in a direct vertical line below the administrator, and it is from this that the name *line employee* comes.

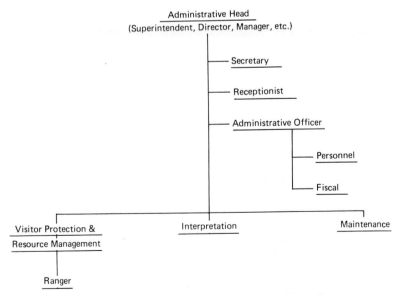

Fig. 2-2b. The organizational structure of a medium-size park.

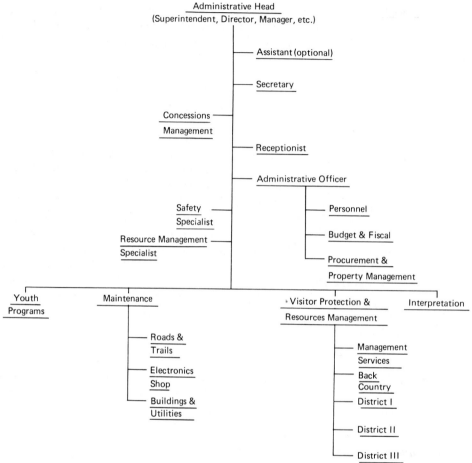

Fig. 2-2c. The organizational structure of a large park.

Delegation of Authority

To choose the right person, and to transfer to that person both the understanding of the task and the sense of responsibility for its execution is a primary function of an administrator.

One of the qualities I would certainly look for in an executive is whether he knows how to delegate properly. The inability to do this is, in my opinion (and in that of others I have talked with on this subject), one of the chief reasons executives fail. Another is their inability to make decisions effectively. [1]

As a basic principle, all authority should be delegated to the lowest possible level. What is the lowest possible level? How is it determined?

Within the functional areas, the authority level should be at the upward point where two or more functions or geographical areas are involved. For example, the park manager must have the authority to discipline all employees within the park, but the manager should not have the authority to purchase over and beyond the monetary limits set for all park managers; someone else has that duty since it encompasses another control center. The granting person should al-

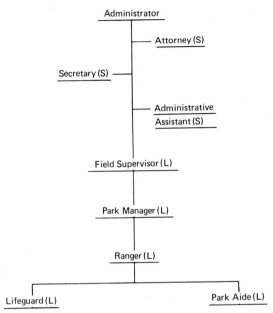

Administrator

Attorney (S)

Secretary (S)

Administrative Assistant (S)

Field Supervisor (L)

Park Manager (L)

Ranger (L)

Lifeguard (L)   Park Aide (L)

Fig. 2-3. A simplified chart showing the difference between staff (S) and line (L) functions.

ways seek to delegate the authority as far downward as possible, asking why any particular decision needs to be at a higher level.

> *There is one final test, in my opinion, by which it can be determined whether an executive is objective and consistent in the practice of delegating authority, and that is this: if he can turn a job over to a junior and then support him in carrying it out in a manner quite different from that which he himself would have chosen.*[2]

Although this sort of independence should be welcomed, supervisory control should be maintained. Remember, when something goes wrong or mistakes are made, much of the blame will travel back up to the administrator who delegated the abused authority.

Responsibility and Accountability. Authority is desired by almost everyone. What is not desired by many is responsibility and accountabil-ity. It is crucial to a smooth-running organization that with every authority delegated there is clearly understood responsibility and account-ability.

Within most governments the law will hold the chief executive responsible and accountable. Logically then, the chief executive retains all authority. In practice, however, this cannot and should not be. The chief executive *must* delegate authority, and a way must be found to place responsibility and accountability along with that delegation of authority.

For example, if the person in charge of fiscal matters is delegated the authority to approve purchases, then responsibility for keeping within the fiscal resources must also be delegated, and this person must be held accountable if the agency spends more than the budgeted amount. Park managers must operate under these same rules, both as delegatees of higher authority, and as delegators of authority themselves.

Areas of Responsibility Document. In order to make the responsibility/accountability concept work, there needs to be an *Areas of Responsibility* document. The document, as prepared at the agency headquarters level, should be indexed and contain data on all division heads, supervisors, assistants, and others serving in areas of responsibility. Similar documents should be prepared for regional personnel, as well as all park units, so that required tasks will be attended to on a routine basis. Only the agency level document is discussed here.

The lead section of the document should be an *agency organization chart* showing the specific job titles and who fills each position (Appendix A at the end of the chapter). In our example all names and secretarial staff have been omitted from the chart. Next comes the Areas of Responsibility section. Normally this would include the head of the agency and subordinates at least three ranks deep on the organization chart.

Following this comes the *responsibilities* themselves, dealt with under the following headings:

1. *Functional responsibilities.* The functions, such as Agency Newsletter, Concessions, or Training Programs, should be alphabetized. The name of the person responsible should be placed across from each function.
2. *Liaisons.* The agency should assign a liaison to oversee every organization, agency, or group in which the agency might have an interest or from which the agency might need help. Those organizations should be listed alphabetically followed by the name of the person acting as liaison.
3. *Committee membership.* For every appropriate committee there should be an individual noted as responsible for monitoring that committee and its workings, and who is delegated to attend their meetings. If the committee is the type for which the agency should have a liaison, the two responsibilities should be placed with the same person.
4. *Readings.* Pertinent magazines and periodicals should be read and the articles worthy of note referred to those who could most benefit by such follow-up reading. Therefore, each publication of interest should be listed, alphabetically, with the person responsible also noted. Whenever possible, the person who is the liaison with a particular organization should also be the person responsible for reading on the subjects concerned, or for reading that organization's newsletters or other publications.
5. *Cross-reference.* An administrator often will want to know all the responsibilities of a particular individual. To speed the process there should be a cross-referencing by name.

The compiling of an Areas of Responsibility document is of limited value if it is not utilized. Ideally, all of the employees of an agency should have a copy for reference. Should the agency not be able to provide sufficient copies, one should go to the receptionist, the mail room, each secretary, and all persons at the executive and supervisory levels. Each region, district, and individual park should have a copy also.

Coordination

Even with the delegation of responsibility and authority, even with the areas of responsibility documented, there will always be the need for active coordination of employee efforts.

Once an organization, be it an agency or a specific park, employs two or more persons, there will always be a tendency for overlapping, duplication, and voids. It is normal for persons within an agency to talk with each other and to be aware of each other's responsibilities. This is also desirable. At the same time, the involved individuals sometimes tend to get into each other's areas of responsibilities. Or, they bend over backward to avoid the potential conflicts, and thus create voids. One of the best methods of averting these situations is to hold regular staff meetings. Brief reports noting actions as they relate to previous goals and actions projected for the future will help employees to keep on course. At these meetings any overlaps or voids will probably be obvious and can be corrected.

Controls

Just as it is important to delegate authority, it is also vital to provide controls, which are procedures established to preclude improper or illegal acts. The *structure* of the agency should provide these controls. Two of the more critical areas needing controls are personnel and fiscal.

Personnel. Controls are needed to be sure the agency does not exceed its authorized level of employment, nor fail to act correctly in regard to other regulations affecting personnel, such as the Fair Labor Standards Act. Therefore, the person controlling these actions must be placed in a structure position high enough in the organization to ensure the needed authority (see Chief, Personnel and Training, Appendix A).

Fiscal. As previously noted, the agency and its units should be administratively structured so as to facilitate fiscal controls. For instance, the person responsible for authorizing the purchasing of goods (Supply Officer) should be placed under a different supervisor than the person paying the bills (Accounts Payable), as shown in Appendix A. This placement alleviates the chances of collusion. In the same manner, the office issuing to the parks the sequentially numbered camping tickets (Management Services) and the office receiving the camping fees (Budget and Finance) should be under different supervisors, as is also shown in Appendix A.

Span of Control

This is a term used to gauge the ability of an individual to *successfully* supervise the work of subordinates. For example, a regional supervisor has several area managers responsible to him or her. These area managers each have several park managers directly responsible to them (see Appendix A). As a continuation of this chain, which repeats the inherent relationship at each level, the park managers will exercise control over rangers or wardens, interpreters, aides, lifeguards, and maintenance personnel. If any of these supervisors must personally oversee too many people working at too complex a variety of tasks, control is lost—the span of control has been exceeded.

There is no established number of subordinate positions that a supervisor "should be able to handle." The span of control will depend primarily on the type of functions performed by subordinates. Some programs, by the distribution of the personnel involved, or by the nature of the tasks involved, require detailed discussion and supervision, while others need only policy direction and a feedback system. The ability of the supervisor is an issue here. Also, some employees require considerable supervision while others need almost none, so the individuals concerned play a part in determining the span. It follows that supervisors must have time to give each subordinate the administrative attention necessary for the development of a positive supervisor–subordinate relationship. This translates into time to stop and talk, to answer questions, and perhaps to listen to complaints and suggestions.

CONCLUSION

There is no one best method of developing agency structure just as there is no one best structure. However, the factors mentioned in this chapter should be taken into consideration when developing structure for any level of organization. Park managers should understand the reasoning that shapes their agency's structure and realize the implications of their position within it.

Changes should be weighed carefully. The organization of most agencies is rearranged far more often than it should be, and far more often than its personnel would like it to be, as those in authority strive to meet changing citizen needs, changing legislation, changing policy directives, and the increasing complexity of recreation management.

General References

Drucker, Peter F. 1974. *Management: Tasks, Responsibilities, Practices.* Harper & Row Publishers. New York.

Hjeltes, George and Jay S. Shiver. 1978. *Public Administration of Recreational Services.* Lea and Febiger. Philadelphia, PA.

Lutzen, Sidney G. and Edward H. Storey. 1973. *Managing Municipal Leisure Services.* International City Management Association. Washington, DC.

Rodney, Lynn S. and Robert F. Toalson. 1981. *Administration of Recreation, Parks, and Leisure Services* (2nd ed.). Wiley. New York.

REFERENCES

References Cited

1. Penney, J. C. as quoted by Raymond Dreyfus. 1964. *What a Supervisor Should Know About How to Delegate Effectively.* The Dartnell Corporation. Chicago, IL.
2. Randall, Clarence B. as quoted by Raymond Dreyfus. *What a Supervisor Should Know About How to Delegate Effectively.* The Dartnell Corporation. Chicago, IL.

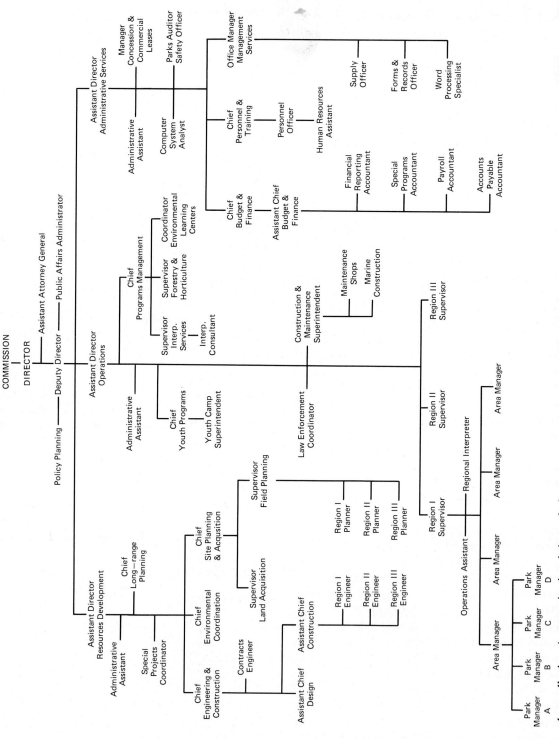

Appendix A. An organizational chart of a large park agency showing the line and staff relationship of the headquarters office. Note the three main divisions. Note also the relationship of Operations with the three regional offices, which supervise several area managers, who themselves supervise several parks. (Modified from Washington State Parks and Recreation Commission.)

CHAPTER THREE

POLICY

When it is determined that an agency shall conduct itself in a certain way concerning a specific action or a specific situation, the result is policy. Policies emanate from legislative actions, court rulings, and agency self-determination. In some instances, policies are a response to social or political change, reflecting new directions, while in other instances a policy may represent a bold thrust by a single person. In the broadest sense policies are guidelines for action. As guidelines, policies give a sense of direction, an assurance of consistency. They seek to ensure that the agency carries out its mandate properly.

Most policies stem from the legislative branch of whatever level of government the agency operates within. In recent years, as government has become more complex, the legislative branch has conveyed to the agency more and more rule-making authority within the rather broad policies it has formulated. As a practical matter this has resulted in a greater amount of policy being set by the agency or governmental executive. A recent example is the abolition of HCRS (Heritage Conservation and Recreation Service) by the U.S. Secretary of the Interior, James Watt.

The formulation of policy is a matter of critical concern. Policy must be broad enough to provide latitude for responsive decision making, yet be specific enough to enable the decision-makers to accurately reflect intent.

RESOURCE POLICY FORMULATION

In the nineteenth and early twentieth centuries a few perceptive North Americans, realizing that the natural resources of the new world, while vast, were not endless, became concerned with the stewardship of these resources. From Catlin, Olmstead, Muir, the two Roosevelts, Pinchot, Mather and Albright, to Hewitt, Udall, Laurance Rockefeller, McTaggert-Cowan, and Leopold, there has grown up on this continent a tradition of love and respect for the natural scene and of action to conserve its values.

These and other leaders have helped to hammer out basic resource policy on a continent where resources were originally so plentiful that waste of them became a habit, and careless exploitation was the norm. Not only that, but decade by decade, the expanding population achieved more leisure time, earned more discretionary income, and found better facilities for travel enjoyment. With these riches of leisure, money, and facilities, the public sought more and better opportunities to enjoy the outdoors. But the same public also put more demand on resources for competing uses. In the years following World War II, this process greatly accelerated as the United States and Canada, released from wartime restrictions, designated millions of acres for subdivisions, industrial sites, highways, schools, and airports. The resources for outdoor recreation—shoreline, green areas, open space, and unpolluted waters—diminished rapidly in the face of these demands. New policies were needed to mediate demands and control use. Certain policies were tried and found wanting in the face of this pressure. Some of these were modified, and, occasionally, new policies were instituted.

The attempt to formulate such policies resulted in legislative battles at the federal level. Administrative problems surfaced within the federal agencies responsible for providing opportunities for outdoor recreation. Similar problems were faced in many state and provincial capitals across the continent. In some instances, they stemmed from conflicts among different interests competing for use of the same resources. In others, it was the matter of responsibility—who should do the job, and who should pay the bill. Private landowners were faced with the problems caused by the public seeking recreation on their land. Each year the problems increased.

This concern over recreation was not new, only intensified. Several state legislatures had evidenced their interest in the establishment of local recreation lands when they created state park departments in the early 1900s. The National Park Service recognized the need for this other level of parks when, in 1921, Director Stephen Mather organized a state park conference. As noted in Chapter 1, the delegates to that conference formed the National Conference on State Parks, which today is known as the National Society for Park Resources, a branch of the National Recreation and Park Association. Although some state preserves had been established before the turn of the century, this first conference initiated organized review and cooperation on the matter of state parks.

In response to the unprecedented demands, state, provincial, county and local recreation areas of various kinds have also been pressed into service to fulfill the continent's growing recreational needs.

Laws Setting Major U.S. Resource and Recreational Policy

As previously indicated, policies emanate from several sources, one of which is the legislative process. In the United States, Congress has had much to do with formulating policy. The following is a list of major actions taken since the conservation and wise use of resources became a recognized issue. Some of these deal directly with land designation, use, and recreation policy, while others are only tangential to these issues. In other instances, these legislative actions set up bodies which in turn formulated policy.

1864   Yosemite Valley and the Mariposa Grove of Big Trees withdrawn from entry as public domain. Granted to state of California for management as a state park.

1872   Yellowstone National Park set aside. First U.S. National Park, and first instance of federal policy in the matter of outdoor recreation.

1891   Forest reserves established (later called national forests). Halted sales of certain public lands.

1906   Act for the Preservation of American Antiquities. Far-reaching legislation to set aside federal lands of historic or scientific interest. Still used by presidents to preserve public domain.

1916   National Park Service Act. Mather's and Albright's efforts to establish a separate parks bureau are successful.

1933   Establishment of Civilian Conservation Corps. Unemployed men doing conservation work on federal and state lands.

1935   National Park System Advisory Board established.

1937   Pittman-Robertson Act passed for the enhancement of wildlife.

1946   Bureau of Land Management established. Consolidated the General Land Office and Grazing Services. Manages large portion of public domain for purposes that include recreation.

1950   Dingell-Johnson Act passed for the enhancement of fisheries.

1958   Outdoor Recreation Resources Review Act(ORRRC). Created a commission to assess current and future recreation needs, and recommend policy. (Their work had such an impact on policy that considerably more about the commission is set forth later in this chapter.)

1960   U.S. Forest Service Multiple Use Sustained Yield Act. Officially acknowledged outdoor recreation as one of the purposes of national forests.

1963   Bureau of Outdoor Recreation Organic Act. Created to carry out salient points of ORRRC recommendations.

1964   Wilderness Act. Set aside certain federal lands capable of affording primitive experiences.

1964   Public Land Law Review Commission Act. Established to coordinate, where possible, the large body of legislation affecting management of public lands.

1964   Land and Water Conservation Fund Act. A means of stimulating federal and state outdoor planning, acquisition, and development by use of matching funds.

1965   National Park Service Concession Policy Act. Standardized policy.

1966   National Historic Preservation Act. Established a new program to identify and preserve historical sites and structures.

1968   Wild & Scenic Rivers Act. Provided for designation and safeguards for wild and scenic rivers to preserve these threatened environments.

1968   National Trails System Act. Designated Appalachian and Pacific Crest National Scenic Trails as initial units of a national system of trails at all levels of government.

1969   National Environmental Policy Act. Established policy on environment, the Council on Environmental Quality, and requirement for an environmental impact statement.

1970   Volunteers in the Parks Program Act (VIP). Encouraged citizens to contribute their time and skills.

1974   Forest and Rangelands Renewable Resources Planning Act. Provided for long-term planning thus permitting better-informed choices.

1975   Eastern Wilderness Act. Designated 16 national forest areas as part of Wilderness System, even though not free of human alteration or not of standard size.

1975   Amended Federal Aid Highway Act. Authorized lake access and bikeways.

1976   Railroad Revitalization and Regulatory Reform Act. Authorized 90 percent federal grants to enable state and local governments to plan, acquire and develop recreation facilities on abandoned railroad rights-of-way.

1976   Coastal Zone Management Act amendments. Established new program of grants to acquire coastal areas.

1976   Land and Water Conservation Fund and Historic Preservation Act amendments. Increased amount of funds for federal and state agencies under these two bills.

1976   Tax Reform Act. Provided tax incentives for preservation of historical structures.

1976   Federal Land Policy Management Act. Public outdoor recreation must be considered as a use for public lands.

1977   Surface Mining and Reclamation Act. Many changes required, giving impetus to recreation in mining areas.

1977   Youth Employment and Demonstration Projects Act. Established YACC on year-round basis to aid parks, forests and recreation areas.

1977 Food and Agriculture Act. Authorized payments to private land owners who allow certain recreational uses by the public.

1978 Heritage Conservation and Recreation Service (HCRS) created to identify, evaluate, and encourage protection of the nation's natural and historic resources, and plan and fund recreation programs. Assumed most of the functions of the former Bureau of Outdoor Recreation, the office of Archeology and Historic Preservation, and the Natural Landmarks program.

1978 Endangered American Wilderness Act. Designated 1.3 million acres in 10 western states as part of National Wilderness Preservation System.

1978 Comprehensive Employment Training Act amendments (CETA). Provided funds for employees in recreation and other areas.

1978 National Energy Conservation Policy Act. Included studies of off-highway recreation vehicles and bicycle transportation facilities.

1979 Archaeological Resources Protection Act. Established process providing for excavation and protection of the resource.

1980 National Wild and Scenic River System. Added 13 wild rivers to system.

1981 Heritage Conservation and Recreation Service (HCRS) abolished. Most duties transferred to the National Park Service.

Other Policy Sources

Policy also emanates from executive actions, other than those taken by a president to generate or veto legislation. From time to time presidents have appointed committees to study recreation issues. Sometimes policy decisions emerged from these sessions and were expressed through legislation and agency action. In other instances, the political climate was not right, and the findings of such bodies went largely unheeded.

Another source of influence on policy is professional groups, such as the Society of American Foresters, or the National Recreation and Park Association, both of which have committees on policy. The various citizen conservation and environmental groups, such as the Sierra Club or the Izaak Walton League, also affect policy by support or rejection of certain measures. Recently some of these groups have combined to block proposed actions through litigation.

The Outdoor Recreation Resources Review Commission. By 1958 Congress had decided that an intensive nationwide study of outdoor recreation should be made. The authorizing act, Public Law 85-470, set forth the mission for the Outdoor Recreation Resources Review Commission (ORRRC). It had essentially three purposes: to determine the outdoor recreation wants and needs of the American people now and what they would be in the years 1976 and 2000, to determine the recreation resources of the nation available to satisfy those needs now and in the years 1976 and 2000, and to determine what policies or programs should be recommended to ensure that the needs of the present and the future are adequately and efficiently met.[1]

This study was made by the ORRRC, a group composed of members of Congress, citizens, and employees who produced a report containing 27 documents, summarized in a single report entitled "Outdoor Recreation for America."

Some of the findings were as follows.

1. That the simple activities are the most popular.
2. That outdoor opportunities are most urgently needed near metropolitan areas.
3. That although across the country considerable land is now available for outdoor recreation, it does not effectively meet the need.

4. That money is needed.
5. That outdoor recreation is often compatible with other resource uses.
6. That water is a focal point of outdoor recreation.
7. That outdoor recreation brings about economic benefits.
8. That outdoor recreation is a major leisure-time activity, and it is growing in importance.
9. That more needs to be known about the values of outdoor recreation.

The national outdoor recreation policy that evolved from the ORRRC study was that: *It shall be the national policy through the conservation and wise use of resources, to preserve, develop and make accessible to all American people such quantity and quality of outdoor recreation as will be necessary and desirable for individual enjoyment and to assure the physical, cultural, and spiritual benefits of outdoor recreation.* [1]

Implementation. This policy has required the cooperative participation of all levels of government and private enterprise. In some aspects of the program government action was required; in others, the private sector has been better equipped to do the job.

Federal. Generally speaking, it seems that the federal government is best equipped to (1) preserve scenic areas, natural wonders, primitive areas, and historic sites of national significance, (2) manage federal lands for the broadest possible recreation benefit consistent with other essential uses, (3) cooperate with the states through technical and financial assistance, (4) promote interstate arrangements, including federal participation where necessary, and (5) assume vigorous cooperative leadership in a nationwide recreation effort. [1]

It is difficult, given the widely divergent entities involved, to fix areas of responsibility for states, counties, and municipalities. However, most park practitioners would concur with the following statements as to which level of government was best equipped to handle certain areas of responsibility.

Provinces and states. (1) Preserve scenic areas, natural wonders, primitive areas, and historic sites of provincial and state significance or regional significance if that region covers two or more governmental authorities. (2) Manage provincial or state lands for the broadest possible recreation benefit consistent with other essential uses. (3) Cooperate with the federal government for technical and financial assistance and in comprehensive provincial or state and national planning. (4) Promote intergovernmental arrangements. (5) Provide consultation service. (6) Provide strong cooperative leadership.

Counties and municipalities. (1) Acquire and develop areas strategically located to best serve the citizens of the governmental jurisdiction involved. (2) Provide program leadership to aid area citizens in learning recreation skills. (3) Cooperate with other agencies and other levels of government.

POLICY DEVELOPMENT AND CHANGE

Only the head of an agency should have the authority to issue policies. This does not imply that only the head should suggest or be involved in the development of policies—far from it. Policies should be the result of much coordinated thinking. This should involve all agency personnel. All relevant data should be made available to the policy maker along with pertinent observations. The wise policy maker will solicit this input (Fig. 3-1).

One of the most difficult aspects of policy formulation is trying to predict the future. There are multiple variables affecting the implementation of policy. Outcomes may be quite different than what was intended. Wengert stated it this way:

The decision-maker is, in short, acting under conditions of uncertainty, created in part by

Fig. 3-1. Two park agency administrators inspect, observe, and question, gathering information that will affect policy decisions. Lake Samish Park, Whatcom County Parks, Washington. (Photo by Grant W. Sharpe.)

limitations of knowledge, in part by limitations of time, and in part by limitations of techniques. Problem-identification and problem-solution in the area of resource policy can obviously be improved by use of planning techniques—by logical analysis and rational calculation. But planning should never be confused with certitude. Rational techniques for identifying resource problems and preparing proposed solutions cannot assure correct answers, but must deal in terms of approximations and probabilities. The technique used may represent the highest level of rationality; it may be mathematically precise. But the non-rational and irrational aspects of human behavior must also be included as a part of the matrix from which policy decisions will flow. [2]

New developments arise both from the public with its new vehicles and outdoor recreation needs, and from government itself as legislation is passed that either centrally or peripherally affects recreation areas. These events will require adaptation of existing policies or the develop-

ment of new ones. It is important that policy adherence be one of the checkpoints in supervision, not only to assure compliance with guidelines, but also in order to recognize the discrepancies that indicate the need for revision or new policy.

A Case in Point—Beach Driving in Washington State

Note that *politics* is very much a part of the formulation of policy. The following case history shows how changing use of a resource called for political decisions as well as policy formulation, and outlines the part played in this formulation by agencies, executives, legislators, the public, and the courts.

The state of Washington has 3740 km (2337 mi) of marine shoreline of which 250 km (157 mi) front directly on the Pacific Ocean. This frontage has varied topography, consisting of both low-bank sandy beaches and high-bluff outcroppings. The beach itself varies in width from zero to approximately 1.6 km (1 mi) of sand resource. Washington's beach is different from similar areas in the United States in at least one aspect. There are no major population centers on this beach and, therefore, there is not the intense push for commercial and high-density living accommodation nor the pressure of hordes of people living "right next door." This relative isolation has also meant that local citizens have developed their own use of the beach and have very strong proprietary feeling about it and their use of it.

Prior to 1966, the beach was administered by the State Department of Natural Resources (DNR) who operated under laws requiring it to receive the highest economic values from lands that it administered. Such uses included mining and oil exploration, and, on the beaches, nonrestricted sand removal and unlimited driving. It must also be noted that established or "historical policy" plays an important role in this case. In the territorial days of Washington, the only easy north-south route near the coast was along the beach. As a result the state had declared the beach a public highway.

In the early 1960s, many Washington citizens became increasingly interested in preserving all state-owned ocean beach lands for conservation and recreation purposes. Several special interest groups began to express concern about the way in which the ocean beaches of Washington State were being administered.

Local and out-of-state beach users were appearing in increasing numbers; local governmental authorities were becoming concerned about the rapidly escalating costs of beach maintenance; health officials were alarmed at the sanitary conditions; families, especially those with children, were concerned about safety. As one father, holding his bruised daughter who had been hit by a car on the beach, painfully put it, "Doesn't my daughter have a right to use these beaches too?"

There was no beach policy per se, only policies that had been formulated for other land resources, yet were being applied to the beach situation. The time was ripe to develop a beach policy and to make a decision as to who would *administer* it. This also meant changing the historical beach-use policy.

During the 1967 legislative session a conservation-minded governor responded to all of these factors and groups by submitting an executive request calling for the administration of the beaches to be transferred from DNR to the Washington State Parks and Recreation Commission (WSPRC).

This bill, containing legislative policy as suggested by the governor, became one of the most controversial bills of the decade as an elected body (the legislature) was asked to consider a request from the elected governor to transfer jurisdiction from yet another elected official (head of DNR) to an appointed body and its director (WSPRC). The controversy becomes more easily understood when one understands that the head of DNR and the legislative majority were of one party, and the governor was of another.

It might well have been that the bill would never have passed had not the legislature agreed that an important issue was at stake, and that policy, not politics, needed their attention. It was decided that the beach administration would stay with DNR if the legislature determined that the best use of the beach was for revenue purposes. Conversely, the administration would be transferred to WSPRC if the best use was for conservation and recreation. The latter use was deemed the best by the legislature. It also set forth several policies within the statute that transferred jurisdiction. One of these dealt with the thorny issue of driving on the beach.

The legislature decreed that all automobile use could not be banned from the beach, but use could be *regulated* by WSPRC. This legislative policy seemed too vague to WSPRC, who asked the state's attorney-general for a ruling of legislative intent. That response indicated, in essence, that WSPRC could ban some of the automobiles from some of the beach some of the time, but not all of the automobiles from all of the beach all of the time. At this point it became obvious that whatever actions WSPRC took, they would probably end up in court; nonetheless, they must proceed as directed.

The following is a brief summary of the steps then taken in the process of formulating a policy for the beach driving issue. Note that a standard planning format was followed.

1. Data gathering. Information and statistics concerning laws governing the beaches and automobiles, accident/death reports from the beach, location and cost of constructing and maintaining beach access roads, and data on need and cost of patrolling were compiled. Drivable sand areas were located and noted on maps.
2. Data analysis.
3. Development of preliminary driving regulations based on data analysis and assumptions.
4. Development of preliminary plan of action leading from preliminary regulations to final rules.
5. Review by a cross-section of staff to provide an opportunity to locate the flaws in the prepared regulations and the plan of action. (All of the steps above were handled

by the director after conceptual approval by the WSPRC.)

6. Presentation of the proposal to the WSPRC, the formal policy maker. (This body approved the proposed policy.)

7. Discussion of the proposed policy with legislators from the directly affected area as well as those on the legislative parks committees.

8. Discussion of the proposed policy with local officials, including county commissioners, mayors, and sheriffs.

9. Briefing meetings with key individuals from groups sympathetic to the proposed policy (held while steps 7 and 8 were in progress).

10. Discussion of the proposal with individuals opposed to the policy.

11. A carefully laid-out media campaign initiated by WSPRC, prior to the holding of public meetings.

12. Public meetings to receive input. These meetings were held both in beach communities and in population centers from which most of the beach users originated.

13. Evaluation of feedback by WSPRC. The staff assembled and analyzed all data received from the meetings and developed a final proposal.

14. Publication of the regulatory plan by the Commission. Final hearings were held prior to legally adopting rules that it believed were consistent with the policy.

Adoption of this plan was not an easy task. The local user population voiced strong opposition to banning automobiles from even small stretches of beach as suggested by the Commission. These local users, as well as some others, wanted to cut up logs for firewood, remove sand, advertise the beach as the longest drivable beach in the United States, and continue their own unrestricted driving (Fig. 3-2).

Those who did not want any restrictions on where automobiles could drive took one last approach to the issue—that of questioning *who* had policy authority. As this book went to press, these citizens have won. In late 1980 the Washington State Supreme Court, in a split decision, ruled that the legislature had *not* conveyed this particular policy authority on the WSPRC, even though this has been its intent. The determination of this policy is now back where it started in 1967—in the state legislature. It is up to that body to clarify the language of the statute in order that the WSPRC will have undisputed policy authority.

Fifteen years have passed and nothing has changed? Not quite. The public of Washington

Fig. 3-2. Washington State's ocean beaches have historically been used as highways. At right a rescue vehicle tows a car stuck in the sand. Fort Canby State Park, Washington. (Photo courtesy Washington State Parks and Recreation Commission.)

State is now better informed. Many more of them have been to the beaches, and many citizens are interested in the issue. The beaches remain a place of wild beauty. The driftwood still piles up 30 feet high, and cars still roar past beach strollers. In time a policy will be formulated that will embody an acceptable compromise.

A Case in Point—Alcohol Consumption in Parks

Policy on this issue is invariably subject to vacillation, yet few policy decisions have as much impact on the *park manager* as does this one.

There are those who favor a comparatively open policy, stating reasons such as the following.

1. Ethnic background—"We always have wine (or beer) with our meals."
2. Honesty—"It is being done now undercover, so let's be honest about our actions."
3. Family rights—"We do it at home and this is our home away from home."
4. Consistency—"Beer and wine are sold and can be consumed in other public places, why not here?"

Those who wish a more restrictive policy state the following reasons:

1. Expense—law enforcement must be stepped up when people are under the influence of alcohol, so costs are increased.
2. Litter—more cans and bottles will be strewn over the park. This increases maintenance costs and looks ugly.
3. Disturbances—there will be more boisterous noise when liquor is allowed.
4. Mores—liquor use is offensive anywhere, but particularly in a family campground.

In between these two policy extremes is the park manager who must administer the written policy while facing those users who insist on established historical use or ethnic rights. And in many instances, the actions of the manager or the ranger or park aide representing the manager will bring about a change in policy. The following situation is typical.

The agency policy states "no alcohol." After a very brief period of practical experience, the new park manager changes his or her phrase from "Sorry, alcohol not allowed" to "Please put it in a paper cup—it's not allowed, you know, but you're OK."

As more "OKs" visit the park, wine and beer bottles appear on the picnic tables and only the "hard stuff" is in the paper cup. Before long visitors and managers are asking "why can't the law be changed?" After all, the rowdy ones can still be arrested under other laws. And so the policy is softened and alcohol is allowed under certain conditions, in certain places in the park.

The chances are that one of two patterns will evolve out of the "alcohol situation" (1) a new manager will take over this park whose actions will depend on his or her background and past park experience (i.e., the enforcement could become more lax or more stringent) or (2) the legislative body might receive so many complaints—from both directions—that it passes new legislation. In either event, the chances are that some alcohol will be consumed and not everyone will be pleased. Of course such violations of the law as consumption of liquor by minors or driving while under the influence, must always be promptly dealt with.

Over the course of time any given park manager will find his or her day brushed (if not deeply affected) by such "policy hassles." The chances are that each manager of significant tenure will also encounter one or more of the following policy dilemmas.

Leash policy Dogs will be forbidden entirely. Then if they are allowed, on a leash. Then allowed on a leash but only if in certain areas. Then forbidden but with the provision of agency- or concessionaire-provided kennels in some tucked-away place. And so it goes until the whole cycle starts again (Fig. 3-3).

Fig. 3-3. A leash law was in effect at this park, but was obviously being ignored by the owner of three German shepherds. Deception Pass State Park, Washington. (Photo by Grant W. Sharpe.)

Noise, especially after 10 P.M. Many people take the city with them—T.V., radios, tape decks, souped-up hot rods, motor bikes, and their boisterous voices. There are decibel laws—rarely enforced. But after bedtime—then what? Most policy makers start out stating all is to be quiet after, say, 10:00 or 11:00 P.M. Then they shift to a selected area for noise—after all—kids have to let off steam don't they? Before long groups become too noisy, too late, and the word comes down to enforce the 10 P.M. rule.

Hang in there, ranger. You will keep control if you are fair, firm, and consistent.

The greatest difficulty may be with consistency, as these last few examples have shown. Policies are generally restrictive, and the public manages to slowly loosen them up until the restrictions have to be tightened again. This too is part of being a park manager—knowing how to live with these inevitable modulations. However difficult it might be to work with "hard and soft" policies under "flexible" direction, the manager may find that easier to cope with than the unwritten policy.

Unwritten Policies

One is not long around an agency before hearing about unwritten policy. There are usually at least two types.

1. The policy is generally well known, but the agency has not set it down in written form. This type of unwritten policy should be encoded as soon as possible. In the meantime, the new employee would do well to remember it.
2. The other type of unwritten policy is much more difficult to deal with and will rarely find its way into print. This situation is the result of certain persons in positions of authority who want things done their way but do not want the "way" to be in writing.

An example of such an unwritten policy might deal with hiring practices. The person in authority might give lip service to equality in hiring while letting it be known behind the scenes that only certain types of individuals are going to be hired. Another such policy deals with purchases that are not controlled by bid rules. Often people in key positions will let subordinates know where the boss wants the purchasing done.

Angry? Bewildered? You don't know where to turn, or what to do? Should you go along? Or protest? Or quit? We suggest you discuss your dilemma with your supervisor, who has probably been in the same situation. Then make up your own mind and act accordingly.

Implementing Policy

Since policies are usually developed and adopted only after considerable involvement by many people, it is reasonable to assume that the employees who administer the policy will need some time and assistance in understanding them. They should be informed as to why the policy was needed in the first place, how it is to be implemented, and under what circumstances.

Once the policy is adopted, copies of it should

be reproduced in sufficient quantity to assure its availability at each park area, as well as at headquarters. It is equally important that time be given to policy matters during the regular in-service training programs so that all are aware of policies, and know that they apply to everyone—from the top administrators down. When new employees are hired, policies should be discussed with them as a regular part of indoctrination.

CONCLUSION

Some policies are matters of routine, and administering them is no great problem. Others, as this chapter has pointed out, are hard to formulate, and may be even harder to enforce. Painful as the administration of policies might be to the manager at times, they are a necessity, and a reality that those aspiring to managerial positions must face. Meeting the needs of the public is a most complex task, as the public is most complex. One of the wonders of our society is how so many divergent people can live, work, and recreate together—not as one—but together.

To protect the rights of the recreationist, to protect our fragile and beautiful parks, and to give the manager half a chance to succeed in this crazy, wonderful mission, we need policies. And, imperfect as they might be, they do guide and validate our actions in a civilized society.

REFERENCES

General References

Dana, Samuel Trask and Sally K. Fairfax. 1980. *Forest and Range Policy: Its Development in the United States* (2nd ed.). McGraw-Hill. New York.

Everhart, William C. 1972. *The National Park Service.* Praeger Publishers, Inc. New York.

McCall, Joseph R. and Virginia N. McCall. 1977. *Outdoor Recreation: Forest Park and Wilderness.* Benziger, Bruce & Glencoe, Inc. Beverly Hills, CA.

Parks Canada. 1979. *Parks Canada Policy.* Parks Canada, Ottawa, Ontario.

U.S. Department of the Interior. 1968. *Administrative Policies for Natural Areas, Historical Areas, and Recreation Areas of the National Park System.* Three Volumes. Washington, DC.

References Cited

1. U.S. Department of the Interior, 1962. *Outdoor Recreation for America.* A report to the President and to the Congress by the Outdoor Recreation Resources Review Commission. Washington, DC.
2. Wengert, Norman. 1967. *Natural Resources and the Political Struggle.* Random House, New York.

CHAPTER FOUR

RECREATION LEGALITIES AND LIABILITIES

Legalities refer to the laws by which park agencies must operate. Liabilities are responsibilities the agency and the park manager assume when that operation takes place—in other words, when a park is open to the public. There are books, volumes, and even complete libraries dealing with legalities and liabilities. Here we are dealing only with those basic legal concepts that are important to park administrators and managers. For anyone who desires more information, sources are listed at the end of this chapter.

LEGALITIES

Lawmaking Bodies in the United States and Canada

The United States and Canada are nations of laws with a marvelous and complex system of checks and balances. For example, a higher court, presumably less susceptible to a conflict of interest on any given issue, might overturn a lower court. And yet a provincial or state legislature or the federal legislative body might pass or change a law which changes the effect of a judicial ruling.

The following paragraphs show governmental levels that have authority over park agencies. The higher level has the authority to supersede the next lower.

Federal Lawmaking Bodies of the United States and Canada

Federal Supreme Courts. The *U.S. Supreme Court* and the *Supreme Court of Canada* will sometimes issue decisions that will affect an agency, particularly in the field of human rights and law enforcement. Also under this heading are laws pertaining to visitors, such as the Official Languages Act of Canada, which states that all official publications must be in both French and English. When dealing with these decisions, the concerned agency personnel should be in close contact with their agency's legal counsel.

Federal Legislative Bodies. The *U.S. Congress* and the *Canadian Parliament* will frequently pass legislation that will have a definite effect on a park agency. Although the method will vary depending on the size of the agency and the level of government in which it operates, someone in the agency should be assigned to keep abreast of these laws. This can usually be done through the provincial or state association of cities, counties, or municipalities. In the United States it can also be done in house by subscribing to the National Recreation and Park Association's *Washington Scene*. Someone in the concerned agency should know the chief staff person of the U.S. House Interior and Insular Affairs Committee and the U.S. Senate Energy and

Natural Resources Committee. Information obtained from these sources should then be made available to agency personnel in the field.

The Congress and Parliament pass laws, the courts rule on the legality and applicability of the laws, but the federal agencies, under the president or prime minister, administer the laws, and within that administration is the ability, authorization, and direction to issue guidelines. It is vital that concerned agencies not only be aware of those guidelines, but play a role in their development. Unless the agency is large, it probably will not be able to do this on its own. These agencies should utilize the services of national organizations such as the National Recreation and Park Association, the Audubon Society, conservation groups, or provincial or state park and recreation associations.

Federal Agencies. Federal agencies that have particular relevance for the park and recreation field are listed as follows.

Canada

Minister of Forestry and Rural Development

Minister of Indian Affairs and Northern Development

United States

Department of the Interior

Bureau of Indian Affairs

Bureau of Land Management

Bureau of Reclamation

National Park Service

Office of Water Research and Technology

Fish and Wildlife Service

Department of Agriculture

Cooperative State Research Service

Extension Service

Forest Service

Soil Conservation Service

Department of the Army

Corps of Engineers

Department of Transportation

U.S. Coast Guard

Provincial and State Government. The governments of the 10 provinces, the Yukon and Northwest Territories, the 50 states, the Virgin Islands, the Commonwealth of Puerto Rico, and the Territories of the Pacific, have variable organizational structures, but they all have courts, legislatures, and executive agencies. The need for close monitoring that has just been stated regarding the federal government is even more important when the relationships under consideration are closer to home, such as provincial government to provincial agencies or state government to local agencies. These latter sorts of relationships will generate far more decisions that, in turn, will have more direct effects.

Supreme Courts. The state supreme court will often issue decisions affecting state agencies. These decisions are published in the court reports called *Supreme Court Decisions* and are readily accessible through the state association of cities, the state association of counties, and local law libraries. This is also true for provincial courts. For an understanding of those decisions, which can often be confusing to the layperson as well as the lawyer, one should rely on the agency's legal counsel.

Legislatures. These bodies will pass many laws directly affecting their state or provincial agencies. The laws are known as statutes and are normally quoted under revised codes, such as the Revised Codes of Illinois (RCI). These statutes or revised codes supersede all other state rules. In some cases, state and provincial law merely supplements local law, and in others it applies only to state/provincial lands and state/provincial agencies and has no effect on local land or agencies.

State government has its own laws and rules relating to lobbying and participation in legislative workings. This might also be true of an agency's particular level of government. These issues and this authority must be clear before an agency can act in the legislative arena. Also, those responsible for such matters must be cognizant of what tasks the state professional associations or societies can perform for them.

Just as at the federal level, where the federal agencies issue rules or regulations that become law, so it is at the state level. Many state agencies will also have power under what are commonly called administrative procedures (or some similar title) to adopt rules that have the power of law, one step below statutes. These rules are usually called administrative codes with the names of the state preceding it, such as the Pennsylvania Administrative Codes (PAC).

At the state level there are fewer agencies to be concerned with, but they must be dealt with more frequently, and there is a deeper involvement than there is with the federal agencies. These agencies will include, by whatever title they might have, parks and recreation, labor and industries, human rights, environment, and natural resources. These formulations are generally applicable to the Canadian federal-provincial relationship also.

Local Governments and Agencies. In almost any given province or state, there are more *local* agencies concerned with parks than the combined total of all the provincial, state and federal agencies in the parks field. These local agencies possess certain similarities from state to state and province to province.

Courts. One similarity among all local levels of government is that there is no city supreme court. This is important to remember, as most lower court rulings that affect two or more jurisdictions will be appealed to higher courts. Therefore, from a local agency's point of view, these courts are not nearly as important as the provincial court or state supreme court or appellate court.

Local Legislative Bodies. These might be a county council, a city council, a special policy or taxing board, a municipal council, or other.

These bodies have the same basic authority over their jurisdiction as the provincial or state legislature does over the entire province or state, subject to the constitutional limitations and the preemptory authority of the state or provincial legislatures. What they enact becomes an ordinance and it is the law in that geographical area.

Local Agencies. Normally the local parks agency does not have the power to make enforceable rules. At the same time, there must be an awareness of what power does exist, and agency officials must become acquainted with the corporation counsel or other persons providing legal advice to local agencies.

Types of Law

Park managers and administrators must be aware of the following facts, opinions, and rulings concerning laws that affect park personnel. These excerpts are from a presentation by Nixon J. Handy, Assistant Attorney General, state of Washington.[2]

> *Common Law.* *The common law consists essentially of several centuries of American and British law and is applicable today where there is no specific statute or constitutional provision controlling an issue. The common law determines the liability of a landowner for injuries occurring upon the owner's land by categorizing the land users and analyzing whether the landowner has met the standard of care owed to that particular class of users. The common law recognizes three essential categories of land users.*
>
> 1. *Trespasser. A trespasser is a person who enters the landowner's property without permission. For the park manager, a trespasser on public land is anyone who passes into an unauthorized area which is clearly marked as such. The common law imposes the minimal standard of care upon the landowner with respect to the trespasser— the duty of not intentionally injuring the trespasser. In most provinces and states, the landowner owes no duty to the tres-*

passer to maintain the land in a safe condition for the trespasser's use.

As far as park managers are concerned, this means that force probably should not be used to remove a trespasser. Certainly park personnel cannot shoot a trespasser and probably shouldn't physically assault a trespasser. A sheriff should be notified if verbal efforts to remove a trespasser are unsuccessful. Excepting the previously mentioned intentional injuries, then, the trespasser is responsible for injuries sustained on another person's land even though it may result from a defective or dangerous condition on the land.

2. *Licensee. A licensee is a person allowed or permitted by the landowner to enter upon the land for the licensee's pleasure or benefit. People entering upon the public land outside planned and marked recreational areas to hunt, fish, trap, remove wood, camp, or hike are probably licensees. They are on the land primarily for their own benefit and the state is making no representations as to the condition of the land. The common law does not require the landowner to be constantly inspecting the land to make it safe for the licensee. If the landowner does become aware of a dangerous condition on the land which the landowner can reasonably expect the licensee to encounter, the common law does require the landowner to either remove the dangerous condition or warn the licensee of it. The landowner does not, however, have a duty to remove or warn of a hazard which is open and obvious—especially if it is reasonable to expect that the licensee will observe the hazard and recognize the risk involved.*

3. *Invitee. Three kinds of invitees exist: First, a person who is invited by the landowner to enter the landowner's land for some purpose or advantage to the landowner, is an invitee. Examples are the businessman, policeman, fireman, or the doctor invited by the landowner for a purpose benefiting the landowner. Second, a person who pays a fee to enter upon another's land, such as a skier or a golfer, is an invitee. Third, a person invited as a member of the public to enter upon land which is held open to the public is regarded as a "public invitee." Typical examples would include persons attending a church, or users of public recreational facilities (Fig. 4-1). The duty the landowner owes to these invitees is the highest legal standard imposed upon landowners. The landowner must regularly inspect the premises for any unreasonably dangerous conditions and must either cure such conditions or warn the invitee of their existence.*

Fig. 4-1. By constructing a facility such as this tire swing, an agency is inviting its use. For this reason it is important to keep maintenance records. (Photo by Grant W. Sharpe.)

One additional category of land users should be mentioned—the small child. Under one doctrine, a landowner who maintains a condition upon his or her land that is dangerous to children because of a child's inability to appreciate the danger, and that the landowner can reasonably expect a young child will be attracted to, must exercise reasonable care to protect children. This "attractive nuisance" doctrine has been applied to railroad turntables, refrigerators, construction projects, and other similar situations. Generally speaking, the doctrine applies to artificial conditions on land, not natural conditions, and applies to children from the approximate ages of 4 to 12.

In the past public agencies have enjoyed immunity from liability for natural conditions on public land through the doctrine of sovereign immunity. This idea originated with the thought that "the king can do no wrong." Today, however, sovereign immunity has been largely abolished by the federal government and most states. In most states standards apply with equal force to public and private landowners. The above general rules of law probably apply to any state with respect to obligations owed to persons coming onto public land. In many states these general rules of law have been modified by recent statutes.

With the abolition of sovereign immunity and with recent court decisions allowing sizable damage awards, many public and private landowners have been reluctant to open their lands for public recreational use, thereby attempting to limit their liability.

Constitutional or Statutory Law. These laws are exactly what they purport to be. Constitutional law is that law as set forth either by the United States or an individual state constitution, while statutory law is either as adopted by the United States Congress or a state legislature. In the United States, the federal constitution is a *grant* of authority, while state constitutions are a *limitation* on authority, that is, if the U.S. constitution does not grant the authority, the federal government does not have it, but if the state constitution does not take it away, the state has the authority.

One typical state statute provides that any landowner, public or private, who opens land to the public for outdoor recreational purposes, without charging a fee of any kind, is not liable for unintentional injuries to such users. The statute does not apply to injuries resulting on the land from known, dangerous, artificial, latent conditions for which warning signs have not been conspicuously posted, and the statute does not affect the attractive nuisance doctrine. Thus, with respect to public recreational areas in many states where no fee is charged, the landowner can only be liable for injuries sustained on such land if the injury was caused by (1) an artificial condition, (2) that was hidden, (3) that was dangerous, (4) that was known to the landowner to be hidden and dangerous, (5) and for which no warning sign had been conspicuously posted (Fig. 4-2).

Fig. 4-2. "If you build it you must maintain it." The handrails and tread boards of this foot trail have been removed by vandals. To prevent injury and a possible lawsuit the trail should be closed and posted as dangerous until repairs can be made. (Photo by Grant W. Sharpe.)

The statute does not affect recreation areas for which an entrance fee is charged and we must presume that the highest common law standard applied to invitees applies to these areas. Where a fee is charged, the landowner must inspect the premises for unsafe conditions and either cure the defects or warn the public of them.[2]

Navigable Waters Laws. Since states and provinces contain navigable waters, all agencies should obtain legal opinion as to what is navigable water and what is nonnavigable water. Stated broadly, navigable waters are those that can be traversed by a small boat. The public has the qualified right to boat, swim, fish, and otherwise use the surface of all navigable water regardless of whether the beds (land under the water) are publicly or privately owned.

In many instances title to the beds of navigable waters, although initially vested in the state, was subsequently conveyed into private ownerships. For example, in the state of Washington, on Puget Sound, something over 50 percent of the tidelands were sold by the state to private owners prior to 1974 when the legislature banned further sales. Transfer of title to the bed from public to private ownership does not change the classification of the water from navigable to nonnavigable.

Human Rights. There has been a continuing development of federal, state, and provincial laws, as well as court rulings, dealing with human rights, especially for women and minorities. This has been particularly evident in recent years. Because these laws change rather frequently, this book will not refer to any of them but will note that all human beings are to be given equal and fair treatment. This has involved certain adjustments to agency procedures regarding personnel. Human rights legislation also means that there needs to be concern about the qualification for both entrance level and upward employment mobility. This is covered more thoroughly in Chapter 7, Personnel Management.

A typical statement pertaining to visitor use that presently is required on all publications in most states is "no person is denied the benefits of (area's name) facilities because of race, creed, color, sex, age, or national origin."

LIABILITIES

In the last half of the twentieth century there has been a sharply increasing demand for areas and facilities to be made available for recreational pursuits. These demands are not only for traditional recreational activities but also for those offering new excitements—and dangers. Recreation involving all-terrain vehicles (ATV), hang gliding, scuba diving, and river running offers good examples. Along with this increase in numbers and broadening of scope there has been a dramatic increase in the number of lawsuits filed, the number of judgments being awarded the user, and in the amount of the awards—some exceeding $500,000.

In Chapter 2, we referred to the relationship between authority, responsibility, and accountability. With accountability comes liability—the ranger's or manager's personal liability and that of the agency. Recent unrestrained litigation and liberal awards make it easy to understand why park personnel would avoid giving medical assistance unless some sort of "Good Samaritan" act has been passed by the state, giving legal protection to anyone attempting to assist an injured person. The same caution applies to facilities, unless the state has a limitation on liability. The best protection lies in proper design, construction, and maintenance of facilities, however.

Fortunately, most agencies will defend the employee who was acting in performance of duty and in a reasonable manner in light of all attendant facts and circumstances. Lawsuits, however, are very expensive and time consuming, regardless of who wins.

Some agencies are self-insured, while others have commercial insurance policies. Some individuals carry a personal liability policy while others do not. The authors are not advocating that managers do or do not take out such a policy. Park managers should make such a determination after consulting with their agency's legal advisor.

Some Recent Representative Cases. The following specific cases, contributed by Nixon J. Handy, illustrate some common liability situations occuring in parks.[2]

Natural hazards. Smith *v.* U.S., *383 F. Supp. 1076 (1974). In an incident at Yellowstone National Park, the Smith family entered the park with their 14-year-old son, Cameron. The family paid the entrance fee and received a brochure which warned that the hot natural pools were dangerous, that they should stay on marked trails, and that parents should supervise their children carefully. After viewing several well-marked thermal pools, the family parked at a paved turnout and walked down an unmarked, unposted trail to a boiling pool with steam arising from it. Cameron, the son, went to the edge of the pool and leaned over to look. The embankment caved in, tumbling the boy into the water. Cameron was severely burned and received permanent scars over most of his body. The court said that even though the family may have been invitees when they entered the park, that status was lost when they left the paved parking area and ventured down the unmarked trail. The court said that it would not be practical nor reasonable to require the Park Service to post warning signs at every thermal pool and said that the defective bank was not a condition which the Park Service could reasonably have been expected to find. Further, the court felt that the Smiths were adequately warned of the danger by the brochure and the obvious and apparent dangerous nature of the boiling and steaming pools. The court finally held that the Park Service met its duty of adequately warning the Smith family of the dangerous condition and that the family itself was negligent by proceeding as they did.*

Recreational swimming areas. Ward *v.* U.S., *208 F. Supp. 118 (1962). The United States leased a swimming area on Lake Hasty in Colorado to a private recreational association. The United States had developed the recreational area and remained active in administering the site even after the lease. A 16-year-old girl, who paid no fee, was drowned while swimming in the pool shortly after several young boys had been playfully ducking her. Her family sued both the association and the United States for negligence. The court awarded a judgment for the family, ruling that the United States, by setting aside the area for swimming, by constructing facilities for that purpose, and by posting signs inviting the public to use the area for swimming, had induced the public to believe that measures were being taken to safeguard activities at the area. The court said the United States therefore had a duty to require reasonable supervision and that it breached that duty in failing to have a lifeguard supervising the area. The judgment for the girl's family was $10,600.*

Wild animals. Claypool *v.* U.S., *98 F. Supp. 202 (1948). A visitor, William Claypool, entered Yellowstone National Park and paid the entrance fee. He received a brochure and asked the attendant ranger if it was safe to camp out—because of the bears. The ranger replied that it was safe. The brochure warned against feeding, aggravating, or inciting the bears. Mr. Claypool camped out one night and then moved to another site. Having seen some bears in the interim, he again inquired of a ranger as to the safety of sleeping outside. The ranger responded that hundreds of people sleep outside in Yellowstone every night and that the bears never attack without provocation. Mr. Claypool camped out once again. At one A.M. a bear attacked his tent and injured him. Mr. Claypool successfully sued the Park Service. As it turned out, three days previously another bear or bears had been involved in an unpro-*

voked night attack, an event unheard of in the park for over 20 years. The day after the first attack, several rangers searched for, found, and killed a grizzly bear believed to be the original assailant. The court held that Mr. Claypool was an invitee and that the Park Service was aware of a new and extraordinary danger of which it had a duty to warn Mr. Claypool. The court held the Park Service liable for the injuries sustained.

Wild animals. Ashley v. U.S., *326 F. Supp. 499 (1964). Another visitor, Mr. Ashley, paid his fee, received his brochure, and entered Yellowstone National Park. While sleeping in the front seat of his car with his right arm resting on the window sill, a bear bit his elbow causing serious and permanent injuries. Mr. Ashley sued the Park Service. The court found that the Park Service had no notice whatsoever of the bear's dangerous propensities and that the Park Service had met its obligation of informing the public regarding bears by issuing the brochure. This opposite result shows that the facts of each case really make a difference in the outcome.*

Hazard Trees

From the preceding descriptions of specific cases it is apparent that lawsuits can arise from many sources. Fortunately, all parks do not have grizzly bears or elbow-biting black bears, but most have trees. For this reason we will look at hazard trees more closely.

The various states' and provinces' immunity statutes might provide the recreational landowner protection from liability for natural hazards, since natural catastrophes, such as those caused by wind, cannot be foreseen. On the other hand attorneys for some agencies have advised that enough loopholes exist in the statutes to justify a *hazard-tree rating program* as one further means of limiting liability. Handy recommends that such a program be implemented in all areas where a fee is charged, where the site is developed, or where signs are posted inviting the public to use a particular place since by taking such action the landowner is indicating the site is safe for public use.[4]

If suit is brought, it is usually to the agency's advantage to settle the case out of court so that precedents do not become established in damage awards against the government. This procedure is less costly to the public purse and the plaintiff gets a better settlement with fewer legal fees. Out-of-court settlements also make sense when one understands that damages from natural events differ in many ways from case to case, so that the application of case law to these situations would often result in inadequate comparisons and unusual, if not incorrect, damage awards.[3]

What Is a Hazard Tree? Mills and Russell describe a hazard tree as one that is defective and, because of its location, may fall (or "fail") and cause personal injury or property damage. For a hazard to exist there must be a valuable target, such as people, a building, or a car, in close proximity. An example of a hazard tree is one near where people have been invited, such as in a picnic area or campsite, a parking overlook, or at an interpretive panel or sign. A defective tree deep in the forest and away from people is not a hazard tree because there is no target.[4]

Since World War II there have been millions of dollars worth of property damage and numerous fatalities and injuries in parks from tree failures.[1]

A healthy tree seldom presents a hazard. With so many different tree species, however, and so many conditions under which they grow, all trees should be suspect of being hazardous. Limbs may fall from a perfectly healthy tree through the process of natural pruning. Shade-tolerant trees, healthy in their natural stands, can become weakened due to sudden exposure to sunlight when adjacent trees are removed during the construction of campgrounds, roads, or parking lots. Shallow-rooted trees may lose their wind firmness when tree removal opens up the stand. Road cuts and trenching for sewer or water pipes often sever roots. The wounded parts become entryways for fungus infection. Soil compaction around trees caused by construction equipment, autos, horses, and humans can weaken trees.

Lightning, frost cracks, and fire scars can expose the inner bark to fungus and insect attack, as can axe and knife wounds caused by thoughtless park visitors.

Mistletoe causes a loss of vigor in otherwise healthy trees. Even the growth habits of trees, such as leaners (Fig. 4-3), volunteer tops, split crotches, and other deformities can create hazards.

Even healthy-looking trees do not live forever, and at some stage of their life their viability is lessened and they can no longer ward off attacks from fungus and insects, nor stand the strain of a

Fig. 4-3. How long will this leaning tree be supported by its neighbor? Note the campsite beneath this deadly example. (Photo by Lynn Mills.)

heavy snowload or strong winds. A good inspector can usually locate the telltale evidence of such weakened conditions as those shown in Figure 4-4. As Mills and Russell state:

> *Failure to carry out periodic inspections and to correct reasonably detectible tree hazards could leave recreation site owners open to costly law suits in the event of a serious accident.*[4]

Managers should acquaint themselves with the details of the liability situation in their particular area, and be well aware of agency policy on this matter.

Inspections. Systematic inspections for hazard trees should be carried out annually. Any tree within falling distance of a campsite, picnic site, interpretive sign, building, parking lot, or any other place where people linger should be examined.[4] According to Mills and Russell, the best time to conduct a hazard tree inspection is in the spring after trees have been exposed to winter storms and before heavy seasonal use. Inspections may also be needed after hardwoods have leafed out or after the occurence of a severe summer storm.

Inspections should be carried out by at least two people, permitting simultaneous views and discussion of the condition of individual trees.

TORTS

A tort is defined as a civil wrong, not arising from a contractual relationship, giving the person who suffers from the wrong a right of action for damages. It is also defined as a breach of legal duty not imposed by contract.

Each state has its own process for handling tort claims. The following description utilizes the federal basis but is applicable for all states in general terms. [2]

The U.S. Federal Tort Claims Act

The Federal Tort Claims Act permits damages to be awarded as a result of claims against the United States for damage to or loss of property

1 Dead tree
2 Dead top
3 Slow growth rate—general decline of the tree
4 Thinning, yellowing, or red crown
5 Leaning tree
6 Dwarf mistletoe brooms
7 Distress cone crop (unusually large numbers accompanied by thinning crown)
8 Foliar insect feeding
9 Large, dead or broken branches and branch stubs
10 Split crotch (hardwoods), weak fork (conifers)
11 Lightning scar
12 Frostcrack
13 Canker rot
14 Wound (trunk or roots)
15 Bark beetles
16 Fruiting bodies (conks) on trunk, branches, or around base of tree
17 Punk knots on trunk
18 Hollow
19 Resin soaking (resinosus) at base of tree and nearby soil
20 Wet looking bark at base of tree
21 Loosened roots (leaning tree)
22 Other downed trees in area with small root ball and rotted roots
23 Broken, rotten roots
24 Root insects

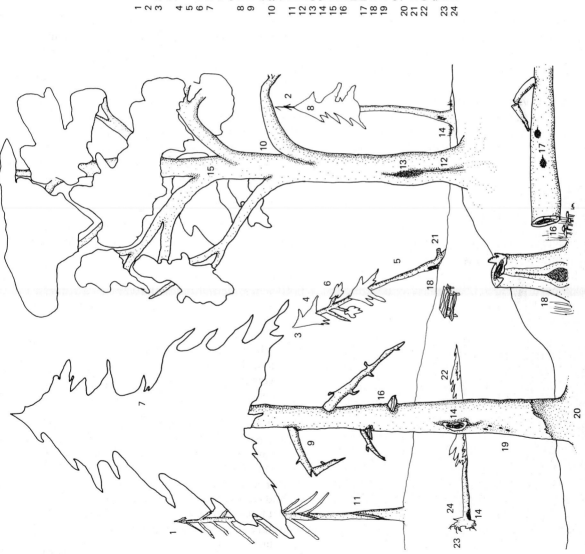

Fig. 4-4.   Tree defects that may result in hazardous conditions are illustrated here. How many can you identify? (Courtesy of Lynn J. Mills and Kenelm Russell.)

or on account of personal injury or death caused by the negligent or wrongful act or omission of any employee of the government while acting within the scope of his or her office or employment. This applies to circumstances where the United States, if it were a private person, would be liable to the claimant for such damage, loss, injury, or death in accordance with the law of the place where the act or omission occurred. The period within which a claim may be made is limited to two years.

The government has no right to recover a judgment from its employee in cases where a judgment has been paid arising from an incident where the government was held responsible as the principal and the employee (agent) was not sued. However, this does not mean that the government may not require reimbursement from the employee for loss or damage to the government property that was involved in the incident.[5]

INVESTIGATING ACCIDENTS

Any action taken by legal counsel must be based largely on the reports that comprise the file, and these papers have their origin, in most cases, at the scene of the accident. Accurate reporting of all essential facts is extremely important. In the typical case that a park manager may be called on to investigate, the opportunity to acquire information is fleeting. Full details should be recorded at the time the accident occurs. This aspect cannot be overemphasized in accidents that occur in parks since the persons involved are likely to be visitors whose homes are many miles away. It is often very difficult to supplement information by correspondence. For this reason, all employees must be instructed in the correct procedure.

Neither the employee, in making the initial report, nor a follow-up investigator for the agency, should state conclusions of his or her own concerning responsibility for an accident. The employee must state all the facts whether such facts are favorable or unfavorable to the agency or to an agency employee. Conclusions as to responsibility for an accident are not only out of place, but, in some instances, may make it difficult to achieve an objective determination of liability, which determination, of course, must be based on facts. When reporting or investigating an accident, it is useful to try to put oneself in the place of the people who may have to use the report. Leave nothing to the imagination. This does not mean that a report should be voluminous or long winded, but never assume that the person who uses the report will be able to visualize adequately a situation that seems obvious to the recorder. Remember, getting the names and addresses of all witnesses is especially important. Failing this, write down license numbers of vehicles, so that names may be obtained later.

Photographs are especially helpful to a person who must mentally reconstruct the circumstances of an accident. An instant self-developing camera and film serves this purpose best since it is known immediately whether or not the accident scene has been adequately recorded.

If there are visual indications that should be noted in the report, they should be described with some care. For example, in the instance of motor vehicle accidents, skid marks or whiskey bottles provide testimony the same as a witness. If there are signs, signal lights, or street or road marks that may have significance, these also should be described. Often weather conditions and visibility are considerably important. The location of the vehicles, if this is a vehicle accident, is especially important, as well as the character of the road and direction of travel of the vehicles. Note that statements by participants in an accident that are made *immediately* following the accident can prove to be of considerable importance in the event there is a trial arising from the accident. Further, if there is a law enforcement officer also investigating the accident, the park should endeavor to obtain a copy of this officer's report to be submitted as a part of the file.

Failure to conform to a required standard of care under the particular circumstances constitutes negligence. There should be included in an accident investigation report not only facts that may show negligence of the government driver but that may also show negligence of the private driver, or some other person, or may show that some special condition contributed to the accident and resultant damages. Information of this kind may be significant in determining whether a claimant was guilty of some contributory negligence that might constitute a bar to all or part of his or her claim, or even be the basis for a claim or counterclaim by the government for damages to government property. It is important that persons charged with the responsibility of determining a claim have information with respect to vehicle ownership. It is desirable, therefore, that the report include an investigation of the ownership of the vehicle to determine whether or not the driver owns the vehicle, and if this is not the case, the investigator should find out by whose authority and for what purpose it was being operated.

Motor vehicle accidents have been emphasized here because today most accidents seem to arise from negligent operation of motor vehicles; however, the same care should be exercised in filling out a report on any type of accident. In parks, where citizens are regarded as guests, and where these guests use facilities that have been constructed for their benefit and enjoyment, injuries can arise from what may seem to be very harmless situations. Recreation agencies have responsibility for maintaining the premises in a reasonably safe condition for the benefit of the persons who may be expected to use them, and this includes its own employees. Any persons who use park facilities are entitled to expect a reasonable amount of attention to their safety while on such premises (Fig. 4-5). Falling is frequently a source of injury and resultant claims against the government. If you are charged with the duty of investigating an injury arising from such an event, be sure that you describe the exact location of the fall and the condition of the premises at the time of the accident. Again, photographs are especially helpful, even though it may be necessary to

Fig. 4-5. In order to miss the leaning tree, drivers in larger recreation vehicles are forced to swing out into the opposite lane as they negotiate the curve. Is there potential for a court case here? Only time will tell. (Photo by Grant W. Sharpe.)

take the pictures some days after the accident occurred.

The following is a sample directive and accident reporting procedure.

Effective immediately, the Accident Form 01 (Appendix A, at the end of the chapter) is to be completed for all accidents occurring on any agency property. Form 01 should be completed by authorized staff immediately after rendering assistance as necessary to the injured party. The completed Form 01 is to be forwarded through the chain of command to the Assistant Director of Operations within five working days of knowledge of the accident.

Form 01 has two primary functions: (1) gather facts to assist in adjudicating claims against the agency and (2) to ensure that the conditions leading to the accident have been changed, as much as possible, to prevent reoccurrence. Thus, recording all the facts in as much detail as possible is essential to its usefulness.

Special attention must be paid to accidents occurring on concession-controlled areas of a park. Each manager with a concession must make contact with the concessioner to effect an agreement to report accidents, occurring on concession controlled property, to the park manager as they occur.

The manager should review such reports. If a serious accident is reported, or the accident might lead to legal action or cause the agency embarrassment, the manager would complete Form 01 on this accident, with the assistance of the concessioner. [6]

SUBMISSION OF CLAIMS

There should be a standard form for claimants who have been injured or whose property has been damaged, who desire to file a claim against your agency. How helpful should an employee be in connection with the furnishing of such claim forms? As a purely legal matter, never volunteer information with respect to the filing of a claim. If an injured person or that person's representative asks about the matter, it is the park employee's duty to inform such persons that they are entitled to file such a claim should they desire to do so, and copies of the claim form should be furnished. There should be no volunteer statement with respect to whether or not the person requesting the claim forms is likely to be successful or should be successful in filing of such claim. On the other hand, it would not be proper procedure or good agency public relations for an employee to be evasive or noncommunicative if it is clear to the employee that the injured person is uninformed and desires to know whether or not there is some way that a claim may be submitted.

This is a point where discretion will be very important. Park agencies desire to create a climate for visitors that makes them enthusiastic supporters of the goals and objectives of the agency. Injured persons, finding out later that there were claim forms available of which they were not aware, might conceivably feel that the agency, rather than just the employee, was not cooperative and cordial. Remember too, that the file of accident reports and other documents usually may be inspected by the claimant on request.

CONCLUSION

For park managers, understanding the laws that affect public safety is important. Managers deal with large numbers of people who are out of habitat and trying out new equipment or driving in unfamiliar terrain. Accidents are inevitable. Professional handling of legal details as well as other aspects of these mishaps is the mark of a competent manager.

Vigilance in the matter of hazards in the park is mandatory. Not only must the public be kept from harm, but the agency must be protected from litigation.

REFERENCES

General References

Bury, Richard L. 1980. *Risk and Accidents in Outdoor Recreation Areas: selected papers.* Dept. Info. Report 80-1. Texas Ag. Exp. Sta. Texas A & M University. College Station.

Driessen, Gerald J. 1972. *Safety and Risk Management in Selected Areas of the National Park System.* The National Safety Council. Chicago, IL.

Dyer, Donald B. and L. G. Lachtig. 1949. *Liability in Public Recreation.* C. C. Nelson. Appleton, WI.

Gaidula, Peter. 1970. *Tree Hazard Control Guidelines and Standards for Use in the Cali-*

fornia State Park System. California Department of Parks and Recreation. Sacramento.

Hadfield, J. S. and G. M. Filip. 1980. *Watch Out! Your Favorite Tree May Kill You! A Guide for Recognizing and Reducing Tree Hazards in Forest Recreation Sites in the Pacific Northwest.* USDA For. Serv. PNW For. & Range Exp. Sta. Portland, OR.

Hjelti, George and Jay S. Shivers. 1972. *Public Administration of Recreational Services.* Lea and Febiger. Philadelphia, PA.

Jubenville, Alan. 1978. *Outdoor Recreation Management.* W. B. Saunders Co. Philadelphia, PA.

National Safety Council. 1974. *Public Employee Safety Guide—Parks and Recreation.* National Safety Council. Chicago, IL.

Page, Joseph A. 1976. *The Law of Premises Liability.* Anderson Publishing Co. Cincinnati, OH.

Rhyne, Charles I., William S. Rhyne, and Stephen P. Elmendorf. 1976. *Tort Liability and Immunity of Municipal Officials.* National Institute of Municipal Law Officers. Washington, DC.

Wallis, G. W., D. J. Morrison, and D. W. Ross. 1980. *Tree Hazards in Recreation Sites in British Columbia. Management Guidelines.* British Columbia Ministry of Lands, Parks and Housing; and Canadian Forestry Service. Joint Report No. 13.

Wright, William B. 1957. Supplemented to 1968. *The Federal Tort Claims Act.* Central Book Company, Inc. New York.

References Cited

1. Gaidula, P. 1973. *Training Needs for Field Personnel in Detection, Evaluation and Control of Tree Hazards in Forested Recreation Areas.* Proceedings of the 21st Western International Forest Disease Work Conference. Estes Park, CO.

2. Handy, Nixon J. 1978. Recreational Resource Management from a Legal Perspective. Paper presented at New Perspectives for Outdoor Recreation II. Fort Warden State Park, WA.

3. Joy, Kerry. Personal correspondence. British Columbia Parks and Outdoor Recreation Division, Victoria.

4. Mills, Lynn J. and Kenelm Russell. 1980. *Detection and Correction of Hazard Trees in Washington's Recreation Areas. A How-to Guide for Recreation Site Managers.* State of Washington Department of Natural Resources. Olympia.

5. U.S. Department of the Interior. National Park Service. 1961. Office of the Field Solicitor. San Francisco, CA.

6. Washington State Parks and Recreation Commission. Olympia, WA.

APPENDIX A

A Sample Accident Form Used by Park Employees Immediately after Rendering Assistance to an Injured Party.

ACCIDENT FORM 01

1. PARK:_____ DATE: _____

2. Person completing form:_____

3. Injured person's name:_____

   Address:_____ AGE: _____

4. Date of accident:_____ Time: _____M.

5. Location of accident._____

6. Explain, in detail, what injury was sustained:_____

   _____

7. Explain, in detail, how the accident was reported to you as having occurred:_____

   _____

8. Did your investigation verify that this is how the accident occurred?

   Yes _____   No_____

   If the answer to #8 was no, explain what your investigation determined happened.

   _____

   _____

   _____

9. If there were witnesses to the accident, list their names and addresses below:

   NAME:_____   NAME:_____

   ADDRESS:_____   ADDRESS:_____

   _____   _____

   PHONE:_____   PHONE_____

10. What treatment was rendered to the injured party?_____

11. Were photographs taken? Yes_____   No_____(If yes, please attach)

12. If vehicles were involved, what were the license numbers?

    _____ _____ _____ _____

13. The following is completed only when a park vehicle is involved in an accident with another park-owned vehicle and/or park property, and the accident occurs on park property.

14. Vehicle #1 _____ Driver:_____
      (make, year, license no., tag no.)
                                          License No.:_____

      Vehicle #2 _____ Driver:_____
      (make, year, license no., tag no.)
                                          License No.:_____

      Estimated cost of repair: _____   _____
                                      vehicle #1   vehicle #2

      Describe park property damaged:_____

15. NOTE: Completing this form does not constitute making a claim for medical or other benefits under the Workman's Compensation law. To file such a claim, your doctor must assist you in filing a Department of Labor and Industries Accident Report Form. This should be done immediately, and in no case later than one year after the injury.

16. What steps should be taken to prevent a reoccurrence of this type of accident?_____

17. Have these steps been taken? Yes_____ No_____

      If no, when and by whom will they be taken?_____

18. _____
      (Signature of person completing form)

CHAPTER FIVE

POLITICS

Politics is neither good nor bad, ethical nor un-ethical. It is the art and science of government. The part of government we are concerned with here is land managing agencies, but this concern must not be too narrow, for it is the *regulation of relations* with other parts of government and with the public that is at the heart of politics as defined in this chapter.

Politics encompasses those skills and abilities that enable administrators to understand and communicate with others in government, as well as with private citizens, so that their agencies not only survive and serve, but succeed in achieving goals and objectives. This works on a personal level too. If you don't survive in your job you cannot serve, and your experience and professional vitality are lost to the agency.

If you work for the government, and most students in park management will be doing so, you had better understand and participate in this sort of politics. All too often practitioners in various governmental endeavors believe that they and their chosen field are above politics. By definition they are *not* above it—they are in the midst of it. It is better, more efficient, and more fun to try to understand and enjoy the world of government in the role of an active participant instead of as an unwilling and suspicious bystander. The administration of a park or other land managing agency is no exception; this too requires understanding and involvement in politics. The management of a single park requires political skill

too; the larger the unit the greater the need, but it is always there. Although the perspective of this chapter represents the view from the top, the tenets set forth will be of value to the student, as well as to all persons engaged in park management, regardless of the level of their position. All agency personnel should have some understanding of how administrators think and why they act in certain ways. Many different requirements must be met in order to keep the agency on course and functioning fully. Some of these are political, and it is with these that we attempt to come to grips here.

GOVERNMENT ORGANIZATIONS

Millions upon millions of words have been written about government—government in abstract, government in specifics, and government in its functional aspects. Often it has been stated that ours is a great nation despite its government. Or, "it is remarkable that government can accomplish anything with its myriad of levels, checks and balances, and complications." We propose to you that ours is a great government at least partly *because* of all these levels and complexities, and that without them, our particular form of government would cease to be.

To be an efficient administrator, a person must know not only his or her own agency, but where it fits into the myriad of levels; how it is funded, what its problems are, and what its future is. To do this, he or she must study the agency's place in the government of the county, state, province, or federal agency.

Within the Agency

To get started on the right foot in political relations, administrators must realize that their agency, be it local, state, provincial, or federal, is only one of many. It is vital for heads of agencies not only to know and understand their own agency, but also the others. Here is a list of goals suggested for a new administrator entering a top position. As lower level management personnel rise in their organization these suggestions will be applicable to them also.

1. Secure, study, and understand all federal, state and provincial, and local laws, ordinances, and policies that directly affect your agency or are applicable to you. This should include everything from the Constitution of the United States or the British North America Act to your state or provincial governing laws down through local ordinances. You should also direct your attention to those laws that are not made by statute or ordinances but by your own particular administrative procedures act.

    In most agencies the technical background needed to assist in securing these laws, and the time to do the research will be lacking. It might be a worthwhile cooperative project with your local college or university to publish such a compilation for the benefit of all in your state or province. As an administrator, a copy of these laws should be on your desk. Once you have it, work closely with your legal people to be sure that you know and understand your role: mandatory in some instances (you *must* do so and so) and permissive in others (you *may* do so and so). You must also be aware of the limitations of your role, and of your agency's purview.

    Although it is important to be familiar with all levels of government, the number one priority is your own. After you are familiar with the laws governing your agency, move up the ladder until you have explored all the way to the top. The reason, of course, is that those laws relating to agencies above you are, in the main, applicable to your agency, too. Then turn to the levels below you.

2. Secure and study the history of your agency. How did it start? Who played the key roles? Where are the skeletons? What great mistakes were made? Read past annual reports and pertinent newspaper articles. Consult with people who have been previously employed by your agency. Talk with volunteers, civic leaders, and the real source—the "old timer." Every town has a historian, and they are not always to be found in the library.

3. As previously stated, yours will be only one agency among the many agencies in your level of government. Each has a boss, or two, or three. Meet with the chief administrator of your level of government and learn what your role is—both per se, and as it relates to other departments, and other levels of government. There will be many times when your beliefs differ from your superiors'. Discuss your beliefs with them, present your input, and then support the agency position. Properly presented, your thoughts and suggestions will be welcomed and considered. If these are not properly presented, you might well be reminded of your subordinate status, and rightly so. Persons below you respect a chain of command; your chief administrator expects the same of you.

4. Your agency might have a board or commission in addition to a chief administrator. If so, get acquainted with the board. Be sure that your understanding of the needs of the agency is the same as theirs. Please note that we have said "theirs." Just as each of us has different views, so will the board members. However, it is vital that even though these individualities exist, the policy, goals, or ob-

jectives are understood and supported by all as a unit.

5. Remember your employees. All too often we check with the powers above, reach an understanding, but then forget those people who really need to know what's going on. At certain levels of management your staff will contact more people in a day than you will in a week or a month. Lack of communication with those further down the chain of command is a common and deeply resented omission. Also, it would be impressive if your employees knew what was going on in your agency when they are questioned by the public, or by employees of other agencies.

There are some skills that study and observation may improve, but that seem almost instinctive in some administrators—particularly those who might be referred to as "politically astute." Knowing which person may be asked for aid and which may not. Knowing when to keep quiet and when to talk, when to confide and when to avoid confidences. Being a good judge of character— knowing other's strengths and weaknesses as well as your own . . . many other items of this sort might be listed, but we will limit ourselves to pointing out that these are indispensable skills, and that a successful career does not allow for too many mistakes in such matters.

These are the primary requirements: knowledge of your agency—its laws and policies, its philosophy, purpose, goals, and objectives. You should know what your chief administrator believes; you and your board should have reached an understanding. You will have met with your employees and given them some ideas of your style of management. You will have taken time to sound out their views. Now it is time to concentrate on the next aspect of politics, interdepartmental relations.

Outside the Agency

The need for awareness and understanding of interagency relationships is paramount. This advice is sound for any level of management. Take time to visit the appropriate people in the other agencies not only to find out how they relate to you, but also what else they do.

There are many reasons for administrators to understand in depth the interrelationships of all agencies. In a government of checks and balances your agency will be very dependent on many other agencies. These agencies will not always get along. Administrators fight for their own agencies, and you must expect that there will occasionally be some ruffled feathers. Astute political practices require that you smooth things over as soon as possible. Having good interagency relations is beneficial to everyone involved.

Another reason for friendly relations is that there may come a time when you will need assistance from another agency. Do you have a control problem your agency can't handle? Your agency should establish and continue to maintain a cooperative program with your community's law enforcement personnel. Give similar thought to your fellow agencies of health, public works, fiscal, personnel, and others.

In your relationships with other agencies it is well to keep in mind that many agencies not originally involved in outdoor recreation now desire to move into this field because of increased public involvement. Also, well-meaning citizens often desire to establish another agency when yours is not as responsive to their suggestions as they believe it should be. Usually this proliferation and overlap is not in the best interest of good government and heads of recreation departments must resist it, tactfully but firmly.

Furthermore, in our society where the higher level of government has tax rights over the lower level of government, the lower level is often unable to provide services because of a lack of money. This brings about a cancerous tendency for higher levels of government to enter into your agency's area of responsibility to "aid" it, even when the services are not wanted or needed.

An understanding of the levels of government and the levels of responsibility is important to political participation in conferences and other interagency activities. Directors must acquaint themselves with the administrators of land managing agencies in other levels of government, as well as those from adjacent states or provinces, should the opportunity present itself.

NONGOVERNMENTAL ORGANIZATIONS

To understand politics, you must also understand the universe around you, the universe into which your world of government and your area—parks—must fit. You must first accept the fact that people—citizens—are interested in their government and also keep in mind that it *is* their government—your too, of course—but also theirs. Also remember that these nongovernment employees have their vocations and their avocations. Just as you are interested in your own local schools, church, and businesses, so are they interested in "your" parks. Just as you are often overly critical of some institutions, not really understanding them, so are they critical of yours.

Insofar as outdoor recreation is concerned, there are two major categories of nongovernmental agencies—those concerned with parks and recreation and those that are not.

Privately Financed Agencies Involved in Parks and Recreation

Many of the semipublic, character-building organizations such as scouting groups, the YWCA/ YMCA or YWHA/YMHA, are involved in the parks and recreation field. Many do a great job in providing areas and programs, and, just as with public park agencies, some do not. Many of these groups have a specific nonrecreation purpose and use recreation as an aid or a means to that end. It is the goal of others to provide the recreational enjoyment per se. Whatever their reason, these groups are a part of your political world. It is the responsibility of the agency director and management to set the example in cooperation, to aid, to coordinate. To do this, administrators must participate politically with these organizations, talk with their personnel, learn of

their needs, determine what they have in common with the agency, and enlist their support. Certainly cooperation and good public relations are indicated at the park manager level also. See Chapter 8, Citizen Involvement, for more on this topic, from the manager's point of view.

Organizations Not Directly Concerned with Parks—The Rest of the Political World

Now it is time to consider participation in the larger, more complicated "outside" political world. The remainder of this chapter will be dedicated to special interest groups, the communications media, and elected legislative officials. An awareness and understanding of these three categories won't cover every skill and subject administrators and managers need to master, but it will keep your nose above the waterline while you learn to swim in the world of politics.

Groups—Organizations, Federations, Clubs

In dealing with these groups, conflicts sometimes arise. You might find yourself between opposing groups that favor different approaches to the same goal, or that have different goals. This usually involves the delicate art of compromising without selling one's soul, which not only can be done, but must be done. Administrators at all levels will have dealings with such groups, and must be able to see the reasons for their varying positions, and find some way to keep them all aware that their views are heard and considered in all events that affect them. By their attitude toward all sorts of conflicting views administrators can set a tone of calm acceptance and consideration. This openness may help the opposing groups to listen to one another, and prepare them for inevitable compromises.

Top administrators must take the time to talk with the presidents of the local chapters of unions, to address the noon meetings of service clubs, and to visit the local newspaper editor. When they do, they must be sure to listen—to listen not only to what these people say, but also to how these people respond to what is said. It must be kept in mind that these are usually solid citizens who probably have lived in their community a long time, possibly even before the agency in question came on the scene. They want their community to be a wholesome place in which to live and raise a family. Administrators must seek and listen to their counsel and tell them about their agency's problems and objectives. This too is politics.

Interest in what administrators might consider "their business" is shared by nearly every group—ethnic, church, youth clubs, environmental councils, special subject matter clubs, business and industry, labor—all are interested and *desire* to participate. In fact, they *will* participate!

In working with these groups there are certain aspects to consider. First, one must do just that—work *with* them. Explore ideas with them and listen to theirs. By doing so not only will better ideas come forth, but you will enlist the aid of needed and powerful allies. Let them champion your ideas and take credit for them. Regardless of whether you are being asked or are seeking the contact, find out about the group. Learn which groups are of prime concern to your agency. Some administrators have a liaison whose job it is to know about particular groups and they assign that person the responsibility of reading their publications. If your position puts you in frequent contact with them, keep an up-to-date record of the clubs in your geographical sphere. The record should contain a listing of the purpose, when they meet, past deeds and present concerns, and officials. There is nothing sneaky or dishonest about doing this. To the contrary, it is due recognition that they are people bound together for a purpose that is of interest to you.

When you speak to groups, have no more than two or three key points to make. Keep in mind that they often don't know your particular field or your function within it. Don't worry about the details of the subject at this time. Make them clear later, when the club members are interested.

Sell concepts—sell ideas. Capture the imagination. "Sell them the fragrance of the steak, not how to cook it." If you don't know how to speak effectively—learn. Join the local Toastmasters or Toastmistresses Club—get some feedback on your speaking problems and correct them.

Important as speeches are, of far greater importance are the people one meets. Do you have a regular news release? If so, don't forget to put the clubs on your mailing list. Use your coffee breaks to make new contacts. The ripples from a pebble dropped in the water spread out to affect the whole pond—your friendly contacts can bring about similar amplification of your messages. Remember that the telephone is an efficient way to open and maintain lines of communication and takes far less time than letters or personal contacts. You might find you don't have enough time to do all this. Get volunteer help. Try to contact representative groups, those who do the coordinating: the chambers of commerce, executive councils of labor unions, and similar groups. By doing so you will expand the contact manyfold.

COMMUNICATIONS

The essence of effective political behavior has been seen to be good communications. Beyond personal contacts comes the outreach to the public through the media. Here are some very practical considerations that anyone in charge of communications should be aware of.

What is the name of the key contact on the local newspaper? Radio station? Television?

What is the deadline date and time for each?

What is the layout and length for articles or releases submitted to each?

What groupings of people are reached using what medium? At what time of day?

What kind of photographs or slides does each want and use?

What will communications representatives take as news and what as promotion?

Radio. As with all types of communications media, the success or failure of radio use depends on how the medium is used, when it is used, and what market is being sought. Three types of materials should be considered.

News Release. Keep it to two paragraphs. Know the audience and when it will be aired. If it is for farmers, have it before they go into the fields. If it is for big city commuters, try to schedule it while they are in their cars.

Public Service Announcements. Radio stations were required to provide regular two- to five-minute spots as a public service. Even though this is no longer mandatory, some of this free time may still be available to your agency. Keep the audience in mind. Enlist the help of other people to put the message across, including politicians and civic leaders. Should you not have the time to do all this, you might find a volunteer who not only has the time but also can do a better job.

Special Features. When you have a subject that deserves a wider coverage, contact the station. They are usually willing to present subjects of particular interest, as they desire to build their listening audience.

Television. Television reaches more people with more impact than any other medium but it is also more exacting in its requirements for materials. This medium wants slides or film strips of human interest stories, and will come to you to shoot them. Be prepared and set up for them. As with the newspapers, they too have three types of presentations.

News Release. This must be very brief and hard hitting. If not really exciting, it is doubtful if it will be accepted. A photograph or slide always helps.

Public Service Announcements. Television has also provided this service, but not as frequently as radio. The films are often shown very early in the morning when the audience is minimal.

Fig. 5-1. A Forest Service employee being interviewed by a TV cameraman in a national forest near Albuquerque, New Mexico. Familiarity with TV techniques and requirements is a valuable asset for public agency employees. (Photo courtesy of USDA Forest Service.)

Special Features. Here is where your message can really have an impact. Of all the types of cooperation television offers, this feature is the most freely available and best suited to your purpose. The television people are willing to come to the park to shoot (Fig. 5-1). Work with them ahead of time—it will pay off.

You will probably need to acquaint yourself with television operations, as they are not well understood by most park personnel. Keep in mind that with educational television you will be allowed to go into much more detail and also will reach an audience that is looking for greater depth. At the same time, you will not reach as large an audience. Conversely, commercial television normally does not want the depth, so you should attempt to arouse interest in that audience so they will want to explore further on their own.

Newspapers. Basically the same rules apply as for radio, except you can usually get more depth. Also, they are far more likely to use a listing of names and also to announce coming events. See that they get a prepared list of correctly spelled names and dates; don't leave it up to the reporter.

Don't forget to apportion the releases between night and morning papers. Learn when the releases are needed for the weeklies and arrange for critical releases to hit both the weeklies and the dailies at the same time.

Talk with the newspaper personnel to find out what they want, and when. Also, keep in mind the difference between a news release and a feature article. Reporters will write the features, therefore you should know who on the paper's staff writes what.

There are several points to consider with all media.

1. Be entirely truthful—not just partially.
2. Rarely ask for a remark to be "off the record." It is better to have no comment at all.
3. Know what you are trying to accomplish and why, then select the medium you wish to use.
4. Respect the exclusive. This means a specific newsperson has contacted you and developed a story. Don't then call a reporter from a competing station or paper to do the same story.
5. News people are human too, and make mistakes—just as we all do. Be understanding. Keep your sense of humor active. Strive to maintain a friendly relationship.

Other Publications. In interpreting the agency's goals and having its policies understood by the public, don't forget the area of publications such as handouts, brochures, and guides. Since a publication takes more preparation time and incurs distribution expenses, it must be considered with even more care and used on a very selective basis. Consideration should be given to publishing jointly with others, including commercial sponsorship. Caution should be exercised to avoid conflicts of policy and other interests in such a venture, however.

THE ELECTED OFFICIAL

Before you can even think about *relating* to elected officials, you must know *who* they are, then *what kind* of people they are. At the risk of offending anyone's intelligence, we feel very strongly about being sure that all of us, first and foremost, accept the fact that they are humans— they are *individuals*. They, too, work for a living—they hunger and thirst—they laugh and cry—they have good days and bad days. Some are married and some are single. They are of both sexes and of varying ages. They have children or are without. Some must provide for a family, sharing in its joys and sorrows.

Right now you might be thinking, "so does every other individual." You are right—yet elected officials *are* different. Let us use state or provincial legislators as an example. They not only have all of the normal pressures that we have, but they have additional intense and conflicting pressures on all sides of political situations. Some of those pressures come from persons who are known as large financial contributors, and that's tough!

And yet, there is more. Politicians are not only individuals—but are also legislators who are members of a political party, subject to party pressures. They are also members of bipartisan interim committees and members of the highest legislative body in each of our states or provinces—our legislatures. Don't forget too that the experience, abilities, and personalities of these persons vary.

Now that we are aware of them as individuals, let's look at what the directors of agencies must consider in their relationship with them. It will be instructive for managers at all levels to understand what the view is from the top.

Know Their Interests

What type of legislation interests these elected officials? Youth? Environment? Taxes? What are their backgrounds, their avocations, their vocations? What committee work interests them? Could it be your agency? Your director will need someone to sponsor park bills. This selection of a sponsor is important both to the agency and the legislator. It does not happen by chance.

Advance Notice of Problems

How does it go? The best-laid plans of mice and men often go astray. When things go wrong, after assaying the problem, the director must notify his or her superior, and the legislators involved. Constituents will contact both and it is only courteous to get the word to the legislators ahead of time. Either way, they will remember how it was handled.

News Releases

There are many types of news releases—some go out over the governor's signature, some the commission's, the director's, a park manager's, or perhaps another employee's. The legislator must not be forgotten. Perhaps the news release should come from that office. Providing this sort of publicity is a way of saying thanks.

Employment

Do you have a job to offer as a lifeguard, park aide, laborer? There are many youths who desire to work and who can do the job. Don't discriminate against them because the dad, or mother, is a legislator. Treat them the same as other applicants. Hire on the basis of ability, including children of political figures and discharge on a basis of inability, no matter what the employee's connections. The key is the ability to do the job.

Making Speeches

As a part of their speech preparation, administrators must know who represents the area in which they are speaking, and try to find ways to mention officials' names in a positive way. These officials will then remember the agency involved in a positive way. One must remember who is on the commission and in the legislature, as well as other important people. If it is opportune to refer to them in the speech, the name must be ready

and correct. That's important at any level of management. If you can't handle it, you won't be making speeches for long.

Openness

One must be very honest with elected officials, even if it hurts. Also, administrators must not leave them out on a limb. If it appears that they are crawling out on a limb on their own and it's going to get sawed off, agency personal must not take the attitude that "it's their problem," but should come to their aid. This means keeping them fully informed on all issues and developments on which they are likely to be making pronouncements.

Ceremonies and Dedications

From the photographing of a small development to the major park dedication, the elected officials who have worked to aid you have a right to share in the fruits of victory. In some instances such a person should be the master of ceremonies or the

Fig. 5-2. Elected officials, who have worked to aid you, should be a part of the park's dedication day. Here Congressman Tom Foley, of Washington State, addresses those attending the dedication of Steamboat Rock State Park. (Photo courtesy of Washington State Parks and Recreation Commission.)

main speaker (Fig. 5-2). In any instance, they should be involved and mentioned in press releases. Photographs of the event should be sent to them.

Party Politics

Unless the head of the agency is an elected official, and the job was acquired by and is dependent on partisan politics, he or she should keep out of party politics. Commissions and legislatures are bipartisan and directors must act accordingly. Officials are asked and urged to take partisan positions, but they must consider their involvement very carefully. The head of the agency must see to it that persons of both political parties act as sponsors for agency legislation. Otherwise the director will be labeled as belonging to a particular party, and this will reduce his or her ability to function effectively.

One of the most difficult times for such administrators is election time. They will be asked to purchase tickets, to endorse candidates, to appear on platforms. Assuming that they are nonpartisan, the following is recommended.

1. No tickets be purchased, or else purchase from all parties.
2. Administrators support no one.
3. If administrators appear on a political platform for one party, they must work diligently to get on a platform for the others.

Remember that the incumbent is the officeholder until and unless defeated. This person is a candidate, but is still the legislator. They may make statements during the election campaign that seem unfair or untrue. Distinguish the subject from the person talking. Administrators must never attack elected officials. Discuss the subject matter, but refrain from personal remarks.

Cases in Point

The following cases are true, and all are examples of political expertise, or lack of it, in action.

Mightier than the Sword. The state park agency needed state legislative approval and also federal approval to secure over $4 million for acquisition of a conservation area in a metropolitan zone. By carefully programming and designing all aspects of a brochure, and the accompanying news releases, and by deciding who was to be involved in the various types of presentations, the agency was successful in securing over $2 million from both the federal and state levels.

Take It Easy. The agency had taken care of a sewage problem in one of its metropolitan area parks prior to a city newspaper's front page expose of the park's poor example. There certainly was reason for a blast against the paper, since the "evil" was corrected before the paper reported it. However, this would not have been politically prudent. At the same time, one can't roll over and play dead. The agency went to the paper, explained what was done and how it came about, and received a favorable report in a later paper. The relationship of the agency and the paper was strengthened and the public was edified, not treated to the spectacle of a quarrel.

Others Will Assist You. Agency 1 had incorrectly and improperly informed a legislator that it was all right with agency 2, a parks agency, if hunting were to be allowed in agency 2's parks. Based on that information, the legislator introduced legislation to allow said hunting.

There are many groups who oppose hunting in parks. One of these groups immediately conducted a statewide campaign, including direct letters to both legislators and the media. Although agency 2 took no position against the bill, and so advised the sponsoring legislator, the bill never came out of committee. An unpleasant interagency wrangle was avoided.

Once Too Often. The agency had a park manager who had a habit of opposing the views or disagreeing with those to whom he was directly responsible.

On one specific occasion the park manager was instructed by superiors not to take a particular action. In spite of the directive, the manager did take the action. Although it should not have, it came as quite a surprise to this manager when he was fired.

Know the Law. The director of an agency fired an employee for justifiable reasons. The employee exercised the right of appeal and was upheld on the basis that the director did not have the authority.

After legal analysis, it was ascertained that the director did not have the legal authority to fire the person, so the legislature was asked to change the law. When this was accomplished the director fired the employee again—this time successfully.

One of Us. The director of a parks agency kept the parks board well informed, particularly in sensitive complex situations. One of these situations involved a second land managing agency, which was headed by an independently elected official.

At a public meeting conducted by the parks board the head of the second agency appeared and spoke strongly against the actions of the head of the parks agency. As a direct result of the close relationship between the board and director, the board not only defended their administrator, but took strong exception to the actions of the elected official.

The Day of Reckoning. The director of an agency believed she was immune from political concerns because she had a partisan board of her own party. She campaigned against the mayor—who won reelection. During the next few years the director financially contributed to the elected mayor's party, believing that she would be forgiven for her actions. As board terms expired and the members of the party in power were appointed, the day finally arrived when a majority of the board was of the party of the mayor, not of the director. The result: a new director.

Stitch in Time. An agency was required to close down some facilities due to a lack of funds. Regardless of all of the right words in the world, this would be very difficult for the voters in the affected areas to accept. The administrator called each of the concerned legislators prior to the closure, explaining why. The legislators not only knew why themselves, but also had the answers for their constituents when the deluge of calls came.

The Park Manager and Politics

Every employee should understand the political world and assist the agency as much as possible through good public relations. In the instance of park managers, this can be done by participating in a service club, speaking at a parent/teacher meeting, sponsoring ''get acquainted'' days, and other actions that bring managers into the life of the community in which they find themselves.

Much in this chapter will seem beyond the purview of the busy manager of a small park with little or no staff and infrequent contact with the big world of politics. Yet if you are in park management you are in politics whether you like it or not, and you will have a far better chance of success if you understand and participate in politics intelligently when the opportunity arises. It will also increase your ability to understand your job and its relationship to state or provincial situations, and to see why top officials behave as they do. With this understanding you can perhaps gauge your interest in a career in administration, which will certainly necessitate your entering more fully into the realm of politics.

CONCLUSION

Park management involves working with people, and usually, with government agencies. It is not possible to ignore political considerations in such circumstances. If you wish to serve, survive and succeed, you must enter into this challenging world. When thoroughly understood and properly approached, politics adds zest to your job, at any level.

REFERENCES

Brown, William E. 1971. *Islands of Hope.* National Recreation and Parks Association. Washington DC.

Clawson, Marion C. 1959. "The Crisis in Outdoor Recreation," *American Forests*, Part I, 65(3):22-31, 40-41. Part II, 65(4):28-35, 61-62, Washington, DC.

Frome, Michael. 1972. *Whose Woods These Are.* Doubleday and Co. Garden City, NY.

Ritchie, James, I. 1969. *How to Work Effectively with State Legislatures.* American Society of Association Executives. Washington, DC.

Wirth, Conrad L. 1980. *Parks, Politics, and the People.* University of Oklahoma Press. Norman.

CHAPTER SIX

FISCAL MANAGEMENT

It would be extremely difficult to segregate any *one* portion of administration and declare that it was the most important. Yet, if one were to do so, the chances are that it would be a toss-up between personnel management and fiscal management.

FINANCING RECREATION

In all probability, the procurement of sufficient funds will always be a problem in the recreation field. There are several reasons for this. In Chapter 5, Politics, the reluctance of park personnel to be politically active was touched on. Whatever the deep-seated reasons for this aloofness, the practical results show in inadequate appropriations. Parks frequently lack a constituent lobby group. In times of tax revolt this lack of representation is disastrous for park funding. It also evidences itself in a lack of awareness and sympathy by the decision makers. Effective support for parks takes many years to build and needs politically competent resource people to handle it. Once again, the call must go out for parks personnel to involve themselves in politics, and to encourage others to do so. We must know where the power is, and use it legitimately and intelligently, or there will eventually come a time when we will be bypassed by those who can and will use the political process. Parks need money to exist; establishment is only the beginning. In difficult times, the fight for funds will be tough; dedication as well as involvement will be required of the professional.

Funding Categories

Some governmental units require that all agency-generated revenues be deposited in the general fund while others permit the agency to use the revenues. Basically, all revenues are organized in one of the following categories.

General Fund. Although the title may vary, all levels of government have a fund to which receipts flow. For the purposes of this chapter, consider the general fund as the depository for revenues that are not designated for any specific purpose and that may be expended in any way the legislative body decrees.

Dedicated Funds. These, as the name implies, are funds that are dedicated to a specific use or a specific agency. For example, the federal Land and Water Conservation Funds are for a specific use but may be expended by a variety of public agencies. The federal Historic Preservation Funds are also for a specific use but for *both* public and private agencies. The federal Dingell-Johnson (fish) or Pittman-Robertson (wildlife) funds are for the purpose of research, and for the purchase and development of game refuges and public hunting grounds, but are almost always for one agency, usually the state game agency. Revolving funds, as noted below, are another type of dedicated funds.*

Revolving Funds. Under certain circumstances the legislative body will permit the agency to establish an account for revolving funds. These are funds the agency both generates and spends within general legislative authority. This is usually done to provide for the replacement of equipment, or for programs, if the income generated completely covers the cost of operating a particular activity or service.

Many agencies find it difficult to secure funds for purchasing equipment. To alleviate that problem they establish a revolving fund for equipment. The equipment revolving fund should be developed at the time the agency originally purchases its equipment with a direct appropriation. Then, in succeeding budget periods, the agency budgets funds on the expenditure side of the ledger to pay itself for the use of the equipment. The amount paid is either per hour (machinery, boats) or per mile (automobile). The amount paid must cover not only the operating expenses (usually gasoline) but also sufficient funds to replace the equipment when it is time for replacement.

When, as mentioned above, some particular activity has a user fee which covers operating costs, an activity revolving fund is set up. For example, perhaps an agency has determined that there is sufficient interest in an activity, such as photography, to start a class. The governing authority has determined that the class must be self-sustaining and operate 100 percent out of receipts, so a revolving fund is established. All revenues go into the fund and all expenses are paid from it.

*There are very few dedicated funds in Canada. For information concerning those few, contact Office of Assistant Secretary of State, Fitness and Sports Branch, Journal South Bldg., Ottawa, Ontario K1A 0M5.

Sources of Revenue

We have now established that all revenues are placed in one or more of three funds—general, dedicated, and revolving. Where and how are these revenues obtained?

Anticipated and Unanticipated Revenues. When an agency prepares its budget, it must estimate and identify planned expenditures and also list all anticipated sources and amounts of revenue.

Revenues received in excess of the amount anticipated are not considered unanticipated and may not be expended by the agency. Only a *new* source of funds is considered as *unanticipated.* For example, the agency anticipates $40,000 from camping fees, all of which is deposited in the general fund. The agency has an extraordinarily busy year increasing the camping fee revenues to $60,000. The $20,000 is not considered unanticipated revenue and usually is not available to the agency.

Unanticipated revenues then, are revenues from a source not contemplated at budget time. For example, a wind storm falls 70,000 board feet of timber. The revenues from salvaging that timber would be unanticipated. To enable salvage, the governing control agency will usually permit the agency to spend the unanticipated revenues up to the amount necessary to log, clean up, and replant, but this may not entail an amount in excess of the amount to be realized from the log sale.

If the agency is a self-taxing district, it may make its own decision as to whether or not it chooses to spend its unanticipated revenues. Should the agency not be a self-taxing district, and most are not, some higher control authority will make that determination when the occasion arises.

Additional Funding—Nongovernmental. Though agencies normally handle funds only from governmental sources, there is a large and variable source of funds available from nongovernment sources. An agency can always use additional funds to acquire, develop, and operate areas, facilities, and programs no matter how many dollars it is allotted from the legislative authority. Some of these needs which require additional funds will be met by volunteers, as set forth in Chapter 8. Some of the other ways an agency might raise funds from commercial and noncommercial sources follow.

Commercial. All too frequently park agency personnel believe they will become suspect if they cooperate with commercial enterprise. This is not necessarily true. A close working relationship with private enterprise could be of great assistance to the agency. Here are a few examples of such cooperation.

1. The production of outdoor recreation guides, park brochures, or agency films could be accomplished as a joint venture whereby the agency provides the text, and the commercial firm provides the funds, and both receive credit.
2. The development and operation of a campground, golf course, or ski area could be managed as a commercial venture under agency rules and regulations. The entrepreneur can make a profit and the public will be served.
3. Granting a private developer a utility easement across agency land could result in a needed development on agency land.
4. The passage of an ordinance requiring that all new subdivisions set aside park areas, or money in lieu of area, can generate lands and funds for an agency.

Noncommercial. One of the major sources yet to be fully tapped for financial revenues for park and recreation use is that of the noncommercial, nongovernmental organization. Within that resource are the foundations.

Canada and the United States have literally thousands of foundations who yearly give away billions of dollars. Some of these foundations are

international; others allocate funds to recipients in a localized area only. It is suggested that every park and recreation agency in North America contact their local library for a listing.*

A municipality, state, or province might choose to organize its own parks foundation. Some, such as the California State Parks Foundation, serve only the sponsoring agency, while others such as the Washington Parks Foundation serve all park and recreation agencies in a geographical area.† In addition to foundations, there are considerable financial resources in the proceeds from bequests and donations.

Additional Funding—Governmental. The government within which the agency is located is the source of these funds. The funds being described here are in addition to the normal funds appropriated from year to year. The subject of grants will be addressed separately as they constitute a major portion of this source of funds.

The first funds to be considered are those offered by the federal governments. Agencies located in the United States should contact the closest regional office of the National Park Service, which keeps an excellent updated list of all such funds. In Canada the information should be sought from the Provincial Community Service Branch and the National Fitness and Amateur Sports Branch.

Other funds are available from the province or state. This information will be available in the provinces through the provincial, cultural, and recreation services. In the United States contact

---

*For more detailed information about foundations, contact the Foundations Center at either 888 Seventh Avenue, New York, NY 10019, or 1001 Connecticut Avenue, N.W., Washington, DC 20036. Also, there is a Foundation Directory published by Columbia University Press, 136 South Broadway, Irvington, NY 10533. In Canada write Association of Universities and Colleges of Canada, 151 States, Ottawa, Ontario, K1P 5H3, for a booklet listing foundations; there will be a charge.

†In Canada contact the local Provincial Community Services Branch.

should be made with the state park and recreation or conservation services.

These funds do not all originate in the park or natural resource area of government. For example, Federal Law and Justice Funds might be available for training and supplying agency enforcement personnel. Federal forest protection funds might be available for communication systems as well as fire fighting equipment, and federal health and welfare funds might be available for sanitation systems.

Grants. As previously indicated, the subject of grants deserves special handling. Grants are available from both governmental and nongovernmental sources. They may be used for capital or operation requirements. They are available to both public and nonpublic agencies as well as to individuals. The art and technique of securing grants is called grantsmanship and is a most important process.

Until the 1970s, in the United States, one could assume that all grants would be dedicated funds and could be used only for a special single purpose. This is no longer the case. With the advent of block grants from the federal government the various lower levels of government have greater freedom of allocation.

In the 1980s, a period of fiscal austerity, it would be well to review all grant sources.

Governmental Grants. These might be federal grants to state or local agencies, state grants to state agencies, or state grants to a lower entity. The latter include those grants from a federal source administered through the states. There are two basic types of governmental grants: the first uses a formula for a determining amount, such as the Land and Water Conservation Funds, Historic Preservation Funds, or Boating Funds; and those that go directly from the federal government to the specific agency, such as the Dingell-Johnson Funds. In the second type no formula is used to determine the amount. These might be through the National Education Association, or Health and Human Services.

Private Philanthropy. As previously indicated, there are vast amounts of monies available through private philanthropy. Success here will also depend on the grantsmanship of the agency. These techniques are becoming so important that intensive training sessions are held weekly some place in North America. Many municipalities, colleges and universities, and private agencies engage persons whose sole function is to procure grants. The activity is becoming so technical that the subject is being added to many college curricula.*

Bonds. Bonds are interest-bearing certificates of debt issued by a corporation or government by which an agency gains immediate access to funds while committing itself to fulfillment of an obligation. Three categories of bonds are mentioned here, but bonds may have many variations and often bear the name of the issuing authority such as "councilmanic bonds."

General obligation bonds. These bonds pledge full faith and credit of the municipality and are paid for by general taxation. General obligation bonds provide for the early acquisition and completion of development with payment prorated over several years, during which time the site is usable.

Revenue bonds. Revenue bonds are not used unless the financed projects return revenues. The revenues produced by specific earning assets are pledged and, as such, the issues are dependent on the governing authority to receive revenues from use of the facility constructed, in an amount sufficient to pay the principal and interest. These bonds have the same advantage as general obligation bonds but the disadvantage of having to make payment on schedule *from the revenue received.*

---

*Check individual college and university catalogs, as well as private organizations such as the Grantsmanship Center, 1015 West Olympic Boulevard, Los Angeles, CA. 90015. The Center also publishes "The Grantsmanship Center News," which reports on all aspects of grantsmanship.

Special assessment bonds. These sorts of bonds are used where special benefits to property are equal to or greater than the assessment. These bonds are used and paid for by the residents of the local area, such as a sewer district. They are often called LIDs, (local improvement districts). Like the general obligation bonds, they pledge full faith and credit of the governing agency.

Special Tax Levies. These are taxes levied against a special source, such as cigarettes or gasoline, for a special purpose such as park development or boating access. This method has the advantage of enabling the agency to predict the amount of revenue and ensure the income over a long period of time.

Fees and Charges. These can be levied for almost anything, depending on past history and policy of an agency. Effective lobbying, or the lack of it, is the key to instituting a charge or to preventing one. Fees are commonly charged for showers, dog kennels, boat rentals, horseback rides, firewood permits, camping, parking, day-use entrance, guarded beaches, special equip-

Fig. 6-1. Fees are a source of income but fee collection has its own costs. This gate attendant is collecting fees at the entrance to Mactaquac Provincial Park. (Photo courtesy of New Brunswick Department of Tourism.)

ment, special instruction, and activity entrance (Fig. 6-1). Of course fees have their own administrative costs.

Some fees are collected directly by an employee from the user. When this is the situation, consideration should be given not only to the cost of collection, but also to the possibility of misappropriation of funds. Fees are also collected by mechanical devices, such as those charged for hot water showers, or gas or electric stoves. The original cost of the unit must be considered, as well as the fact that there are still personnel costs for the collection of the monies and for maintaining these mechanical devices. There also is the cost of vandalism and stolen monies. Sometimes fees are collected by an employee from honor boxes where users are requested to deposit the amount due. Again, employee costs as well as the potential for misappropriation must be considered. The possibility of theft or use without payment must also be taken into account.

Additional fees may be charged for out-of-area visitors. This decision will undoubtedly be made by the legislative authority. Perhaps you, as a park manager, will have to explain this charge to an irate out-of-area visitor. Should those who don't pay area taxes use area facilities without an extra fee? In 1980, 9 of the 50 state parks agencies had special charges for out-of-state users. These were Delaware, Idaho, Maine, Nebraska, New Hampshire, Oregon, Vermont, Washington, and Wisconsin. There are many states and provinces where extra charges are made for hunting and fishing licenses for non-residents.

CONCESSIONS

The subject of concessions is of great importance. In North America, the term "concession" as it relates to park use, means a space or privilege within a park for a subsidiary business or service. Examples are overnight accommodations (Fig. 10-7), places to buy food, rent canoes, or obtain rides accompanied by interpretation (Figs. 6-2, and 6-3). These outlets are not only a potential source of income but also a key factor

Fig. 6-2. Concessions in parks provide useful services and are a source of income for the park. Transporting visitors for a fee is an example of such a service. These tour boats carry thousands of visitors through a lush river valley to Fern Grotto in Wailua River State Park on the island of Kauai, Hawaii. (Photo courtesy of Hawaii State Parks.)

in park operation. For this reason, concessions are being handled as a major unit within fiscal management.

The fundamental problem of *who* should apply services must be dealt with at the outset. It is the policy of some agencies that all services should be provided and operated by the agency itself. Others believe that certain services should

Fig. 6-3. The boat tour guide, a concession employee, is seen interpreting the Fern Grotto at Wailua River State Park. The site is important to the history of native Hawaiian rituals. (Photo courtesy of Hawaii State Parks.)

be provided by private enterprise whenever possible.

This decision will be governed by agency policy. There is something to be said on both sides. The profitable activity would not be there at all were it not for the agency, therefore perhaps the agency should reap the benefit. Also, the undesirable aspects of concession operation can be eliminated or lessened if the public agency handles these tasks. On the other hand, private operators will pay a business and occupation tax, a leasehold tax, and will provide a net income to the agency if they handle these sales and services. Proponents of this view claim concessioners can be controlled with proper safeguards. Once an agency determines its basic philosophy, it should adopt a policy to guide it in future considerations.

Concession Policy

If a concession-type service is contemplated, the agency must determine if it is already being provided in close proximity to the park. If the answer is yes, then the service should not be provided in the park. If the answer is no, then service should be provided in the park. Should agency policy require that all services are to be agency provided, standard operating procedures should be followed and no further explanation is needed.

However, should the agency policy provide for concessioners there are two possibilities. (1) When it is reasonable to assume a profit can be made, the special service should be granted to private concession operators. (2) When it is not reasonable to assume that a profit can be made, the service should be provided by the agency. The reason for this approach is that the agency already made the decision that the service was necessary and was not being provided close by. Therefore, it should be provided even if it is not a money maker.

This last point arises from a philosophy of holding the monetary return to the agency secondary to the public service provided by the concessioner. There will invariably be an outcry from business interests if the agency puts itself in a position of competition with the private sector.

The required buildings are usually built by the agency for financial reasons as well as esthetic ones, as concessioners can seldom get financing to undertake such construction on public land. The concession has to pay the park a certain percentage of its gross, based on graduated rates, and customarily it also must pay an initial contract fee.

Manager-Concessioner Relationships

With the granting of a concession, the agency creates a very delicate twofold relationship between the agency, the park manager, and the concessioner.

Business. The concession operation is a private business venture, one that must return a profit in order to provide an incentive for the concessioner to serve the public. Business management, unfortunately, is not normally part of the education of the park manager. Yet the manager must oversee the total park operation, including the concession. This situation often causes difficulty.

One of the problems lies in the quality of goods handled in gift shops. Part of the public is outraged by imported "junk" being sold in what they perceive as a natural area. On the other hand, they might not buy expensive local arts and crafts if they were for sale. The "junk" might sell and help the concessioner stay in business while handling less lucrative but necessary services. Also, the manager will be concerned that the concessioner usually charges higher prices than do merchants in nearby towns. However, the manager must remember that the transport and personnel costs are higher, while the season is shorter, for the concessioner.

Living. Park and concession personnel usually live and work in close proximity. As a result it is essential that a friendly atmosphere marked by open communication prevail between park and concession personnel. There is ample opportunity for friction here, considering the complications of families, housing, life-styles, and agency regulations.

Concession employees in particular traditionally cause problems. They arrive green, go right to work, then explode into the backwoods and mountainsides on their too-brief free time, hike too far, and often get hurt, lost, or stranded. They need orientation to the park—especially if it is a large one—yet in the busy early days of the season they seldom get it. This presents a real challenge to the park manager.

Controls

The park manager is the on-site agency administrator of the concession agreements within the boundaries of the park. To do that job effectively, it is crucial that the manager be fully cognizant of the authority under which he or she operates. Administrative duties usually include, but are not limited to, assuring the following.

1. The operation is in basic compliance with the terms of the agreement.
2. The hours of operation are adhered to unless otherwise authorized by the manager.
3. The facility and premises are maintained in a clean, safe, and sanitary condition.
4. Operating personnel are clean, courteous, and qualified to serve the public.
5. The inventory is adequate to meet reasonable expected demands.
6. The operator is maintaining a daily cash-flow sheet. This does not need to be checked daily but must be ready for spot checks.

In addition, it is essential that the park manager be familiar with and subscribe to the agency's policy relating to public service concessions. The concession operation is an integral public service function under the manager's command, and the concession operator is an extension of the park family. When viewed in this light, it should be obvious to the park manager that assistance and guidance expended on behalf of the concession operation is not only an obligation, but will reflect managerial competency. In other words, if you can't handle the concessioner smoothly, what kind of a manager are you?

Misunderstandings. Certain segments of the public have strong views regarding concessioners and their selection. Those who dislike the practice of allowing private concessioners in parks use some of the following arguments.

1. *There is no competition.* The public often believes that the bidding documents are developed to allow only a single favored bidder. Federal, state, and provincial laws guard against this possibility, and it rarely occurs.
2. *Creature comforts ought not to be introduced into park areas.* Some people don't want the civilized comforts for themselves, thus believe there should be none available for anyone. Unless these Spartans comprise a proven majority, their wishes cannot be fully adhered to. Certain basic services are expected, especially if they are not available elsewhere.
3. *Personal bias can and will play a part in the decision if contracts are awarded, whereas if the selection is based entirely on the best financial bid, that bias will be eliminated.* Contracts are not always awarded to the low bidder but, more often, to the concessioner who provides the best public service consistent with protection of the resource.

How does the U.S. National Park Service handle its concessions? Congressional policy is "to encourage and enable private persons and corporations to provide and operate facilities and services deemed desirable for the accommodation of visitors." William Everhart in *The National Park Service* writes very succinctly on this topic. Here is an excerpt:

The only reason for licensing a business concern to operate a concession in a national park is to provide a service that is needed by the public. The only way the concessioner can stay in business and provide the service is to make a profit.

The Park Service insists, as it presses concessioners for improved or expanded services, that of course it appreciates the fact that the concessioners' operations must be profitable. Concessioners are equally emphatic, as they attempt to remain solvent under trying conditions, that they are also concerned with protecting national park values. To many people, conducting a business for profit in a national park somehow doesn't seem right. To the concessioner, who is constrained both by the rules of free enterprise and government regulation, a profit of less than four percent doesn't seem quite right, either.

Paying what seems to be a rather high price for a hotel room, which may turn out to be something less than lavish, and standing in a long breakfast line while a college student with more weighty matters on his or her mind boils the eggs beyond the requested three minutes may cause many a visitor to echo Stephen Mather's declaration that this kind of treatment doesn't add much to a vacation trip. Letters to senators or congressmen or the Secretary of the Interior will compare service and prices in the parks unfavorably with those outside the park. The injured parties generally threaten to take their business elsewhere, and concessioners often wish that they could do the same.[1]

Everhart also mentions the perennial concessioner problems—the short season, the long haul for supplies, the labor difficulties—and notes these same factors also operate to raise construction costs on the facilities.

Early or late in the season, travelers complain if the concessioner is not open to serve their needs, but profits melt in light visitation periods. Weather, earthquakes, eruptions, gas prices—the concessioner may be seriously affected by these, yet must fulfill the operating agreement. There is a high risk of business failure, and thus visitors must pay more for services in remote areas. All these difficulties provide a continuing source of discontent which managers must learn to weigh properly, while not allowing it to color their relationship with the concessioners.

Canada chose an entirely different system. Here enclaves were established within the national parks as town sites, where, with little restriction, competition among private business people was allowed to determine the range and quality of services available to the public. This method has not been without its problems. The Canadian national park administration has had to become involved in municipal affairs and this has greatly complicated the task of park management.

Regardless of which approach has been taken in the matter of concessions in parks, most administrators and concession operators find the relationship fraught with difficulty. It must be handled with good sense and good will, and with the full knowledge that it is an integral part of fiscal management.

BUDGETING

A budget is a fiscal road map to aid the agency in getting where it wants to go within the laws governing the agency. It is a tool that forces the agency to realistically review its priorities and place them within the limits of available funds. It is a bookkeeping process which tentatively establishes income and expenditures. All agencies and units of agencies will have a budget and must learn to operate within its restrictions.

Over the course of time, with changes in administration, agencies will sometimes be instructed by higher authority to bring in a budget request of a *specific amount*, while at other times the instructions will be to submit a budget request which reflects what the higher authority believes the agency *needs*. Regardless of which method is used, the agency might also be directed to submit the details via the *program budgeting system* (PBS) or by some other breakdown.

Types of Budgeting

Specific Amount Budgeting. "The boss" will dictate the amount. The boss will be different people at different levels, but the boss is the boss and the amount indicated must be on the bottom line. The usual disadvantage of this type of approach is that many worthwhile programs never get considered.

The advantages of this system are that time will not be spent developing programs that will not be authorized (no matter how badly needed), and that every avenue will be explored in order to do as much as possible within the set resource. Such an approach may necessitate use of volunteers, as discussed in Chapter 8, Citizen Involvement.

Current Level Budgeting. This implies that the agency will fund the same programs and to the same degree for the next budget period. In addition to the advantages and disadvantages noted for the specific amount budgeting, this type has other disadvantages, such as precluding shift in programs as needed during the budget period. Also, with cost of living increases and inflation, current level is actually a decrease and will necessitate the reduction or elimination of one or more programs.

Some current level budgets include current level plus cost of living, plus extended programs, plus new programs. These options provide the decision makers the opportunity to know how much money it takes to conduct the existing program. The budget should also contain explanation of what it would take and what would be the benefits of extending existing programs, as well as of initiating new ones.

Need Budgeting. Budgeting is a year-round activity. Practically speaking, the budget should be developed on the basis of need no matter what the instructions are, as it is the only way to plan for the future and to continually strive to fulfill that plan. This is the prime advantage to *need* *budgeting*. The disadvantage is that the agency might spend considerable time developing programs which will never be funded.

Zero-based Budgeting.

Here the agency assumes that it has no monies and, therefore, no personnel and no program. From that zero base the agency builds its budget, based on priority. Note that few agencies are required to conduct zero-based budgeting even though it is often discussed. The zero-based process is advantageous as it forces the agency to carefully consider its priorities. It is also very time-consuming, as the budget request must be prepared from the ground up each year.

Program Budgeting System

World War II brought many changes including the program budgeting system. Since those early Pentagon days many agencies have developed a variety of offshoots of this system. Under this system the decision-making agency, be it the city council, the office of the mayor, or whoever, requires the budget to be presented in set program categories so that the decision makers know not only how much an individual agency is requesting, but how much each agency is requesting for a specific function or program. Park budget requests would be categorized under such headings as maintenance, historical areas, publications, and so on. A specific item (such as publications) could be traced across all agencies. Then the decision makers can add up all of the requests within a given function or program area and act accordingly. From this type of analysis decision makers may notice potential duplications or voids, as well as imbalance in specific areas.

Budget Preparation

Most agencies divide the agency budget into two main categories, capital and operating. Here, operating budget will cover recurring activities such as salaries, utilities, goods, and services. Capital

budget will deal with items that are not recurring, such as land acquisition, development, and major equipment (see Chapter 9).

After an agency receives instructions as to the type of budget to prepare and the form in which to present it, what comes next?

Very specific directions should be issued to the employees concerning budget preparation. These directions should include time limitations, as well as any instructions as to which type of park activities are currently being requested by the administration, such as more lifeguards, and what is being downplayed—perhaps publications.

As budgets move up the chain of command, various components should be combined so that when the final budget reaches the top decision maker, the needs are classified by categories as well as by operating divisions. It must be assumed that budget requests to a higher authority will be reduced; therefore attention to priorities is crucial. Priority should be indicated by the position of the item on the list. One should be prepared for all budget cuts to be made from the bottom up. Priority is also necessary as items higher on the list frequently affect other priorities and the results become more complex if one of these is cut. Also, the budget will be prepared with more thought if the persons involved are aware that cuts will be made by priority.

Special attention should be given to information dissemination regarding new programs and additions to existing programs so that personnel will not only do the preparation in a uniform way but also will not waste time. For example, if the governing body definitely rules out a new campground at park X, then there is no sense in placing it in the budget, or if there is to be no increase in the number of park aides, managers should be aware of this and adhere to the directive.

The top-level personnel in the agency should review budget instructions for clarity, practicability of dates, and other such matters. The following is an example of the type of instructions the park manager might receive for budget preparation.

Budget Preparation—Instructions and Responsibilities. The budget process is a lengthy ordeal that consumes thousands of hours throughout the agency. However, it is a process necessary to good government and the agency's chances of success are directly related to the preparation and presentation.

The budget process should generate a good deal of thought rather than mechanical busy work. It is to be hoped that the time spent in computing dollar figures can be minimized, thus allowing time for the more important purpose of logically constructing justifications for proposed budget changes. Managers are to indicate the projected expenditures for the upcoming fiscal period and justify any required changes. Managers will also be provided worksheets to justify new positions and equipment. Any additional justification that might help in selling part of the budget may be included.

To minimize the accounting done by the park managers, the finance office will do as much of the actual accounting as possible. The fiscal staff will provide the current level of expenditures for salaries and will show salary increase costs and health insurance increase costs. The manager will not need to be concerned with justifying current level unless he or she knows a good reason for reducing that current level. For instance, if a park has seven permanently assigned positions and the manager believes that one of these positions is no longer necessary, the fiscal office needs to know why.

The park manager should show what increases of current levels are proposed and provide the necessary justification. That is, if you believe you are justified in increasing your total number of park aides by six persons, you will provide the justification and the fiscal office will compute the necessary salary and benefit allowance.

Following are two examples of possible budget change proposals.

Example 1: Assume a one-time expenditure was made during the current year but is not anticipated next year. The budget request would reflect a negative change for a nonrecurring cost.

Example 2: Assume that legislation requires a mobile home safety door in each park-owned mobile home. This legal mandate should be stated. Any increase to the budget that can be shown to result from some legislation will be much easier to justify.

If there are concerns not reflected in this document please contact the fiscal officer. All items of change will have to be given priority within each division and within the agency. This will be accomplished through meetings between each division's administrative staff and between division heads and the Director. Finally, of course, the Commission (Board) will determine the final priority position of each change. [2]

What Happens Next?

Park managers and park staff give considerable thought, time, and effort to preparing a budget. It is natural that they want to know what happens to the budget after it leaves the park. This information should be given to the park manager at the same time the budget instructions are issued. The manager needs to understand the different inputs as the budget grows through the various levels, and the high probability that many changes will be made. To continue to build staff morale and confidence, the fiscal office should also inform park managers as to the reasons for any changes.

Operating Impact

Earlier in this chapter, note was made of the differences between capital and operating budgets. There is an additional aspect to the discussion, and it is called *operating impact*.

Most agencies will be directed to present their

budgets with at least a major division between those funds necessary to operate what they have (operating budget), and those necessary to effect major improvements and acquisitions (capital budget).

The preparation of the capital budget is similar to preparing the operating budget. However, there is a major difference: the capital budget should contain an *operating impact*.

Operating impact is the name given to the amount of operating funds that need to be added to the operating budget *if the agency is successful* in receiving appropriation for the capital request. The operating impact must include planning and engineering costs as well as operational costs, such as for rangers, utilities, goods, and equipment—all part of the operation once the proposal becomes a reality.

Furthermore, as more funds are expended for capital, and more line staff are added, there will be need for more support staff. Therefore, the addition of support staff in the agency's payroll, fiscal, clerical, and supply sections should be considered.

Getting It Approved

All of the budget preparation effort will be of little avail if the legislative body does not pass the budget. For this reason the park manager will undoubtedly receive some special instructions from the director.

The manager might be instructed to invite area legislators to the park to view certain needs that are reflected in the budget request. News coverage might also be suggested. The manager might also be instructed to be at a budget hearing or, perhaps, to stay away. It is important that the manager and supervisor understand each other and the reason for the instructions.

Obviously, there is much more to the passage of a budget. Successful agencies work year round to get the budget passed. This continuing effort becomes, in fact, a high-priority item among the agency programs.

ACCOUNTING

Assume now that the legislative body has passed the budget. It is time to set up the books and implement accounting. Accounting is not just bookkeeping. It is a dynamic process that shows if we are following the fiscal road map we laid out when budgeting. It includes the following.

1. Knowing income.
2. Knowing expenditures.
3. Knowing cash flow.
4. Knowing what is committed via a contract (purchases) for which the service or item has not yet been received. These are called *encumbrances*.
5. Estimating correctly what services will have been used prior to the actual billing, such as electricity and water. These are called *accruals*.
6. Knowing where you are, compared to where you should be, fiscally.

Handling of Funds

The chances are that either the agency or the governmental entity in which the agency operates will have very specific rules concerning how park managers will requisition goods and supplies and, subsequently, how the agency will make those purchases and account for the goods. The securing of equipment requires at least seven separate actions. This complexity tends to irritate the park employee who is trying to get something done.

First, and perhaps most important, the employee must identify the equipment needed to do the job. All too often the wrong item is received because the person needing the item was not sufficiently accurate or specific.

Then the paperwork starts. The first piece is the *requisition*. The requisition does not give the authority to purchase. It is the document that contains the information needed to assist the purchasing people in making decisions.

The purchasing people now determine if sufficient funds are available and in the proper account. Next, the item required either "goes to bid" to select a vendor or a vendor is selected from a predetermined listing.

A *purchase order* is then sent to the vendor who is to provide the equipment to the park. After the park employee verifies that what was received was the ordered item, the vendor is paid.

Inventories. No matter what your level of authority in the park, *you* will be responsible and accountable for some inventory of equipment. When you arrive at your new post it is mandatory that you, as a manager, know what equipment is your responsibility. You need to be certain the equipment is all present and in good shape before you become accountable for it. This process should be on paper and signed by at least one person in addition to yourself.

Furthermore, once you have accepted the inventory, you need to be careful as to what you loan to your fellow employees located in the next park. Obtain a receipt, as you are the person who will be held accountable, which could mean *financially.*

New items received at your park need to be recorded by whatever process is used by your agency. Transfer of items to another park or deletion as a result of breakage should also be recorded.

When you are being transferred to another duty station you will want to have a signoff from a higher authority indicating that your inventory was satisfactorily accounted for.

Handling Cash. Nearly all full-time park employees will handle cash some time. When you do, remember certain basic facts and rules. Regrettably, some citizens will believe that you are trying to pocket some for yourself. Therefore you need to be constantly alert and not give anyone cause to wonder about your handling of money.

To assist you, here are two suggestions. (1) Give and receive receipts whenever possible and (2) never mix *your* cash with that of the *public.*

Don't "borrow for a day" from the petty cash fund or other such account with the thought that you will repay it tomorrow. No matter how well meaning your plan, sometimes tomorrow never comes and then you are in trouble. Most agencies have a means of keeping a close watch on these matters, such as by use of auditing procedures.

Internal Auditor. Agencies are audited by designated authorities within the states or provinces, as well as by the appropriate federal authorities should they expend any federal funds. Regular audits, by their nature, are conducted as late as a year or more after the end of the fiscal period being audited. As a result, any improper procedure by park personnel will continue for that length of time as the person will not be aware that it is not acceptable. In the case of illegal procedures, these too will continue until brought to light. Also, any irregularities or downright thefts of funds can grow to major, noncorrectable proportions in such a length of time. These situations can be alleviated, if not completely corrected, by use of an internal auditor.

This internal audit service must be on a continuing basis with reports filed regularly. The internal auditor should be responsible to and report to one of the two top people in the agency.

An internal auditor will not prevent misappropriation of funds, nor eliminate use of improper fiscal procedures. However, a competent internal auditor will enable an agency to be more responsible financially. This interim check might also save some very worthwhile personnel from developing bad habits, by providing preventive guidance.

CONCLUSION

The importance of competent fiscal management cannot be overstated. Quite a few park professionals either lose their jobs or are placed in secondary management roles because of lack of ability in fiscal management. It is hoped that this chapter will stimulate the student as well as the practitioner of park management to gain more knowledge and experience in fiscal matters, and to recognize their importance in career development.

REFERENCES

General References

Artz, Robert M. and Hubert Bermont. 1970. *Guide to New Approaches to Financing Parks and Recreation.* Acropolis Books. Washington, DC.

Hormgren, Charles T. 1974. *Accounting for Management Control.* Prentice-Hall, Inc. Englewood Cliffs, NJ.

Howard, Dennis and John L. Crompton. 1980. *Financing, Managing, and Marketing Recreation and Park Resources.* William C. Brown Co. Publishers. Dubuque, IA.

Lothian, W. F. 1977. *A History of Canada's National Parks.* Vol. II. Parks Canada QS-7034-020-EE-AI. Ottawa.

Spears, Charles R. 1978. "Generating Park Revenue." *Trends.* The Park Practice Program. National Recreation and Park Association. Arlington, VA.

Trudeau, Richard C. 1981. "Creative Financing in a Cutback Era," *Trends.* Park Practice Program. National Recreation and Park Association. 18(2):18–24. Arlington, VA.

U.S. Department of the Interior. Heritage Conservation and Recreation Service. 1979. *Fees and Charges Handbook.* Washington, DC.

U.S. Department of the Interior. Heritage Conservation and Recreation Service. 1979. *Foundations . . . A Handbook.* Washington, DC.

U.S. Department of the Interior. Heritage Conservation and Recreation Service. 1979. *Land Conservation and Preservation Techniques.* Washington, DC.

U.S. Department of the Interior. Heritage Conservation and Recreation Service. 1980. *Scrounging.* Washington, DC.

U.S. Department of the Interior. Heritage Conservation and Recreation Service. 1981. *Federal Assistance Guide for Park and Recreation Professionals.* Washington, DC.

U.S. Department of the Interior. National Park Service. 1982. *Cutback Management.* Washington, DC.

U.S. Department of the Interior. Park and Recreation Technical Services. 1981. *Cost-Cutting Stategies for the Park and Recreation Agency.* Washington, DC.

U.S. Department of the Interior. Park and Recreation Technical Services. 1981. *Energy Planning and Management for Parks and Recreation.* Washington, DC.

References Cited

1. Everhart, William C. 1972. *The National Park Service.* Praeger Publishers. New York.
2. Washington State Parks and Recreation Commission, Olympia, WA.

CHAPTER SEVEN

PERSONNEL MANAGEMENT

Gifford Pinchot said, *The first condition of success in any job is not brains but character. Over and over again I have seen men of moderate intelligence come to the front because they had the courage, integrity, self respect, steadiness, perseverance and confidence in themselves, their cause, and their work.*

In most outdoor recreation agencies the greatest percent of the total operating costs will be for personnel. Not for the square footage of space they occupy, nor for the telephones, paper and other supplies they use, nor for the gasoline they consume—but for the actual personnel—their wages and fringe benefits. People are costly. Their wages keep going up, and those fringe benefits (medical, retirement, Old Age Survivor's Insurance, to name a few) continue to increase. Therefore, although sound fiscal management is vital, the proper staffing and the proper utilization of that staff is, collectively, the single most important aspect of sound administration, both for the costs involved and for the quality of work that these people will do for the agency that hires them.

Effective personnel management seems to be a blend of two distinct competencies. One involves knowledge of the mechanics of administration, such as hiring, types of positions, and conditions of employment. The other depends on the ability to lead and inspire others. Requirements for the first can be gained through experience; requirements for the second are more elusive. Training and observation might help, but skill in this latter area seems to come naturally to some, not at all to others.

HIRING

Persons responsible for hiring must take the time, have the patience, and exercise the skills necessary to recognize the type of person who will succeed on the job. Procedures must be developed that aid the comparison process. The agency must develop certain criteria to use in filling the vacant position and compare applicants to the criteria, not to each other.

Defining the Skills

Before starting the process of recruiting personnel, it is crucial to determine what skills are needed to do the job. What is preferred in educational background and experience, especially experience relative to the position in question, and what personal qualities are needed to do the job?

There are many ways to determine what skills are needed. One procedure is to make a list of all the performances each job requires with the estimated emphasis (time requirements) for each of these. This list is often called a CQ (classification questionnaire) or KSA (knowledge, skills, and abilities). Perhaps this can best be done by having the supervisor of the position develop the list of skills needed in order of importance. Priority on this list will not always be given to the skill most frequently used. For example, supervisory tasks might consume only 15 percent of the person's time, yet supervisory skills could be the most important requirement. Another aid in developing the list is to ask advice from the person leaving the job.

Recruitment

Recruitment is the process used to locate the best qualified people and to interest them in applying for the position (Fig. 7-1). After determining the job to be done and the minimum qualifications needed to do it, there is the question of legal constraints, which is covered under Rules Governing Hiring, later in this chapter. When these have been taken into account, an application form should be designed to elicit the necessary information from the applicants.

The potential applicants must be located and informed of the opening. At this point a recruitment bulletin is developed, usually a single sheet of paper containing pertinent data about the job

Fig. 7-1. A park employee, standing at right, discusses employee recruitment methods of his agency with a visiting outdoor recreation class. These informal sessions give students a realistic picture of agency expectations. Pacific Rim National Park, British Columbia. (Photo by Grant W. Sharpe.)

requirements, minimum qualifications, salary, and process for applying. The bulletin should also contain basic information the potential employee needs, such as job title, job location, and some data about the job from the classification questionnaire.

Agencies frequently provide these bulletins to colleges and universities, professional societies, and to other agencies as well as making direct contacts with these same organizations to ensure wide dissemination of the job opportunity and qualifications. The guidelines set forth here are basically aimed at recruitment of persons *into* the agency. However, nearly all of the suggestions are also applicable to those employees applying for a different job within the agency.

There are many ways an agency can obtain information about applicants to enable it to select the best possible person for the job. These include a combination of the following factors.

1. The completed application form along with requested materials such as grade course transcripts, letters of reference, list of past employers, and work experience.
2. Telephone or in-person discussion with references, past employers, peers, and subordinates.
3. Examining college transcripts with particular emphasis on achievement in the courses related to the job to be filled. Where possible, look for subsequent improvement in low grades as a measure of the person's ability to adapt and learn, as well as for consistent high achievement.
4. Examination—written or oral.
5. Personal interview.

Examination

Prior to the examination, the list of applicants is checked to certify that all applicants meet minimum requirements. These might include education level, certain skills and licenses, and specified experience in certain types of jobs.

The people who make the certified lists are now further identified by one of two types of examinations.

1. A review panel examines all of the data provided in the applications and other sources. Often this consideration ranks the applicants on the basis of education and training (called E & T) or knowledge, skills, and abilities (KSA). Sometimes the ranking is affected by a weight system whereby certain characteristics are given more value than others. These values are as set by the supervisor in preparation of the original document, the KSA, or classification questionnaire (CQ).
2. A review panel might also administer a written or oral exam. Since the persons taking the examination have already met minimum qualifications, the examination should be geared to discover and reflect the particular skills and characteristics needed for the job. For example, if law enforcement is an important requirement, then the examination should reflect the applicant's knowledge and experience in this area. As a general rule, the oral examination should be given in the latter stages of the selection process when only top choices are left, as it usually entails the presence of a panel, making this form of examination costly.

The oral examination panel might include persons who are qualified in park management but who are not from the agency concerned. For this reason, and to assure uniformity of standards, the hiring agency should provide the examining board with some guidelines. At the same time the panel must be cautioned against favoring any applicant by its manner of questioning. The following are examples of questions which an examining panel might use in determining the strengths of individuals being considered for entry-level park ranger positions. They will probably supplement these with questions coming out of their own area of expertise or interest.

1. Why do you believe you are qualified to work for this agency?
2. What do you believe your experiences and education could contribute to this park organization?
3. What do you know about this agency, its objectives, purpose for existence and structure?
4. What are your long-range goals?
5. How would you handle the situation if your superior gave you an order you believed to be unethical or illegal?

Members of the examining panel are often asked to make note of their impressions of each individual interviewed. These are confidential, and are for the use of the administrator responsible for the final decision.

Personal Interview. The lists have been certified and the examinations have taken place. It is now time for the supervisor in question to interview the top candidates. This might be done in person or by telephone. It is necessary for the supervisor to be able to chat awhile with each of the candidates, as by this time all candidates are capable of doing the job but all might not harmonize with the agency or the particular method of operation of the supervisor. By talking with applicants for a few moments, another dimension of their personality can be observed.

Selection

Once the final choice is made and the successful applicant has been congratulated, matters yet to be covered would include moving expenses, starting date, starting salary and any special conditions of employment. The unsuccessful candidates should also be thanked for applying and should be notified that the vacancy has been filled, *after* the successful applicant has accepted the position.

The technical and legal aspects of the selection process will be set forth by agency rules. These should be clearly understood before starting the hiring process and should be followed throughout.

Probationary Period

This period of time, usually six months, is an important part of the personnel selection process. During this time employers should carefully and continually review the new employee's work. Regrettably, few employers utilize this probationary period properly.

There are four basic reasons why the probationary period is significant.

1. There are some persons who are outstanding in tests but inadequate on the job, and others who do mediocre work on a test, but who function very well in the actual situation. Six months should be sufficient to find this out.
2. In most parts of North America, it takes six months to effectively observe new personnel, particularly field personnel, in both the busy and the slow season.
3. It allows the agency to determine if the employee fits the agency, and gives the employee an opportunity to see if the agency fits his or her expectations and career plans.
4. It provides the employee a chance to adjust to the new job and begin to perform up to capability. Should the employee not work out, termination at this time does not involve the legal steps necessary for permanent employees.

TYPES OF POSITIONS

Those being hired full time usually will be in one of two basic categories: Civil Service positions or exempt positions. Civil Service positions are also referred to as "covered." The titles might differ from place to place, but the concepts are still the same.

Civil Service

Most agencies will be required to hire one of the top three on the Civil Service register of names provided by the personnel department. There are some deviations from this practice. For some jobs an agency may select from an "open register" any person who has met the minimum qualifications and passed any required examination. Another variation is "3 plus 3" whereby an agency may hire from the top three, as noted above, plus the top three minority persons who are on the register, though they are not in the top three from an examination aspect.

Another variation is the reduction-in-force (RIF) register, which usually takes precedence over all other hiring registers. For instance, should lack of funds necessitate the elimination of a Ranger II position, the person presently filling that position would have the right to take a lateral position from a person who has less seniority or to take a lower position (Ranger I) in the same way. Close coordination with the employee's labor union is advisable when implementing RIF. There also are transfer and promotional registers, and sometimes an agency can use "selective certification" where particular circumstances warrant such specifics as, perhaps, a husband and wife team for live-in supervisors at a youth camp.

Exempt Positions

Basically, an exempt position is one that may be filled by the hiring authority without reference to any register. Often this position may be filled without reference to specific requirements. This latter point will vary from agency to agency and even from exempt position to exempt position within an agency. What is true for hiring is equally applicable for dismissal, as persons filling these positions can be dismissed without cause. The agency head and staff reporting directly to this person are usually in exempt positions.

Special Employment Categories

The trend continues for increased employment of other than full-time regular employees. Sometimes the wages of these employees are budgeted, such as for park aides and lifeguards, while at other times these are a nonbudgeted addition, such as enrollees in federally funded special programs that usually change, at least in title and often in thrust, with every change of administration. It is important that management personnel, at any level of authority, be aware of these hiring opportunities.

Part-time Employees. Part-time employees could either be engaged on a full-time (eight-hour day) basis in positions such as lifeguard or park aide, work only part of the year (seasonals), or could work less than full time (standard number of hours per week) over the year and be known as "less-than-full time" employees. Other similar combination of days and parts of the year are possible.

Whether seasonal or less-than-full time, these employees enable the agency to augment its staff with specialists during the busy season without having to employ them when there is little for them to do. These positions also afford the opportunity to engage college students in the summer, thus providing them with needed income and valuable experience while at the same time giving the agency the opportunity to hire qualified individuals and to see them in operation. A special type of college program is that of the intern, which affords an agency the opportunity to employ a *volunteer* who is highly motivated to work and learn, as park work is that person's chosen profession. In this way professionals-in-training will be able to consider the agency as a potential place of employment, and the agency can carefully screen the intern as a potential employee. These programs vary in length from a college quarter on a part-time basis, to a given term, staggered over two or more years, on a full-time basis.

Conservation and Work Training Programs. The decade of the 1970s saw a great increase in federal government programs and funds for the hiring of special groups. It is worthy of note that during that period of time the U.S. Government spent over $64 billion on these types of programs,

the most recent being the Comprehensive Employment and Training Act (CETA). Agencies using these funds should always keep in mind that they should be for *supplemental* personnel as on any given day the monies might be canceled. Such was the case in 1981 when the administration canceled CETA. At the same time, an agency should be ready to hire supplemental employees when such funds are available, as their work can be most useful.

Volunteers. Some park managers believe they could not operate without volunteers, while others say they cannot operate with them. However, there is a place for volunteers in every agency. This subject is covered in Chapter 8, Citizen Involvement.

RULES GOVERNING HIRING

Authority

Usually the authority to engage, dismiss, or severely discipline an employee is set forth by the legislative body of the government in which the agency is located. The administration of any agency must be aware of its legal authority *and* of the rights of the individual.

Conditions of Employment

Conditions of employment include such matters as pay, sick leave, vacation, hours and places of work, dress code, behavior, and many other factors. Conditions of employment emanate primarily from three sources: statutes, union contracts, and agency policies and rules.

An agency must define the performance requirements and the type of person needed to do the job. It is important that persons being hired know what is expected of them. These expectations constitute the conditions of employment, and the agency must apprise the new employee of them. An orientation session should be held at the main office, covering the "needs to know" information applicable to all employees. This should be followed by another briefing at the place where the new employee will work.

The main office staff must take the time to be sure that incoming employees understand the rudimentary items that "oldtimers" take for granted. Some of these may be quite foreign to the newcomer. These include pay scale, retirement, vacation, holidays, sick leave, disability pensions, liability for accidents or injuries, training programs, time charts, organization line charts, policies, procedures, purposes, goals and objectives. New employees should be introduced to people within the agency and made to feel welcome and at ease. To have a happy employee this should be done the first day.

One should not assume anything, but should go over, or delegate a fellow employee to go over, the "inside items"—location of restrooms, time and duration of coffee breaks, funds for gifts

and flowers, and other such matters. New people must know what is expected of them, and how their part of the organization operates (Fig. 7-2).

Managers will probably be assigned to orient new field employees (after the newcomers receive the basics at the main or regional office) not only to park office routine, but to the park itself and to its equipment. In all, there is a large amount of material for new employees to familiarize themselves with, so some careful thought should be given to accomplishing this task in the best way both for the employees' peace of mind, and the agency's good order and proper functioning.

Affirmative Action

Affirmative action is the title given to a program developed in recognition of decades of discrimination in hiring and promotional practices with

Fig. 7-2. Orientation of new employees is an important part of a manager's job. Here at Lake Meridith National Recreation area, Texas, the manager explains a policy matter to a new employee. (National Park Service photo by Fred E. Mang, Jr.)

regard to women and minorities. Agencies are requested to develop a paper that reflects the present status of the agency's affirmative action, the goals it has set to remedy the situations, and the method by which the agency will bring about these goals.

Agencies continually monitor their programs, usually with a specific person assigned that role. Often this person is called the Equal Employment Officer (EEO). It is critical to the program that top-level personnel be fully committed to its success.

Conflict of Interest

Due to the nature of many jobs in the field of outdoor recreation and park management, there will be frequent and varied opportunities for holding a second job outside the agency in consulting, landscaping, or sales, for instance. To be certain that the agency and employees are both above reproach, there is usually a policy providing guidelines for acceptable outside employment. There also should be, although frequently there is not, a standard way employees can request permission for such employment.

Unions

Unionization is not new in park agencies. Although its initial and main thrust was in the labor and maintenance areas, in many agencies all park personnel now are union members. When one becomes an employee in an agency that has a union, membership is either obligatory (closed shop) or there is the option of joining or not joining (open shop).

Whether one does or does not become a member of the union is not germane to this chapter. What is important is that all employees of the agency adhere to the conditions of employment and, that if they are union members, they be participating members. Not only is this good policy generally, but will ensure that the agency has adequate representation at every level within the union.

TRAINING

Individuals normally come to an agency with at least the standard requirements of formal education and experience indicated by hiring requirements, but as in all employment situations, they must learn a great deal on the job. It is important that the employer and employee discuss possible training opportunities. Often employees are unaware of training opportunities and are, therefore, missing out on ways to increase their ability to serve the agency and, at the same time, to enhance their own careers.

Pretraining

It would be desirable if every employee could undergo training prior to being placed on the job. Unfortunately, very few agencies can offer this opportunity for full-time year-round personnel. On the other hand, seasonal employees are usually hired in such quantity at a given time that a pretraining session can be held. Pretraining should include a thorough orientation to the agency's organizational structure, philosophy and policies, procedures, and benefits. The pretraining should also include "how we do it" information about the specific job the person will be starting.

In those agencies that cannot train prior to the person actually commencing work, pretraining sessions should be held once or twice a year for the employees who commenced employment since the last pretraining session.

On-the-Job Training

The supervisor (this may be the park manager) should spend considerable time with the new employee during the first several weeks. Frequent attention will be welcomed and not considered stifling if the supervisor does it in a manner that builds the employee's confidence. The employee must be made aware that this is common practice, and be introduced to the necessity of establishing checkpoints. As this person shows evidence of understanding a particular part of the job, the supervisor should expose him or her to another facet of the operation.

EVALUATION

All of us want to know how we are doing, so evaluations should not be a frightening experience. The process of evaluation should be taking place constantly, not only when there is an improvement to suggest, but also at a time when honest compliments can be given. The more formal evaluation usually requires a checklist of some sort, in writing, signed by both persons. It is usually performed at three specific times: (1) midway in the probationary period to let the new employee know how he or she is doing, (2) just prior to the end of the probationary period, which is the time to decide to keep or not keep the employee, and (3) every year thereafter.

Such evaluations are enhanced if they list goals to be accomplished and contain a plan, worked out between the two individuals, to help implement the goals.

MOVEMENT

Agency personnel will be moving constantly. Sometimes that movement will be a lateral transfer, at other times, an advancement. Sometimes it will be a reduction in force for various reasons and sometimes a straight-out dismissal. Let us take a look at the various categories.

Transfer

Before considering transfers for any reasons, an agency administrator must check with the personnel officer or legal council to be certain what authority exists. In some instances the employee's approval for any type of transfer might be needed, while in other agencies transfers can be at the agency's will or for cause.

A transfer should be considered a valuable tool. In some instances it provides the opportunity for an employee to gain wide-ranging experience in a planned program of career development. In other instances it might be necessary to

separate two employees who have tried, but who are unable, to reconcile personal differences, while in yet other cases the employees might not do well in a particular geographical area. It may be the family of the employee that precipitates the move. Frequently, obtaining suitable schooling for children is the reason for requesting transfer to another area. Regrettably, sometimes transfers are used either to force an employee to resign or to make an unsatisfactory employee someone else's problem. This should not be done.

Whatever the circumstances, the supervisor and the employee should clearly understand the reason for the transfer and make sure there is agreement on details such as moving expenses and the date of transfer.

Before considering the filling of any vacancies within the agency with promotional or open-register competitive candidates, the employer should do the following.

1. Encourage any employee, who desires to do so, to apply for the position by filing a written intraagency transfer request with the agency's personnel officer.
2. Consult the intraagency transfer register composed of the names of employees who have requested transfer.
3. Consider all employees filing for transfer to the vacant position.

Advancement

As previously noted, one of the legitimate desires of employees is the opportunity for growth within the agency. Growth comes in many forms, including skills, knowledge, and advancement.

It is the responsibility of each supervisor to be aware of the desires of the employees, including their goals as they relate to advancement within the agency. There are many employees who are happy and doing a commendable job right where they are. If one believes that all jobs are important to the agency, then the supervisor must approach employees with that attitude rather than "what is wrong with you—why don't you want to advance?'' Some employees do not wish to advance, and many of these shouldn't. The Peter Principle, which states that employees advance until they reach their level of incompetency, is certainly applicable here.[2] However, there also are many who might be happier and receive more job satisfaction if they were given the opportunity to advance.

Unfortunately, a stigma seems to be attached to both the supervisor and the employee if a person advances to a position and does not succeed. An ideal, and not unrealistic, way to deal with this would be to consider the advancement as a trial period. If it doesn't work out, the experience should not be considered in a negative light. At this time an evaluation should be conducted to determine the reasons for the employee's lack of success. If the problem is correctable, a training program might be initiated, looking toward the time when the employee might again be eligible for the position. Of course, the agency must keep the former position open for the trial period.

Reduction in Force

There will be times when an agency must carry out a reduction in force (RIF). This might be caused by a cut in the budget or by the abolition or reduction of an activity. Whatever the cause, occasionally an agency will be obligated to dismiss persons who are doing a good job and who would otherwise not have been dismissed. There are often laws or policies dealing with how such reductions must be implemented. This is usually a major item in union contract negotiations. Since any such reduction will be disruptive, it is critical that the reduction-in-force plan be developed as far in advance as possible.

Dismissal

Later in this chapter, under Supervision, we will discuss general discipline. For the purpose of this chapter, ''Dismissal'' will be considered the ultimate in disciplinary action.

Because dismissal action is often challenged, and sometimes overturned, and because of the amount of time and effort dismissal action takes, those in authority will often not dismiss an unsatisfactory employee, but will place the person in a position where their actions, or inaction, will do the least harm. This method of handling a personnel problem is not recommended. Once it has been determined that the employee in question has been properly instructed in the first place, and informed of any failings or improper actions, and when it has been decided that there is no position in the agency where this person can be of value—and it has been determined that this employee will not not resign—then dismissal is in order.

The entire procedure must be carefully coordinated with the agency personnel officer. It should also be noted that an employee should never be asked to resign unless the agency is prepared to dismiss this person if they choose not to resign.

Exit Interview

When an employee leaves the agency there should be an exit interview, whether the employee is leaving as a result of dismissal, resignation, by reduction in force, or due to the end of season or temporary employment. Through a properly conducted interview, the agency can gain valuable information about supervisory practices, work condition, employee attitudes, and other matters. Subjects for discussion in the exit interview should include reason for leaving, agency strong and weak points, supervision of the employee, suitability of performance evaluation, and adequacy of the pay scale in relation to the job responsibilities. There should also be a request for suggestions for the improvement of personnel management.

SUPERVISION

If the follower hasn't followed, the leader hasn't led. What characterizes the successful leader? Mental ability, breadth of interests and aptitudes, language skills, maturity, motivation, social orientation, leadership skills, and integrity— all are necessary to a successful leader.

The administration develops policy and provides overall direction for the organization. The employees are engaged in the day-to-day operations. The supervisor is the person in between, and for most parks this is the park manager. It is the supervisor's responsibility to plan, organize, lead, control, and staff. The supervisor should do the following.

1. Plan the work of the unit. Determine the amount of work per person and assign it, trusting the people to whom it is delegated.
2. Determine if the amount and quality of work is according to plan.
3. Put the right people in the right job.
4. Organize the unit properly in order to carry out the plan.
5. Provide leadership in decision making.

The supervisor should be willing to criticize (tactfully) if criticism is called for. The supervisor is in that position because of knowledge of what needs to be done and how to get it done. Constructive criticism is an indispensable part of supervisory skills.

Behaviorial Skills

According to data reported in Bergen's book *Organizational Relationship in Management Action*, the majority of over 200 managers who participated in a survey agreed, "The most important skill an administrator can have is the ability to get along with people." In that survey, management related this ability above intelligence, decisiveness, knowledge, and job skill.[1]

Bergen suggests these seven rules for successful handling of people.

1. Perfect your self-control—the meanest, toughest, orneriest critter you will ever handle is yourself. If you can learn to handle yourself, handling others is simple.
2. Appreciate and praise—there is always a shortage of appreciation and praise. And the

average person is starved for it. That's why— in dealing with people—praise is the most powerful tool at your command.
3. Stress rewards; avoid punishments. In dealing with people, remember that they will work harder to gain a desirable reward than they will to avoid punishment.
4. Criticize tactfully—most of us love to dish it out but find it very hard to take. So, remember, tactless criticism generally makes people so angry that it does more harm than good.
5. Always listen—everyone likes to express an opinion, especially to the boss. That's why a good boss is always a good listener.
6. Explain thoroughly—give your employees every bit of information you can about the agency's plans and problems. Show them that you feel it is important that they know what's going on.
7. Consider your employees' interests as you would your own—nothing will win support faster than the knowledge that you have their interest at heart.[1]

Conceptual, human relations, and technical skills are the three main skills needed to be a competent administrator. University-level courses dealing with outdoor recreation and agency in-service training courses should emphasize the development of skills necessary to getting along with and leading people.

Job Attitudes and Incentives

For the supervisor to be able to use the human skills effectively, there is also a need to understand the employees' job attitudes and incentives. Many studies reflect the fact that supervisors and employees do not view employees' needs in the same light. These studies show supervisors have tended to think in terms of wages, job security, and promotions, while the employees have viewed their needs as appreciation for work accomplished and being made to feel a part of the team.

It would be well for everyone to remember that all humans—including supervisors—have the same basic needs to express creativity, to gain recognition, and to experience achievement. It will make the role of the supervisor and employee much easier and more effective if each is able to understand and perhaps even help fulfill the needs of the other.

Communication

Few processes have had as much written about them as has communications and yet few processes are so little understood, so poorly executed, and so often forgotten. We must understand that organizational goals can be achieved more effectively by creating a responsive flow of communication. Communication is what the humanitarian approach to administrative behavior is all about. How many times have we heard the bitter complaint "Nobody told *me*." Or, "They keep us in the dark." Or, "The right hand doesn't know what the left hand is doing." Communications failure, perhaps caused by lack of sensitivity, is the root cause.

An increase in the amount of information flowing through organizational channels does not necessarily mean that the channels of communication are open and being used properly. The information and directions that flow downward through formal channels are only a small part of the total communications operation. No matter how elaborate the system of formal communications established within an organization may be, this system will always be supplemented by informal channels. Every agency has a grapevine. Administrators must learn how it works, and use it.

Scheduling

Proper scheduling, which means putting the right person on the job at the right time, is paramount to getting the job done. First comes the identification of what needs to be done, then scheduling, then the implementation, and last, the evaluation. Without intelligent scheduling of subordinates by their supervisor, much time, effort, and money can be wasted.

At agency headquarters, or in the larger park units, times will be set for jobs. These time allocations might even be on data cards so they can be processed to determine the total amount of time and cost for a job or a series of several jobs.

In scheduling personnel it is important not only to schedule for maximum job results but also for maximum personal satisfaction of the employee—and these may not always be the same. Some tasks are more menial and less challenging than others. Some require technical knowledge while others do not. Some afford the opportunity to place persons outside of their job classification as a learning opportunity, and should be so utilized. When scheduling, a supervisor needs to take monotony, fatigue, and other factors affecting the employee, into consideration. One must also be flexible and be thinking of alternate scheduling in case there is a change in the weather or other disruptions of the schedule.

Discipline

With advancement comes the opportunity for wielding power—judging, complimenting, and advancing subordinates. Unfortunately, the responsibility for disciplining subordinates accompanies these more pleasant tasks. Perhaps because it is an unpleasant task, it is commonly not done well, either in method of execution or in the results obtained.

Discipline is needed for a variety of reasons. The usual one is failure to do the job. Should discipline be oral or written? A slap on the wrist or dismissal? These are the choices and each needs consideration.

When failure to do the job is the complaint, it should be assumed first that the supervisor has not properly communicated to the employee the information necessary to get the job done. When this possibility has been checked, the next assumption must be that the person did not understand it. It is only after both of these possibilities have been covered that one must assume that the person is not able to do the job and must be placed somewhere else, or let go.

Unwillingness to do the job is also a matter for disciplinary action. This is a separate consideration from the above and must be dealt with as such. It might be that the person has just reasons such as an unreasonable supervisor or unpalatable working conditions. If this be the case, the cause should be remedied. On the other hand, if the attitude has no basis in external circumstances, then the person, if not able to be retrained, must be let go.

Disobedience calls for disciplinary action. Again, the supervisor of the person giving the order must first be certain that the order was understood and was just and reasonable. If not, the situation should be corrected. If the order was sound, the disciplinary action might be suspension or dismissal.

Violation of laws is cause for disciplinary action. This might include theft, falsifying records, or violations of any number of statutes or rules, such as sexual harassment or using controlled substances while on duty. When this occurs, your agency's legal advisor should be contacted.

In any of the foregoing situations, there are certain rules to be followed to preserve the dignity of the employee, as well as that of the supervisor, and his or her position within the agency.

1. Never discipline in front of others, unless the recipient forces you to do so.
2. Meet with the employee personally. Look the person in the eye.
3. Assume that this person is innocent of both wrongdoing and intent to do wrong.
4. Document the charge against the employee precisely, in unemotional terms.
5. Hear the person out.
6. Outline the disciplinary action clearly.
7. Inform the person of appeal rights and who within the agency might be of assistance.
8. If action other than dismissal is taken, do not refer to the disciplinary action again, either to the concerned employee or to the others. It should be a closed book and noted by the supervisor only as a reminder, if neces-

sary. No discussion of it should take place with anyone else.
9. If the action is suspension or dismissal, follow up the meeting with a letter.

CONCLUSION

During your working life you will work for, work with, and be in charge of, people. In all these situations it is vitally important to be aware of effective personnel management. Also, as employers and taxpayers, each of us must be concerned with the fact that much of the resource agency's funds will be expended on personnel costs. Any effort to reduce these costs through humane and skillful management will benefit us all. There are numerous books, articles, courses, and discussion groups to help us gain skills in dealing with our fellow human beings. Take advantage of these. Remember what you learn, and practice your skills at every opportunity. Learn to control yourself, and to direct others when called upon to do so. These abilities will stand you in good stead in every phase of management, and will be of crucial importance in the forwarding of your career.

REFERENCES

General References

Beckley, John L. 1947. *Let's be Human.* Duell, Sloan, and Pearce. New York.

Donovan, J.J., ed. 1968. *Recruitment and Selection in the Public Service.* Public Personnel Association. Chicago, IL.

Dreyfack, Raymond. 1964. *What a Supervisor Should Know About How to Delegate Effectively.* The Dartnell Corp., Chicago, IL.

Drucker, Peter F. 1974. *Management. Tasks. Responsibilities. Practices.* Harper & Row Publishers. New York.

Ginzberg, Eli. 1980. *Employing the Unemployed.* Basic Books, Inc. New York.

Grossman, Arnold H. 1980. *Personnel Manage-*

ment *In Recreation And Leisure Services.* Groupwork Today, Inc. South Plainfield, NJ.

Hjelte, George and Jay S. Shrivers. 1978. *Public Administration of Recreation Services.* Lea and Febiger. Philadelphia, PA.

Hobbs, Daniel G. 1981. "Productivity Through Worker Incentive and Satisfaction," *Trends.* Park Practice Program. NRPA. 18(2):35–44.

McConkey, Dale D. 1965. *How to Manage by Results.* American Management Association. New York.

Rodney, Lynn S. 1964. *Administration of Public Recreation.* Ronald Press, New York.

Shafritz, Jay M. 1977. *The Public Personnel World: Readings in the Professional Practice.* International Personnel Management Association. Chicago, IL.

The Royal Bank of Canada. 1962. *The Communication of Ideas.* Montreal, Canada.

References Cited

1. Bergen, Garret L. 1966. *Organizational Relations and Management Action.* McGraw-Hill Book Co. New York.

2. Peter, Laurence J. and Raymond Hull. 1969. *The Peter Principle.* William Morrow and Co., Inc. New York.

CHAPTER EIGHT

CITIZEN INVOLVEMENT

Citizens can be involved in park management by performing tasks under agency supervision, by participating in decision making through information input or by membership in a general interest or a special interest group. There are differences between the essentially personal assistance offered by individual volunteers and members of general interest groups, and the policy-influencing advisory role sought by user groups or those groups whose members express a broad concern for environmental affairs. This chapter recognizes these differences and clarifies them through the framework of volunteers: individual and group, followed by special interest groups, which will be discussed separately.

Just as few individuals make major decisions without soliciting ideas and input from several sources, so within an agency the person responsible for decision making must obtain aid. This can come from within the agency, from other agencies, and from private citizens or groups of citizens.

Citizens provide assistance in the decision-making process and play an important role in the implementation of decisions. They inform the agency about special needs, generate feedback about facilities and programs planned or provided by the agency, and reflect public opinion concerning the agency itself. Correct handling of public input can assist continued growth of the park agency and its services, help resist infringement by other departments and aid in avoiding

crippling reduction during times of limited financial resources (Fig. 8-1).

VOLUNTEERS

Reasons for volunteering include a desire to serve, a need to learn about one's community, a seeking of recognition, or a wish to share interest and knowledge with others. Business and industry management frequently encourage employees to volunteer their services in community work, thus providing another incentive for citizen involvement.

Involvement can be passive, such as by re-

Fig. 8-1. Agencies must find ways to stimulate citizen interest in the decision-making process. Here Forest Service employees are receiving public involvement training. Albuquerque, New Mexico. (Photo courtesy USDA Forest Service.)

sponding to a questionnaire, or active, through offering help and making a definite commitment. Some citizens who wish to be involved will contact the agency; others need to be sought out. However they present themselves, volunteers are needed and should be welcomed, whether by the director of the agency, a park manager, or an employee at some other level within the park agency. Volunteer assistance in various aspects of park management is becoming more important as budget cuts decrease park manpower. Perhaps it might become necessary to have certain parks entirely cared for by volunteers, or to have certain sections of linear parks maintained in this way.

How and where are volunteers found? How should needs be presented so that potential volunteers are attracted? How do we identify the ones who are willing to serve as individuals? How do we identify those who want to serve only within a group?

The first thing that should be done in order to answer these four questions is to compile two lists.

1. List the jobs/functions/services in which the park or agency needs help—help beyond that which can be hired on the official payroll. These needs could include instructors, office workers, research aides, or persons to oversee a special time-consuming project such as a historical garden or living history costume preparation.
2. List individuals and groups who want to aid the park or agency. Where does one secure these names? As a start, contact retirement organizations, conservation organizations, recreation groups, churches, service/fraternal groups, college outdoor recreation classes, and the National Center for Volunteer Action.

Once these two lists have been prepared, match the first list to the second and contact the volunteers—perhaps a key volunteer can be found to accomplish this organizational work and assist in running the volunteer program.

The Individual Volunteer

Individual volunteer involvement presents far greater opportunities and advantages to the agency than do groups. The individual volunteer is able to perform some of the same services as an employee and costs the agency comparatively nothing. They can be used on a regular basis from daily to once per week. Such persons can be utilized at the agency headquarters in general services, as a consultant, or for special needs. An example might be a retired business executive aiding in budget preparation. Volunteers can assist at individual parks, as well as working at agency headquarters. Most park managers would have no difficulty in utilizing a variety of volunteer services, such as clerical and organizational work, special interpretive situations, or sign preparation or repair.

Individual involvement also presents problems. Individuals may require close supervisior and sometimes cause disruptions. Often they are not deeply committed and cause frustration by not showing up where and when scheduled.

General Interest Groups

These groups are usually broad in scope and purpose, and will offer assistance even if they do not benefit directly. Service clubs fit this category.

Scouts or other youth groups who do benefit directly may build trails for the experience and public service entailed, as well as for individual recognition within the group (Fig. 8-2). Volunteer search and rescue groups have proven extremely helpful to recreation agencies at all levels.

Citizen Boards

A citizen board differs from a special interest group in that it has a much broader base of interest. The importance of the citizen board was summed up nicely in a presentation by Earl T. Groves, Chairman, Board of Trustees, National Recreation and Parks Association, when he made the following comments.

Fig. 8-2. Scout groups are an excellent source of volunteer assistance. These young men are rebuilding trail at Mount Rainier National Park under the supervision of park rangers. (Photo courtesy of National Park Service.)

There are many advantages to citizen involvement in recreation and park programs. Enumerating just a few of these, we can recognize that citizen participation creates the feeling that we, as citizens, have a voice, whether directly as a board member, or indirectly, through a board member that we may know and feel free to talk to. It is a democratic approach, and one that gives visibility and credibility to recreation and park programs in a community. Board members provide, usually at no charge, advisory and consultive services that are of great value. Many of these citizens are also involved in other community activities and provide communication with other public agencies as well as private and voluntary organizations. The citizen members are involved in the business community and have contacts with private businesses and industries, as well as with wealthy citizens. These contacts can lead to substantial contributions and financial support. With the right approach contributions of land and facilities for recreation and parks use can often be generated through these contacts. [1]

There are two primary types of citizen boards—policy and advisory. There is also the administrative board, but it is rarely found in the parks field.

Policy-making Boards. The policy board is either appointed by the head of the particular level of government such as a governor or minister, or elected by the citizens of a particular geographical area, such as a park and recreation district. As noted in Chapter 2, Structure, the policy board usually has the right of hiring and dismissal of the park agency director. It is generally accepted that citizens are assured of a broader interest in their park needs through the policy-making board, whose membership provides a wide range of experience as well as representation of the total geographic area. Those citizens who are interested in park matters are able to express their opinions to a board member who lives close to their location. The staggered appointment of park board members usually provides that a majority of the board will survive a change in the appointing authority, thus decreasing the potential for partisan political maneuvering.

The board members should be informed by the appointing authority as to what is expected of them in both time requirements and responsibility. They should be told what authority they have—and do not have.

For the board to be properly involved, the park agency director should regularly communicate with the chairman, and, to a lesser degree, with the total board. The board should be actively involved in the decision-making process even when the director is the one to make the decision. They should be solicited for ideas and should be involved in the pleasurable aspects of decision making as well as the unpleasant.

Advisory Boards. There are many types of advisory boards or committees. They are operated in various ways and for many purposes. They often give advice to the director or the elected executive. They may be specialists in a particular subject or represent a geographical area. Sometimes a committee for a specific purpose will be appointed by a park manager to function at that park only, although they are usually appointed by the director. Advisory committees can provide considerable constructive support to a park agency if used properly and if provided sufficient supportive assistance. With careful selection such a committee can provide a community level sounding board for the department, and can broaden the basis of public support for the agency's endeavors. Advisory committees can also help alleviate the stigma of insensitivity that is attached to many government agencies having little or no input from the public which they serve. There must be adequate recognition for the services and accomplishments of the group, or of outstanding committee members.

There are some problems with advisory committees. The required liaison and other departmental supportive services involve considerable staff time. If the advisory committee is to be an effective group, the projects or programs must have a real purpose and need. The act of establishing such an advisory committee represents a commitment on the part of the department for involvement in that service and in that program.

The committee findings and the recommendations must be carefully considered and used in making decisions if the agency is to establish and maintain an image of integrity and credibility with the public. This does not mean that all recommendations must be accepted and acted on.

There are basically two types of advisory boards: terminal and ongoing.

1. *Terminal.* These committees deal with a specific subject matter or with a definite goal: a specific problem that needs resolving, or a general subject for a stated period of time. It is important that these committees end their term of service cleanly at the appropriate time.

It is normally easier to keep the interest of a terminal committee, as they usually are composed of persons who are interested in the partic-

ular subject matter or they would not be willing to serve in the first place. Also they know there is an end to the road and this generates a sense of urgency and accomplishment.

2. *Ongoing.* In government situations where strong executive control is required or desired, the ongoing or continuing advisory committee provides the necessary public involvement to ensure that the taxpayers' needs are being met or at least considered. In other words, such a board helps the agency present full service within budgetary and policy limitations. The administrative authority of the agency still rests in the hands of the executive branch of government, yet the advisory board can serve as a buffer for repercussions from decisions made by the agency, thus freeing the agency administrator from various outside pressures (Fig. 8-3).

The ongoing advisory committee is one of the more difficult to deal with, and yet one of the

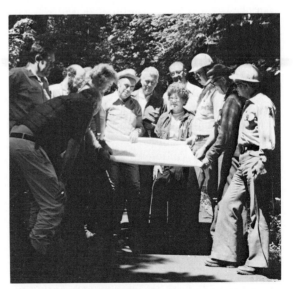

Fig. 8-3. A citizen advisory committee meeting on site with Forest Service officials to discuss the routing of the Pacific Crest National Scenic Trail through private land. (Photo by Grant W. Sharpe.)

most rewarding if the agency is able to handle it properly. Ongoing advisory committees have a tendency to believe that they are in management and, when they make decisions and give them to the person who appointed the committee, often forget that they are giving advice that will not always be followed. At the same time, their input is useful. These individuals reflect their constituents' as well as their own diverse backgrounds. It is important that they be heard.

There are many ways to establish advisory committees. The state of California has published *Citizen Participation,* which not only lists committees created by it up to the date of the publication, but also advises citizens how they should approach the state should they want to form an advisory committee. See general references at the end of the chapter.

"Friends" Groups

The *friends* group is one category that should be given consideration during times of monetary difficulties. Friends often start through their own initiative, to assist an agency in a particular need. Sometimes they continue, in the role of *friends of the park*, while at other times the organization may terminate, such as when the promotion of a bond issue is over.

Sometimes they will actually become a bona fide partner with the government entity whereby the government provides the area and facility and perhaps the major maintenance while the friends raise funds, provide minor maintenance, and operate the facility. An interesting example is Stone Mountain Park near Atlanta, Georgia, which is a self-supporting park created by the state, and developed and operated by a committee appointed by the state.

Docents

Here, volunteers take a course conducted by the agency to ready them for working with park visitors in a teaching or guiding capacity. The creation of a docents program should be considered for certain types of areas and for certain types of activities, particulary ongoing indoor programs. For example, in certain museums there are excellent docents programs where people learn to become tour guides for the museum.

Evaluation

Can volunteers be evaluated? Should they be evaluated? Yes, and in the same way that paid employees are, impartially, and on an ongoing basis. If workers, volunteer or paid, are informed of desirable and undesirable qualities and performances at set intervals over the duration of the job, they have the chance to strengthen weak points and maintain good ones. If they undergo a firm, fair evaluation, they feel useful and that they are being taken seriously. If a volunteer is not doing a good job and fails to improve, thus becoming a detriment to the program, then that person can and should be dismissed as any paid employee would be.

A report at the time the volunteer leaves the agency is done in much the same way as the evaluation, but with a different goal. Its goal is to provide a record of the volunteer's job experience, to be used as a reference for rehire, or for the benefit of future employers.

Evaluation of the supervisor and the staff by volunteers is already in use in some agencies. The intent of such an evaluation is to gain an understanding of the needs and wants of volunteers, to make sure their suggestions are under consideration, and to obtain an outsider's view of operations to which the volunteer has been exposed.

Volunteer Recognition

Evaluation will bring to light certain individuals who have done outstanding work and give the agency or manager an opportunity to give such persons recognition and thanks (Fig. 8-4). Recognition can take many forms. Special volunteer banquets can be held annually, or more frequently. Volunteers can be provided with certificates of appreciation signed by an important personage such as the head of that level of government or a representative from the legisla-

Fig. 8-4. Citizens should be given visible recognition and thanks for their public service. Here a volunteer has just been presented a certificate of appreciation for volunteer work. (Photo courtesy of Long Island State Park and Recreation Commission.)

tive branch. The local newspaper and other news media might do special articles on volunteers. This publicity serves to attract others to volunteer. Volunteer workers can also be recognized for their contributions at meetings of the legislative body of the appropriate level of government.

SPECIAL INTEREST GROUPS

Increasingly in North America, citizen involvement through activist groups is affecting land management decisions. These groups are questioning and shaping policy at the federal, state, provincial, and local levels. Agencies must find ways both to give these citizen activists access to the hard information they require and to incorporate their demands into the decision-making process (Fig. 8-1). If agencies do not keep communications open and practice good relations, they run the risk of having their policies and practices criticized and perhaps distorted in the media, or debated piecemeal at hostile public meetings.

In North America we have long accepted special interest groups, perhaps first under religious auspices and then in politics. Acceptance, of course, does not imply agreement. Many people feel pressure groups or lobbyists or special inter-

est groups are, at best, necessary evils—unless of course it is *their* special interest. A special interest group in this context is usually a collection of people who are interested in a specific activity or a specific use of an area. That does not sound too bad, but sometimes they want to exclude other users, and that causes difficulties.

Often a group will favor the agency position on one issue, and oppose it on another. For example, a group interested in the preservation of a natural area might join with a group desiring land for hunting. If successful in securing the area, the two groups might move to opposite sides when the question becomes "should hunting be allowed?"

These activists may often be found among the ranks of volunteers helping individually or as a group within a park agency. ATV or horseback groups work with backcountry rangers to provide access and facilities and to create good will for their groups, both with the agency and with the general public. For other organizations, their main sphere of operations is in policy formulation, and they are usually well represented at public meetings and hearings, often by salaried personnel. Their services and contributions can also be utilized by appointment of individuals from such groups to advisory or citizen boards.

Advisory committees from special interest groups can be very effective. The special interest committees can also create problems when the park agency's concerns do not align precisely with the committee's established priorities. For example, an advisory committee established to give programming direction to the department concerning disabled visitor use might generate enough enthusiasm, interest, and participation to identify needs far beyond the capabilities and regulatory limitations of the agency. Committee members can become disillusioned rapidly if such a situation is not handled properly. Sometimes an umbrella-type advisory committee functions better for an agency. This would mean an outdoor recreation advisory committee that appoints subcommittees within its own framework; in this example, one dealing with facilities and programs for the disabled based on the foreseeable and long-term needs. This subcommittee would seek input from various groups representing handicapped visitors and relay it to the main or umbrella committee, which would oversee or cover all these matters, and keep them in control and proportion as part of their advisory function.

PUBLIC MEETINGS AND HEARINGS

There is another type of citizen participation somewhat different from volunteering. It is that form of involvement that occurs through public meetings and hearings.

It has not always been so, but today in North America more and more citizens are attending and participating in public meetings regarding park activities and policies. These meetings are held to seek public input into the decision-making process and to serve as a means of disseminating information. In the United States, the National Environmental Policy Act of 1969 requires public agencies to seek out and take into consideration all viewpoints on proposed actions involving federal funds.

The typical *public meeting* is somewhat relaxed in nature, often allowing considerable interaction among those present. Usually this sort of gathering is not officially recorded and is not conducted under rigid rules. An increasingly popular form of public meeting, stressing small size and informality, is the workshop. Here techniques such as sitting together at tables, thus facing one another at close quarters, are used to promote mutual understanding.

A more structured type of public meeting is the *hearing*. During the hearing the citizens have the opportunity to have their names registered and their views, along with the formal presentations, placed on the record. The hearing is often prescribed by law and must be conducted under set rules. The agency legal counsel has the duty of deciding when a hearing is required.

Regardless of the level of government in which your agency operates, it is important to be familiar with the laws, rules, and policies governing such hearings. In nearly all instances these rules will include a requirement for the placement of an official notice. This posting will undoubtedly include everything from a notice on a city hall or post office notice board to the formidable looking Federal Register carrying notices of a proposed federal action. The register is available at any federal agency office.

Stimulating people so they will come to a public meeting is a difficult task and must be well thought out. One of the best methods is direct contact with the various interest groups discussed earlier. This is particularly true when the subject matter is not very exciting. The usual media channels should be considered, as should the posting of extra notices. For hearings, the agency will probably need to place an official paid notice in one or more newspapers of general circulation.

Conducting a meeting dealing with a highly controversial subject is a difficult task. Sometimes the agency will conduct such a meeting itself while other times a competent, disinterested outsider will be asked to handle it. As the new practitioner often learns all too quickly, the person conducting the meeting will frequently be the park manager or a ranger. Whoever conducts the meeting needs to be aware that the crowd could become unruly. Suggestions 5, 6, and 7 in the following list will help when the atmosphere becomes tense. As a last resort, postpone the meeting until tempers cool.

1. Notify appropriate persons, including the news media, in ample time, and state the agenda clearly.
2. Arrive at the site in plenty of time to take care of basic communication needs. Are the microphones working? Is there water for speaker or chairperson? Are there chairs for all? Is there directional signing on access roads, building, hallways, and doors? Is the slide projector working? Are there pencils and paper available? Is a copy of the agenda available for everyone, if appropriate? These preparations set a tone of calm

and openness that reflects favorably on the sponsoring agency. Don't depend entirely on others to see to these details. Delegate them, but *be there* to see that these things have, in fact, been done.

3. Keep the staff team small. Don't give the impression of intimidation by bringing a whole stable of experts. Too many representatives might also signal apprehension. Often a staff person will play the role of an expert witness such as a backcountry ranger testifying concerning the establishment of use limits. What ever the reason for staff involvement, a cardinal rule is "don't speak unless asked."

4. Use registration cards. An example of such a card is seen in Figure 8-5.

5. Receive all suggestions without comment; a debate should not be conducted at this sort of meeting.

6. Allow no cross examination of speakers by persons in the audience.

7. Find light moments and capitalize on them. To laugh at ourselves is to gain perspective and release tension.

8. Try to summarize, as seems advisable, at least at the end of the meeting or hearing.

9. Listen to what people are saying, not only with words but also by body language. Also, be cognizant of what they are *not* saying.

10. Make no exceptions to the rules.

11. Accept written comments, and advise people these will receive as much consideration as the oral comments.

Generally, new or innovative programs of some magnitude are apt to find better public acceptance if they are preceded by public meetings. The meetings do several things for the program

---

ATTENDANCE REGISTER

Registration is optional, however, we welcome the opportunity to record your attendance at this meeting and would appreciate indication in advance of any subject about which you may wish to make a statement.

Location of Meeting _____ Date _____

_____ _____
   (First Name)   (Initial)   (Last Name)   (phone)

_____
   (Address)   (Street or Route)   (City, State or Province, ZIP)

_____
   (Occupation)   (Organization Represented)

DO YOU WISH TO MAKE A STATEMENT? _____ Yes _____ No

If "yes," please specify subject: _____

Fig. 8-5. An attendance register form. It may be used as a means of calling on people who wish to make a statement, as well as a record of those attending the meeting.

and the department. They offer an excellent way for the agency to receive suggestions and to get feedback. They provide an opportunity for public education about departmental services and the potential benefits of the program itself, promoting greater public understanding, and, perhaps, eventual acceptance.

In the conduct of such meetings it is essential that the department identify and invite all persons or groups desiring to be heard. Those who are identified as in opposition to the program should also be invited. Quite often, because of the nature of the program, it is possible to have cosponsorship or multiple sponsorship of meetings. This is usually desirable since it broadens the exposure of the meeting to the general public and avoids the appearance of imposing ideas from above.

PUBLIC RELATIONS

In parks and recreation work, public relations means little more than the ability of people of an organization to express themselves to those they serve to the end that all may profit through understanding. [2]

Through skillful public relations, an agency can ensure that the public is aware of its objectives and operations, and that decisions affecting the public are based on the agency's knowledge and understanding of that public. The public makes vital decisions at the ballot box. People get their information in large part from the mass media, which serves as a source for attitudes and actions, so it behooves the agency to pay attention to its communications with the media. This function is most effectively handled through a public affairs officer.

Park agencies are constantly engaged in public relations, for better or for worse. Avoidance of this sort of communication is impossible, since in every contact any agency personnel has with the public—through news releases, speeches, letters, phone calls, on the sidewalk or on a self-guiding trail—the agency is sending a message. This is true even if not one word is spoken. As the public

deals with agency personnel it becomes aware of their attitude, and as the public uses its parks, it takes note of the park's general appearance and upkeep. These, too, are forms of communication, and are thus powerful public relations tools.

There are several ways of communicating with citizens for sound public relations including the following.

Letters

Few things show the character and purpose of an organization better than its mail, both incoming and outgoing. The outgoing mail carries the message and the quality of its source. The incoming mail brings the proof of failure or success. It is of the utmost importance that letters should be alive. Dry, formal, official letters stamped all over with pallid impersonality, are poison. [4]

When sending a letter, whether initiating it or in response to one received, one should not only be aware of the audience, but also of the specific purpose for which the letter is being sent. In the book, *The Modern Executive's Guide to Effective Communication*, Parkhurst lists basic purposes of the business letter: (1) to ensure accuracy (2) to make transactions binding (3) to furnish complete records (4) to provide the least expensive communication (5) to make contacts (6) to promote goodwill (7) to talk more effectively and (8) to buy or sell goods. [3] (In the case of park agencies, the discussion of services would be of paramount importance, rather than buying or selling goods.)

News Releases

A news release is far more complicated than a letter in that it might well be used by all three news media. Remember the audience is as varied as the total listening, viewing, and reading audience of the area covered. These releases can be very effective for reaching a large audience. Refer to Chapter 5, Politics, for more details.

Telephone Calls.

With the exception of face-to-face meetings with park visitors, managers will probably have more personal contact with citizens by telephone than by any other single method. Here are some time-tested suggestions for using the telephone to better public relations.

1. Answer the telephone as quickly as possible and explain any wait or holding.
2. Greet the caller pleasantly.
3. Identify yourself.
4. State or find out whether or not the person being asked for is in or out before you ask who is calling.
5. For callbacks, be sure to get the telephone number and the name correctly.
6. Be attentive.
7. Use the citizen's name.
8. Try to end the call on a pleasant note. Be brief. You are busy and should assume that the caller is also.

The Employee

By far the most important person in all public relations is the *employee*. All of the news releases, all the letter-perfect letters, and all those excellent telephone conversations totaled up will not have one fraction the impact the agency employee will have, on or off the job. Employees are also citizens of the community and as such are ambassadors to that community. Therefore, the agency should inform its employees on policy matters and of the agency position on current debates, as well as insisting on neat appearance and politeness on the job. Employees should be periodically reminded of how important they are to the creation of a favorable image for the agency.

CONCLUSION

There is no replacement for the goodwill of the community, and the interaction with volunteers and groups, if properly handled, will help supply understanding and support for agency objectives.

Volunteers have proven themselves very helpful in the past. In an era of stringent budgeting they are invaluable. Creative thinking involving both citizen and agency personnel on the subject of volunteer assistance is now more important than ever.

Park agencies and park managers must also be responsive to public opinion from beyond the volunteer ranks, and be legitimately active in forming that opinion. Involving citizens is our best hope of both serving and pleasing them.

REFERENCES

General References

Brown, William E. 1971. *Islands of Hope*. National Recreation and Park Association, Inc. Washington, DC.

California Department of Parks and Recreation. 1974. *Citizen Participation*. Sacramento, CA.

Creighton, James L. 1977. *The Use of Values: Public Participation in the Planning Process*. Synergy Consulting Service. San Francisco, CA.

Fazio, James R. and Douglas L. Gilbert. 1981. *Public Relations and Communication for Natural Resource Managers*. Kendal/Hunt Publishing Company. Dubuque, IO.

Feeny, Bob. "Senior Citizen Park Maintenance Corps." *Trends*. Park Practice Program. NRPA. 18(2):25–27.

Gebler, Charles J. 1982. "Off-season, Off-site Interpretation" in *Interpreting the Environment* (2nd ed.). Grant W. Sharpe, (ed.). Wiley. New York.

Heberlein, Thomas. 1975. *Principles of Public Involvement for National Park Service Planners and Managers*. Department of Sociology, University of Wisconsin, Madison.

The Institute For Participatory Planning. 1978. *Citizens Participation Handbook For Public Officials and Other Professionals* (3rd ed.). Laramie, WY.

Irland, Lloyd C. and J. Ross Vincent. 1974. "Citizen Participation in Decision-Making. A

Challenge For Public Land Managers," *Journal of Range Management.* 27(3):182–185.

Sontag, William H. 1981. "Quality Interpretation Through Citizen Involvement," *Trends.* Park Practice Program. NRPA 18(2):8–11.

References Cited

1. Groves, Earl T. 1978. From a speech presented to National Recreation and Park Association. Asheville, NC.

2. Lykes, Ira B. 1962. "Preparing for Good Public Relations—A Bridge between the People and the Service," *Park Practice Guidelines.* Published by National Park Service, Washington, DC.

3. Parkhurst, Charles C. 1962. *The Modern Executive's Guide to Effective Communication.* Prentice Hall. Englewood Cliffs, NJ.

4. Pinchot, Gifford. Taken from "Ideal Public Administration as Visualized by Gifford Pinchot." Published by University of Washington, College of Forest Resources, Seattle, WA.

PART THREE

THE RESOURCE

PART
THREE
THE RESOURCE

CHAPTER NINE

PLANNING, LAND ACQUISITION, AND DEVELOPMENT

Park managers have to deal with the consequences of planning in a general way, and with the consequences of actual development in a most specific way. This overview of planning, acquisition, and development, and the implementing processes involved, will introduce the student or new manager to an important phase of park agency operations. Insight into the responsibilities and difficulties may illuminate some park management problems.

Planning is a process widely used, and confusion arises when we try to define it narrowly or to confine discussion of it to one chapter. Planning enters into land acquisition and classification and is inherent in such chapters in this book as Facilities, Policy, Fiscal Management, and Citizen Involvement. As a framework for addressing problems, planning is a major factor in Maintenance and Safety, Environmental Concerns, Depreciative Behavior and Vandalism, and Conflicts.

PLANNING

There are many definitions for planning. It has been defined as "an activity concerned with the systematic collection, analysis, organization and processing of technical information to facilitate decision making."[1] Another definition tells us that "planning is the process of preparing in advance and in a reasonably systematic fashion, recommendations for policies and courses of action (with careful attention to their probable

by-products, side effects, or spill-over effects) to achieve accepted objectives in the common life of society."[2]

In this chapter, planning will touch on the process of determination of need, the involvement of the manager, and the steps leading up to a plan document and site plans. Development will encompass budget preparation, staffing, the review and approval process, and construction.

In discussing planning and development, especially from the manager's viewpoint, all park areas could be said to fall in one of the following categories.

1. The park is well established, handling its visitor load, changing activities, and use patterns with minimum stress on the resource and with only minor difficulties for the users and park staff.
2. The park is well established but needs modification. Perhaps its facilities need updating (including changes to meet energy conservation, sanitation requirements or disabled access), or perhaps it is a question of measures to limit danger to the users or to the resource. Time and changing use patterns eventually put most parks into this category.
3. The area is a new one, still in the planning stage, with site design plans yet to be drawn up and approved.

In the last two situations the contributions of a manager who is dealing with, or has at some time dealt with, a similar situation or site could be most useful. In agencies that have effective checks and balances and that follow proper procedures, a manager, or another representative from the field staff, is required to sign off on site plans at a certain point in the proceedings. One factor in the smooth operation of parks in category number one might be that managers were involved in their planning and development.

Planners

As a result of the relative youthfulness of the park profession and of the fact that several skills are needed to comprehend the planning of land use, planners come from many disciplines—they can be landscape architects, civil engineers, urban planners, or graduates of one of several planning programs now offered in Canada and the United States. Some planning tasks are handled by planners who are staff employees, while others are contracted out to private firms.

Whatever the planner's background, the best plans are produced by a team approach. Here the planner has access to expertise from foresters, soil specialists, interpretive specialists, biologists, civil engineers, geologists, historians, and archeologists—persons from disciplines pertinent to the site in question, including, it is to be hoped, the park manager and maintenance personnel.

Planners are not decision makers; the agency director or the park board or commission has this responsibility. However, in their deliberations, these decision makers must rely on the planners' presentation of the situation, on those alternatives the planners may have chosen to prepare, and on the planners' expertise. It is imperative therefore, that planners provide accurate data and a fair analysis of those data.

Determination of Need

There are different levels within land-use planning, primarily identified by the area addressed, including nationwide, regional, state or provincial, agency, area, and, finally, development or site-design planning.

Planners at these various levels must anticipate the needs of the public from their particular vantage point, determine potentially suitable areas and their optimum capacities, and plan park facilities and services to meet public needs. They frequently must estimate costs for development and operation. This must be a continuing function that considers competitive demands for land use within the total recreation requirements of their level of planning responsibility.

Information, such as inventory, classification, and use limits for current and projected parks, must be gathered. Objectives are set in light of this information, and a program outlined for systematic accomplishment of the objectives. Attendance statistics and use data must be studied, keeping in mind that use statistics are molded by the facilities available. The varying tastes of users for convenience or primitive situations, or some intermediate state of comfort, must be assessed and taken into account. Different experiences are provided by various public land managing agencies and by the recreational facilities offered by the public sector, and all these opportunities must be factored into determination of need.

Planners do have established mechanisms to help in determination of need. In the United States, each state must have on file a Statewide Comprehensive Outdoor Recreation and Open Space Plan (SCORP), which provides the basic data for recreational acquisition and development by state and local agencies.

The section of this chapter entitled "Land Acquisition" deals with the various ways in which an agency might acquire such lands.

Canada also has collected appropriate data for broadly based recreational planning starting with the Canadian Outdoor Recreation Demand Study in 1967. Provinces have conducted similar studies, as well as producing provincial models of the Canada Land Inventory. Data from these studies helped establish systems planning processes, which seek to identify and provide a diversity of recreation experiences for Canadian citizens.

In addition to these national plans in both countries, agencies may have their own outdoor recreation plans, and most parks have a master plan giving long-range direction for all facets of that park's development.

Planning Concerns of the Manager

The following headings represent a useful method of sorting out the various ways planning affects managers. Perhaps these categories will also offer new insight into the planning process at the level of the individual park.

Location. The park manager shares with the planner a concern for the overall layout of the park. This includes an interest in circulation patterns, modes of transportation, and levels of density of development. The planner needs to locate facilities so the park staff can observe camping sites, picnic areas, and other high-use areas. The same attention needs to be given to visitor safety. Typical planning concerns here might include location of the source of water, location of sanitary facilities, location of garbage collection points to avoid attracting animals into sleeping areas, the placement of lighting fixtures where needed for safety as well as for surveillance to deter vandalism, and the best location for emergency exits from both structures and forested areas.

Preservation. Most managers express a sincere interest in the preservation of the resources of their areas, and they can speak with authority about the need to employ protective strategies in planning. For example, exposed tree roots, eroding hillsides, chewed-up shrubs, muddy paths, and other signs of human and vehicular impacts are typical management problems that might be prevented or lessened by planning techniques, based on a thorough knowledge of soil and vegetation types as well as observation of visitor-use patterns. Planners' judgments about park location and correct layout of facilities are critical considerations in the matter of preservation.

Operations. The manager is responsible for the staffing of the park and for its budget requirements, therefore this person will be very interested in personnel and operational costs of the facilities and use areas being designed by the planners. The distinction between development funds, needed on a one-time basis, and those funds needed annually for operation is important. After the planners have rolled up their blueprints and the engineers have built the roads and facilities, and both have gone on to a new project, the manager must be able to *manage* the results, and the operating costs *must* be reasonable.

Maintenance. Considerations that suggest the need for manager-planner dialogue in operational matters hold equally true for maintenance. What is built must be maintained, and maintenance requires personnel and money. Careful consideration must be given to this consequence in the planning process so that maintenance costs will be kept within acceptable limits. Managers asked to review site design plans must seek advice from maintenance personnel if they themselves are not familiar with materials and design possibilities that would be appropriate and economical on the sites in question.

Production of General Plans

The standard planning phases adapted by Bradley for interpretive planning[3] will be used to give the management student an outline of the planning process. Descriptions have been modified to make them representative of all planning processes.

Identifying Objectives. As guides to specific action, objectives must state an overall purpose, consider the implications of action to achieve that purpose, and identify a specific target and course of action to reach that target.

Data Collection. In terms of Driver's definition,[1] this phase might be called the *sine qua non* of planning; the gathering of facts in an intelligent and evenhanded way—facts as best they can be determined by approved scientific methods— not guesses, not projections of present statistics, not wishful thinking or hearsay. Pertinent data must be compiled on use and users, present and potential, and on the characteristics of the resource base.

Analysis of Data.   Examination of all data and their prospective interrelationships occurs during this phase. This should be a consultative process with experts in such disciplines as ecology, sociology, economics, soils, transportation planning and forestry, to name only a few. Bradley suggests this should provide a reasonable understanding of the resource, the user, and the management strategies and patterns possible, given these data.[3]

Synthesis of Planning Choices.   Several different courses of action, any of which will fulfil the stated objectives, should be delineated from the foregoing analysis. The planner's creativity and specialized knowledge should find expression here, always guided by the objectives and channeled by economic restraints and the public readiness to entertain nontraditional ideas.

The different possibilities must be sufficiently developed in this synthesis so the decision makers can ascertain the advantages and disadvantages of each course of action and judge how well each might fulfill the objectives. Their choice of a plan, or of a modification of a plan, or perhaps of a combination of plans, is the final step in the synthesis phase.

Production of a Plan Document.   The selected plan must now be elaborated. This includes the impact statement required by the jurisdiction in which the proposed park will lie.

Implementation.   Careful orchestration of developmental phases is required: (1) to produce the planned results (2) to avoid undue delay to other capital projects and, (3) to produce these

results economically and without exceeding the allowable and estimated environmental impact. The material discussed under Development in this chapter represents the implementation phase as could acquisition of the required land.

Evaluation and Revision.   This process should be operating during all phases of planning, but must be formally instituted at this point. Do the plan results meet the stated objectives? (Fig. 9-1) A periodic review of monitoring results, plus attention to feedback from independent sources should enable evaluation and guide revision.

The plan document should provide an accurate base map indicating existing conditions on the land as well as all proposed changes. These include boundaries, access and other roads, utilities, previous use, existing and proposed developments, vegetative cover, open space, unusual features, and soil types.

Facilities should be located precisely enough so that no substantial facility relocations should be necessary for the preparation of the more detailed site design plans. There should be a written narrative report explaining what is in the plan

Fig. 9-1.   Public use of facilities must be monitored to determine if the objectives of planning have been fulfilled. At right planners observe a recreation area undergoing heavy use. Merwin Park on the Merwin Reservoir near Mount St. Helens in Washington State. (Photo courtesy of Pacific Power and Light.)

and the justification for these elements. At certain stages of the procedure there must be opportunity for both public and agency feedback (see Chapter 8, Citizen Involvement).

For our purposes, we will pick up this sequence where the approved area or park plan is being translated into the more detailed site plans necessary to generate the development process.

Site Planning. In a classic planning process, working with land not previously developed for recreation purposes, the area or general development plan would be the source of specifications for the site plans. In many instances, of course, the park already exists and is adding a new facility, or is having an existing facility modified, so this situation is then the genesis of the site plan (Fig. 9-2).

Site planning locates structures and activities on the ground—or to quote Lynch, "in three dimensional space." He goes on the say "a plan necessarily disturbs a site, but it should enhance and not violate it, whether it practices conservative adaptation or bold rearrangement."[4] Graceful integration of the proposed facility into the web of environmental relationships requires sensitivity. This in turn demands the expenditure of time by several disciplines gathered into a team headed by the regional planner. The first result of their observations and decisions will be site plans, whether for a building or other facility. Decision makers must pore over these, perhaps calling for agency or public review of the proposals and specifications.

Have the planners come up with a visitor center that is compatible with the site? Are correct proportions maintained between slopes and flat areas for the amphitheater? Is the potential of natural areas exploited? Are the shortcomings of the site adequately compensated for? The reviewers of the plans must be thinking of the potential use of the area. Have the planners considered suitability of soils? Degree of accessibility for disabled persons? Availability of water? What about conflicting visitor use? Separation in time

Fig. 9-2. Park planners check the elevations of a breakwater prior to the construction of a new marina. Great Salt Lake State Park. (Utah State Division of Parks and Recreation photo by Kay Boulter.)

and space, so often suggested as the resolution of problems raised in Chapter 14, Conflicts, may have to be implemented in the site plan. What about all the other variables inherent in these plans? Deliberations involving site plans are also dealt with under Planning for Park Facilities, in Chapter 10, Park Facilities.

Not only must requirements of the visiting public or resident employees be fulfilled as far as can be foreseen and resources guarded from overuse but budget considerations must not be forgotten. These must be addressed at all stages, certainly not least in facilities design and layout. What are the implications of a certain architectural style, a particular exterior finish, a specific window design in terms of energy loss or maintenance? Not only that, but how can the arrangement of the facilities on the site limit use to those areas most capable of withstanding impact? Is the *time* as well as the *effort* required to maintain a facility being computed by the planners? Is the potential for vandalism being considered?

After approval, site plans are translated into detail plans or preliminary engineering design, intended to illustrate the final project features (Fig. 9-3).

Fig. 9-3. Details of a park project are being readied by this park planner in Utah. (Utah State Division of Parks and Recreation photo by Kay Boulter.)

LAND ACQUISITION

In order for people to participate in outdoor recreation, particularly in modern industrialized and urbanized societies, land and water areas must be set aside for this purpose. Forethought is necessary in this situation, for no matter how much money is appropriated, no matter how many people are hired, it will be for naught if the land and water on which to base recreational pursuits is not secured for public use. The factor of time cannot be ignored here. In areas near large population centers other uses may well preempt recreational use if a well-planned program of acquisition is not employed to secure suitable land.

There are four important factors adding to the recreational space problem.

1. Millions of visitors from other countries are using parklands across the breadth of North America.
2. Our own citizens are using these same parklands more and more frequently.
3. Today there is far less open space owned by private citizens or companies available for our citizens and foreign visitors to use. This results in greater use of public parks and recreation areas.
4. Technology has made access to these lands easier and has vastly increased the demands for special areas to handle particular needs.

Despite strong statements from national leaders citing the need for more recreational areas, acquiring needed parklands has become increasingly difficult, particularly in urban areas where needs are greater but where conflicting demands are more formidable.

Fig. 9-4. An example of flood plain that might better be zoned for recreational use. Snohomish River, Washington. (Photo courtesy Army Corps of Engineers.)

There are some positive aspects to the land acquisition situation, however. Land is often zoned for recreation because experience has proven this to be the best use. Flood plains are an example of areas where other uses are not practicable because of periodic flooding. Recreational uses on such lands can adjust to the inconvenience without danger to human life or serious economic loss (Fig. 9-4).

Another bonus has resulted from the general decline in railroading, resulting in the disuse and abandonment of over 50,000 miles of track in the United States alone. Alert citizens across North America have recognized the recreation potential in this unexpected resource and have worked diligently to acquire abandoned railroad rights-of-way. These long, narrow, often scenic strips of land have proven to be excellent opportunities for public hiking and biking trails (Figs. 9-5 and 9-6).

There are several ways recreation or park agencies can acquire land. These include purchase, donation, condemnation and transfer. There are also other means of securing the use of an area, without purchase.

Methods of Gaining Ownership

An agency must be willing to negotiate with the landowner. At the same time, the rules governing the availability of funds also govern the flexibility an agency has in such negotiations. These include appraisals, relocation costs, use privileges, and time sequences.

Purchase. Areas are acquired in fee title when all rights in the area are obtained. If the area is purchased in less than fee title, this implies some restrictions on rights. Frequently it is mineral rights that are at issue.

Fig. 9-5. These two photographs were taken at the same location. The upper photo shows the abandoned railroad tracks. After 10 years, numerous committee meetings, public hearings featuring apprehensive landowners living adjacent to the tracks, and negotiations with railroad owners, a linear park was established. (Upper photo courtesy Burke-Gilman Trail Park Committee. Lower photo by Grant W. Sharpe.)

Fig. 9-6. Numerous facilities were constructed to ameliorate relationships with skeptical landowners along the route. These included car parking access for this non-motorized-use trail, plantings for screening, chain-link fencing in some areas, viewing platforms, signs, picnic tables, and restrooms such as the ones seen here. The new trail is used by people of all ages for both recreation and commuting. Burke-Gilman Trail, King County, Washington. (Photo by Grant W. Sharpe.)

Donation. Agencies often make known their need for recreation lands through public speaking engagements, interviews, and other media in order to attract donations. Furthermore, agency personnel should attempt to alert attorneys and clergy to their needs, as these persons are frequently contacted by people interested in making donations of land.

The offer of a donation of land should be considered in the same light as all other acquisitions—the agency must analyze whether the area should or should not be acquired for park purposes. If the area is desirable and should be accepted, the necessary actions should take place regardless of what level of government might best administer the land. If the suitable agency is not interested or not able to act at the particular time, some agency should accept the donation and act as a holding agent.

What should the agency do if the parcel of-

fered is not desirable? They should try to have the donor allow the agency to accept the donation with the understanding and written agreement that the land may be put up for sale or trade for more suitable park land. In most instances, a donor of land benefits through a tax write-off. This entire transaction must be worked out very carefully between the agency legal counsel and the donor.

Some provinces and states have established park foundations to seek and receive donations. These foundations can be of great assistance to an agency, as they help people realize the rewards associated with this sort of generosity.

Stipulated Deed. This is the method commonly used to give land to an agency when there are conditions as to what may or may not be done with the land. An example would be the donation of a parcel of land that must be used for recreation or it would revert to the owner. This would preclude using this parcel for sale or trade in order to consolidate holdings or lessen management problems.

Condemnation. The bad word! No one likes to wear the black hat, and, like the villain closing in on the weary widow, foreclose or condemn. However, sometimes an agency must institute condemnation proceedings. Assuming for the moment that the agency head has such authority, he or she should use condemnation when necessary and not feel guilty because of it. Before exploring the condemnation procedure, let us look at some reasons why an agency might need the land for the public good and thus decide to institute such proceedings.

Identified Resource. The first reason for condemnation is based on the agency's state or provincial plan, as discussed earlier in this chapter. An identified resource refers to land that has already been selected as suitable and necessary to the agency plan.

Inholdings. For various reasons an agency might find itself with a private parcel inside the boundaries of one of its holdings. The owner might choose to develop a facility not in keeping with the park atmosphere, or might prevent the

Fig. 9-7. Inholdings create problems of incompatible use. The private house, here in Antietam National Battlefield, Maryland, is an example of the difficulties of trying to establish a historical milieu with modern buildings close by. (National Park Service Photo by Cecil W. Stoughton.)

park agency from accomplishing a logical development. To eliminate such problems, attempts to acquire the inholding should be made, and condemnation may be necessary (Fig. 9-7).

Natural Boundaries. Rivers, mountains, or lakes form natural boundaries for many land areas. Unfortunately, all too frequently an existing park's boundary is artifically set, that is, it does not follow the natural boundary. For instance, it may stop 9 m (30 ft) from a wide river. Such parcels of land cause many administrative problems, and agencies will sometimes condemn to acquire them.

Threat of Incompatible Use. There will be a time when the possibility or actual fact of incompatible use dictates acquisition—such as the threat of a motorcar raceway next to a natural area.

The actual condemnation process involves one or both of two actions. The first is establishing the *right of eminent domain* which means, in essence, seeking a court ruling that states that the governmental entity needs the area for the welfare of the public. Need, as seen by the agency, has just been discussed under the types of condemnation. However, this does not mean that the court will see the situation in the same light. The agency will have to convince the court of this need. Should the court not rule in favor of the agency, the action is stopped. Should the court rule in favor of the agency, the *right of eminent domain* has been established. The next phase is that of establishing the price.

Sometimes the landowner desires to sell the property, but for considerably more money than the agency believes the parcel is worth. When such is the case the condemnee waives the right of forcing the governmental entity to prove *eminent domain* and enters into what is commonly called *friendly condemnation.* It derives the title from the fact that the owner wants to sell and the only dispute is the amount of purchase.

Condemnation is not desirable. It costs the agency time, money, and sometimes causes resentment in a community. It frequently places hardships on those whose property is being condemned. For these and other reasons, it is highly desirable to identify the nature of the problem and attempt to resolve it in other ways.

Managers can perform a particularly useful service here in recognizing those areas that would affect the park if incompatible uses were established. They should strive to keep informed on projected sale or land use charges in the area, and alert supervisors about them.

Transfer. Transfer of jurisdiction between agencies and between local, county, state provincial, and federal government is a process frequently used in order to follow legislative mandate or to adequately represent all types of areas in systems planning. Hundreds of parks exist today as a result of the transfer process. Some resistance might be made by one agency to what might be termed "raids" by another. These controversies such as the one concerning the jurisdiction and size of the area set aside around Mount St. Helens in the state of Washington are of great interest to the student of land use politics.

Use without Ownership

Lease. This arrangement is usually for a set period of time and for a specific purpose. The rental fee is commonly based on the value of the property and paid on an annual basis. An example would be the utilization of land belonging to the U.S. Bureau of Land Management, from whom, until 1977, an agency could lease land for 50 cents per acre or purchase for $2.50/acre. Section 42 (11) of the Federal Land Policy and Management Act of 1976 provides for the acquisition of such lands by public agencies for purposes of recreation and historic monuments, at no charge. Another example would be a county leasing land from the state government for recreational use.

Use Permits. These are issued usually at little or no fee for an indefinite period of time, but with a provision for revocation. Typical situations would be use of the space under electrical transmission lines for a trail right-of-way, or use of a bridge or pier for fishing.

Development Rights. This method assures the continuation of present use, and does not involve purchase of the land. For instance, an agency might purchase development rights from the owners of a golf course. That use, golf, and no other, would then prevail on that land. This is commonly done on farm lands to ensure the continuation of agricultural use.

Prescriptive Easements. These are gained when an agency claims, and is awarded, the use of a parcel of land on the basis of a number of years of similar use by the public. For example, walking rights over a beach or across open space might be secured by such an easement.

Scenic Easements. These are similar to development rights, but they differ in that the owner is paid the amount necessary to preclude any changes that would detract from the scenic aspect. Such an easement might involve a setback on a bluff overlooking a white water river, private land adjacent to a park, or an inholding next to a roadway.

DEVELOPMENT

The land envisioned in the regional area plan has been acquired, the planners have provided a plan document, and now a tangible structure, or some other modification of the area is to become a reality. At this point in the chapter, a flow plan may prove helpful (Fig. 9-8).

Financing the costs of construction is a very important phase of development. Here final project features are illustrated and estimated construction costs are projected. At this point too, the agency starts perfecting its capital budget for legislative review.

Budget Preparation

The information contained in Chapter 6, Fiscal Management, on budget preparation is also applicable here and will not be repeated.

Only those budget details that specifically relate to the capital budget will be dealt with here.

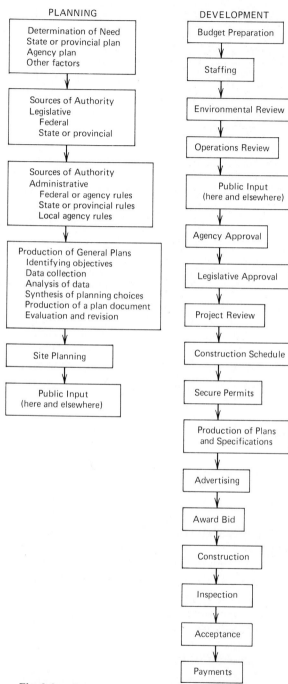

PLANNING

Determination of Need
State or provincial plan
Agency plan
Other factors

Sources of Authority
Legislative
Federal
State or provincial

Sources of Authority
Administrative
Federal or agency rules
State or provincial rules
Local agency rules

Production of General Plans
Identifying objectives
Data collection
Analysis of data
Synthesis of planning choices
Production of a plan document
Evaluation and revision

Site Planning

Public Input
(here and elsewhere)

DEVELOPMENT

Budget Preparation

Staffing

Environmental Review

Operations Review

Public Input
(here and elsewhere)

Agency Approval

Legislative Approval

Project Review

Construction Schedule

Secure Permits

Production of Plans
and Specifications

Advertising

Award Bid

Construction

Inspection

Acceptance

Payments

Fig. 9-8. A generalized flowchart for the planning and development of a park.

Capital Budget. The capital budget request deals with monies for acquisition and development of new areas and facilities as well as *major* renovations and repairs to extend the life of existing facilities. (This is in contrast to the operational budget, which is the day-to-day money used to run the agency.)

The development part of the capital budget is usually set forth in a long-range *capital needs program* of 6 to 10 years with a specific capital budget request that spans 1 or 2 years. The latter program requires much more specificity including a showing of need and also design in some degree of detail.

The Process of Development

Staffing. Depending on the size and scope of the capital development program, a varying amount of personnel with professional and technical training is required to prepare the budget. These people must gather appropriate data to develop all documents necessary to implement the program. Some will stay on the project until it is completed; others will help only in certain areas at specific times. To assure a balance of expertise, this project staff usually includes planners, engineers, environmentalists, and at least one representative, perhaps a manager, from the field staff. The maintenance department should also be represented at some point.

The responsibility for preparation of the budget for capital development projects should rest with the planning unit and must be closely coordinated with other technical staff. In addition to those aspects already noted, environmental and operating reviews are required.

Environmental Review. Preliminary environmental project review must be undertaken. The environmental impact statement (EIS) consists of estimating the effect of the proposed construction on the site. This information is deduced from environmental data, such as studies of flora and fauna.

Permits. The agency should also review pertinent regulatory documents and move to obtain the required permits. In both planning and development there are many situations that require permits before work can proceed. These fall under federal, provincial and state, and local agency rules, and reflect the areas of concern each of these levels is responsible for.

Operations Review. Design features now must be reviewed by the field staff with estimated operating start-up cost and annual operating costs identified. These cost figures are then to be placed with, and become a part of, the budget document and are to be added to the operating side of the appropriations (if the capital request is funded).

Public Input. There will be public input from many sources and at different times during the planning process. Some will be received during the "determination of need" and even more during the "environmental review." Depending on the scope of the project there also might be a special public meeting or hearing (see Chapter 8, Citizen Involvement).

Agency Approval. When these internal reviews are completed, this budget document takes its place with other agency budget documents and is assigned some point of priority within the agency budget request. Then, all agency budget requests are considered—compared—and submitted by "the authority" in his or her annual request to the legislative body. The "authority" will be the governor if the budget is from a state agency. In the case of a park district, that person would be the park director.

Legislative Approval. Some of the methods used to gain legislative support were discussed in Chapter 5, Politics, and Chapter 8, Citizen Involvement. For the purposes of this chapter, it will be assumed that the legislative body has passed the request.

With rare exception, not only will the legislative body not consider a request for construction funds (capital budget), but neither will the board, manager, or approving authority do so, unless the request is reasonably specific. The authorities will recognize that the agency cannot be precise, but a high degree of accuracy will be expected. They will also demand a high probability of completion if the funds are to be forthcoming.

Construction

Some considerable time has elapsed between the preparation of the budget request and its final legislative approval. Furthermore, even more time will pass before the project can assume its place in the agency schedule. During that period of time any number of events might have taken place which would drastically change the scope of the job, or even cause its cancellation. Therefore, the agency now needs to have a project review.

Project Review. The planner initiates this review, considers apparently needed changes, summarizes the recommendations and coordinates the review by other staff persons so that it is clear that they all approve the changes in the project. Quite frequently they will not all approve proposed changes.

Unresolved differences of opinion over changes in the project are sent to the higher levels, as necessary, for a final decision. These persons will likely be the same ones who originally approved the project. Following this review there should be no further changes to the project without the approval of the chief of engineering.

Construction Schedule. In order to ensure that all projects are started and completed within the appropriation period, a project implementation schedule designating specific time periods for each project phase (field data, permits, design and construction) should be prepared. The project schedule must take into consideration such items as weather, potential interference with public use, permit requirements (for instance, no work to be done in the stream bed during spawning season) and any other requirements affecting the construction program.

Permits. It is now time to prepare the final environmental documentation and secure any permits not previously obtained. Sometimes minor revisions in project scope or design will be necessary to comply with permit requirements.

Decision to Proceed. The final decision to proceed or not to proceed with project implementation is now made after review of the final project design permits, and environmental documentation. The agency budget and finance office need to be contacted to verify that the funds for the project have been set up.

Production of Plans and Advertising. The engineering division is responsible for the production of plans and specifications. These documents must be sent to all who have indicated an interest. They must also be advertised for bids in the appropriate journals, in most places titled by the town or city name, such as the *"Midvale Daily Journal of Commerce."* This solicitation must be handled according to the public bidding procedures applicable to the particular province or state. Bid openings should be brief and conducted in a professional manner with all participants well oriented in standard bid opening procedures.

The plans have been approved, the appropriations made, the bids let and the contracts awarded. The contract documents must now be prepared. These are the contract, the performance bond, the bid proposal sheet and a complete set of specifications. It is now time to start construction in accordance with the agency construction schedule.

Inspection. There are two stages of inspections during construction. That which is done during construction is known as "on-site" while that done just prior to the agency accepting the project is known as "final."

On-Site Inspection. The more major or complex the project, the greater the need to have an on-site agency inspector present during all construction hours. Regrettably, this is often impossible and frequently incorrect quantities or products of inferior quality are used. The on-site inspector should keep records of quantities and other items pertinent to payments. The inspector usually keeps a construction diary. Any changes in the on-site construction due to unforeseen problems will need to be written up officially as a *change order.* This process is expensive and time consuming.

Final Inspection. The final inspection is actually two phased. A "punch list" is submitted by the agency inspector. This shows the contractor what the agency believes needs to be done before the project is accepted and the contracts paid. (There are different versions of the derivation of this construction jargon. One version is that a hole was punched beside each item on the list as it was completed.) Taking care of these requests constitutes the second phase. After the inspector believes the project is properly completed, the agency "signs off" as having accepted the project.

Another interesting part of this stage as it develops is the phenomenon of the public, living adjacent to the area under development, also appointing themselves as inspectors. They will not only give on-the-job advice but will write their legislative representatives about various aspects of the work in progress.

Guarantees and Payments. Project failures that are a result of poor workmanship or faulty materials and equipment (generally within one year of the project acceptance) are replaced at the contractor's or supplier's expense. The agency usually protects itself by requiring of the contractor a one-year performance bond. This type of bond, paid for by the contractor, is a financial assurance that the work will be done as specified, both as to quantity and quality.

Each public works contract is backed up by a 100 percent performance bond and liability insurance. In addition, the contract should specify a certain number of days for completion of the work with a clause requiring payment for authorized extensions to complete construction work.

In spite of all good intentions by contractors and agency inspectors, there will, in all probability, be something wrong with most new facilities. It would be optimistic to expect all projects to be built right the first time. The chances are the park manager will need to do a little rearranging or "fixing" even on new facilities—be they campgrounds or visitor centers.

CONCLUSION

Few decisions made in park systems are more long lasting or more obvious than those made in planning, acquisition, or development. If mistakes are made they seldom go away or lend themselves to easy solutions. All three of these phases require masterful orchestration of many processes. These processes are vulnerable to change and political exigencies. The appearance of a park complete with facilities ready to serve the public represents the culmination of a long and complex process.

REFERENCES

General References

Lykes, Ira. 1981. *Fundamentals of Park Technology.* Associated Faculty Press, Inc. Gaithersburg, MD.

O'Brien, Jan J. 1977. *Construction Inspection Handbook.* Van Nostrand Reinhold Co. New York.

Jubenville, Alan. 1976. *Outdoor Recreation Planning.* W. B. Saunders Company. Philadelphia, PA.

References Cited

1. Driver, B. L. (ed.). 1974. *Elements of Outdoor Recreation Planning.* The University of Michigan Press, Ann Arbor, and Longman Canada, Limited, Don Mills, Ontario.
2. Woodbury, Coleman. 1965. "The Role of the Regional Planner in Preserving Habitats and Scenic Values." *Future Environments of North America.* Natural History Press. Garden City, NY.
3. Bradley, Gordon. 1982. "The Interpretive Plan" in *Interpreting the Environment.* (2nd. ed.). Grant W. Sharpe, (ed.). Wiley, New York.
4. Lynch, Kevin. 1972. *Site Planning* (2nd ed.). The M.I.T. Press. Cambridge, MA.

CHAPTER TEN

PARK FACILITIES

Definitions of the word *facilities* tell us it derives from the idea of making things easy or convenient. It is certainly more convenient for visitors to drive on paved roads to a well-established campground rather than to look for a place to pull off the highway and pitch a tent. Managers need campgrounds too but for different reasons. Large numbers of people cannot be allowed to wander around an area without provision of toilets, tables, or trails, nor can they be permitted to trample fragile areas. For the manager, then, facilities assist in establishing reasonable control and concentration of visitors. For visitors, access, comfort, and safety are the primary benefits of facilities.

It should be kept in mind that the term "facilities" covers many areas and structures. For instance, not only the picnic table, but the site the picnicking area occupies, the associated buildings, utilities, trails and signs, as well as the parking lot used by picnickers—all these are "facilities." Any humanly constructed, improved, and maintained structures or improved and maintained areas are designated as facilities.

Managers must keep the facilities in good condition despite heavy or even depreciative use. They must also maintain and operate the equipment needed to care for these facilities. In some instances park managers will be responsible for new installations or will help plan revisions of facilities. An understanding of facilities, their categories and uses, is therefore appropriate knowl-

edge for the manager. Knowing how and why facilities were constructed will not necessarily make the job of maintaining them easier but might lessen the frustrations involved.

Facilities vary greatly from park to park. A manager of a provincial park in Alberta or a state park in Montana would probably shudder at the thought of a 5500-car parking lot just for swimmers, or a picnic area parking lot large enough to accommodate over 1000 cars. Both of these may be found on Long Island Sound at Sunken Meadow State Park, only 40 miles from New York City (Fig. 10-1). Areas near large popula-

Fig. 10-1. The size of these parking lots, which together accommodate approximately 6700 cars, reflects the fact that they are only 40 miles from New York City. Note the bridge and footpath allowing access to the beach from the picnic area at left. Sunken Meadow State Park, New York. (Photo courtesy Long Island State Park and Recreation Commission.)

Fig. 10-2.   In order to locate parks near population centers it is often necessary to acquire and develop ordinary or even unattractive land. The upper photo shows county, state, and federal officials inspecting a former gravel pit that is being used as a dumping ground.

The lower photo shows the same site 10 years after the development and installation of facilities. Sacajawea Community Park, King County, Washington. (Upper photo courtesy of Bureau of Outdoor Recreation. Lower photo by Grant W. Sharpe.)

tion centers with high visitation differ greatly in their facility needs from parks located a considerable distance from major population centers.

As a side issue, not important to the visitor, but important to the park manager and the agency budget director, grades and pay scales of managers are directly linked to the amount of facilities within a given park. The more facilities a park has, and the greater their complexity, the higher the pay grade of the manager. What this really means is that as you advance in knowledge and experience within the ranks of park managers, you will be trusted to operate and maintain more and more of these expensive things called facilities.

People can be said to go to parks basically for a *park experience*, which means different things to different people. Whatever it is, the park experience is closely related not only to the park's natural attractions but also to its facilities. For some visitors, of course, absence of facilities is the criterion for choosing a certain area.

As we have seen, certain parks contain outstanding natural resource amenities that attract certain user groups. It would be nice if every park had a scenic attraction, a spectacular view, or some cultural amenity. In order to locate parks near population centers, however, it is often necessary to acquire and develop rather ordinary land (Fig. 10-2). In such instances, it is the park's location and facilities, not its impressive landscape, that attracts visitors.

Most parks have the basic facilities, although the quality and quantity varies greatly from park to park. But isn't it true also that the facilities themselves attract certain user groups? It seems quite obvious that picnic areas attract picnickers, campgrounds attract campers, and boat launching ramps attract boaters. A large, modern, well-developed campground attracts different people then does a small primitive one. A paved road attracts different users than does a gravel road. What is not so obvious is which came first, the facilities that attracted the users or the users that necessitated the facilities. Actually, in most situ-

Fig. 10-3. Which came first, the people or the facilities? Here it seems the people did, as they appear to be cooking a meal in the middle of the road. Circa 1900. (Photo by William H. Wilcox. Courtesy of Historical Society of Seattle and King County.)

ations these forces have worked together (Fig. 10-3).

People who visit the same park year after year may do so because they like the park "just the way it is." They may feel possessive about a certain part of the park, even seeking out the same campsite each year. A loyal clientele may suddenly become antagonistic if drastic changes are made. For example, visitors might come to a park because it offers good fishing on a lake where access to the water is by small car-top boats or canoes. The planner or manager might believe a further service could be rendered if a boat launching ramp were installed to benefit all boaters, including those pulling water skiers. An astute manager would carefully determine the need for such a facility, as well as inviting discussion on the change with present park clientele through public hearings, before making such an "improvement."

Barrier-Free Facilities.

Outdoor recreation activities are appealing to nearly everyone, regardless of ability or disability. Activities that remain inaccessible simply because of architectural barriers automatically shut out a significant segment of the North American population.[11] Obviously all areas in all parks, forests, and reserves can't be available to all visitors, but older facilities that are being refurbished, as well as all new facilities being considered, can eliminate most structural barriers through careful design.[11]

In the United States the *Architectural Barriers Act of 1968* notes that "Any building or facility, constructed in whole or part by federal funds must be made accessible to and usable by the physically handicapped." State, provincial, and local laws often have legislation requiring all public facilities be accessible to all people.[11]

Facility Costs

The cost of facilities has many variables, including labor costs, distance from suppliers, availability of materials, weather factors, site conditions, standards required, and initial planning costs, which might include delays for public hearings and time spent on the filing and acceptance of environmental impact statements. Most managers will have to depend on the agency headquarters to determine the cost of new and rehabilitated facilities through bidding and other contract procedures. The relationship of these costs to the available monies will determine the quality of the facility, the size, and many other factors including whether or not it will be built at all.

Not all types of facilities are capital construction projects. Some, such as signs, picnic tables, fireplaces, or components for footbridges are made in prison industries, centralized agency

workshops, or in the parks themselves, frequently during the off season.

FUNCTION OF FACILITIES

It is difficult to imagine the average park area without facilities. Facilities do the following.

1. They serve the needs of park visitors.
2. They protect the park from visitor impact.
3. They are necessary to the management and maintenance of the park.
4. They create a park image—either favorable or unfavorable.

Although facilities may add to the appearance of a park, they also intrude on park resources. Facilities cost money, they are expensive to maintain, and they are a focus for vandalism. Vandalism must be addressed by design, placement, and special consideration as to materials (see Chapter 13, Depreciative Behavior and Vandalism). Where possible, facilities should be constructed of materials indigenous to, as well as in harmony with, the natural environment.

Facilities must not infringe on unique areas or be placed where there is unusual or endangered flora or fauna. In the past, too many parks were unduly manicured or overdeveloped simply because the park "looked better that way." Today some park agencies make it a policy to have up to 80 percent of the park acreage in a natural condition, benefiting both wildlife and the people who wish to see wildlife.[2]

PLANNING FOR PARK FACILITIES

When determining the kind and extent of facilities the planner must consider the following factors.

1. How is the site to be used?
2. What is the amount and kind of land and water available?
3. Will the land support the expected visitor

load and activities without excessive deterioration?

4. Can the proposed facilities be maintained with a modest increase in the personnel and materials budget or will substantial increases in one or both be needed?

The Park Master Plan

To answer these questions a *master plan* must be developed and followed. Some master plans present park objectives in the broadest terms, serving only as guides to the development of more detailed plans, including facilities location. Other master plans, for small parks, may be so specific as to spell out in detail the location and type of roads, trails, utilities, buildings, and other facilities. An approach taken by many park agencies, which combines these two types, is to have specific plans for facility design and development within the more general master plan.

These more specific *site plans*, which serve to portray in detail the type and location of all park facilities, are known by several names, and serve several functions.

1. Assure coordination between the park and its neighbors.
2. Establish land use priorities.
3. Guide the designer in the preparation of detailed plans for each facility.
4. Show relationships between various park facilities.
5. Provide a basis for determining cost estimates.
6. Give agency administrators a reference for preparing construction priorities.
7. Provide the maintenance staff with a reference guide to all park facilities.

The four facility functions listed earlier show us that facilities provide user satisfaction and serve as management tools. Using these as criteria, the planner might look at proposed facilities under the following headings.

Suitability to the Site Is there harmony between the proposed facility and the natural landscape? Is there harmony between various facilities? How much of the natural setting will have to be altered to construct the facility?

Esthetics Is the facility attractive in its own right and neither too unconventional nor too ordinary?

Adapability Can the proposed facility be expanded to meet new demands at a reasonable cost?

Suitability for Maintenance Will this design raise or lower maintenance costs? Has this design proven elsewhere to be relatively low in maintenance costs?

Safety Do design and materials provide maximum safety for both visitors and staff?

Vandalism Potential Will the design leave the facility vulnerable to vandalism, or will it discourage vandalism? Will broken or defaced facilities be easily restored?

Access Is the facility readily accessible to all visitors including disabled persons? Is traffic flow and direction obvious for both foot and vehicle traffic? Is night lighting adequate?

Energy Efficiency Is the facility designed for minimizing heat loss in cooler months? Does it make provision for cooling in the warm season? Are the energy requirements reasonable? Is lighting achieved with minimum wattage?

Cost/Effectiveness Is the design actually the least expensive, or would spending more on the construction be offset by reduced maintenance and vandalism costs as well as increased life of the facility?

Construction Costs Does the design entail unnecessary or expensive construction costs, such as earth removal and grading? Are the materials difficult to secure?

Architectural Conservatism Is the facility in keeping with traditional design found in parks in this geographical region? Will visitors complain about the facility being too costly or unnecessarily elaborate? Is the design compatible with existing facilities?

EXPERIENCE WITH PARK FACILITIES

Does the fact that facilities are new guarantee trouble-free management? Assume that the planner has done his or her homework well, considered the climatic and topographic factors, water availability and the desirable and undesirable features of the site, and, after asking specialized user groups for comment on the facility design, has put together a good plan with several options for the decision makers.

The "best" design is picked, contracts let for construction, and within a year or so the new park with its shiny new facilities is ready for the public. The new manager arrives, the park is dedicated with the local politicians in evidence, and the shakedown period begins.

The park, it turns out, is far from complete. Construction scars need to be effaced and screenings must be planted. The visitors arrive, going into places the manager doesn't want them, just yet. The sign system, it turns out, leaves something to be desired.

What was designed for low density appears to be receiving high-density use. Some trails will need paving. Picnic table pads might be necessary. No emergency or overflow camping area was provided, yet everything is already full.

A vault toilet placed in a wet area is slowly surfacing. Some trees blow down during a windstorm. Initials are appearing in the smooth-barked trees in the campground. Children have to be rescued from nearby cliffs. The chlorinator in the water supply system breaks down. A tree catches fire because of fireplace location. Cattle from an adjacent farm are in the campground after breaking through the new fence. A camper

wedges his huge recreation vehicle between two trees damaging everything involved. Someone has broken into the coin box in the shower house. A camper complains about the noise coming from the adjacent group camp and threatens to punch someone in the nose.

Fortunately, things ease up after awhile. Not all of these hypothetical problems are a result of faulty design; some might be the result of faulty construction; some are policy related, others due to inexperience or bad luck. But good facility design and location can lessen or avoid at least some of these problems.

Space does not permit detailed information on the design of specific facilities. The interested student of park management is advised to read any of the references cited at the end of this chapter, particularly the books by Douglass and Jubenville, the U.S. Forest Service publications, and the many pages dealing with facilities in the Park Practice Program.

Our treatment here will stress manager-related concerns under the headings (1) Buildings, (2) Day-Use Areas, (3) Overnight Areas, and (4) Support Facilities (needed in both day and overnight areas). A certain amount of overlap is unavoidable. For instance, charcoal grills are mentioned as features of both day use and overnight areas, but they are not discussed in detail until the section entitled Support Facilities.

BUILDINGS

These are difficult to classify, as they can be found in any of the categories that follow, yet they do form a special unit of park facilities. Some buildings serve the public, but most are for park employees, serving park management and maintenance needs. These include administrative buildings, utility buildings, shop structures, employee residences and dormitories, entrance stations, and perhaps a historical building or two. Buildings intended for park visitor use are bathhouses, restrooms, and visitor centers or museums. Some parks have concession buildings such as food services, lodges, and buildings that house rentals of various kinds.

Since buildings stand out prominently, it is particularly important that design and construction materials should complement the park values. These materials should be selected for appearance, durability, and ease of maintenance. Building location should provide easy access yet be in harmony with the natural aspects of the area. At the beginning of this chapter it was suggested that facilities in general be constructed of material indigenous to the area and in harmony with the environment. This is particularly true for park buildings.

DAY-USE AREAS

These offer facilities for picnicking, swimming, boating, trailheads and trails, impromptu games, interpretive areas, and winter sports areas. Day-use areas should be designed to be readily accessible, esthetically pleasing, functional, and to require minimal maintenance. Facilities for each of the above uses will be considered separately.

Picnic Sites

Picnicking, which basically involves eating outdoors, often with family or friends, is one of the most popular daytime recreation activities in North America. Some people prefer to picnic in isolation with their family, others do not object to, or may even enjoy, large groups. Picnicking can take place anywhere, but is enhanced if there is some shade, reasonably level ground, and a view. At least some sites and the paths leading to them should be firm and level, equipped with totally accessible and usable facilities, and identified with the International Symbol of Access (see Fig. 18-12). If the picnic area is near water the sites should be set back, unless the sites are on rock, to prevent shoreline impact. Facilities include tables and fireplaces or charcoal grills at each site and a nearby trash receptacle, water supply, toilet, and central parking. These facilities keep people concentrated in areas designed

for this use, consolidating the problems of cleanup and maintenance, and confining soil compaction.

The fireplace or charcoal grill should be set away from trees and permanently anchored. The trash container should be obvious to the visitor, accessible to maintenance crews, and yet blend into the surroundings. The water supply and toilets are usually centrally located. Attempting to provide shade at each table is unwise because picnic use puts too much compaction on the feeder roots of trees and eventually kills them.

Group picnic areas should be separated from the family picnic area. In group areas the tables are closer together and more formally arranged. Fireplaces or grills are not needed with each table. A picnic shelter containing stoves, water, and tables, and that provides overhead protection from sun or rain, may be found in either group or family picnic areas.

The number of persons to be accommodated per acre in picnic areas is generally fixed by agency policy, based on the park's proximity to population centers and the number that can be accommodated without deterioration of the site.

Barrier devices or curbing will be necessary to confine vehicles to parking areas, for everyone wishes to drive right up to the tables, and will, if not deterred. Signs will be needed for management purposes.

Swimming Areas

Swimming takes place in pools, ponds, lakes, reservoirs, streams, rivers, and oceans, and is a major day-use activity. Freedom from pollution and hazards is essential. Beaches should not be developed where there are strong currents, steep dropoffs, or other conditions that create a safety problem for swimmers. The average water temperature during the swimming season should be above 20° C (68° F).

Facilities might include a sandy or pebble beach, a grassy area upslope from the beach, toilets and a change house or dressing room for each sex, a central parking area, trash receptacles, drinking fountains or hand pumps, an anchored float, and a roped-off area or buoy markers designating the outer boundaries of the swimming area. Approximately 75 percent of the swimming area should be in depths of 1.5 m (5 ft) or less. Various signs will also be needed.

A small play area for impromptu games, such as frisbee tossing or touch football, contributes to the enjoyment of the area. A fast-food concession stand near the beach is a convenience some park visitors really enjoy, but it adds to the litter problem.

Disabled persons' access consists of a firm pathway or boardwalk built from the parking lot to water's edge, with a rubber mat laid directly on the sand. Handrails give disabled swimmers added assurance of safety.[11]

Boating Areas

Most park managers will be concerned mainly with boats that can be transported either by car-top or on trailers. The major facilities involved are launching ramps, docks, fuel facilities, parking for cars and trailers, adequate turn area, and toilet and garbage facilities. Launching, boating and fishing regulations must be posted. In some areas fish cleaning facilities might be necessary.

Trailheads

The trailhead is a point where users transfer from road vehicles to trails or vice versa. Users could be hikers, walkers, horse or bike riders, or in winter, snowmobilers, cross-country skiers, or snowshoers.

From the facility standpoint, these areas are relatively uncomplicated. The trailhead consists of a central parking area convenient to the trail. Facilities may include toilets, drinking water, garbage cans, an information bulletin panel and trail-use signs. If horses are used on the trail, a hitch rack is usually necessary. A load-unloading ramp might be needed if commercial packers use the trailhead.

Care must be taken not to overdevelop a trailhead. The size of the parking area should be

closely related to the designed use or optimum capacity of the trail system (see Chapter 12, Environmental Impact). Also, the facilities here must be carefully considered in order to avoid unrelated use. If, for example, tables and fireplaces are provided at the trailhead, it is difficult to prevent the site from becoming a campground for other park visitors who do not intend to use the trail.

Trails

Trails are linear corridors, usually well defined, generally leading the user away from and back to "civilization." The purpose is to permit visitor access to the resource with a minimum of impact. *Walking trails* are short and provide access to nearby points of interest for the casual hiker or stroller. A popular walking trail is the self-guided interpretive or nature trail. The walking trail should take full advantage of a variety of views, vegetation types, and other points of interest. Walking trail standards include such requirements as numerous bends in the trail, easy grades, benches, hand rails near potential hazards, and footbridges or boardwalks over wet areas and sensitive sites (Fig. 10-4). The tread should be treated with some surfacing material such as wood chips, bark or soil cement. Paving might be required in certain areas of heavy use.

Hiking trails, on the other hand, are designed for the more experienced and rugged hiker and encompass longer distances and rougher terrain. Grades may be up to 12 percent or more. Reaching scenic vistas is an important consideration in hiking trail location. Since hiking trails run across hillsides to gain elevation, switchbacks as well as cuts and fills are usually necessary. Soil erosion must be held to a minimum by use of drainage techniques such as culverts and water bars.

Other types of trails include equestrian, bicycle, snowmobile, and cross-country ski trails. Each type has standards of design, and the trail planner must understand these differences of construction, location, and vertical and horizon-

Fig. 10-4. The elevated boardwalk serves to separate visitors from the trail environment without inhibiting their enjoyment of it. This channeling of visitors is in contrast to letting them roam at will, causing damage to the vegetation. Sunken Forest, Fire Island National Seashore, New York. (National Park Service photo by Cecil W. Stoughton.)

tal clearing needs. As we will see elsewhere, keeping these users apart by time, season, or physical separation is frequently necessary (see Chapter 14, Conflicts).

There are likely to be problems on a trail entering or leaving a park to or from another ownership, particularly if the regulations governing the adjacent land differ from the park's. Examples would be leash laws for pets, carrying of guns, campfire permits, motorized vehicle use, and smoking while traveling.

Playground Facilities

Not all agencies feel it necessary or appropriate to provide play apparatus. Most playgrounds are found in the activity-oriented structured recreation parks, but occasionally such facilities are found in state and provincial parks. Some are even found in national recreation areas. The management purpose of these facilities is two-

fold: to provide children with an opportunity to use large muscles and to "let off steam," and to concentrate their activities in a small area, usually in or near a campground, picnic area, or wading area. Equipment includes simple culvert crawlthroughs and hideaways, swings, sandboxes, whirls, climbing bars, overhead ladders, and slides.

Impromptu Game Areas

Resource-oriented parks do not usually provide facilities for organized sports or athletic events. If they are provided, the standards are usually less than league requirements. The policy on providing sports facilities varies greatly even within agencies, however.

Once a pattern of use is established it may be difficult to stop. For example, local pressure to provide space for a soccer field, complete with goal posts and white lines, could lead to tournament play and the need to provide more fields. A policy on such use is clearly needed.

Level, open space is usually sufficient invitation for visitors to start an impromptu game of baseball, soccer, or football, or to throw frisbees, sail kites or fly model airplanes. Such space should be separated from picnic areas and campgrounds if possible. Some parks provide backstops or goalposts, shuffleboard courts, and horseshoe pits. Visitors often bring their own equipment for badminton or volleyball. Sandy beaches and other small areas, including septic tank drain fields, are ideal for many of these uses.

Interpretive Areas

Basic facilities for interpretive areas include simple bulletin boards or exhibit shelters and interpretive signs. Exhibit shelters may be located at trailheads, en route between parking areas and the attraction, and at the attraction itself. Interpretive trails, utilizing either signs in place or numbered posts keyed to leaflets, provide access with a minimum of disturbance to natural or cultural areas. These trails, designed for intensive use, require constant maintenance and for this reason should be less than 1.6 km (1 mi) long. Wildlife observation blinds and platforms provide access to native wildlife species for close study and photography. Some parks offer the convenience of a visitor center that contains restrooms, offices, an information desk, exhibit rooms, and an auditorium.

Most interpretive facilities are intended for day use. An exception is the amphitheater, designed for evening presentations on the natural and cultural history of the area. Seats, projection booth, screen, and an amplification system with speakers; a fire circle, and a short access trail, are usually components of such a facility. Newer units have a rear-screen projection system that eliminates the projection booth at the rear of the audience. Most amphitheaters are located in or near campgrounds, and are reached by walking. Some may have a central parking lot for patrons coming from other areas.

Winter Sports Areas

The criteria used to determine if a site is suitable for winter sports activities include snow texture and depth, slope steepness and aspect, wind, temperature, avalanche potential, slope clearing costs and protection from erosion, the availability of electricity, and accessibility.

Winter sports include such activities as downhill skiing, cross-country skiing, snowshoeing, ice skating, snowmobiling, and snow play. The area often requires warming facilities, a food and hot drinks stand, restrooms, equipment rental, first aid station, and lockers. These comforts and conveniences will require housing in a ski shelter, hut, or lodge.

Downhill skiing requires a lift device, and the types vary greatly from simple rope tows to elaborate chair lifts, or cars (called gondolas or trams) that are suspended on wires. Cross-country skiing requires a safe system of relatively level trails, separate from snowmobile trails. Both types of skiing will probably require plowed parking at the trailhead. Sliding areas for snow play must also be separated from other winter sports, and this activity must be confined to treeless slopes in order to avoid accidents.

OVERNIGHT AREAS

Overnight areas include campgrounds, group camps, and lodging areas. Each should be designed to provide a pleasant experience for visitors and should be separated from day-use areas in order to avoid conflict between user groups.

Campgrounds

The campground is perhaps the prime example of a park facility serving as a management tool. It limits visitor impacts to a specific area thus reducing damage to the overall recreation complex. It allows concentration of services, maximum surveillance and safety measures, and social interaction among users. From its beginning the campground has been designed to accommodate automobiles—the means most North Americans

Fig. 10-5. Campgrounds were made necessary by the advent of the family car, and from their inception they have been designed to accommodate automobiles. This nostalgic 1936 photo was taken in Heckscher State Park, New York. (Photo courtesy Long Island State Park and Recreation Commission.)

have used to reach the site. The family car gave people the mobility to participate in the camping experience (Fig. 10-5).

Even though extensively and carefully planned, the area supporting the campground will undergo considerable modification over time. Vegetation, soils, and wildlife populations are all altered through initial construction and continued visitor use, as cited in Chapter 12, Environmental Impact. Such deterioration is one of the costs of providing overnight accommodations for people in the forest environment. When a park is small and the campground is comparatively large, modification will be more apparent than in a park where the campground comprises only a fraction of the total park acreage. If they bear in mind that the objective is to protect the rest of the park while confining the impact, managers can be more tolerant of visitor-imposed damage. Trees singed by campfires, the cutting of wiener sticks from shrubbery, exposed roots (Fig. 12-7), erosion from shortcutting, and enlargement of campsites to accommodate specific

visitor needs are impacts that must be kept to a minimum by wise and vigilant management, but they can never be completely stopped. These problems come with the convenience and control that campgrounds also provide. When one considers the alternative to the developed campground—extensive litter and sanitation problems, campfires out of control, intrusion of tents and vehicles everywhere, as well as other problems connected with dispersed road recreation—the campground, with all its problems, seems preferable in most situations.

As Wagar points out, camping is an essential ingredient of outdoor recreation.[12] For many visitors, staying in a campground *is* the recreation experience—the campfire, the cooking, the renewed contact with the elements, the change of pace, getting away from some of the comforts and conveniences of home—all these factors, and no doubt others we have not yet recognized, contribute to the camping experience.

On the other hand, campgrounds are regarded by some visitors as primarily inexpensive, convenient, and relatively safe stopovers en route to other places. For yet others, campgrounds are a base of operations, a place to stay while exploring, fishing, or hiking.

All this leads one to believe there needs to be a wide spectrum of campground designs to fulfill the needs of the camping public. Most authorities agree with this conclusion.[3,4,6,9,12] Diversity has been considered in the planning process, and visitors would do well to seek out their preferences. Some developments, such as traveler's camps, have 15 sites per acre with camp sites side by side. No attempt is made to screen out distractions or to preserve the natural values of the area. Forest camps usually have 50 m (150 ft) between individual sites and the natural values will be left reasonably intact.[12]

Campground sizes vary greatly, as does the array of facilities offered. The purpose of the campground, the amount and kind of suitable land available, construction costs, demand forecasts, proximity to travel routes, and agency pol-

icy all dictate the general design of the campground. Design should allow the closure of some units for vegetative rehabilitation, as well as for convenience of fee collection and trash pickup during the off season. Campground components are considered under Support Facilities later in this chapter.

The developed campground size ranges from a small area with three or four sites and a simple pit toilet to those with an elaborate road and sign network, several hundred units, flush toilets and showers, and an amphitheater. These large campgrounds require a sophisticated sanitation system. Local sanitation laws often dictate the type of sanitation facilities used in campgrounds.

A typical campsite or unit should consist of a parking spur and an adjacent use area containing a table, fireplace or grill, and tent space (Fig. 10-6). Barriers may be used to confine the car to its parking space and protect the table from damage. More elaborate sites come with complete sewer, water, and electrical hookups for recrea-

Fig. 10-6. A campsite showing a fireplace, table, and barrier rock. Space for a tent is provided also (at far right). Ralph River Campground, Strathcona Provincial Park, British Columbia. (Photo by Grant W. Sharpe.)

tion vehicles. Areas with more than 25 camp units should have a holding-tank dump station. All these components will be considered under *Support Facilities,* later in this chapter.

Campers seek different experiences from their camping. Some want the sociability and security of having other people nearby. Some bring with them most of the conveniences of home, including radios, tape players, and television. Others want isolation or at least peace and quiet. Purists bring with them only the essentials for sleeping and eating. It's all called "camping," and this variety of styles again shows the need for a diversity of offerings in order to satisfy the needs of the camping public.

The campground often becomes the park manager's main problem because it is where people, many of them strangers, concentrate for overnight or longer. It's the city transplanted to the woods. Some problems are related to the design of the facility, some are not. Aside from the social problems of noise, pets, and other annoyances, here are some common campground problems related to design.

Confusing entrance and road layout.

Campsites and parking spurs not level.

Group camp too close to family campsites.

Materials chosen with no concern for ease of maintenance or protection from vandalism.

Campsites too close together.

Campground too close to a major hazard.

Campground size inadequate to meet demand.

Campground too close to day-use facilities.

A road passes near campground creating a high incidence of theft.

Shortcuts taken in design and construction materials in order to economize.

Water or sanitation facilities inconveniently located for many sites.

Campsites not diverse enough to accommodate a wide range of recreational vehicles.

All sites designed for single vehicles only.

No screening vegetation between campsites.

Insufficient parking for guests or visitors.

Inadequate campsite barriers.

Trail system poorly signed.

Other problems, arising from policy decisions rather than the design of facilities, include those resulting from a differential fee system, an inadequate reservation system, and insufficient staffing and materials to properly maintain the campgrounds.

Group Camps

Group camps, also known as Organizational Camps, Environmental Learning Centers, and by other similar names, are often found on public recreational lands. They are used for educational and social purposes, by school, scouting, church, and other groups that have a common interest requiring members to live together for a few days. Demand for such areas is usually heavy and reservations must often be made a year in advance.

Basic facilities include a road and trail system, parking lots, sign system, headquarters building for staff offices, kitchen facilities and a dining hall, first aid room, cabins or bunkhouses for staff and campers, shower and toilet structures, water supply for both domestic use and fire control, classrooms, clubhouse, and other indoor recreational space. A swimming area is highly desirable, as is outdoor space for organized sports and nature activities. Miscellaneous facilities include shelters, fire circles, and perhaps a caretaker's residence.

Group camps should be isolated from all other park facilities to lessen distractions and assure privacy and safety for group campers, and to protect other park users from the noise associated with group camps.

Standards and safety practices for group camp facilities, particularly the water supply, sewage treatment, and living quarters, might be dictated by local health agencies. Information on standards and accreditation requirements for health and safety practices may be obtained by writing the American Camping Association (ACA). (See General References.)

Lodging Areas

Such facilities range from simple housekeeping tent units to housekeeping cabins to elegant lodge facilities complete with opportunities for dining. The policy on guest cabins and lodges varies with agencies: some provide and maintain them, others build and then lease them to a concessionnaire, others are concessionnaire built and maintained, still other agencies leave the matter up to the private sector outside the park boundary. Some park agencies have found the operation of lodging to be a profitable business (Fig. 10-7). These kinds of facilities increase the opportunity for a larger segment of the population to enjoy the park or recreation area, as not everyone cares to camp, and lodging areas provide an alternative.

SUPPORT FACILITIES

Support facilities are those structures and amenities that provide water, sanitation, parking, safety, convenience, and access. These support facilities or utilities are needed in both day use and overnight areas as well as in the area housing park personnel.

Service facilities, shops, offices, and employee residences should be located away from recreational use areas, and, where possible, confined to locations that do not have resource values attractive to the public. Electricity and telephone services will be required; lines should be placed underground.

The Water Supply

Providing a continuous, safe, clean water supply for the park and its visitors is a major task for park managers. The needs of visitors include water for drinking, cooking, washing, and sanita-

Fig. 10-7. The state-owned Western Hills Resort on Fort Gibson Reservoir, near Wagoner, Oklahoma. (Photo courtesy Division of Lodges, Oklahoma Tourism and Recreation Department.)

tion. The park needs include additional water for residences, fire protection, and irrigation.

Because of past inadequacies and present high standards, public health agencies have a great deal to say about the park water supply, including its source, method of transport, storage, method of purification, and final dispersal to visitors. Water may be cold, taste good, and look clean, but these attributes are no guarantee that it is potable (safe to drink). Any water source can be contaminated. All water must be tested frequently. Water taken from a lake, reservoir, or spring may require chlorination.

Early in the planning of a park the average daily water needs, as well as peak demands, must be estimated. Then it is necessary to determine if this amount of water is available from either a groundwater or surface source. Groundwater is frequently more readily available and less costly to develop for use than is surface water.

Water demand varies with the kind of facilities that are in place. A park with pit toilets has one level of demand, one with flush toilets another. Add to this a shower house, laundry house, rental cabins and a group camp, and the demand increases dramatically. For example, in a campground with pit toilets the average daily requirement per person is about 21 liters (5.5 gal). In a campground with showers and flush toilets the daily requirement of water per person could be as much as 100 liters (27 gal). Some writers estimate a much higher use.[7]

In a given park the water supply may come from several sources. In most instances the preferred source is a drilled well with water pumped to various outlets. This requires electricity, of course. Sources other than groundwater are streams, springs, lakes, and reservoirs—this water reaching the area of use by gravity in most instances. Springs must be fenced, boxed, and covered with a lid. Hand pumps must be boxed to prevent contamination. Maintenance includes annual cleaning to remove sand, silt, algae, and salamanders. Often a collecting or storage tank is needed to provide a reserve supply for peak demand. In colder climates, provision must be

made for weatherproofing or draining all pumps, pipes, and storage tanks to prevent freezing.

Where a water supply is utilized away from developed areas, such as along a trail, the visitor should be encouraged to boil or chemically treat any water obtained for drinking or cooking.

Toilets and Sewage

Toilet facilities, ranging from modern flush toilets to primitive pits, are necessary for any recreation development.

Flush Toilets. These are costly to build, have a high water-use rate, and require a reliable water supply. Water is used as a carrier of the waste through sewers to the local sewage treatment plant. When such a plant is not available, as in most outlying parks, sewage is handled through a septic tank and drain field, or an aerator-lagoon system. To accommodate a septic tank drain field system, the soil must ''perc,'' that is, be suitable to accept the effluent from the drain fields.*

These are only two of several types of waste disposal systems used in parks. In very heavy use areas the sewage treatment plant can be quite elaborate. Some plants treat the effluent according to such high standards that it may be discharged into park streams.

Toilet buildings should be well lighted, ventilated, and painted. The fixtures should be securely anchored to the floor or walls and all pipes hidden from view in order to reduce vandalism. Skylights permit natural light to enter (Fig. 10-8). In some regions solar collector panels can be used to heat and cool the building.

A waste treatment alternative is *static pile composting*, a simple and economical means of rendering raw sewage into organic soil condition-

---

*To determine the suitability of the soil a simple percolation test is made. It is essentially a hole dug in the soil and wetted for several hours. The rate at which the water level in the hole falls is used as a measure of the soil's capacity to accept drainage. The percolation rate will vary from hole to hole in the same soil type.[5]

Fig. 10-8. Round log supports give this flush toilet building a look of rustic simplicity, yet it is a very expensive facility to build. Not illustrated are the accompanying septic tank and drain field, located across the road to the right. Newhalem Campground, Ross Lake National Recreation Area, Washington. (Photo by Grant W. Sharpe.)

ers. Organic materials such as sawdust or woodchips are utilized to absorb human waste. The waste, stacked in a cone-shaped pile, is decomposed by microbial activity over a period of several weeks. Equipment needed is a front-end loader, used for mixing and piling waste, and blower system, used to draw air through the pile. The end result is an odorless, useful soil conditioner.[10]

Research is continuing in the disposal of waste, particularly in backcountry areas, where high use in combination with thin soils create serious problems.[8]

Pit or Box Toilets. A pit toilet is a hole in the ground with a wooden structure over it. When the hole fills the toilet is moved and the site is covered with soil. These structures have not disappeared from the park scene. They are used in

such areas as small and remote campgrounds, in picnic areas, at trailheads, small swimming areas, and in winter-use areas where freezing weather forces the closure of flush toilets. They are also used where soil percolation is poor, and where water is unavailable.

Vault Toilets. An improvement over the pit toilet is the vault type or chemically sealed vault toilet. This type is more costly to build, it must be pumped out periodically, and the pumping is a continuous cost. Also, it must be accessible to pump out trucks that transfer the waste to sewage treatment plants. Its advantage is that it need not be relocated and is more sanitary than a pit toilet. This type of toilet is particularly useful in areas with a high water table.

One of the major problems with vault toilets is improper use. As mentioned above the vaults require pumping out. Beverage cans, plastic, rocks, sticks, rolls of toilet paper, and other debris that visitors throw into the toilet damage the pumping mechanism. This creates a serious management problem since contracting firms will not pump at any price if their equipment is going to be damaged. The park manager must somehow convince visitors to use these facilities for the purpose intended and not as garbage cans. Here is an opportunity to use interpretation as a management tool by devising a sign that could persuade visitors to look after this facility for their own sake.

Attractive portable fiberglass box and hold-tank toilets that sit on top of the ground are available commercially and might be necessary in very wet areas, at special events, or where permanent facilities have broken down. In some parks a supply of these is kept on hand, and, as the need arises, they are shifted around. This rotation might also include summer- and winter-use areas. These new toilets are miniature treatment plants, some injecting air into the holding tank to induce bacterial destruction of waste while others use recirculating odorless oil to carry waste products through a settling tank. In the latter model the waste sinks and the oil is filtered and used over again.

Fig. 10-9. The holding-tank disposal facility for recreation vehicles. The vehicle is driven over the depression, the holding tank hose is lowered into the drain opening, the tank valve is opened and the holding tank is drained. Emigrant Lake Campground, Jackson County, Oregon. (Photo by Grant W. Sharpe.)

Dump Stations

Most recreational vehicles today are self-contained, which means they possess toilet holding tanks. To prevent people from emptying these tanks along lonely country roads, provisions must be made for convenient dumping stations. A few gasoline stations offer customers the service of draining their holding tanks. However, to be most effective, the service must be available where the toilet is being used, in the park itself. Dump stations are usually placed somewhat inconspicuously on a pull-through just inside the park on the exit side of the road system. The station itself is quite simple. It consists of a concrete pad over which the recreation vehicle is driven. The pad contains a drain hole leading to a huge holding tank. There is also a hose and water supply used for washing down any spill and for replenishing the vehicle's holding tank (Fig. 10-9).

Refuse or Trash Receptacles

The all-important garbage can, litter barrel, or trash receptacle is usually made of metal or plastic. Those made of metal might be steel oil drums

with one end removed, or aluminum cans or wire baskets designed to hold trash. Some parks have a take-it-home policy and don't provide such receptacles. Most park managers find it impossible to get along without them.

These cans must be readily available to visitors and maintenance people alike. Most are painted green and have the litter logo on the outside. To prevent loss they must be chained in place. Even if not anchored with a lock, having a special mounting or base suggests to park visitors that cans should not be moved closer to their site or taken home with them. A supportive base also prevents animals from tipping cans over—a major irritation to employees who have to clean up the mess. This speaks well for having tight-fitting lids in order to keep rodents, flies, and birds from entering the container. The relatively inexpensive but durable 55-gallon drum has the disadvantage of being heavy even when empty; it becomes a backbreaker when full.

Heavy-duty plastic liners make pickup and disposal of garbage a more efficient and less unpleasant task and keep the cans cleaner. Trucks are available today that make loading easy (Fig. 11-4). Some parks now use large containers and self-loading compaction trucks, particularly where visitor use is heavy and great amounts of garbage are generated daily. Where practical, private contracting of refuse pickup should be considered. This frees employees for other duties and relieves the park from having to dispose of mountains of garbage.

Raccoons, porcupines, rodents, and even domestic dogs can become a nuisance if refuse is not handled properly. Extreme care must be exercised in placement of cans or dumpsters if the area is bear habitat. Deaths and injuries can result from attracting bears to camping areas.

The Road System

The park road system includes entrance roads, public access roads, service roads, and parking areas. As these roads provide the main circulation and access to the park features, their location must be carefully considered to avoid affecting sensitive areas.

Park roads should be located to take best advantage of the topography and scenery with a minimum of disturbance to park features. Designers try to keep cut-and-fill slopes to an absolute minimum in order to reduce road scarring. Where the scenery is favorable and the topography permits, parking is provided to enable visitors, particularly the driver, an opportunity to view the scene in a more relaxed manner. These overlooks may include drinking water and toilets, interpretive signs, picnic tables, and a trailhead for a short walking trail.

Park roads are built to different standards than are major highways and are not designed for high speeds or exceptionally heavy vehicles. They may have sharper curves, steeper grades, and narrower widths since they are intended for restful, leisurely driving. These standards also make park road construction less expensive than highway construction.

Unfortunately some drivers do not realize that road standards are different within the park, and therefore they do not adjust their speed. On the road leading into the park appropriate signing should emphasize the fact that the visitor is entering a territory requiring different driving behavior. A sign posting the park speed limit doesn't tell the driver *why* he or she should go slower, and the result is frequent confrontations with park rangers or, worse yet, frequent accidents. Interpretive skills will be required to communicate this message. Entrance roads should be few in number to limit administrative problems.

Access roads provide visitors admittance to campgrounds, picnic areas, food and lodging sites, and other developed recreation opportunities. Here again speeds are much reduced for safety reasons. The use of speed bumps might be appropriate.

Use of service roads is usually limited to park employees for maintenance, fire control, or other emergency access. These roads are posted as service roads and often have physical barriers at their entrances to keep visitors out.

From a maintenance standpoint, the road system requires considerable attention. For every unit of road there is double the roadside to maintain. Vegetation keeps invading the roadside, loose soil fills the drainage ditches, catch basins and culverts fill with blocking debris, trees fall across the road, and visitors keep tossing out garbage that we politely call litter. The signs need replacing, the grass and weeds must be mowed, the road surface must be patched, and the center stripe must be repainted. Gravel roads need to be bladed to control drainage, to remove loose material, to fill ruts, and to level washboard. Dust might have to be controlled in heavy-use areas. The road system requires constant attention from the park staff.

Parking Areas

Parking lots are intended to provide temporary storage for visitors' cars in an area where the planner, and presumably the manager, want them. They are also an excellent management tool for regulating numbers of people, distributing them evenly over a park, and protecting the rest of the park from damage.

Parking lots are a major component in the design of any park layout. The size and shape vary because of basic requirements. Most are for group day-use activities, such as picnicking and swimming, and often one lot can be designed to serve several activities. On the other hand, some lots serve a specific activity, such as a boat launch area, or, as in the case of overnight camping, as a private parking slot in the form of a spur or pull-through.

Most park visitors, particularly those staying overnight, wish to be close to the vehicle that brought them to the park, for convenience, and for security reasons—both theirs and the vehicle's.

In locating a parking lot the planner must consider several factors: the traffic problem it will create or solve, the proximity of the lot to the activity it serves, the extent of intrusion on the activity and on the natural landscape, the size, the potential for expansion should it be needed, and impact on the site.

Large lots may be necessary where heavy use demands the accommodation. Where possible the planner tries to break up solid parking areas with a median strip between parking lanes, and to blend the development into the natural surroundings. Tree plantings provide shade and soften the harshness of paving and rows of cars, providing a suitable transition to the more natural area beyond. To prevent problems such as cars slipping their brakes, all parking areas should be level.

Special care should be taken in the design and construction of parking areas for amphitheaters to ensure that vehicle lights will not interfere with the presentation on the screen.

The parking facility cannot be designed to accommodate peak holiday use. Even on ordinary weekends the lot may fill and people will have to be turned away. On such days traffic will become congested at park entrances and people will park along the shoulders of the approach roads thus causing problems in another jurisdiction. Parking *must* be limited to the designed capacity of the parking lot; limitations were imposed to operate in just such situations to protect the resource from overuse.

Traffic Control and Parking Barriers

These are intended to keep cars where the planner and the manager want them, on the roads, parking lots, and parking spurs. The individual barrier device is made of a variety of materials including native rock boulders, precast concrete or wood posts, logs, or concrete or wood curbing. Guardrails, made of steel or wood railings, are another type of barrier. These are mounted on concrete or masonry posts. The purpose of the traffic control device, as the name implies, is to protect the visitor from dangerous places, and to protect park resources from visitors. Rows of trees and shrubs serve as living barriers along roadways, but are not too effective in campgrounds, where continuous abuse from autos eventually kills barrier vegetation. The simplest

yet most effective barrier is street curbing. Urban dwellers understand its purpose. In contrast to this, the large log or boulder presents a challenge. Visitors seem to want to move such barriers out of the way, as though they were there by chance and simply represent an inconvenience. Barriers should be esthetically pleasing, or at least not offensive, while meeting safety and administrative requirements.

Signs

Visitors depend on signs for guidance, information, and safety. Managers use signs to inform visitors of hazards, regulations, and to control traffic. Where recreational uses might overlap signs are necessary to assist in the avoidance of conflict. Signs should intrude as little as possible on a site, yet be conspicuous where needed. The size of the sign and letter size varies with use and agency policy. A person on foot reading a sign has a different need than someone traveling in a car. Wording should be brief and positive, and the text should be in lowercase letters. Some parks maintain a file of sign messages on word processing equipment or computers. The scripts are easily retrievable and don't need to be rewritten should the sign be stolen or damaged and need replacement. A note of caution: the wording on a sign might be grounds for a lawsuit in case of an accident. It is essential that the agency legal staff review the proposed wording on any signs used for administrative purposes.

Sign materials are usually wood or metal or a combination of these. Posts are made of concrete, metal, or durable or preservative-treated wood. The choice of material is often ruled by problems of weathering, vandalism, maintenance, and the replacement costs. Park or agency policy also may be decisive; for example, some agencies require all sign panels be made of metal. In others, particularly the older parks, the signs are all made from wood (Fig. 10-10). The lettering is sometimes routed directly on the wood, or it might be painted or silkscreened on the wood or metal.

Carefully maintained signs foster an attitude

Fig. 10-10. This arresting and highly photogenic entrance sign is located at Newcastle Island Provincial Park, near Nanaimo, British Columbia. (Photo by Grant W. Sharpe.)

of respect for the park and its facilities. Directional signs leading to the park are most often the responsibility of another agency, usually the highway department or department of transportation. Where possible a *Sign Manual* covering agency policy on specifications, construction methods, maintenance, and ordering procedures should be used. If none exists, one should be written, following the fine examples already established by some agencies. Initiating a sign system is not as simple as well done examples might lead us to believe. As was so aptly stated in *Parks:*

> *It is simplicity itself to make and erect a sign. It is very much harder to make and erect a sign that says what you want it to, remains legible and attractive throughout its planned life, offends nobody and does not cost the earth.* [1]

Community Kitchen or Picnic Shelter

Used by small to large groups in inclement weather or hot sun, this concrete-floored structure is usually roofed with open sides (Fig. 10-11). It commonly contains large wood-burning stoves or metered gas or electric stoves, sinks equipped with running water, serving counters,

and picnic tables. This facility is usually located near the group picnic areas. If constructed of wood it must be made of pressure-treated timbers to extend its life and reduce maintenance costs. The design should fit the landscape. Some modern shelters are constructed of precast concrete frames and laminated wood beams and can accommodate anywhere from 1 to 50 or more picnic tables.

Picnic Tables

The picnic table is the basic facility in picnic areas and campgrounds. The style and condition of the tables are major factors in the appearance of the site. They must be sturdy to withstand concentrated abuse and exposure to the weather. Picnic tables are commonly made of pressure-treated wood, precast concrete, masonry, fiberglass, metal (usually galvanized iron pipe or aluminum tubing), or a combination of these materials (Fig. 10-11). The hardware should be

Fig. 10-11. Note the interesting features of this picnic shelter with its undercover tables and community stoves. Although the tables in the foreground (each with its own charcoal stove) are positioned very formally on a hardened surface, the whole facility is attractive and "natural" looking. The upswept lines of the roof, its flamelike crown, and the sturdy rockwork of the buttresses all contribute to this effect. Lake Sammamish State Park, Washington. (Photo by Grant W. Sharpe.)

rust resistant. On those parts of the table and bench where bare skin or food comes in contact with wood, toxic preservatives such as pentachlorophenol should not be used. A high-quality wooden table is usually finished with exterior varnish, plastic, or other synthetic finishes.

The choice of table design is governed by suitability and availability of materials, custom, cost, and the type of park and landscape. For example, massive rustic tables usually blend with the scenic qualities and use demands of a national park or forest, whereas a light wooden and metal table may better fit a neighborhood park.

A standardized design within a park or park system is advantageous as it allows for interchangeable parts, ease of transportation and storage, and most important of all, mass production in construction. Some park agencies construct their own tables during the slack season, others depend on institutional labor, and still others purchase their tables from commercial suppliers. The popular wooden table of a few years back, utilizing round peeled logs for the underparts and machined wood for the seats and tops, is giving way to the all-machined wooden table or to one with pipe legs simply because the latter lends itself better to mass production methods and generally costs less to maintain.

Maintenance is important in determining the life of a table. The tables and benches should be constructed so planks can be removed every few years for refinishing. A smooth surface is more attractive, easier to wipe clean, and less likely to snag clothing. Also, a defaced or weathered surface may invite more carving or other abuse. Broken and unsafe parts, loose hardware, and unsightly surfaces should be promptly repaired. A current problem is scorching of table tops from portable charcoal grills. An asbestos pad secured at one end of the table top will prevent such scorching.

Lighter tables are convenient for park personnel, but also make it possible for visitors to move the tables. Generally the policy is to anchor tables in place to prevent theft and the tendency to ever-expanding site deterioration. In heavily used areas the table site should be hardened with a concrete pad, gravel, or wood chips (see Figs. 3-1 and 10-11).

Outdoor Stoves and Grills

The dream unit that could be used for an evening campfire, convert to a waist-level cooking stove, and yet be theft proof, indestructible, and easily fabricated in the park shop is not yet on the market. Some designers have come close, but, in the meantime, compromise is still necessary.

Probably no park facility has undergone a more complete transition than the park stove or fireplace. It has gone from a simple ring of rocks to an elaborate fireplace with firebox, grill, and chimney, to the all-metal, waist-level, pipe-supported grill that can be swiveled to face the wind. Several ground-level stoves have been built that permit easy cleaning, swivel to face the wind, have adequate flat surface to hold several pans and don't disintegrate when cold water is thrown on hot parts, but they are still backbreakers when used for cooking.

The waist-level charcoal grill is convenient for cooking but is not practical for the evening campfire. Perhaps it's asking too much of a facility to serve both purposes, cooking and campfire. Therefore, perhaps one should place the high grill in day-use areas, and the ground stove in overnight sites. The design is a matter of meeting local needs. The manager can expect complaints from both kinds of users.

Fireplaces or Stoves

These are found in the community kitchen or picnic shelter. The design includes a chimney for smoke draft, a metal or brick firebox, a steel grill, and brick or native stone masonry on the outside. Perhaps there will be a built-in fuel bin. Such a facility is expensive to build and subject to damage from freezing and thawing in cold climates. Once common outside, they are gradually being replaced with cheaper ground-level stoves. Their use in picnic shelters is probably not as great as it once was, since there are many convenient ways of cooking and transporting hot food rather than firing up the big stove and cooking on site.

Fire Ring

The fire ring is used largely at night for "recreational fires" for social gatherings, for wiener or marshmallow roasts, or for warming. It is constructed of plate or metal or corrugated culvert set in the ground. The ring size varies depending on use from 0.6 m (2 ft) for family groups to 2 m (6 ft) for small campfire programs or skating pond warming fires. The fire ring is usually circled with benches or logs.

Trail Bridges

Trail bridges must serve hikers, bicyclists, horseback riders, and maintenance vehicles. In some instances one bridge must do all of these, in other places it may be designed to support foot traffic only. Materials for trail bridges include concrete or wood supports, wood stringers, and wood decking. Laminated arch beams are also used. All wood must be seasoned and treated with preservatives. Most footbridges over shallow stream crossings need not have handrails; however, a footbridge over 1 m (3 ft) high should have at least one handrail. Rustic-style footbridges are suitable in a forest setting and are often photographed as background for family pictures.

Docks

These are needed to provide access to water for swimming, fishing, or boat mooring. One dock should not be expected to serve all three purposes because of the conflict between uses and the specific design needs. Use should be limited to that for which it was designed; for example, swimming should be prohibited from fishing and boat docks.

Bottom and water conditions vary greatly. Some bottoms are soft and will accept driven piles, others, because they are rocky, will not. The water surface may fluctuate greatly between summer and winter, daily in tidal areas. In some areas there will be thick ice that can rip a dock apart.

Some docks must be designed to float in order to fluctuate with the water level. Flotation is provided by large steel drums, styrofoam, or logs. Other docks, of a cantilever design, are built out over the water and can be raised above the ice level in winter. Some use permanent rock cribs as foundations; here the decking is removed before the lake freezes over. In others everything is portable and must be removed before the winter freeze. Where winters are mild and the lake level relatively constant, docks can be built on piling in a more permanent manner.

Boat Ramps

The ramp, usually constructed of reinforced concrete slabs, should be at least 3 to 4.5 m (10 to 15 ft) wide and be long enough to be usable at any water level. On some reservoirs, this can be a considerable distance during the drawdown. The preferred grade is between 8 and 15 percent. The water beyond the ramp should be free of hidden obstacles. A trailer parking area is necessary; boaters will appreciate one designed with drive-through stalls.

Separating the ramp from the swimming area will reduce conflicts and minimize swimmer contact with propellers and with pollution from oil spills.

Lifeguard Towers

These structures are used by lifeguards while on duty at swimming beaches. They should be high enough to provide an unobstructed view of the entire swimming area, since the lifeguard is in charge of all beach and water activities.

A sign should state that these towers are intended exclusively for the use of lifeguards, and no one else should be on them, whether or not the guard is on duty. A sign should also inform the public of the hours when lifeguard protection is available.

A roof or umbrella should be available to

shade the person on duty. Other equipment needed by the lifeguard includes a megaphone, a first-aid kit, blankets and stretcher, a surfboard or torpedo buoy with rope, and a lifeboat with oars. A two-way radio would be advantageous if the park uses such a system.

Bathhouse

The bathhouse is a change facility for swimmers and may include lockers, a hose or shower, toilets, and separate dressing rooms for men and women. When a food concession is part of the bathhouse operation, the concessioner usually is responsible for this facility. The one exception would be the first-aid room, which is usually the lifeguard's responsibility.

In parks where the visitor load is relatively small, a simple change shelter may be all that is necessary. The structure is often roofless so that it can be dried by sunlight. Care must be exercised that nearby trees or cliffs do not provide "viewpoints."

Bulletin Boards

These are located at roadside pulloffs, overlooks, trailheads, trailsides, near historical structures, or at other points of concentration in parks where essential information or interpretative messages are provided for visitors (Fig. 10-12).

A wide overhanging roof provides protection from rain and helps reduce glare. The plate glass covering, which protects the materials, should slope outward at the top to further reduce glare and annoying reflections. This sloping surface also reduces the amount of bird droppings that accumulate on the glass.

Materials used vary greatly. Some consist of outdoor plywood and metal posts, others use sturdy timbers and a roof of shakes or shingles. Massive structures of timbers and stone masonry are found in areas of heavy snowpack.

Useful bulletin board materials include maps, information on what to see and do, where camp

Fig. 10-12. A bulletin board containing a park map, park brochures, and specific park information. Post barriers and curbing form a protective island for this orientation facility. Discovery Park, Seattle. (Photo by Grant W. Sharpe.)

purchases may be made, park services, regulations, and messages for visitors (see Chapter 18, Care of Visitors). Interpretation, if offered, should be concerned with features in the immediate area.

Park Benches

Benches are used at skating rinks, overlooks, beaches, amphitheaters, and along walks and trails. The foundation is usually precast reinforced concrete; the legs are usually buried in the ground to prevent theft or damage. The wooden seats and back slats should be treated with non-irritating preservative or paint. Where vandalism is frequent, benches should be constructed entirely of concrete, even though these are less pleasant to sit on.

Plantings

These are facilities also, in the broad sense, since many shrubs and small trees are brought in and planted. Plantings beautify an area, break up monotonous developments, provide shade, and control traffic and erosion. Vegetation between campsites provides privacy and screening, and in other areas can hide landfills or maintenance buildings and equipment.

Plants are also a focus for problems. Theft and damage are ever-present possibilities. In parking lots trees shed their leaves, break up pavement with their roots, or drop their limbs. Trees will eventually fall and are thus a potential liability, as was discussed in Chapter 4, Recreation Legalities and Liabilities.

ENERGY AND FACILITIES

Certain park facilities require energy in the form of fuel or electricity for heat and light. The cost of energy will in all probability continue to increase, so energy-saving devices should be considered in the design of all new park buildings. This would include the use of insulation, weatherstripping, and building materials that resist heat transfer. Consider also solar panels in the roofs of park buildings, including the water supply for restrooms, shower facilities, and pools. Park managers along coastal areas, mountains, prairies, or other windy areas should consider the use of windmills to generate electricity. Park agencies should assume a leadership role in utilizing solar heating and wind systems.

How can the park manager contribute toward energy conservation? Stopping waste is one way. Other methods include having employees walking or riding bicycles when possible rather than driving, turning off lights when not needed, turning down building thermostats, checking insulation in all appropriate areas, reducing water consumption to save both water and electricity for pumping and heating, and promptly repairing dripping faucets. Recycling aluminum cans and other materials should be considered. Perhaps a volunteer group could undertake this task.

Energy conservation will require cooperation from both employees and park visitors. Imaginative interpretation could assist in making energy conservation goals important to both groups.

Managers must have a firm commitment and be willing to inconvenience themselves in order to set a good example.

CONCLUSION

Park facilities may be built to prevent visitor impact, to channel visitor use, as a convenience to visitors, to prevent theft or vandalism, to fulfill safety requirements, to enhance the quality of the park experience, to provide utilities, to assist in management operations, or to comply with the law. In both planning and replacement, informed choices are necessary in order to avoid basic problems.

Managers come and managers go but the facilities stay, aging and enduring, eventually wearing out or perhaps losing out in popularity. Other facilities, of one kind or another, will probably replace them. Maintaining these facilities and seeing that they are not misused is a very important part of the manager's job.

REFERENCES

General References

Adams, Robert L., Robert C. Lewis, and Bruce H. Drake. 1973. "Outdoor Recreation Facility Cost Estimates." From *Outdoor Recreation: A Legacy for America,* Appendix A, An Economic Analysis, Bureau of Outdoor Recreation, USDI. Washington, DC.

American Camping Association. 1980. *Camp Standards with Interpretations for the Accreditation of Organized Camps.* ACA. Martinsville, IN.

Fight, Roger D. 1980. *Planners Guide for Estimating Cost Per User-Day of Proposed Recreational Facilities.* USDA Pacific Northwest Forest and Range Exp. Stn. General Technical Report PNW-110. Portland, OR.

Goldthorpe, Arthur. 1980. "Access Requirements for Disabled in National Parks," *Parks Magazine.* 4(4):13–15.

Olson, Don. 1981. "Energy Saving in Ohio State Parks," *Trends*. Park Practice Program. NRPA. 18(2):12–17.

Orr, Howard R. 1971. "Design & Layout of Recreation Facilities," *Recreation Symposium Proceedings*. USDA N. E. Forest Exp. Stn., Upper Darby, PA.

The Park Practice Program. Includes four periodicals: *Trends, Design, Guideline,* and *Grist*. National Recreation and Park Association. Arlington, VA.

Sharpe, Grant W. (ed.). 1982. *Interpreting the Environment*. (2nd ed.). Wiley. New York.

"Trends in Energy Management". 1982. A complete issue of *Trends* consisting of 16 articles devoted to energy and park management. Park Practice Program. NRPA. 19(3): 1–48.

U.S. Department of Health, Education and Welfare. 1967. *Manual of Septic-Tank Practice*. Public Health Service Publication No. 526. Washington, DC.

U.S. Department of Health, Education and Welfare. (nd). *Environmental Health Practice in Recreational Areas*. Public Health Service Publication No. 1195. Washington, DC.

U.S. Department of Housing and Urban Development, and The American Society of Landscape Architects Foundation. 1976. *Barrier Free Site Design*. Washington, DC.

U.S. Department of the Interior, Bureau of Outdoor Recreation. 1967. *Outdoor Recreation Planning for the Handicapped*. Prepared in cooperation with the National Recreation and Park Association, Washington, DC.

U.S. Department of the Interior, Bureau of Outdoor Recreation. 1977. *Recreation for Special People*. Outdoor Recreation Action, Report No. 45, Washington, DC.

Wernex, Joseph J. 1979. "Successful Methods of Design and Construction for Managing Impact on Trailbike Trails," *Recreational Impact on Wildlands Conference Proceedings,* Ruth Ittner (ed.). Forest Service USDA; National Park Service, USDI. Seattle, WA.

References Cited

1. Allwood, John and Ray Taylor. 1980. "Signs of the Times," *Parks Magazine*. 5(1):20–21.

2. Austing, Ron. 1978. "Land Management in the Hamilton County Park District," *Park District News*. Cincinnati, OH.

3. Brockman, C. Frank and Lawrence C. Merriam, Jr. 1979. *Recreational Use of Wildlands* (3rd ed.). McGraw-Hill. New York.

4. Douglass, Robert W. 1982. *Forest Recreation* (3rd ed.). Pergamon Press, Inc. Elmsford, NY.

5. Hill, David E. 1966. *Percolation Testing for Septic Tank Drainage*. Bulletin No. 678. Connecticut Agricultural Exp. Stn. New Haven.

6. Jubenville, Alan. 1976. *Outdoor Recreation Planning*. W.B. Saunders Company. Philadelphia, PA.

7. Landsberg, H. H. 1964. *Natural Resources for U.S. Growth*. Johns-Hopkins. Baltimore, MD.

8. Leonard, R. E. and H. J. Plumley. 1979. "Human Waste Disposal in Eastern Backcountry," *J. For.*, 77(5):349–352.

9. Michigan Department of Natural Resources. (nd). *Field Manual*. Parks Division. Lansing, MI.

10. Patterson, James C. and Carole Sue Rodgers. 1979. "Static Pile Composting—A Waste Treatment Alternative," *Grist*. Park Practice Program. NRPA. 23(3):17, 23–24.

11. U.S. Department of the Interior. 1980. *A Guide to Designing Accessible Outdoor Recreation Facilities*. Heritage Conservation and Recreation Service. Ann Arbor, MI.

12. Wagar, J. Alan. 1963. *Campgrounds for Many Tastes*. USDA Intermt. Forest and Range Exp. Stn., Ogden, UT.

CHAPTER ELEVEN

MAINTENANCE AND SAFETY

MAINTENANCE MANAGEMENT

The objectives of a park maintenance program are to keep the park environment clean, healthy, and safe, and to conserve public monies by conscientious care of facilities and lands. Maintenance entails care of park buildings and other structures, including their indoor facilities such as heat, water, sanitation, and light systems; care of beaches and grounds, including soil, turf, shrubs, and trees; repair of roads and trails; and care of all park equipment. Proper stewardship of these will not only result in a smooth-running economical operation but will reflect favorably on the agency that administers the park.

Maintenance also includes:

1. Routine repairing, refurbishing, refinishing, replacing, and cleaning the present facilities and equipment or their components to counteract normal wear and tear and to repair overt damage.
2. Constructing new facilities or components of facilities as well as modifying, adding to, or altering existing facilities or their components.
3. Constructing products for recreational use, such as fireplaces, picnic tables, and similar items.[4]

As Rowe points out, maintenance is the antidote for depreciation, which may be defined as a decrease in value due to wear and tear. Though depreciation is inevitable, the life of a facility or piece of equipment may be extended significantly through proper maintenance. As costs rise (for both replacement and new construction) it becomes imperative for park managers to better maintain what they already have. Planned maintenance actually earns money through increased operating efficiency because power and fuel costs are reduced.[6] Money is saved also through the avoidance of lawsuits that arise from charges of negligence.

Maintenance is more than reacting to emergency situations. It means looking for trouble. Maintenance management therefore encompasses preventive (routine and planned) maintenance, which includes the periodic inspection of equipment. In this way replacements and minor repairs can be made, perhaps preventing a costly breakdown.

The following factors affect the maintenance operation: the type of visitor use a park receives, the seasons of use, the original design of the park, its latitude and altitude, its labor relations, and such environmental factors as weather, topography, soil types, and vegetative cover.

The title "maintenance manager" may refer to the park manager or his or her assistant, or, as in the instance of larger parks, it may be a person who deals specifically with the necessarily more complex maintenance tasks. The maintenance manager, especially in the latter instance, must be exceedingly versatile and knowledgeable. Experience in budgets, personnel management, equipment and facility use and repair, and public relations is necessary to meet the demands of the position of maintenance manager in a large park. In a small park the manager will have to meet many, perhaps all, of these challenges. All personnel should be involved in maintenance, no matter what the size of the park, in such matters as litter pickup or noting equipment in need of repair.

Maintenance Standards

Once park maintenance objectives, such as those cited in the beginning paragraph, are agreed on, standards are established to help achieve those objectives. As Sternoff and Warren point out, "Maintenance standards describe the conditions that will exist when maintenance tasks have been successfully completed."[7] Once standards are established, conditions must be monitored to see if they are being upheld. Because of local conditions each park will need its own standards and schedule of inspections. Various methods of planning these inspections will be discussed later in this chapter.

Time schedules and budgets may have to be adjusted as current conditions are measured against the standards. Are standards being met or slighted? Is time being wisely spent? Perhaps better scheduling and supervision are required. Perhaps the maintenance routine is taking too much time and energy because standards are unrealistically high. These possibilities must be kept in mind when monitoring conditions and allotting time.

Maintenance and the Public Image

Good maintenance procedures are often unappreciated, as they may never be noticed by most park visitors. In fact, visitors usually take for granted the fact that lawns are mowed, restrooms cleaned, garbage cans emptied, grounds free of litter, and that the drinking fountains are working properly. Seldom will they write letters when things are in "mint" condition. Let something

appear rundown or out of order, however, and complaints will be forthcoming.

Maintenance staff members usually come in contact with park visitors more frequently than any other park personnel. For this reason, an accurate general knowledge of park resources, a reasonable conversational ability, a pleasant demeanor and neat personal appearance are standards that managers might keep in mind when hiring and training employees (Fig. 11-1). A slovenly or rude employee or an employee who can't answer questions intelligently and cheerfully creates an unfavorable impression for the park agency.

Maintenance employees must be assisted in gaining understanding of the agency and its objectives and the importance of their role in achieving those objectives. Pride in work is necessary. One step in developing this pride would be representation in the decision-making process, as well as at normal staff meetings.

Since they perform services for the total park management operation, the maintenance staff should not look on their work as merely custodial or menial, but should be encouraged to view it as

Fig. 11-1. Maintenance personnel do more than maintenance work. Members of the maintenance staff are often the only employees park visitors see. Here a park gardener assists visitors with a travel problem. Lake Sammamish State Park, Washington. (Photo by Grant W. Sharpe.)

an integral park of park management. It must be pointed out to them that it is their work that keeps all other programs running.

Maintenance and Park Design

All too frequently, maintenance problems are, at least in part, the result of poor planning and design. Present recreation pursuits are not always the ones for which the park was originally designed, and this creates unavoidable difficulties. However, even in new parks planners have sometimes been too removed from the day-to-day problems of the maintenance staff, and consequently have designed areas and facilities which produce unnecessary problems for the maintenance division. Then, too, in today's cost-conscious world, architects and contractors occasionally slight the requirements of good maintenance practices in order to keep the construction costs within available funds.

One way to avoid, or at least alleviate, such irritating and costly planning mistakes, as discussed in Chapter 9 (Planning, Land Acquisition, and Development) is through a checkoff system during the design phase. Selected members of the maintenance staff should be allowed to study the design to determine if the plans will result in extra maintenance effort and costs. Examples of things to look for would be the location and number of electrical outlets, ease of access to plumbing facilities, the use of inappropriate building materials (requiring early replacement), inadequate surface finishes (making cleaning difficult), or wood in contact with the ground, which may cause deterioration of the wood at an unacceptable rate.

Maintenance Personnel Management

Park managers not directly involved in maintenance should not isolate themselves from the maintenance staff, but be available in order to encourage good communications. When possible the park manager should involve the maintenance staff in the budget and planning processes as well as other park functions.

The staff must be kept on the alert and positively motivated. This can be accomplished in part by the supervisor being aware of both successes and deficiencies in employees' performances, by helping to correct any shortcomings, and by being ready to reward employees for improvement. Outstanding performance should be recognized by merit increases or job advancement. Certain staff members should be given an opportunity to expand their horizons through the additional training cited below.

Many maintenance positions are entry-level positions, paying the minimum wage. The total work force, however, ranges from laborers to highly skilled mechanics and tradespeople, with the salaries improving greatly at the upper levels. Opportunities should be provided for motivated employees to advance.

In some instances park personnel may not have the expertise or equipment to accomplish certain projects and the work may need to be contracted out. Repairs on sophisticated sanitation systems, motors, and electronic apparatus are examples. Frequently the smaller or less complicated construction jobs could be done by park staff (day labor) just as effectively. In most instances the park staff can do a given job for less than a contractor, because no profit is required. Another reason for in-house work is that park maintenance crews usually have greater sensitivity and dedication to the work, resulting in less damage to the area than might be incurred by a contractor crew.

Since the maintenance staff must be able to repair almost anything found in the park, a wide variety of skills is required. Larger parks usually have a separate maintenance division employing mechanics, plumbers, electricians, carpenters, and painters. In some smaller parks one or two persons do all these tasks. In even smaller parks, the park manager or assistant manager will have to do most maintenance jobs, since there is no one else around. This requires park managers to have or acquire considerable practical skills and abilities, including knowledge of plumbing, wiring, and repair of small engines. It must be stressed that this test of self-reliance comes to most park management graduates at some point in their careers.

The Maintenance Supervisor.

A maintenance supervisor may be necessary in a larger park with considerable maintenance. Maintenance supervision requires a wealth of talents. Such persons must have technical knowledge of equipment, and an ability to plan and implement a functioning maintenance program. Supervisors must prepare budgets for future programs, supervise human resources, be responsible for safety, assist in the actual work, act effectively in emergencies, supervise construction projects, and even advise the park manager on matters related to chemical control of vegetation, safety problems, pollution abatement, energy conservation, and other environmental issues.[6]

Today maintenance is in a dynamic state, ripe for the world of computers—computers to receive, analyze, and disseminate large amounts of maintenance information with great speed and accuracy. Mathematical models already determine the staff, equipment, materials, and time needed for certain jobs. New sanitation and water systems, as well as solar heating devices need elaborate monitoring systems requiring new skills of maintenance supervisors.[2] Today, some sanitation plants are so complicated that codes require an engineer or certification of an employee to operate the system. Maintenance supervisors must be either widely knowledgeable persons or surround themselves with talented individuals to supply the broad range of experiences and skills now needed.

Maintenance Employee Training

Maintenance personnel must have training consistent with the level of work they are expected to perform. Certain permanent maintenance staff will need additional training in order to keep pace with technological advancement. This can come through on-the-job training, attending workshops, taking correspondence courses, or though training opportunities made available by equipment manufacturers. Many agencies have provisions for tuition reimbursement for vocational night courses at community colleges. Also, with so many seasonal people entering and leaving the maintenance work force each year, there is a need for seasonal on-the-job training for new employees.

As park ambassadors, the maintenance staff must be trained in public relations, park cultural and natural history, park policy, rules and regulations, and personal appearance standards, as well as the technical and safety skills required for the job. It is the park manager's duty to assure that subordinates receive suitable training. In some instances the training may be left to other experienced employees; however, the manager must monitor the apprenticeship to ensure that the training proceeds in a satisfactory manner.

Maintenance personnel are involved in most aspects of park management. Therefore, when practical, the employee's training should be as broad as possible, scheduled on a task-training timetable (Fig. 11-2). In this example, the names of the employees are placed at the left, and different tasks are placed along the top. As the employee becomes trained in the various tasks, a mark or the date is placed opposite the name. Such a timetable informs the supervisor of an employee's progress, and facilitates work scheduling to expose each staff member to the learning situations indicated by the chart. A similar chart could be devised for attendance at lectures, such as those covering park orientation, agency history, public relations, safety and first aid, and emergency medical training.

The better informed the employee, the better the total park operation. Also, the promise of continuous on-the-job training may attract and help retain good personnel. As Espeseth stated, personnel need to know what is expected of them, how to do the job properly, what is available to help them do their job better, how they fit into the organization, and how they can advance themselves.[1]

	Task						
Employee	Mowing	Sharpening Tools	Power Saw	Post Hole Digger	Shop Tools	Dump Truck	Dumpster
Jones	X		X			X	
Smith	X	X		X	X		X
Hanson					X	X	
DeKalb	X		X			X	
Kline		X	X		X	X	

Fig. 11-2. Employees' task-training timetables are used for record keeping. The X indicates a date that would be entered when the task has been mastered.

Planning and Scheduling Maintenance Work

The objectives of programming maintenance work into a schedule are (1) to increase to the highest degree possible the *productive utilization* of the maintenance staff, (2) to coordinate the work to minimize interference between other maintenance groups or individuals, (3) to coordinate with other park activities to minimize interference with, and from, these other programs, and (4) to provide the best possible services with the available resources of personnel, equipment, and materials.[4]

Job Scheduling and Labor Efficiency. Scheduled (routine) maintenance work is done periodically according to a predetermined time schedule. Such schedules should yield the following information.

1. *What* needs to be done.
2. *Where* it needs to be done.
3. *How* it should be done.
4. *When* it should be done.

Types of scheduled maintenance include the following.

1. Facilities examination and repair (buildings, signs, trails, bridges, roadways).
2. Grounds keeping (mowing grass, weeding).
3. Landscaping (vista clearing, trimming shrubbery, planting ornamentals and barrier species).
4. Cleaning (garbage hauling, policing grounds, janitorial services).
5. Preventative maintenance routines (vehicle lubrication and service, equipment lubrication, heating and ventilating service).
6. Operating routines (pumping plants, swimming pools, sump pumps).[4]

There are three types of maintenance services: emergency, routine, and planned. *Emergency service* is required when a facility demands attention (e.g., a broken water pipe or a plugged toilet). *Routine service* is given on a regular basis to keep equipment and facilities running efficiently (e.g., lubricating equipment and cleaning restrooms). Routine service also includes maintaining grounds, such as mowing and filling in holes. *Planned service* means specific maintenance scheduled on a time basis without waiting for an emergency, yet not on a routine basis. Examples would be roofing a comfort station every 10 years, or replacing truck brake linings every

50,000 miles. The head of maintenance determines which category has priority. Labor, equipment, and supplies must be coordinated for maximum efficiency. A lot of time and effort can be wasted in maintenance work. Haskell lists the following reasons.[3]

1. Waiting for orders in the morning and at noon.
2. Looking for the foreman to find out what the next job is.
3. Visiting the site to find out what must be done.
4. Unnecessary trips to stores.
5. Return trips for tools.
6. Searching for the foreman in order to get a supply-withdrawal authorization.
7. Unnecessary trips back to the shop when another job is in the vicinity of one just completed.
8. Dispatching three people to a job that two could very easily do.
9. Waiting for workers from other crafts to start or finish.
10. Looking for the job site.
11. Confusion and backtracking because of countermanded orders.
12. Waiting for other employees to vacate a site.
13. Trying to make up for insufficient information on blueprints.
14. Searching for materials that are on order but have not yet arrived.

The solution to most of these delays is effective scheduling of work crews, equipment, and materials. Scheduling should occur at least one day in advance, although some projects may need a week or more of lead time. Work schedules should be set up within normal work time, allowing overtime only in emergencies, and then holding it to a minimum. A detailed map of the park in the maintenance office as well as a checkout board listing job site and estimated time of return for each crew or employee might be helpful. New equipment, new techniques, revised procedures, policy changes, and similar matters should be noted on a central bulletin board or through an efficient memorandum system.

Record Keeping. The work accomplished, materials used, staff required, and time required should be recorded. This provides information for weekly, monthly, and annual reports. Interested parties know what has been done and when, and these data provide them information for planning future projects as well as cost figures for budget preparation.

Seasonal Workloads. Because park visitation is seasonal, resulting in heavy workloads for a short period, the staff is also expanded seasonally to accommodate these increased maintenance needs. Some parks defer certain types of maintenance work, such as new construction, tree trimming and removal, equipment and building repair and painting, until after the busy visitor season has ended. Such a plan keeps experienced personnel on the job throughout the year and provides a base on which to build the temporary maintenance staff the following season. These employees will be needed to train seasonals the following years, as well as to contribute their expertise to the job itself. Managers cannot release skilled employees such as these each season's end, and then expect to rehire them the next year. Their abilities will command steady employment elsewhere if the manager cannot arrange the work schedule to keep them on the payroll year round. Unfortunately many park agencies cannot afford to keep skilled construction labor on the payroll all year, thus major developments and skilled services may have to be contracted out. Also, there are many highly qualified maintenance "retirees" who only want seasonal employment.

As mentioned above, the key to successful operation and maintenance is a carefully planned and faithfully followed work schedule and the following factors should be considered:

1. Season of year.
2. Priority of work items.
3. Expected public use.

4. Capabilities of the park staff.
5. Limitation of work hours, time off, annual leave, and restrictions governing overtime.
6. Varying weather conditions.

The answer to *when* it should be done is considered in the following example of a work schedule, contributed by Michigan State Parks, based on the four seasons of the year.[5]

1. *Summer work schedule* (June 1 to September 1). Priority is given to routine maintenance and cleaning of public use areas and buildings. At this time major maintenance and new construction is of secondary priority and will not be scheduled.
2. *Fall work schedule* (September 1 to December 1). As there will be some public use of parks at this time of year, the fall work schedule will be a combination of routine maintenance and operational activities with major maintenance and construction projects.

Emphasis should be given to those outdoor jobs that must be completed before winter sets in. It is a good time for painting building exteriors, landscaping, seeding, and making repairs to structures and utility systems.

This schedule should also include the many jobs necessary to close the park for the winter, such as equipment lay-up, draining water and sanitation systems, and winterizing buildings.

3. *Winter work schedule* (December 1 to April 1). Weather conditions are such that only certain kinds of work can be accomplished during this period. Much of the work can be done inside, such as equipment repair on stoves, tables, benches, as well as tuneup and repair of trucks, tractors, and mowers (Fig. 11-3). Interior building repairs could also be taken care of at this season. Weather permitting, some outside work such as tree trimming, tree moving and thinning, regraveling, hauling fill, and reroofing buildings could be

Fig. 11-3. An example of a winter work project. Every five years the tops and seats of these picnic tables are removed for refinishing. Most of the damage is from vandalism. Miracle Beach Provincial Park, British Columbia. (Photo by Grant W. Sharpe.)

scheduled, as well as work that can be done outside regardless of temperatures.

4. *Spring work schedule* (April 1 to June 1). This is the time to complete those projects that could not be accomplished during the fall and winter, and that must be completed in order to ready the park for the summer heavy-use season. During this period inspection is called for to make sure everything is in good condition and ready for the public.[5]

Michigan's severe winters make its work schedule more rigid than might be the case for a more southern state, such as Florida. However, Florida has its own set of seasonal changes, advantages, and disadvantages. The maintenance manager must know the visitor use pattern and the weather and proceed accordingly.

Equipment

Most workers want to do the job as quickly as possible while expending the least physical effort. This means using labor-saving machines, rather than hand tools. The equipment needed varies with the job to be done. However, the equipment available will vary with the size of the park and its financial resources. All parks need standard cleaning equipment for the daily care of restrooms, but not all parks can afford elaborate aerial tower trucks used for tree trimming and removal. Some equipment may be shared between parks on a scheduled basis, or rented if it is to be used only a few times a year. Shared mobile equipment allows fewer pieces of costly equipment to be used in more areas.

Equipment selection is important. High-quality, rugged, industrial-grade equipment with a

Fig. 11-4. Good equipment saves time and money, and so equipment must be selected carefully. Consultation with the people who must operate such equipment may prevent problems. This garbage truck was designed for efficiency of loading and unloading. Pacific Rim National Park, British Columbia. (Photo by Grant W. Sharpe.)

long life span is usually the most economical. Machines requiring continuous repair are seldom available when needed, and this is annoying, disruptive, and costly. When purchasing, seek the advice of the mechanics who must maintain a machine, and of the person who has to operate it. Their experienced counsel will probably save future headaches, and pay off financially in the long run (Fig. 11-4).

When selecting equipment there are other questions one should ask. Will this machine do the necessary job? Can parts be easily obtained? Is it easily serviced? Is it dangerous to operate? Can inexperienced help operate it? Will it be a safety hazard to park visitors?

Specialized equipment such as stump removers, crawler tractors, concrete mixers, power saws, and front-end loaders should be used only by trained personnel. No employee should be allowed to operate any equipment unless he or she understands its purpose, its operating technique, and its basic care and maintenance (Fig. 11-5). A signout system for equipment gives the maintenance supervisor better control.

The manufacturer's manuals that accompany new equipment should be kept on file in the maintenance office. Where practical, a copy should also be available with the equipment. These should be read and understood by the operator before using the equipment. The servicing and storage instructions should be read carefully, and observed.

The Inventory. An inventory record should be kept for all tools and equipment owned by the park. The list should include name, cost, date of purchase, serial and model numbers, specifications, warranty data, and storage location. The data from hour meters should also be recorded. Equipment should also have records kept on dates of routine maintenance, as well as repair costs of parts and labor. Such records are invaluable for purposes of budgeting, determining costs of specific tasks, planning for scheduled maintenance, and reporting thefts.[7] In some instances the recording of hours of use or miles of service on equipment is utilized for scheduling routine maintenance as well as servicing and repair.

Servicing and Repair. All equipment is covered by warranty for a certain length of time, *assuming normal servicing*. After the warranty has expired, of course, it is still necessary to carry on routine servicing such as lubrication, oil changes, filters, battery testing, installing antifreeze, spot painting, and performing minor repairs and adjustments.[5] Some work will have to be done in commercial repair shops by skilled workmen if the park staff is not equipped for such work.

The Maintenance Manual

Each park manager should see that a maintenance manual is prepared as a guide to the step-by-step procedure of working with all equipment and facilities. It should include the manufacturer's service and repair suggestions. This manual serves as a ready reference for new employees as well as those not able to remember the minor details of a particular maintenance activity.

Fig. 11-5. Seasonal park employees are being checked out on the proper operation of a mower by the maintenance supervisor. Lake Sammamish State Park, Washington. (Photo by Grant W. Sharpe.)

SAFETY

The Park Safety Program

This program aspires to prevent injuries, occupational diseases, deaths, building fires and wildfires, motor vehicle collisions and property damages, and law suits against the agency and its employees.[8]

The basic objectives of the park safety program are the reduction of accidents involving agency staff, park visitors, and concession and contractor personnel. Each employee must accept responsibility and maintain constant alertness to prevent accidents both on and off the job. Each person should report hazardous conditions or unsafe practices and take steps to eliminate them where indicated. Accident prevention thus becomes a part of that person's job description. The employee must believe in safety, practice safety, and insist on safe working conditions if accidents are to be avoided. According to the Michigan Department of Natural Resources, most accidents do not "happen"—they are caused—by carelessness, negligence, thoughtlessness, or failure to observe simple rules of safety. Proper supervision can eliminate these causes.[5]

Maintenance and Park Safety

A safety study revealed that of all the park-related occupational injuries, 66 percent involved maintenance personnel (National Safety Council). Yet it is the maintenance division that usually has the responsibility of taking corrective action against unsafe conditions in the park. There are several reasons for this apparent contradiction. The maintenance staff works more with tools and other high-risk equipment than do other park employees. Many maintenance employees are young seasonals, often with no previous work experience and limited safety knowledge. Their work takes them to isolated areas where supervision is often limited. Also, maintenance workers frequently work along roads and are thus exposed to moving vehicles.

The reason for a park having a safety program for its employees is the same as it is for industry: to reduce losses, both human and monetary. Measuring human loss is difficult. How does a manager measure personal pain or family grief? Monetary losses are more easily measured. These include the costs of medical bills, the worker's wages while recovering, the time spent in investigating accidents, and the loss of the services of an injured park employee.

Most agencies are covered by some type of industrial insurance. The rates charged to the agency are reflective of the payments made for injury to employees. Therefore a safe program also saves money.

All levels of government require their park systems to have a work safety program. If there is no state operated safety program, employees may be covered by OSHA (Occupational Safety and Health Act of 1970) in the United States. In Canada each province has its own work safety program, usually under a workman's compensation board. Such work safety programs set the standards for the member agencies.

Park Safety Officer. All parks should have a safety officer, appointed by the park manager, to chair the park safety committee. In smaller parks the manager might be the safety officer. Each division should delegate a member to attend the park safety committee, which should meet regularly with the park safety officer. The park safety effort will not succeed without the *continuous active support of the park manager.*

The following are the duties of the park safety officer, or that officer's equivalent.

1. Initiate the park safety program.
2. Chair the park safety committee.
3. Work closely with all division heads, stressing the importance of "setting the example" of safety.
4. Make safety publications available to all supervisors and employees.
5. Prepare and give safety talks to all park personnel.

6. Work closely with concession and contractor personnel to achieve cooperation and compliance with safety rules, requesting them to designate safety officers. These officers should become members of the park safety committee.
7. Periodically inspect all park areas for unsafe practices and conditions. This includes concession operations and privately contracted construction sites that might constitute a hazard for employees and park visitors.
8. Initiate corrective action on hazardous situations.
9. Keep records of all accidents, their causes, location, and related details.

In addition to a park safety officer, there should be an agency safety committee that should have representation from each division. The agency safety officer should also serve as a resource for the park safety officer.

The Safety Committee. The safety committee can help reduce losses in parks of all sizes and is organized as follows.

1. Each department or division should have at least one person on the committee. Bigger departments or divisions should have two or more representatives.
2. The committee should be made up of both line personnel and management.
3. The committee should make inspections and give recommendations to the park manager. It must help spread awareness of safety among all park personnel.
4. For those agencies of sufficient size to afford an internal auditor, that person should be on the park safety committee. When the auditor inspects the park for fiscal concerns he or she should also check for safety features.

Inspections—Maintenance and Safety

It is difficult, in most instances, to separate safety inspections from maintenance checks. Since the task of checking is a long and detailed

one, they could probably be combined. One purpose of inspections is to see if the park is operating properly. For example, a spring inspection would be for the purpose of seeing if the park is ready for the summer season. A summer inspection tour would be a check on maintenance standards and the proper handling of park visitors. This sort of inspection is frequently made by a higher authority than the park manager and might not be announced. Such inspections include grounds, buildings, facilities, and equipment safety monitoring, as well as pointing out any weakness in maintenance performance levels.

If only to avoid poor ratings the park manager should make his or her own routine inspections. However, concern for the park and visitors should be the main reason for inhouse inspections. Reports of inspections and repairs must be kept in the park files. These actions and dates are evidence of sincere and positive accident prevention efforts, and serve as a means of protection against tort claims. Visitors have a right to assume all park facilities are routinely checked for safety, and that repairs are made when indicated (see Fig. 4-1). The responsibility and importance of making prompt and adequate repairs must be impressed on employees. Accidents may not be completely preventable, but there is no excuse for cursory inspections or slipshod repairs. Should the park manager have no financial resources to implement such repairs, the area should be closed, or the particular piece of equipment should be withdrawn from public use.

Safety Detection Guide

To make sure facilities are inspected on a regular basis, each park should have safety inspection schedules for all facilities, including playground equipment, docks, buildings, grounds, parking areas, roads, and trails (Fig. 11-6). All items should be listed with a space for checkoff and comments. The inspection sheet should include (1) the name of park, (2) the facility, (3) the date, (4) the name of inspector, (5) the condition of facility or area, and (6) suggested corrective action as required.

Fig. 11-6. Park employees on a safety inspection of picnic area facilities prior to the busy summer season. Such inspections are a part of preventive maintenance. (Photo by Grant W. Sharpe.)

In order to assist the park manager or safety inspector to make the most complete inspection possible, a checklist, adopted from the National Park Service, will be found in Appendix A at the end of this chapter. It offers a reasonably comprehensive hazard review of conditions and facilities. Purely maintenance concerns, such as painting and roof conditions, could also be checked at this time. Individual parks are advised to make deletions or additions as needed. Note any unsafe acts of workers or visitors seen during the inspection tour, and suggest corrective action.

Employee Safety Training

The park manager must see to it that all employees are properly trained for the jobs they are expected to do. This includes pertinent safety information. Necessary first aid and rescue equipment must also be on hand and periodically inspected.

Training should include how to recognize potential hazards, the proper safety clothing and equipment to wear (shoes, goggles, gloves, and hard hats), the proper approach to lifting bulky

objects, the method of handling volatile fuels, and the care and handling of hand and power tools (Fig. 11-7). There are numerous other aspects, depending on the operation involved. Training methods include preemployment safety training packets, demonstrations, showing film and slide programs, bulletin boards, and home study courses. It is extremely important that skillful, dynamic instructors be given this task. Otherwise the employees may tune out the information, yet appear to have had adequate instruction, since they attended the program.

Safety should be a part of every orientation and training program for new employees. Safety meetings should be held weekly, perhaps at the start of the day, keeping them limited to 5 or 10

Fig. 11-7. Employees should be trained in recognizing potential hazards, and be required to wear protective clothing and equipment. Note the hard hat and goggles being work by this employee. Maintenance shop, Chaco Canyon National Monument, New Mexico. (National park Service photo by Fred E. Mang, Jr.)

minutes. Review any accidents that may have occurred since the last meeting. Also, suggest hypothetical situations and ask for responses on safety procedures. Demonstrate a different safety technique at each session. Short written quizzes could be handed out and answers discussed at the same meeting. Short safety sessions should also be on the agenda of every staff meeting. This way all employees will be kept apprised of the safety program and its effectiveness. Periodic half-day or all-day safety training sessions should be considered.

Fire presuppression is an important part of park safety, also. Since the maintenance staff will probably form the backbone of the fire fighting crew the relationship is a close one—a subject dealt with extensively in Chapter 16.

Employment consideration could be given to seasonals who have completed standard first aid training courses. Also, offer short courses for park personnel in first aid, emergency medical training, vehicle traffic control, water safety, skiing safety, mountain climbing and rescue work, and other special park needs. The instructor should spend time and thought preparing these sessions. Get help outside your agency when possible. Safety posters should be displayed and changed periodically. Safety is everyone's business.[8]

CONCLUSION

Maintenance, more than any other park function, is needed year round and is needed regardless of park visitation. Even if the park is "mothballed," maintenance is needed. Maintenance—its personnel, equipment, and supplies—consumes a major portion of the park budget and deserves the attention of top management.

A park's safety record carries a message about management's ability to foresee problems and prevent them, as well as its ability to keep employees at all levels "up to speed" on safety. Maintaining a good record requires a deep conviction of the importance of this subject along with creative energy intelligently directed.

REFERENCES

General References

Espeseth, Robert D. 1982. "Risk Management," *Trends*. Park Practice Program. NRPA 19(2): 25–30.

Lawson, Quinton Y. 1982. "Conflict—Security vs. Life Safety," *Trends*. Park Practice Program. NRPA 19(2): 13–17.

U.S. Department of Agriculture, Forest Service. 1976. *Health and Safety Code. Your Guide to Safe Practices.* Superintendent of Documents, U.S. Government Printing Office, Washington, DC.

U.S. Department of the Interior, Heritage Conservation and Recreation Service. 1980. *Maintenance Impact Statement Handbook.* Washington, DC.

Utah State Department of Highways/Roy Jorgensen and Associates. Jan. 1976. "Performance Standards for Maintenance," *Trends*. Park Practice Program. NRPA.

Wilcox, Arthur T. 1982. "Maintenance Standards," *Trends*. Park Practice Program. NRPA 19(2): 10–12.

References Cited

1. Espeseth, Robert D. Jan. 1976. "Planning for Maintenance Management," *Trends*. Park Practice Program. NRPA.

2. Everhardt, Gary. Jan. 1976. "Maintenance as a Career," *Trends*. Park Practice Program. NRPA.

3. Haskell, Theodore J. 1970. "Scheduling Maintenance Functions: Getting the Right Things Done." From *Park Maintenance for the Administrator* Proceedings 1970. Park and Recreation Administrators Institute, University Extension. University of California, Davis.

4. Judd, Joe. 1970. "Management Control of Maintenance." From *Park Maintenance for the Administrator* Proceedings 1970. Park and Recreation Administrators Institute,

University Extension. University of California, Davis.

5. Michigan Department of Natural Resources. (nd). *Field Manual*. Lansing, MI.

6. Rowe, Gerald A. Jan. 1976. "Introduction," *Trends*. Park Practice Program. NRPA.

7. Sternloff, Robert E. and Roger Warren. 1977. *Park and Recreation Maintenance Management*. Holbrook Press, Inc. Boston, MA.

8. U.S. Department of the Interior, National Park Service. 1969. *Safety Handbook*. Washington, DC.

APPENDIX A   SAFETY INSPECTION CHECKLIST

DATE: INSPECTOR: PARK UNIT:	SATIS-FACTORY	INADE-QUATE	COMMENTS
Park Entrance:			
Condition of paving			
Deceleration turnouts			
Approach markers			
Entrance sign			
Checking station maintenance			
Traffic stripes			
Lighting			
Traffic controls			
Seasonal hazards			
Rock or tree hazards			
Reflectorized markers			
Parking Areas and Roads:			
Condition of paving			
Intersections			
Signs			
Guardrails			
Parking turnouts			
Danger trees			
Tree or rock falls			
Emergency phones			

DATE: INSPECTOR: PARK UNIT:	SATIS- FACTORY	INADE- QUATE	COMMENTS
Seasonal hazards (ice, slides, washouts)			
Reflectorized markers			
Traffic stripes			
Lighting			
Garbage cans			
Trails: Drainage			
Condition of surface			
Footbridges			
Guardrails			
Signs			
Garbage cans			
Piers and Docks: Signs			
Railings			
Pilings			
Lifesaving equipment			
Ladders, ramps, steps			
Decking surface			
Garbage cans			
Cleats secure			
Beaches: Broken glass			
Debris			
Marker buoys			
Lifeguard stand			
Navigation aids			
Garbage cans			

DATE: INSPECTOR: PARK UNIT:	SATIS- FACTORY	INADE- QUATE	COMMENTS
Utility Centers:			
Entrance signs			
Electric services			
Water systems			
Fencing, gates			
Wood and metal shops			
Storage areas			
Machinery shielding			
Flammable rags			
Safety maintenance			
First aid supplies/services			
Power and hand tools			
Power mowers			
Fire suppression equipment			
Fire hydrants			
Fuel storage			
Paint storage			
Furnace room			
Roof drainage			
(Maintenance concerns)			
Residence Areas:			
Signs			
Roads			
Walks			
Lighting			
Flammables			
Fire hydrants			
Electric services			
Fire escapes			

DATE: INSPECTOR: PARK UNIT:	SATIS- FACTORY	INADE- QUATE	COMMENTS
Fire suppression equipment			
Garbage cans			
(Maintenance concerns)			
Administrative Building, Visitor Center: Entrance signs			
Interior signs			
Electric services			
Water systems			
Sanitation			
Emergency shelters			
First aid supplies/services			
Slippery floors			
Steps and ramps			
Guardrails			
Drinking fountains			
Automatic sprinklers			
Fire hydrants			
Fire suppression equipment			
Fuel storage			
Safety posters			
Furnace room			
Storage rooms			
Emergency exits			
(Maintenance concerns)			
Concessionaire Units: Entrance signs			
Electric services			
Water systems			
Sanitation			

DATE: INSPECTOR: PARK UNIT:	SATIS- FACTORY	INADE- QUATE	COMMENTS
Service area			
Warehouse			
Fencing			
Mobile equipment			
Ropes and guy wires			
First aid supplies/services			
Food handling			
Flammables			
Ladders, steps			
Boat-handling area			
Fire suppression equipment			
Contractor Units: Signing of detours			
Maintenance of detours			
Materials hauling and storing			
Fencing and barricades			
Shoring trenches and cuts			
Water			
Sanitation			
Lighting			
Scaffolding			
Mobile equipment			
Ropes and guy wires			
Night lighting of hazards			
First aid equipment			
Hard hats			
Fuel storage			
Flammables			

DATE: INSPECTOR: PARK UNIT:	SATIS-FACTORY	INADE-QUATE	COMMENTS
Explosives			
Firearms			
Ladders			
Rigging			
Welding			
Power tools			
Hand tools			
Fire suppression equipment			
Grounds (picnic, camping):			
Signs			
Condition of surfacing			
Restrooms			
Water systems			
Electric services			
Visibility on curves			
Fences			
Barricades			
Stoves and grills			
Picnic tables			
Garbage cans			
Danger trees			
Interpretive devices			
Holes, ditches			
Playground equipment			

CHAPTER TWELVE

ENVIRONMENTAL IMPACT

The previous chapter dealt with the care of facilities, which are certainly part of the park environment. In this chapter the park environment is considered from a different aspect, that of its natural resources: soil, water, vegetation, and wildlife. These four resources are closely attuned. An impact on one will often result in an impact on at least one of the others.

As attendance in park areas increases, greater presssure is put on these fragile park resources. What limitations should the manager impose on the number of visitors in order to reduce this pressure? What level of damage is tolerable? How does the manager judge the point at which crowding or trampling is destroying the very park resources the visitors came to enjoy? Is this concern with limiting use the province of the park manager?

There are no clearcut answers to these questions. Agencies vary in their ability to react to problems of this kind. However, park managers must train themselves to be aware of environmental impacts and try to pass any concerns they have along the chain of command.

All natural resources are subject to human manipulation. Unfortunately, past environmental alterations have sometimes been characterized by opportunism and inadequate planning. The consequences of this in regard to soil, water, vegetation, and wildlife have frequently been disruptive of natural processes. Dumping of raw industrial and municipal waste into streams and lakes, de-struction of soil through poor agricultural practices, and eradication of cover and intensive unregulated hunting are examples of negative manipulation.

SOIL

All terrestrial life depends directly or indirectly on soil, yet today most people have little or no understanding of it. Except as used for potted house plants, flower gardens, or lawns, soils are seldom considered by urban dwellers. Farmers, on the other hand, look on soils as the source of their livelihood. They understand soils' fertility, productivity, perhaps even their origin. Terms like mineral content, coarseness, acid or alkaline soils, heavy soils, and soil porosity are part of the farmer's vocabulary. One can understand the farmer's interest, but why should soils be a concern of the park manager?

Parklands are not commonly managed for agricultural crops, forest products, meat, or other consumptive purposes. Therefore, managers might not expect parklands to deteriorate in any way while under their care. Unfortunately, parklands also suffer from overuse. The park manager must be able to recognize, and should try to control overuse, since management implies stewardship of all resources.

Often lands not valuable for anything else are made available for outdoor recreation. Millions of acres of forest-and grass-covered lands in

North America have been found to be substandard for agricultural purposes; these are lands that never should have been plowed. Most have reverted to grasslands for grazing, to timber-producing lands, and to a lesser extent, to parklands, with some being used for intensive outdoor recreation. Failure as croplands or timberlands probably means the fertility was low, or the growing season too short. The suitability of such lands for recreation may be questionable but often they are only lands available for that purpose. This is one reason managers have difficulty retaining covering vegetation.

Most park managers take charge of areas that have been long established, so these managers were not there when campgrounds, picnic sites, park trails, waste disposal systems, or other facilities were located. Possibly topography, slope, drainage, and other factors were considered at that time, but mistakes may have been made. Unforeseen circumstances may now frustrate the original plans. This is particularly true of those circumstances related to visitor impact, such as soil compaction and erosion. Managers, then, often inherit some tenacious problems.

Soils are a basic resource of natural systems, and variations in soil conditions usually are evidenced in related parts of the system. A change in *soil type*, for example, may be associated with changes in vegetation or water quality, or erosion potential.

For these reasons soils play an important role in recreation planning. Some knowledge of their properties is useful to the manager. *Soil texture* or particle size distribution is an important property that affects soil management. The following categorizes the various soil particle sizes and their engineering capabilities.

1. *Gravel* is coarse, with particles over 2 mm in diameter. It is well-drained, stable material that will support heavy loads.
2. *Sand* is 0.05 to 2 mm in diameter and is gritty to the touch. It also drains well and holds up under heavy loads. When dry, sand lacks cohesion and must be confined. Fine sand is less stable when saturated and tends to flow if not confined.
3. *Silt* is 0.002 to 0.05 mm in diameter, is barely visible, and feels smooth to the touch. When dry it lacks cohesion, remains stable but compresses under loads. When wet it becomes very unstable, and it heaves when frozen. In a disturbed state it is subject to wind erosion.
4. *Clay* is under 0.002 mm in diameter, and individual grains are invisible to the naked eye. When dry, it is cohesive and supports heavy loads. When wet, clay becomes plastic, slippery, and impervious. Porous soils lying over clay are subject to slippage on slopes greater than 10 percent. Clay is also subject to wind erosion if powdered, such as on trails or roads.
5. *Peat* soils are of organic origin, fibrous to the touch, dark in color, and lack cohesion. They are unstable and will not normally support development. They are usually associated with high water tables, either at present, or at sometime in the past.

There is a direct correlation between the type of soil and the feasibility of recreation development, such as roads, trails, building foundations, or sewage drainfields. Yet we must look beyond particle size and engineering properties and consider other aspects of soils as they affect management practices.

Soil Profile

When we cut downward into the undisturbed soil, we find individual horizontal layers called *horizons*. These horizons make up the *soil profile*. Every undisturbed soil has its own characteristic properties and peculiar arrangement of horizons. In fact, in North America there are over 75,000 individual kinds of soils, each being different from the others in physical and chemical properties.

The soil profile's upper layer (above mineral soil) is decomposed litter derived from dead

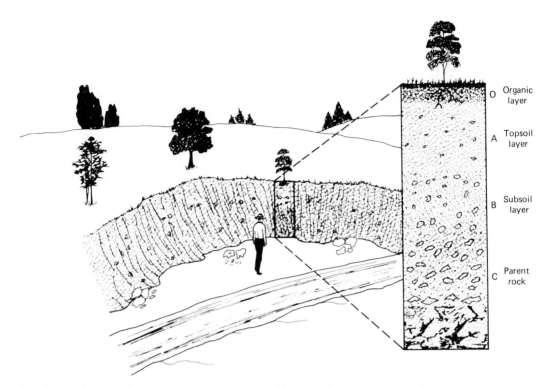

Fig. 12-1. A generalized illustration of the principal layers or horizons that constitute the soil profile. Note the darker organic matter at the top, and bedrock at bottom. In practice these horizons would be subdivided into numerous subhorizons, underscoring the differences in organic matter, chemical composition, soil inhabiting organisms, seasonal fluctuations of ground water, and geologic origin of the parent material.

plants and tiny animals. The original forms of plants or animals may or may not be recognizable in this *O* (organic) horizon (Fig. 12-1). Organic matter contains many essential plant nutrients that are released by microbial decomposition processes.

The topsoil, or next layer of the profile, also contains considerable amounts of organic matter mixed with the mineral soil. This upper layer, usually gray or black, is called the *A* horizon. It is in this layer where most of the roots from surface vegetation are found. Leaching, the process by which water percolates down through the topsoil carrying dissolved material along with it, takes place here.

These dissolved materials are moved downward by soil water into or through the *B* horizon, which is normally immediately below the *A* horizon. This *B* horizon is called the subsoil, and contains less organic matter. In moist climates the *B* horizon contains an accumulation of clay-type materials and iron oxides brought downward by leaching. In dry climates, in addition to the oxides and clay, there are usually deposits of other soluble minerals such as lime or gypsum. Also, some minerals may be brought into the *B* horizon from below through evaporation of soil water.[13]

The *C* horizon consists of decayed or disintegrated parent rock grading downward into unweathered bedrock. The boundaries of these various layers of the soil profile may or may not be well defined.

Not all soils are found in close association with their parent material; many have been transported some distance. Wind-blown soils include sand dunes, volcanic ash, and loess (a silt-sized material). Water-transported soils are found in floodplains, alluvial fans, and deltas. Another example of transported soils are those that have developed from the rocks carried and pushed ahead by glacial ice. In many instances the soil found in a given area may have resulted from a combination of the situations and agents mentioned.

Most soils are mineral (inorganic). This means their organic content is very low, usually 5 percent or less. Organic soils, on the other hand, which generally lack substantial mineral content, are found in bogs and marshes and are often called muck soils or peat. We are concerned here with the more common mineral soils.

Composition of Mineral Soils

The four major components of mineral soil are minerals, organic matter, air, and water. The *mineral* content is composed of rock fragments that have been formed by weathering. The soil particles range in size from coarse gravels to sand, to silt, and very fine (nearly microsopic) particles of clay. In a typical silt loam topsoil, about 45 percent of the volume will be mineral matter.

Organic matter in mineral soil results from the accumulation of decomposed plant and animal residues. This is constantly being consumed by soil organisms such as earthworms, insects, rodents, and microorganisms and therefore must be constantly replaced. Approximately 5 percent of the total volume of a silt loam topsoil is organic matter, but this varies significantly with climate.

The remaining 50 percent of the soil volume is pore space, which is occupied in nearly equal quantities by air and water. As one increases, the other decreases. For optimum plant growth the balance between air and water space must be carefully maintained.

Air in the pores of soil is not the same as air in the atmosphere. In the soil, air has a higher relative humidity. It is seldom continuous but is found in pockets or pores. The carbon dioxide content is higher and the oxygen content lower.

Soil water is a solution that supplies nutrients to plants. Just after a rain or artificial sprinkling, the water is readily available to plants. However, as it is consumed or evaporates, that which remains is tenaciously held in pore spaces or as a tight film around the soil particles. As the soil dries this moisture becomes less available to the plants.

Of interest to people who work with soil is *soil productivity*, the ability of a soil to grow plants. Soil productivity is determined in large part by the nature of the topsoil and subsoil. The topsoil is the major zone of root development and supplies most of the water and nutrients available to plants. The permeability and chemical nature of the subsoil, even though not always penetrated by roots, have some influence on the topsoil's potential for plant growth.

Soil Erosion

One of the park manager's biggest environmental problems may be soil erosion. Since it takes anywhere from 50 to 100 years to build 2.5 cm. (1 in.) of soil, this vital resource must not be wasted. All soils erode, but some do so more quickly than others. The rate of erosion is dependent on several factors: vegetation, soil characteristics, precipitation, topography (soil slope), wind, and animal and visitor impact.

The influence of soil characteristics on erosion is difficult to determine in that soil factors are difficult to isolate in the presence of vegetative factors.[7] The dynamics of soils themselves are not completely understood.

Wind erosion is most common in arid and semiarid regions, but also occurs in humid areas, particularly during dry weather periods. Wet soils are not susceptible to wind erosion. When the moisture content of soils is lowered by hot, dry, winds, wind erosion may take place. Vegetative cover is the best way to alleviate wind erosion in park areas. In dry regions, windbreaks of trees and shrubs and picket fences are useful in reducing wind velocities and trapping drifting soil.[2]

Water is the chief cause of erosion; over a period of centuries water action can level mountain ranges. Running water is the major contributor to erosion; however raindrop splash serves to detach soil and, under certain conditions, to transport it. Vegetative cover is a major deterrent to raindrop impact and erosion.

Rainfall's contribution to erosion has been studied extensively on agricultural lands but information for park areas is scanty. Data from agricultural experiments tell us the rainfall factors that bear on erosion are raindrop size, rainfall intensity, and total rainfall.

On bare soils, raindrop splash provides the detaching force that begins erosion. Level soils or soils at a low angle are subject to soil splash but actual soil transport is minimal, even when rainfall intensity is high. Downhill transport increases with slope angle and reaches its maximum where slope steepness and rainfall intensity are greatest (Fig. 12-2). Sand-size material is especially susceptible to splash erosion.[7]

Recreation Impact on Soils

Recreation development is often the cause of soil erosion through topographic modification as well as the clearing of vegetation. Heavy equip-

Fig. 12-2. The impact of a raindrop striking wet soil is illustrated in this photo sequence. The drop of water, a sphere about 3 mm (⅛ in.) in diameter, is traveling at the rate of 9 m/sec (30 ft/sec) when it strikes the soil. The force pushes the wet soil outward in all directions and throws particles of soil and water to distances of 0.6 to 1.5 m (2 to 5 ft). The resulting crater is about four times as large as the raindrop. (Photo courtesy of USDA Soil Conservation Service.)

Fig. 12-3. Because of intensity of use, campground and picnic area soils are particularly vulnerable to trampling. Note the lack of ground cover in this park near Redding, California. (Photo by Grant W. Sharpe.)

ment used in construction alters soil porosity, which affects the infiltration rate.

The manager will have no problem recognizing erosion caused by construction, but what about the effects of visitor use on soils? If a manager permits unrestricted trampling on soils and vegetation, the natural attractiveness of a recreation area is threatened. Because of the intensity of use, the soils of campgrounds and picnic areas are particularly vulnerable to trampling (Fig. 12-3). Campground soil should be the type that will withstand compaction yet maintain its fertility to support plant growth.

Site wear indicators are bare soil, soil compaction, loss of ground vegetation, dead trees and windthrow, trees with exposed roots, and an increase in site size.[8] Physical changes are not easily noticed unless there is some form of environmental monitoring such as photographs of the same site taken every few years. Manning indicates the detrimental effects of trampling may be

described in a seven-step soil impact cycle (Fig. 12-4).[18]

In the Quetico-Superior canoe country of Minnesota and Ontario, studies showed the *A* horizon of campsites was reduced in thickness an average of 65 percent below that of adjacent unused control areas. This loss of litter and humus was attributed to loss of ground vegetation, mechanical reduction resulting from trampling, surface runoff that increased with soil compaction, and the practice of raking litter to improve the appearance of the campsite and reduce fire hazard.[6]

Recreation area soils must support heavy traffic by people, vehicles, and sometimes, horses (Fig. 12-5). Helgath, in her study of trail deterioration in the Selway-Bitterroot Wilderness in Idaho and Montana, noted *trail location* to be more important than the level of visitor use in causing deterioration of trails. A trail system with the same amount of use throughout showed variable amounts of deterioration depending on

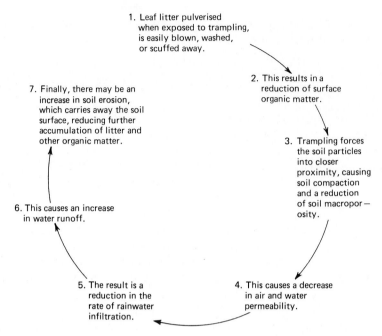

1. Leaf litter pulverised when exposed to trampling, is easily blown, washed, or scuffed away.

2. This results in a reduction of surface organic matter.

3. Trampling forces the soil particles into closer proximity, causing soil compaction and a reduction of soil macropor—osity.

4. This causes a decrease in air and water permeability.

5. The result is a reduction in the rate of rainwater infiltration.

6. This causes an increase in water runoff.

7. Finally, there may be an increase in soil erosion, which carries away the soil surface, reducing further accumulation of litter and other organic matter.

Fig. 12-4. A seven-step soil erosion sequence. (Adopted from Manning.[16])

Fig. 12-5. Erosion from motorcycle use on range land in Idaho. The trails worn by the dirt bikes soon become gullies. Henry Creek Canyon. (USDA Soil Conservation Service photo by R. Neil Sampson.)

a variety of site factors. She noted some trail grades of 15 percent eroded more easily than steeper 30 percent grades, the variable being the soil type through which the trail ran. One stretch of trail had only a 5 percent grade, but, since it was located on a fine-textured soil, it suffered very serious erosion. Rerouting the trail around the vulnerable soil type, or installing planking across it would correct this.[10]

Intensive recreation use does affect underlying soils, although there is some difference of opinion regarding the nature and extent of this influence. The primary change seems to be through the physical compaction of soils from either pedestrian or vehicular traffic. Such compaction causes changes in bulk density, soil moisture, and infiltration rates. Ketchledge and Leonard also point out that hiking boots (with cleated rather than smooth soles) cut and roughen the soil surface. The soil loosened by these boots is easily eroded by runoff water.[11] Many park managers are encouraging park visitors, as well as their employees, to switch from heavy lug sole boots to lighter boots with flat soles, or even to running shoes. The use of light shoes results in less damage to trail treads as well as requiring less energy while hiking.[32]

According to Lull, the amount of compaction depends on five major factors: weight of the compacting agent, previous use, soil type, amount of organic matter, and moisture content. Moisture content is mentioned as most important because resistance to compaction decreases as moisture content increases. The moisture acts as a lubricant, weakening adhesion between particles.[17]

Once land is stripped of vegetation most soils have little resistance to erosive forces. Rainstorms of high intensity can be expected to generate tremendous quantities of sediment.[7] Dirt roads and trails both deteriorate from rainsplash erosion when there is no protective tree canopy overhead to absorb rain energy. Vegetation, then, is an important deterrent to soil erosion through its interception of raindrop impact and through its root system holding soil in place. Unfortu- nately, vegetation is often difficult to maintain in recreation areas where human use is heavy.

Soils and the Park Manager

Given the information that recreation use changes certain soil characteristics, what are the implications for managers of recreation areas? Probably the most important is that soil information must be utilized in the process of planning any new recreational developments, and when considering changes in existing areas. If possible, new facilities should be located on soils most suitable for the given type of development. According to Dotzenko et al., campgrounds located on soils with high organic-matter content should be easier to develop and maintain.[5]

The suitability of soils for waste disposal will be an important consideration and may dictate whether or not developments requiring waste disposal facilities are possible in a given area. This factor will certainly influence the decision as to the type of waste system utilized.

In locating trails for hiking or other uses, care should be taken to avoid unstable or highly erodible soils. This should lessen the impact of trails and make them less costly and easier to maintain.

A knowledge of soil and methods of reducing soil deterioration should also be applied to park maintenance. One of the more important points is the value of maintaining a protective covering of leaf litter and humus to improve filtration, protect the soil from compaction, cushion the effects of beating rain, and reduce runoff.[22,27] Since the thickness of the top organic horizon is reduced by the management practice of raking off the litter and humus to improve appearance and reduce fire hazard, it may be necessary to find other ways to meet these objectives.[6] Another maintenance practice that might need modification is the timing of watering when used as a cultural treatment for vegetation. Water applied just prior to periods of high use could increase damage to soils and vegetation through trampling.[27] Similarly, measures should be taken to reduce water runoff on hiking trails, through the use of water bars and culverts.

As mentioned in the beginning of the chapter, it is frequently the case that parklands are available simply because the soil types were not suitable for agriculture, timber production, or because the land lies in a floodplain. This may mean the manager will inherit some very severe problems.

How does the manager recognize and deal with an "inherited" soils problem? Watch for certain signs while making periodic tours of the area. Are buildings settling and cracking? Is water puddling where it once drained? Is soil sliding or washing away in places where vegetation used to grow? Are basements dry or do they flood under certain conditions? Does the soil in the drain field absorb moisture so slowly that the sanitation system becomes a health hazard? Learn the drainage patterns of the area by driving or hiking around immediately after a storm. If you see a change in patterns, or a warning sign, get professional assistance.

Park managers need not feel uncomfortable about lack of soil knowledge. Soil scientists with government agencies are available to assist in classifying, mapping, and describing soils so that they may be used to their best purpose. In soil survey work the soil scientist walks around the area, stopping frequently to dig into the soil and study its properties. The field work is supported by laboratory testing of soil samples collected in the field. Soil maps are made with accompanying descriptions. These show the planner and manager the location and extent of different soils. From this, decisions can be made on safe uses of the soil or adjustments and corrections of present use. Soil maps are especially informative to the manager wishing to expand facilities in the park. Soil surveys show soil wetness, overflow hazards, depth to bedrock, hardpans, tight layers, erodibility, clay layers that crack when dry and swell when wet, and hazards of slippage on slopes. Surveys show the location and extent of different soils and provide information about their proper-

ties to a depth of about 6 ft. Soil maps are available for most of the United States and the populated regions of Canada.

A farmer using a soil in the wrong way may suffer losses for a year or two but can usually correct the problem the next year. A park planner must be right the first time, otherwise buildings crack, roadways sink, and trails wash out. If you inherit poor planning, attack the problem intelligently; perhaps it can be lessened. At least knowledge of the cause and nature of the problem will lessen your frustration. The bibliography at the end of this chapter includes several textbooks on soils for those requiring further information.

WATER

Before beginning a discussion of water in recreation areas, it seems appropriate to briefly mention the hydrologic cycle, as represented in the diagram (Fig. 12-6). Water falls from the clouds either as hail, snow, or rain, the form of precipitation depending on the air temperature near the ground. Some water is evaporated before it reaches the ground. Of water that does reach the earth, some flows over the surface to enter streams. Some penetrates the soil, to a depth and in an amount determined by the characteristics of the soil. The thicker and more decomposed the humus, the more water the soil will hold although soil particle size also plays a role here. Some water becomes part of the groundwater system and moves laterally, eventually feeding into streams, lakes, or oceans. Part of this groundwater is used as water pumped from wells, some is taken up by vegetation and used for growth, and much is transpired by trees, going into the air as water vapor. The transpired water, plus the water evaporated from the surface of streams, lakes, and the ocean, is returned to the clouds; and the hydrologic cycle is completed. Water is available at several points during the hydrologic cycle to serve the needs of plants and animals. It is also available to serve humans

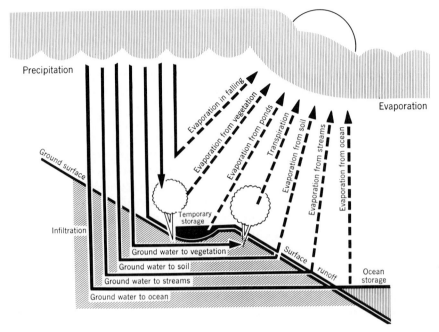

Fig. 12-6. The hydrologic cycle, showing the movement of water from the atmosphere to the land and ocean, and back to the atmosphere. Note the relationship of the precipitation and evaporation to soil and vegetation. (From *Introduction to Forestry.*[21])

in many ways including domestic water supplies, transportation of wastes, food production, water power, navigation, and recreation.

Water and Outdoor Recreation

Most recreation activities are directly dependent on water; it is difficult to imagine an outdoor recreation area without it. Water is important for many reasons, the most basic being for drinking. Water is essential in most kinds of recreation area sanitation systems. It is also the limiting factor in whether an area can support swimming, boating, sport fishing, waterfowl hunting, and such winter sports as skating, skiing, tobogganing, and snowmobiling on ice or snow. Water has great attractive powers, whether it is at rest as a pond, lake, or reservoir, or in motion as a flowing creek, a river, pounding ocean surf, a geyser,

or a waterfall. Hearing the sound of water is also part of the recreation experience.

A safe water supply, then, is needed as a base for safe, clean, recreation activities. Maintaining this safe supply is part of the manager's job.

Some outdoor recreation areas are located in natural floodplains. It is assumed that this is the wisest use of the land, even though there is the expectation that the land will be inundated periodically. Were it not for the periodic flooding the land would probably not be available for recreation but would be in some more remunerative use.

The Esthetic Aspect of Water

Visitors to recreation areas perceive bodies of water in various ways, depending on their expectations and desires. A person interested only in sightseeing looks at water differently than a person whose orientation is toward fishing, waterskiing, or swimming. The exposure visitors have already had to water also affects their attitude toward it. For example, people who live in a desert environment regard water differently from those who have lived near it throughout their lives.

Most people are naturally attracted to water. They like to stare at it, walk along it, throw rocks into it, play in it, boat on it, or just listen to it. They generally prefer to camp near it when given a choice and will climb to various heights to look down at the waterscape. Water in its many forms appears in photographs and paintings. People often linger at footbridges to look into the water below. Why is this? Perhaps it fascinates us because water vistas are always changing. The water depth, its clearness, its color, the patterns created by the mirrored shoreline, the patterns created by the wind ripples on the surface—all contribute to the changing water scene. There is for some a sense of danger and mystery in larger bodies of water, a realization of an alien element that we must approach with respect and enter into with caution.

Water adds richness and diversity to what otherwise might be a very ordinary landscape, and it supports many species of plants and animals that also fascinate and delight visitors. Therefore, protecting and maintaining the quality of the water in a park deserves the manager's close attention.

Recreation Impacts on Water— Pollution

Water, for many of the uses just cited, will need to meet certain federal, state/provincial, and local standards for quality, often stated in biological, physical, or chemical terms. The quality of water available as a recreation base might be lowered both by natural processes and human influence. Visitors to the park may contribute to water pollution. An oil or gas spill caused by careless use of an outboard engine causes pollu-

tion. Soil erosion also contributes to the deterioration of water quality.

Industrial, agricultural, or urban pollutants often enter a river upstream from a recreation area and render the water useless for all purposes except enhancement of the view. Even this esthetic value may be impaired if it is known that the water is polluted.

Sediments carried into lakes affect plant life in two ways: by obscuring sunlight and thus interfering with photosynthesis, and by burying plants. Silt pollution also smothers fish eggs and may seriously affect aquatic insects that serve as fish food. Chemical wastes kill plant and animal life, often many kilometers from the source. Thermal pollution, the release of hot or cold waters into lakes or streams, affects the fish population. Diseased animals are also sources of waterborne diseases that cause intestinal disorders in humans. A fecal parasite *Giardia lamblia* is known to exist in wildlife throughout North America, particularly in the Cascades and Rocky Mountain regions, and can be transmitted to humans through water. It causes giardiasis, perhaps better known as beaver fever or backpacker's disease.

Evidence of pollution includes water discoloration, floating material, oil slicks, and objectionable odor. Sometimes the water looks and tastes all right, but diarrhea or abdominal pains in users signal contamination. Pollution should also be suspected if there is a change in aquatic life, especially in plant species and population. When pollution is found within the park the manager must see that adequate warning is given to park visitors in order to protect visitor health. When in doubt as to the degree of pollution in any form and its effect on park visitors and park values, the manager should learn where advice is available within the agency by discussing the problem with the supervisor. Following the chain of command is *always* the correct procedure. It might also limit embarrassment such as resulted in the case of the park manager who alerted persons outside his agency about pollution in a lake and caused quite a stir, only to find that the "pollution" he had noticed was pollen drifting on the lake's surface.

Parks on large lakes may be exposed to pollution, particularly if the lake is used for industrial purposes, if it is ringed by agricultural lands, or if it is used for transportation. While park managers must rely on local, state or provincial, or federal environmental legislation to eventually alleviate such problems, they should be aware of these regulations and be able to discuss any infraction of them when called on to do so. At the same time, managers must do all in their power to prevent or terminate park-related pollution. Advice and help on sediment levels and pollution are usually readily obtained from a variety of sources once the problem is identified.

The manager should not confuse lake eutrophication with pollution. *Eutrophication* is the natural aging process of lakes, and takes place independently of human activities. In this process a lake traps nutrients draining in from the surface of the surrounding basin, and from groundwater inflow. According to Greeson:

> *Enrichment and sedimentation are the principal contributors to the aging process. The shore vegetation and higher aquatic plants utilize part of the inflowing nutrients, grow abundantly, and, in turn, trap the sediments. The lake gradually fills in, becoming shallower by the accumulation of plants and sediments on the bottom and smaller by the invasion of shore vegetation, and eventually becomes dry land. The extinction of a lake is, therefore, a result of enrichment, productivity, decay, and sedimentation.*[9]

The park manager can extend the life expectancy of a lake by controlling those factors that speed up eutrophication. For example, the excessive fertilization of parklands with nitrogen and phosphorus contributes to algae growth. Keeping roads and trails away from a lake shore, along with other erosion control methods, will help reduce sediments. Keeping a tree cover around the shoreline keeps water temperature down. Dredg-

ing is a direct means of reversing the eutrophic process.

Every lake is different, and rates of eutrophication vary. Retarding the aging of lakes is a complicated process, requiring specialized knowledge. Caution is advised in tampering with such a critical system, lest the control methods upset the fine balance and make things worse. Once again it becomes apparent that the park manager must seek professional assistance in matters of this sort, starting with the immediate supervisor, and then, with permission, consulting with specialized personnel inside or outside the agency.

VEGETATION

Native vegetation is considered a valuable resource for any park. Its presence at park entrances, along roads, around buildings, and generally throughout the park is often perceived as that factor that makes the area "parklike." It usually stimulates appreciation for the park environment, particularly when the area outside the park has been noticeably modified.

Unfortunately, some parks are devoid of much of their original vegetation. Many areas have previously been used for farming, timber production, grazing lands, or military or industrial sites. Such uses often drastically modified the natural vegetation. On the other hand, some parks are established on areas where vegetation has been unmodified by human activity or by recent forest fires.

Plant Succession

Space doesn't permit a full discussion of plant succession, but the manager should at least be aware that the composition of the vegetation in a park is not static. Assuming that moisture is available, any bare soil area will eventually support plants. After a disturbance such as the removal of plant cover by fire, wind erosion, tree harvesting, or trampling by humans or animals, the basic stage of succession begins, provided the disturbance ceases. Seeds are introduced into the bare area by wind, birds, or other carriers. The first plants to grow in the open sunny area are called *pioneers*. Their presence modifies the site, and eventually a new series of plants begin to appear, having a somewhat different tolerance for shade than do the pioneers. These *intermediate plants* may occupy the site for many years but they too will eventually lose out to a new community, referred to as the *climax* stage.

The successional stages cited here are only theoretical. There are numerous environmental factors that influence plants such as soil moisture, temperature, light, and soil nutrients; thus the stages of succession are difficult to distinguish.[23]

With a changing overstory (trees) there is a change in the understory (ground cover) that in turn affects such things as erosion and water quality, as well as wildlife, through habitat changes. Once again the interdependency of natural resources in park areas is illustrated and managerial concern with all aspects of these resources is shown to be necessary.

The Role of Vegetation

Vegetation serves many purposes. We have already seen the importance of vegetation in controlling erosion and intercepting precipitation, as well as the esthetic value plants have for most people. Plants play other roles also and many of these are of importance to the manager.

Vegetation and Visitor Interest. Visitors to parks are often more than casually interested in the vegetation found in park environments, particularly the varied tree, shrub, and wildflower species. Some parks have unusual or rare plants, large trees, or vegetation having cultural significance. The park manager can enhance visitor enjoyment by interpreting the vegetation through the various media cited in Chapter 17.

There are other important aspects of vegetation for the manager to consider in his or her role of protector of parklands.

Plants and Energy. In the presence of sunlight the leaves of plants take in carbon dioxide from the air, and water from the soil. Through a chemical reaction called photosynthesis, plants produce a carbohydrate that is sent to all parts of the plant less than a year old. This new growth contains stored energy that is used by other living things. Oxygen, a by-product, is released to the atmosphere where it becomes available to all forms of plant and animal life for respiration.

Plants and Wildlife. In addition to providing food and oxygen for wildlife, vegetation serves another important function, that of providing wildlife habitat. As land outside parks becomes increasingly modified by urban sprawl and through farm and forestry practices, certain wildlife species become even more dependent on parklands for suitable cover and nesting sites. Vegetation usually provides this needed habitat.

Vegetation and Soil. Plants eventually die and decay, their remains becoming available to other plants. When decomposed, vegetation increases the water-holding capacity of the soil. Plants also facilitate soil aeration through root decay. Some plants add nitrogen to the soil through nitrogen-fixing bacteria that fasten on the root nodules of leguminous plants, as well as on the root structure of some trees.

Vegetation as a Site Indicator. Certain species of trees, shrubs, and other plants grow in poorly drained soils. Others are found only in dry sites. Still others are found in open sunlight, while some tolerate total or partial shade. Lists here would be pointless since the species combination varies widely throughout North America. A local list of vegetative site indicators should be obtained and studied by the manager.

Vegetation and Microclimate. Plants serve as indicators of microclimate. The species that occur, their growth rate, and their health are all indices of subtle climatic changes. Plants differ according to the direction the slope faces, and they also indicate frost pockets and windy sites by composition and condition. Taller vegetation also modifies the microclimate, as one readily notices when moving from direct sunlight into the shade of the forest canopy.

Vegetation as a Screen. Plants can effectively cover unsightly areas or special park operations such as dumps, maintenance sheds, or service areas. They can serve as screens along park boundaries, and provide privacy around employee residential areas. Thorny species are also used to channel visitor movements.

Vegetation as a Sound Barrier. The ability of vegetation to impede sound transmission is not great, so it should not be relied on for sound reduction where the sound source is close by. To be most effective, special plantings must be made, (i.e., shrubs in the foreground, trees in the background), along with a specially constructed landform in the center of sufficient height to screen the sound source from view.[4] Where distances are great [300 m (1000 ft) or more], trees may be only slightly better for absorbing sound than the same distance left in open space. The effectiveness of trees to absorb sound varies with their size, density, type, and position relative to the sound source.[15]

Tolerance of unwanted sound (or noise) varies with the individual. Some noise is judged annoying if it appears to that person to be inappropriate or unnecessary. The sound of a barking dog, motorcycle, or electric generator late at night in a campground while visitors are trying to sleep would be more objectionable than the same sound in the daytime. Furthermore, the owner of any of these three "noisemakers" would react to them differently than would a nonowner at any time, day or night.

Vegetation and Wind Velocity. Trees dissipate the force of wind by acting as vertical barriers in its path. The best example of this is the wind-

breaks or shelterbelts of the great plains, where the winds are affected on the leeward side for a horizontal distance of over 40 times the height of the trees. Soil evaporation is reduced, transpiration from vegetation is diminished, drifting snow is checked, and the movement of soil is lessened.[23] Picnic sites or campgrounds in windy areas might benefit from such plantings.

Miscellaneous Contributions. Though not as important in parks as in areas under cultivation, vegetation's greatest contribution to humans is in providing foods (fruits and vegetables), fuel, plant pigments (dyes), shelter (forest products), fibers, clothing, spices, beverage plants, decorations, latex, chemical derivatives, containers, furniture, wood novelties, tobacco, and drugs. Only in unusual circumstances are any of these projects of significance in park areas, although some outdoor recreation opportunities might be available in certain commercial forests and farms, and berry picking and mushroom collecting are allowed in most recreational areas.

Problems with Vegetation

Some plants are classified as weeds, perhaps because no one has found a use for them. Often it is because they are not indigenous, and having no natural controls they crowd out native species or harm our well-being, our livelihood, or our recreational activities. Currently the greatest recreational problem seems to be with Eurasian water milfoil and similar exotic water plants that choke lakes and waterways and bring boating and swimming to a halt in certain areas. Water intakes are clogged, fishing is made difficult or even dangerous and ecological relationships are seriously disturbed.

Positive identification and treatment are tasks for specialists, but park managers must watch closely for any unfamiliar waterweed, especially near boat ramps, as early detection is important in eradication attempts.

Visitors coming in with boats and trailers must

be persuaded to examine their equipment for plant fragments of any kind before putting their equipment into the water. Interpretive assistance should be sought in order to design the most effective signs possible, and other media should also be considered to help alert the public to the problem and elicit cooperation. Although the spread of these weeds seems inevitable, an attempt is being made to slow their spread until more effective controls can be developed.

Turf management and vista clearing are also important parts of most park manger's responsibilities. The first requires routine attention; the second, judicious intervention.

The growing of crops to produce controlled substances is a problem on some remote recreational lands. This situation is dealt with by law enforcement agencies, confining the role of the manager to one of discreet surveillance and prompt reporting.

Recreation Impacts on Vegetation

When considering impact on vegetation a distinction should be made between the overstory (trees) and the understory (ground cover). The latter contains the reproduction of tree species, as well as woody shrubs and herbaceous vegetation. Certain activities impact one layer but not the other; the degree of impact differs, and certain impacts can be injurious to one but beneficial to the other layer.

Some of the impact of recreational use on vegetation is apparent even to the untrained eye. Consider the smooth-barked trees that have been scarred by initials (Fig. 13-5). Certainly these carvings mar the beauty of the tree. Once a tree is marked, subsequent visitors add their contributions. Rough-barked trees also have problems as visitors frequently hack into the bark in order to use it in starting campfires. Axe blazes and other wounds serve as entry points for disease and insect infestation. Firewood cutting of live trees takes its toll, as does removal of vegetation to enlarge a campsite.

In a study of the Quetico-Superior canoe country of Minnesota and Ontario it was found that many pine saplings had been cut for tent poles by canoeists, only to be burned for a campfire by a following party not needing the poles. More saplings were cut by later parties, which essentially reduced the number of pine in the younger age classes.[6] It was interesting to note in the same study that campers preferred sites with pine cover; however, that cover type will eventually disappear if this depreciative use continues.

The recreation impact on vegetation is primarily by trampling. The above canoe campsite study found that 80 percent of the ground cover was lost with only light use.[6] Both cover abundance and the number of plant species present is reduced. LePage, in a study in a new campground in northwestern Pennsylvania, found that the original ground cover, not able to withstand continued pressures from trampling, was replaced by more resistant species. Grasses have a greater tolerance to trampling than do dicotyledonous herbs.[12]

Damage is most severe in the central portion of campsites where foot traffic is heaviest and the protective litter layer is lost first.[14] With each year of use the area covered by natural vegetation in a campsite can be expected to shrink, until the site is either barren, or populated by a few resistant species that have replaced the original plant community. Dry summers are particularly hard on vegetation, both from the standpoint of available water and the fact that hotter summers may increase visitor use in recreation areas, putting even more stress on the vegetation.

After a few years of use a site can be expected to widen, especially if the understory is sparse and easily cleared away and there are no physical barriers to impede expansion. As sites show wear, people tend to extend their activities into the vegetation. Merriam et al. found that site expansion was a major phenomenon on sites lacking rock walls or dense shrubs. New tent locations were chosen as older ones become dusty or bare of vegetation.[19]

Fig. 12-7. Exposed tree roots lace this four-wheel vehicle trail on the Little Natches River, Mt. Baker-Snoqualmie National Forest, Washington. (Photo courtesy of USDA Forest Service.)

Where soils are thin [less than 30 cm (1 ft.) deep], the tree cover is often rooted in only 16 cm (6 in.) of soil. Therefore, the slightest amount of surface erosion will expose tree roots (Fig. 12-7). Exposed roots are subject to drying and mechanical damage, and the ability of those trees to withstand strong winds is also affected.[6]

The cutting of woody sticks for cooking purposes (toasting wieners and marshmallows) also has an impact on campground shrubbery. Another problem is that fireplaces produce toxic ash, which in concentrated form may harm nearby tree roots. Drainage from fireplace areas tends to spread this toxic material. Campers' fires may spread, and under the right conditions, kill adjacent vegetation. Also to be noted is the scalding of bark and injury to the cambium, which may occur when a hot gas lantern is hung in contact with a tree trunk.

Management Treatments of Deteriorating Sites

Obviously, vegetation is going to deteriorate in newly opened recreation areas. Even light use eventually results in loss of ground vegetation at campsites. Observers of a new area can expect to find a reduction in the abundance of cover within a year or two, as well as a reduction in the number of plant species present. LePage, in the same study previously cited in Pennsylvania, found campsites that had received 150 camper days of use throughout the first summer averaged less than 10 percent loss in the vegetative cover; however, loss of vegetation cover increased to 60 percent for 300 camper days of use. It was thought that restricting the average amount of use to 200 campers or less per season might minimize loss of cover. However, such restrictions may not be feasible in light of continuing demands for recreation space. It seems such restrictions only postpone the inevitable.[12]

When managing areas for recreation, consideration must be given to the ability of native and suitable introduced species to withstand recreational use and abuse. Studies by LePage show that such plants as blue grass (*Poa*), path rush (*Juncus*), and clover (*Trifolium*) demonstrate tolerance to trampling.[12]

The astute manager will experiment with site rehabilitation methods, and keep records of those factors influencing the success or failure of the remedial attempts. Rehabilitation methods include delaying the opening of sites early in the spring when the ground is damp and easily compacted, and the spreading of thin layers of straw on bare spots at the close of the season to trap windblown seed and hold it in place until spring. Consider loosening and aerating the soil, or bringing in new topsoil, and adding mulch. Revegetate bare areas with species resistant to drought and trampling. It may be necessary to close damaged sites for a year or two in order to effect rehabilitation.

Ripley attempted to evaluate the durability of various tree and shrub species on three national forests in North Carolina.[21] Similar lists for other regions would be useful, but few exist. As a manager you may be frustrated by a lack of research dealing with vegetation native to your region. It would be advisable to look for resistant characteristics in indigenous species. Woody shrubs may be more desirable than herbaceous ground cover due to their greater durability. Species with thorns or dense branching serve well to define site boundaries. Jute matting is useful in site rehabilitation as it helps hold soil in place and gives new plants a chance to get started beneath a protected covering (Fig. 12-8). Useful information will be found in writings on silvicultural practices, shade tree management, and landscaping. Until more specific research is done dealing with the vegetation of recreation sites, managers will have to utilize information from other fields, and integrate it with their own knowledge and best judgment.

The recreation manager must carefully consider and evaluate the nature and degree of visitor use and abuse as well as the impact of planned management actions. As suggested earlier, much of the attraction of a recreation area is of an esthetic nature and thus the vegetative character could have an influence on the level of user satisfaction derived from the area. Silvicultural treatments are used on commercial stands to produce timber; it might be possible to adapt these treatments to produce healthy vegetation that enhances the quality of recreation.

Although each visitor contributes to the deterioration of a recreation site, there is no general awareness of this, unless, of course, the damage is deliberate. Normal wear and tear produces no sudden results, even in new areas, where, as we have seen, 80 percent of the original ground cover may disappear with only light use. The cutting of tent poles, wiener sticks, and other campsite needs increases site deterioration to an even greater degree. Any management attempt to restore damaged sites or to extend their period of usefulness must be accompanied by an interpretive visitor-education program. Visitors should be made fully aware of the problem through park

Fig. 12-8. Jute matting is frequently used to hold soil in place, and like a great gauze bandage, gives new plants a protective covering. Cascade Pass, North Cascades National Park, Washington. (Photo by Grant W. Sharpe.)

interpretive programs and informed of how they can assist in slowing the deterioration. Vegetation can be used as a management tool. It can be used for fencing, screening, controlling users, as a wildlife attractant, a soil stabilizer, and a modifier of microclimate.

The general references at the end of this chapter offer further reading on the improvement and maintenance of vegetation in recreation areas. Chapter 4, Recreation Legalities and Liabilities, discusses the liability problem of danger trees in developed recreation areas.

WILDLIFE

Wildlife forms the basis of certain types of recreation and can be a complement to yet other recreation activities. The recreational enjoyment of wildlife can be separated into nonconsumptive uses (wildlife photography, bird-watching, and other generalized or specialized wildlife observation) or consumptive uses (fishing, hunting and trapping). Both types of uses may fall within the spectrum of activities that an area offers to recreationists, especially if they occur at different seasons.

The park manager must realize that there are divergent viewpoints where wildlife is concerned. Some people like to hunt; others don't and are often vociferous in their opposition to this sport. At present the per capita hunting population is on the decline, at least in the United States. The major factors responsible for the decreasing number of hunters are urbanization, a shrinking accessible land base for hunters, and the reduced game habitat due to agricultural practices. At the same time the proportion of people interested in watching wildlife, without killing it, is on the increase.[30] The current romantic view of nature, and the revulsion toward killing animals evidenced by segments of the North American public, probably reduce the proportion of hunters in the population as a whole.

Wilkins points out that hunters have been responsible for most of the pioneering work and much of the money that implements wildlife con-

servation programs. These efforts stayed the rapid decline in population of many game animals in the early 1900s.[30] Traditionally, financial support for wildlife has come from license fees paid by fishermen and hunters, and the federal taxes on guns, ammunition, and fishing tackle. Thus, it is the hunters and fishermen who are responsible for supporting the game departments that have brought about an increase in many species of wildlife. These species are now annually harvested through carefully regulated limits and seasons. Because of the increase in numbers, this wildlife is also seen and enjoyed by the nonhunting public. Competition between consumptive and nonconsumptive users of wildlife will no doubt increase in the years ahead, and more confrontations between the two groups can be expected. Here is where recreation area managers could use interpretation as an effective tool to reduce the number of such confrontations. Through interpretation, the nonconsumptive user can learn the values of hunting and other wildlife management techniques. Similarly, hunters can be made to realize that others have a legitimate claim to the same land for nonconsumptive wildlife purposes.

Problems with Wildlife

Wildlife provides pleasure for park visitors, but also creates problems for park managers. Animals may leave the park and feed in nearby orchards or on field crops, or a park may become overpopulated with a species that causes damage to park vegetation. Beaver and muskrat build dams and may back water onto adjacent landowners' property as well as onto parklands. Beaver have been known to leave the park area and cut down trees on nearby residential lands. As mentioned elsewhere in this book they also transmit diseases that cause sickness in humans. Park wildlife might transmit disease to livestock on adjoining agricultural lands. Certain mammals such as skunks, fox, and bats might endanger the lives of park visitors since these animals are subject to rabies. Rattlesnakes, copperheads, and other poisonous snakes create problems in camp-grounds and along trails. Bears are a serious problem in many larger parks, as are moose, elk, and deer in the rutting season. Deer are frequently killed in collisions with vehicles, and serious injuries often result to the drivers, passengers, and cars. Wildlife might be harassed, chased away, or killed by visitor-owned domestic pets. These sorts of problems must be anticipated by the manager and a policy formulated in order to deal with them as effectively and consistently as possible.

Wildlife for Nonconsumptive Purposes

Hunting is permitted in some parklands and not in others. Since much is written on wildlife management for consumptive purposes, we will direct our comments chiefly to the management concerns regarding nonconsumptive aspects.

In a unmodified environment the wildlife population is kept in balance through predator-prey relationships. Where predators such as cougars, wolves, and other carnivores have been eliminated, hunting is necessary to control the prey population. Where such harvesting is not permitted, the animals may become so abundant that they damage the habitat. It is most difficult to maintain balanced animal populations in such areas.

The vegetative cover pattern will determine the abundance and distribution of wildlife present. Since altering the habitat to increase the carrying capacity for one species may reduce it for another, the park manager should understand the interdependence of habitat and wildlife populations.

Wildlife Habitat

In order to maintain ideal wildlife populations in a park, the manager will have to maintain a suitable habitat, which includes food, water, nesting and escape cover, and bedding, roosting, and feeding areas (Fig. 12-9). One of the greatest threats to wildlife everywhere is the disappear-

Fig. 12-9. Wildlife viewing is a universally popular activity. Here Canada geese are being observed by visitors to Kensington Metropark, Milford, Michigan (Photo courtesy of Huron-Clinto Metropolitan Authority.)

ance of such habitat. Wildlife dependent on a particular habitat usually perish if that habitat is altered or eliminated.

Thousands of acres of lakes and marshes which once sheltered wildlife have been drained for agricultural purposes. Lands devoted to housing, industrial sites, and intensive cultivation were once wildlife habitat. Considerable privately owned wildlife habitat, however, is still open to hunting, as are most lands in public ownership. There are, of course, regional differences in available lands and in attitudes toward admitting hunters, and even fishermen for that matter, onto lands used for special purposes.[24]

Some larger parks provide considerable habitat, particularly parts of parks with minimal development or access. The manager can improve habitat for certain species by leaving large snags and standing dead trees. Birds such as woodpeckers depend on these old-growth trees to provide cavity-nesting areas. The manager must be realistic however when the decision is made to leave dead trees standing. The location of the snag, extent of decay in the wood, and fire susceptibility are all factors to consider. A nesting site in a dead tree can hardly justify a million-dollar lawsuit brought against the agency by an injured park visitor. Such trees should not be left near camping sites, parking lots, or other high-risk target areas.

Many of the land-use practices available to farmers, ranchers, and foresters are available to the park manager. These would include food production, water development, and cover and wetland improvement.

Food production is the practice of planting tree and shrub species that produce fruit and browse beneficial to wildlife. Oak, hickory, beech, gum, cherry, mountain ash, dogwood, wild plum, crab apple, persimmon, and service berry all produce wildlife food, called *mast*.[31] Providing *browse* (the leaves, twigs, and shoots of trees and representative shrubs) is another means of assuring food for wildlife. The game department in your area can recommend suitable species for browse planting.

Water developments are projects designed to supply water for the purpose of improving wildlife habitat. Such devices include reservoirs, small ponds, and water catchments. Professional assistance is advised for such projects.[31]

Cover improvement includes providing both protective cover and nesting cover. Protective cover offers hiding places from severe weather and safety from predators. Hedgerows, brushpiles, and plantings for roosting are part of protective cover planting. Nesting cover includes providing ground cover, den and nesting trees, and, where indicated, artificial nest structures.[31] Diversity of habitat is the key consideration.

Wetland improvement provides wetland for waterfowl and fur-bearing mammals by means of developing marsh interspersed with open water areas. Controlling water levels through ditching and dredging and the use of such structures as dikes and spillways is also part of wetland improvement.[31]

The park manager should become familiar with these options, but he or she is urged to consult with wildlife authorities, for improperly planned or executed habitat projects can be harmful to wildlife.

Water and Animals

Fur Mammals. Aquatic fur-bearing animals, such as otter, mink, muskrat, and beaver usually elicit great visitor interest. Laws vary as to whether or not these mammals are protected in parks. Where possible, the habitat of these interesting aquatic creatures should be managed in a manner that contributes to their survival, while making them available to visitor observation. This may be effected through the park interpretive program.

Aquatic Birds. Marsh or aquatic birds also have great appeal for visitors and their habitat should be maintained through the usual conservation practices of controlling soil erosion and pollution, as well as the provision of adequate pond development and nesting opportunities. Park managers should consider means to protect such birds as geese, ducks, swans, coots, rails, and other shorebirds. Examples of protection include provision for vegetative cover, domestic animal control, and isolation from visitors.

Fish. Some park areas provide for visitor viewing of fish populations in small ponds or through windows in stream profile chambers. Most park areas with fish populations permit fish harvesting, with the take usually being regulated by fixed seasons and catch limits. Because of the popularity of recreational fishing in park areas, visitor impact on the resource is usually heavy and fish management measures are often necessary.

The environmental needs of fish include cover for protection from their enemies, adequate space, suitable spawning sites, favorable water temperatures, and a year-round food supply.

Possible stream management techniques are the regulation of water flow, temperature, and water fertility; control of competitor fish; watershed protection to prevent siltation and reduce high-water damage; and pollution abatement.[29]

Pools can be built of logs or boulders; these can provide hiding and resting places in streams.

The natural beauty of the stream should be maintained by avoiding the use of materials or methods that give the pool or stream channel an artificial appearance.

The stocking of gamefish is necessary in lakes and streams where waters are deficient in either food or suitable habitat, and sport fishing is an established usage. Advice from fish specialists is advisable before considering stream channel manipulation or other fish improvement projects.

Impact of Visitors on Wildlife

Many animals are wary of humans and are secretive in their behavior. If human pressure becomes too great they will leave the area and a less timid species might move in. Those that move out might perish if they were not able to compete with the resident species of the area they migrate to.

Most visitors do not discriminate between campground hangers-on (the animal opportunists, which increase with the presence of humans) and truly wild species. Most people are as pleased to see a raccoon, which readily adapts to humans, as a badger, which does not. Feeding a Canada jay tidbits from the picnic table provides this visitor with pleasure just as stalking the pileated woodpecker pleases the birder. These opportunist species provide visitors a feeling of being in touch with nature. This contact is part of the attraction of park areas. For these reasons a manager probably need not worry about the withdrawal of the less tolerant species from areas of moderate to heavy use. The majority of visitors will not even miss them. On the other hand, the complete withdrawal of certain animal species may have a serious effect on the park. The loss of owls or hawks, for example, might set loose a population explosion of rodents in the area.

MANAGER RESPONSE TO ENVIRONMENTAL IMPACT

The reader may legitimately ask at this point, now that he or she has read about environmental impact, what can be done about it? At the beginning of the chapter, it was asked what limitations the park manager should impose on the number of park visitors in order to reduce environmental degradation. In some park areas perhaps nothing need be done about it. After all, as some writers have pointed out, parks are for people and will inevitably deteriorate with use. Yet, if the very feature that people came to see is being destroyed by visitor impact, we have a reason to consider protecting the feature. It then becomes necessary to take a hard look at the park we are trying to manage. Some parks are so heavily impacted that the best solution appears to be paving extensive areas. This is the extreme situation, and most readers of this book, it is to be hoped, will not ever find themselves in this unhappy situation. At the other end of the spectrum is the park established to protect and preserve some unique, rare, or special resource. There is no reason visitors should be allowed to destroy such an area, certainly not unknowingly.

In between is the ordinary, commonplace park that is there for visitors' relaxation and enjoyment, to help them get away from their workaday world and where a change of environment is what they are looking for. In this situation there will be considerable impact, but it must be kept under control. Here extensive site manipulation may be needed to hold the soil and vegetation in place, and *some* paving may be necessary.

Visitor impact is largely from visitors doing exactly what they want to do, although poor park design can contribute to impact. Viewing a sunset, walking along a lakeshore, looking out over a view spot, walking to a picnic site, playing frisbee, or simply having a picnic can cause site deterioration if enough people engage in the activity on the same site. Most visitors would not recognize their activities as harmful to the resource. They see themselves as visiting the park for recreational activities and causing deterioration is probably far from their minds—in fact they are usually unaware of it. Even people attending an interpretive activity, presumably to heighten their awareness, can cause site deterioration if the activity is not handled properly.

With a continued increase in use on the same

land base, as is presently happening in North America, and without skillful management, it can be assumed people will eventually trample, pollute, devegetate, and disturb the wildlife throughout the park systems. The need for more intensive management becomes apparent. The park manager may employ direct control measures, indirect control measures, or a combination of the two.

Direct Control Measures

These include controlling soil erosion by planting durable vegetation, spreading bark or wood chips, straw, or gravel on worn areas. Water causing detrimental erosion must be contained.

Trampling of vegetation can be controlled by establishing trails, planting thorny species, or providing barriers.

If campground soil is poor and regeneration slow, additives of peat, wood chips, and fertilizers may be necessary. Planting durable species and watering and protecting them until the soil and vegetation can withstand intensive human activity should be attempted. A complete rest for a season or two may be indicated. Where the site is going to be left bare, such as in a campsite, graveling might be necessary to prevent erosion.

As we saw in Chapter 10, facilities and their location provide not only visitor comfort but they also control or prevent environmental problems.

Indirect Control Measures

Park visitors are seldom aware of the changes effected by sheer visitor impact. Through an interpretive program of educating and informing visitors, and resulting alteration of visitor behavior, the wear and tear on sites can be reduced.

In most instances, it is possible for the park manger to limit the number of people allowed in a park. Certainly the manager can limit, within reason, the conflicting activities of park visitors. Some parts of the park containing unique, fragile, or rare environments may have to be rigidly controlled; perhaps human activity will be proscribed in some areas. In other areas a balance

will have to be attempted between use and overuse. This brings us to a discussion of use limits.

Use Limits

How does the park manager know when a park has reached its capacity? How does one determine that further admissions will cause irreparable damage?

Carrying Capacity. Years ago wildlife and range managers coined the term *carrying capacity* to indicate the numbers of animals that a given habitat could support before the habitat deteriorated from overuse. More recently the catchy phrase has been applied to park management in an attempt to limit the use of recreational lands, either before or after deterioration becomes obvious.

The original intent of using the carrying capacity concept was in determining "how many people were too many." It was concerned with the ecological or biological impact of people on the site. As more researchers and other disciplines got involved, the idea of social and psychological carrying capacity was formulated. This dealt with such things as crowding, noise, esthetics, and the perception of a "park experience."

Some experts in the field define carrying capacity as follows.

That character of use that can be supported over a specified time by an area developed at a certain level without causing excessive damage to either the environment or the experience of the visitor.[16]

The ability of a recreation resource to sustain or support a user population at a measurable threshold based upon specified goals and standards.[20]

Recreational carrying capacity is the level of recreational use an area can withstand, while providing a constant and sustained quality of recreation.[28]

The number of persons for which an area can provide recreation while maintaining the conditions that originally made it desirable for that purpose.[26]

These definitions were not written by park managers but by researchers, people equipped with the sophisticated skills needed to measure environmental or social change. From the manager's standpoint the term *carrying capacity* for recreational use is too imprecise and confusing, and thus relatively meaningless, particularly when research help is not available. Even when standards are established and monitoring takes place, the results may come too late for practical remedial measures. The term "use limits" seems more readily understood, and will be used in the remainder of this discussion.

What recourse does a park manager have? Agency policy has much to say about the number of people that are acceptable on what amount and kind of land. The design of an area also implies certain limits. For example a campground with 30 m (100 ft) spacing between campsites indicates an attempt at providing natural surroundings. A closer spacing, say 10 m (33 ft) provides little chance for maintaining undisturbed area between sites. The first, with four sites per acre, will obviously suffer less impact than the second, with about 17 sites per acre. In this instance agency policy as expressed in campground planning has established the use limits of the area.

Use limits vary with the ability of the park's environmental components to accept human impact. For example, some plant species have greater tolerance than others to human impact. Even the same species can vary in its abilities. Plants growing near the limits of their environmental niche will have much less chance of surviving human impact than those in optimal habitat.[3]

Managers' experience and expectations affect their views. What appears to be a deteriorated site to a manager new to an area, may not have appeared deteriorated to the previous manager, who, seeing the area every day, did not note change taking place. Determining what is acceptable damage or change and what is not acceptable becomes a *judgmental decision*. Thus we see each manager, having a unique set of values, could have his or her own idea of what is excessive environmental impact.

Use limits are elastic. As Bury points out, they can be increased by such management practices as watering, fertilization, and durable species selection. Another means is by hardening the developed sites through the use of gravel, wood chips, and paving. Also, interpretation leading to visitor education can reduce the impact on a site. Finally, shifting use to underused sites can better distribute the visitor load.[3]

There is one slightly different approach to use limits, and this is what Alldredge calls *facilities capacity*. This is the "engineered number of people which installed facilities can handle."[1]

Architects of both buildings and landscapes use capacity concepts when determining the intended use of the features they design. For example, in a visitor center auditorium the number of seats determines how many people will be let in; in a parking lot it is the number of parking spaces that limit access; in a campground it .is vehicles (one per campsite) that control numbers.

The manager must see that this design capacity is not exceeded although the reasons for imposing restrictions are not always obvious. With regard to the visitor center auditorium, it may be for safety reasons imposed by fire regulations; in the parking lot example the motive could be to reduce the impact on vegetation; in the campground it might be prevention of overload in the sewage disposal system. Such common sense limitations of use are easily determined and are certainly within the manager's purview.

There is material available on carrying capacity per se, including the results of considerable research.[25] Interested managers should peruse this literature if the concept seems useful to them.

CONCLUSION

Without some milepost or benchmark, deterioration or its rate is difficult to determine. Studies and photographic records should be made of an area when it is *new* to determine what is there and in what quantity and condition. The environmental impact of visitors must be measured over time; it cannot be a single point determination. Several years of observation are usually needed before an assessment can be made regarding the resistance of the site and the severity of the impact. Historical photos can help, as well as writings and personal accounts, but unless studies of some sort have been made, impacts must be measured with the park's present condition as the criterion.

Ecological transects and plots, photographs, and elaborate lists of plants and animals and their abundance and sociability are needed to determine present levels. Even before the austerity of the late 1970s and early 1980s it seemed impractical and unrealistic to hope for such studies except under the rarest of circumstances.

It thus devolves on the manager to determine as best he or she can the seriousness of the environmental impact, to seek advice from specialists who can offer management suggestions, and to make management decisions based on observations and common sense. Law enforcement and interpretation are other tools available to the manager to help protect park landscapes from excessive deterioration. Park design and the proper number and location of facilities are also factors the manager should be able to count on to help stave off unacceptable levels of damage.

REFERENCES

General References

Aitchison, Stewart W. 1977. *Some Effects of a Campground on Breeding Birds in Arizona.* USDA Forest Service General Technical Report RM-43:175–182.

Armson, K. A. 1977. *Forest Soils: Properties and Processes.* University of Toronto Press. Toronto and Buffalo.

Barton, Michael A. 1969. "Water Pollution in Remote Recreational Areas," *J. Soil and Water Conserv.*, 24(4):132–134.

Beardsley, Wendell G. and Roscoe B. Herrington. 1971. *Economics and Management Implications of Campground Irrigation—A Case Study.* USDA Forest Service Res. Note INT-129. Intermt. Forest Range Exp. Stn., Ogden, UT.

Bogucki, Donald J., John L. Malanchuk, and Theron E. Schenck. 1975. "Impact of Short-term Camping on Ground-level Vegetation," *J. Soil and Water Conserv.*, 30(5):231–232.

Bradley, Jim. 1979. "A Human Approach to Reducing Wildland Impacts," *Recreational Impact on Wildlands Conference Proceedings*, Ruth Ittner (ed.). Forest Service USDA, National Park Service USDI, Seattle, WA.

Chubb, Michael and Peter Ashton. 1969. *Park and Recreation Standards Research. The Creation of Environmental Quality Controls for Recreation.* Tech. Report No. 5. Dept. of Park and Recreation Resources, Michigan State University, East Lansing.

Clark, Roger N. and George H. Stankey. 1979. "Determining the Acceptability of Recreation Impacts: An Application of the Outdoor Recreation Opportunity Spectrum," *Recreational Impact on Wildlands Conference Proceedings*, Ruth Ittner (ed.). Forest Service USDA, National Park Service USDI, Seattle, WA.

Cole, David N. 1978. "Estimating the Susceptibility of Wildland Vegetation to Trailside Alteration," *J. Applied Ecology*, 15(1):281–286.

Cole, David N. 1981. "Managing Ecological Impacts at Wilderness Campsites: An Evaluation of Techniques," *J. For.*, 79(2):86–89.

Cole, David N. 1982. *Wilderness Campsite Impacts: Effect of Amount of Use.* USDA Forest Service Research Paper INT-284. Intermt. Forest and Range Exp. Stn., Ogden, UT.

Cowgill, Peter. 1971. "Too Many People on the Colorado River," *National Parks and Conservation Magazine*, 45(11):10–14.

Dawson, J. O., D. W. Countryman, and R. R. Fittin. 1978. "Soil and Vegetative Patterns in Northeastern Iowa Campgrounds," *J. Soil and Water Conserv.*, 33(1):39–41.

FitzPatrick, E. A. 1980. *Soils: Their Formation, Classification and Distribution.* Longman Inc. New York.

Herrington, Roscoe B. and Wendell G. Beardsley. 1970. *Improvement and Mainte-*

nance of Campground Vegetation in Central Idaho. USDA Forest Service Paper INT-87. Intermt. Forest and Range Exp. Stn., Ogden, UT.

Holmes, Daniel O. 1979. "Experiments on the Effects of Human Urine and Trampling on Subalpine Plants," *Recreational Impact on Wildlands Conference Proceedings,* Ruth Ittner (ed.). Forest Service USDA, National Park Service USDI, Seattle, WA.

King, J. G. and A. C. Mace, Jr. 1974. "Effects of Recreation on Water Quality," *J. Water Poll. Cont. Federation,* 46(11):2453–2459.

Larsen, James A. 1980. *The Boreal Ecosystem.* Academic Press. New York.

Leonard, Raymond and H. J. Plumley. 1979. "The Use of Soils Information for Dispersed Recreation Planning," *Recreational Impact on Wildlands Conference Proceedings,* Ruth Ittner (ed.). Forest Service USDA, National Park Service USDI, Seattle, WA.

Mann, Donald L. and Ken Dull. 1979. "Six Years of Site Restoration at Lyman Lake," *Recreational Impact on Wildlands Conference Proceedings,* Ruth Ittner (ed.). Forest Service USDA, National Park Service USDI, Seattle, WA.

Matheny, Sandy J. 1979. "A Successful Campaign to Reduce Trail Switchback Shortcutting," *Recreational Impact on Wildlands Conference Proceedings,* Ruth Ittner (ed.). Forest Service USDA, National Park Service USDI, Seattle, WA.

Ream, Catherine H. 1980. *Impact of Backcountry Recreationists on Wildlife: An Annotated Bibliography.* USDA Forest Service General Technical Report INT-84, USDA Intermt. Forest and Range Exp. Stn., Ogden, UT.

Schultz, Richard D. and James A. Bailey. 1978. "Responses of National Park Elk to Human Activity," *J. Wildl. Management,* 42(1): 91–99.

Settergren, Carl D. 1977. "Impacts of River Recreation Use on Streambank Soils and Vegetation—State-of-the-Knowledge, *Proceedings: River Recreation Management and Research Symposium.* January 24–27, 1977. USDA Forest Service General Technical Report NC-28.

Teschner, D. P., G. M. DeWitt, and J. J. Lindsay. 1979. *Hiking Impact on Boreal Forest Vegetation and Soils in Vermont's Northern Green Mountains.* Research Note SNR-RM 6. University of Vermont, Burlington.

Tracy, D. M. 1977. "Reaction of Wildlife to Human Activity Along the Mount McKinley National Park Road," unpublished master's thesis, University of Alaska, Fairbanks.

Waggenet, R. J. and C. H. Lawrence. 1974. "Recreational Effects on Bacteriological Quality of an Impounded Water Supply," *J. of Env. Health* 3(1):16–20.

Weaver, T. and D. Dale. 1978. "Trampling Effects of Hikers, Motorcycles and Horses in Meadows and Forests," *J. Applied Ecology,* 15(1):451–457.

Young, Robert A. 1978. "Camping Intensity Effects on Vegetative Ground Cover in Ilinois Campgrounds," *J. Soil and Water Conserv.,* 33(1):36–39.

References Cited

1. Alldredge, Rendel B. 1973. "Capacity Theory for Parks and Recreation Areas," *Trends.* Park Practice Program. NRPA. 10(4):20–30.

2. Buckman, Harry O. and Nyle C. Brady. 1974. *The Nature and Properties of Soils* (8th ed.). The Macmillan Company. New York.

3. Bury, Richard L. 1976. "Recreation Carrying Capacity—Hypothesis or Reality? *Parks and Recreation,* 11(1):22-25, 56–58.

4. Cook, David I. and David F. Van Haverbeke. 1972. "Trees, Shrubs, and Landforms for Noise Control," *J. Soil and Water Conserv.,* 27:259–261.

5. Dotzenko, A. D. 1967. "Effects of Recreation Use on Soil and Moisture Conditions in Rocky Mountain National Park," *J. Soil and Water Conserv.,* 22(5):196–197.

6. Frissell, Sidney S., Jr. and Donald P. Duncan. 1965. "Campsite Preference and Deterioration in the Quetico-Superior Canoe Country," *J. For.*, 63(4):256–260.

7. Farmer, Eugene E. and Bruce P. Van Haveren. 1971. *Soil Erosion by Overland Flow and Raindrop Splash on Three Mountain Soils*, USDA Forest Service Res. Pap. INT-100. USDA Intermt. Forest Range Exp. Stn., Ogden, UT.

8. Geockermann, K. 1972. "Physical Change on Newly Established Wilderness Campsites," unpublished masters thesis, College of Forestry, University of Minnesota, Minneapolis.

9. Greeson, P. E. 1969. "Lake Eutrophication—A Natural Process," *Water Resources Bulletin*, American Water Resources Association, 5(4):16–30.

10. Helgath, Sheila. 1975. *Trail Deterioration in the Selway-Bitterroot Wilderness*, USDA Forest Service Res. Note INT-193. Intermt. Forest Range Exp. Stn., Ogden, UT.

11. Ketchledge, E. H. and R. E. Leonard. 1970. "The Impact of Man on the Adirondack High Country," *The Conserv.*, 25(2):14–18.

12. LePage, Wilbur F. 1967. *Some Observations on Campground Trampling and Ground Cover Response*. USDA Forest Service Res. Pap. NE-68. Northwest For. Exp. Stn., Upper Darby, PA.

13. Leet, Don L. and Sheldon Judson. 1971. *Physical Geology* (4th ed.). Prentice-Hall, Inc. Englewood Cliffs, NJ.

14. Legg, Michael H. and Gary Schneider. 1977. "Soil Deterioration on Campsites: Northern Forest Types," *Soil Sci. Soc. Am. J.*, 41(1):437–441.

15. Leonard, Raymond E. and Sally B. Parr. 1970. "Trees as a Sound Barrier," *J. For.*, 68(5):282–283.

16. Lime, David W. and George H. Stankey. 1971. "Carrying Capacity: Maintaining Outdoor Recreation Quality," *Proceedings, Forest Recreation Symposium*, Syracuse, NY. USDA Forest Service Northeast Forest Exp. Stn., Upper Darby, PA.

17. Lull, Howard W. 1959. *Soil Compaction on Forest and Range Lands*. USDA Forest Service Misc. Pap. 768. Northeastern Forest Exp. Stn., Upper Darby, PA.

18. Manning, Robert E. 1979. "Impacts of Recreation on Riparian Soils and Vegetation," *Water Resources Bulletin*, American Water Resources Association, 15(1):30–41.

19. Merriam, L. C., Jr., C. K. Smith, D. E. Miller, and others. 1973. *Newly Developed Campsites in the Boundary Waters Canoe Area: A Study of 5 Year's Use*. University of Minnesota Agric. Exp. Stn. Bull. 511, Forest Service 14.

20. Pfister, Robert E. and Robert E. Frenkel. 1975. *The Concept of Carrying Capacity: Its Application For Management of Oregon's Scenic Waterway System*. Oregon State Marine Board, Salem.

21. Ripley, Thomas H. 1962. *Tree and Shrub Response to Recreation Use*. USDA Forest Service Res. Note No. 171. Southeastern Forest Exp. Stn., Ashville, NC.

22. Settergren, C. D. and D. M. Cole. 1970. "Recreation effects on soil and vegetation in the Missouri Ozarks," *J. For.*, 68(4):231–233.

23. Sharpe, Grant W., Clare W. Hendee, and Wenonah F. Sharpe. 1984. *Introduction to Forestry* (5th ed.). McGraw-Hill Book Company. New York.

24. Shields, James T. and Gustav A. Swanson. 1971. "Places to Fish and Hunt—The Problem of Access," *A Manual of Wildlife Conservation*, Richard D. Teague (ed.). The Wildlife Society. Washington, DC.

25. Stankey, George H. and David W. Lime. 1973. *Recreation Carrying Capacity: An Annotated Bibliography*. USDA Forest Service General Technical Report INT-3. Intermt. Forest and Range Exp. Stn., Ogden, UT.

26. Sudia, Theodore W. and James M. Simpson. 1973. "Recreational Carrying Capac-

ity of the National Parks," *Guideline.* Park Practice Program. NRPA. 3(3):25–34.

27. Wagar, J. Alan. 1964. *The Carrying Capacity of Wildlands for Recreation*, For. Sci. Monogr. 7.

28. Wagar, J. Alan. 1974. "Recreational Carrying Capacity Reconsidered," *J. For.*, 72(5):274–278.

29. White, Ray J. 1971. "Stream Improvement," *A Manual of Wildlife Conservation*, Richard D. Teague (ed.). The Wildlife Society. Washington, DC.

30. Wilkins, Bruce T. 1971. "Non-harvest Aspects of Wildlife Management," *A Manual of Wildlife Conservation*, Richard D. Teague (ed.). The Wildlife Society. Washington, DC.

31. Yoakum, James D. 1971. "Habitat Improvement," *A Manual of Wildlife Conservation*, Richard D. Teague (ed.). The Wildlife Society. Washington, DC.

32. Zaslowsky, Dyan. 1981. "Looking Into Soles and Other Weighty Matters," *Audubon*, 83(2):60–63.

PART FOUR

USE AND PROTECTION

CHAPTER THIRTEEN

DEPRECIATIVE BEHAVIOR AND VANDALISM

The term *vandalism* is a *management* concept. Youths on their way home after the taverns close don't decide to *vandalize* the street tree plantings—they are just having a little fun, clipping the young trees off with their car bumpers. Teenagers out for a day at a state park want to leave a memento of the visit there and of their feelings for each other—they aren't vandalizing—just carving their names together on an aspen tree. Even the more violent acts of destruction such as wrecking restrooms are no doubt exciting games and challenges to those involved. Their older brothers did it—the guys from another high school or town "wasted a rest stop on the Interstate"—so they too want to show their strength and daring.

The point here is that the term vandalism represents the view from the top. It is a term used by the establishment: owners, managers, taxpayers—not by the perpetrators. Because of this one-sided view, and because the term generalizes and thus masks a complex of acts and motives, it is imprecise. Its imprecision tends to confuse the issue when one is searching for motives or means of abatement.

Users of the words *vandal* and *vandalism* should remember these are not accurate descriptions of a person or an act. It is no wonder that many writers spend a lot of time trying to define and categorize these terms. We will do this too, but let us remember to use these words advisedly and try to see beyond to the person, the setting, and the motive.

WHO ARE THESE "VANDALS"?

The original Vandals were a group of Teutonic tribes active from 400 to 536 A.D. In 406 they crossed the Rhine to Gaul but were driven out. Crossing the Pyrenees, they settled in Spain for a generation. In 428 they set sail for Africa, 80,000 strong. The Vandals forcibly occupied much of Roman Africa, including the port of Carthage, which became a pirate stronghold. In 455 they attacked Rome, systematically emptying it of its treasures and destroying public buildings. Early writers called similar acts "vandalism."[1] Possibly those northern tribes saw themselves as justified in overpowering a careless decadent enemy, and not as wanton destroyers. However, because of their reputed role in the sack of Rome, the word came to be associated with ignorant malicious destruction of the beautiful, the artistic, or the venerable. In modern times the meaning has enlarged to include all sorts of antisocial acts directed toward public or even private property. The implication still remains that those who destroy are barbaric and unappreciative of civilization's benefits.

Looking at the profile of apprehended violators, it appears that today the vandal is not restricted to a specific tribe, income, race, sex, or

Fig. 13-1. Even concrete picnic tables are not immune. Vandalism generally requires no skill or body of knowledge, as do more complicated crimes. (Photo courtesy of National Park Service.)

age group. There is, perhaps, no such thing as a "typical vandal." It nevertheless seems to be true that most persons apprehended in connection with Harrison's definition of vandalism (page 197) are male, and many are in their teens. Petty's study of vandalism in national parks and forests found that over half of all apprehended vandals lived within 35 miles of the vandalized site. Less than one-fourth lived between 35 miles and 100 miles, while the remainder lived over 100 miles away.[21]

Research on vandalism generally pertains to vandalism in schools, churches, public transportation facilities, private automobiles, and homes but may usually be applied to vandalism in park environments as well.

Vandalism generally requires no skill or body of knowledge as do more complicated crimes such as bank robbery, picking pockets, or "hotwiring" a car prior to theft (Fig. 13-1). Given access and the requisite physical strength, almost anyone is capable of vandalism, although at times great ingenuity is used to defeat protective measures.

DEPRECIATIVE BEHAVIOR

As a beginning in understanding the complexity of these terms, we will take the idea of vandalism apart and examine its components. We will do this through another management construct, *depreciative behavior*. This construct might offer a more productive way to categorize the types of problems involved, and will itself enclose a category termed vandalism.

Depreciative behavior is defined as any act that detracts from the social or physical environment. In what is essentially a *result analysis* Harrison uses the following three categories.[15]

Result Analysis

Nuisance Acts. Included in this category are making excessive noise (shouting, playing radios loudly, permitting dogs to bark); allowing pets to run loose; draining camper waste water on the ground; littering; short-cutting trails; picking wildflowers; writing obscenities on walls; defecating on floors, or any other acts the results of which are inherently transitory, although they may in some instances accumulate in permanent damage.

Legal Violations. This category encompasses campground violations (cutting of trees for firewood, camping in closed areas); thefts of park property (signs, tools, tires, gasoline); thefts of visitor possessions (food, cameras, binoculars, money, camping equipment); traffic violations; and any other serious violation of park regulations. In a strict sense, all acts in these three categories are illegal, but there is a difference in management response, and these are the sort for which there are specific agency or civil prohibitions, so a warning or citation is the result (where possible).

Vandalism. In contrast to the two previous categories, vandalism *per se* results in defacement or scars. It is defined here as any *act that willfully defaces or destroys some part of an outdoor recreation area resulting in increased costs to the manager or lessening the appeal of the area to the visitor.* More specifically, vandalism is the damage or defacement of facilities, such as buildings, picnic tables, benches, signs and interpretive devices, or of natural, cultural, or geological features.

In order to arrive at effective preventive techniques, it is important to understand the different types of motives that underlie vandalism. Harrison grouped vandalistic acts by their result. Cohen on the other hand, delineates five *motivational* categories: acquisitive, tactical, vindictive, playful, and malicious.[8] Madison suggests an additional category, which he calls "erosive,"[19] making six in all. He sees the first three as having an objective; they are not mindless, wanton, or meaningless (as he feels is true of the last three) but are committed for personal gain, to attract publicity, for revenge, in spite, or in protest. Although they were formulated on a more general basis, these categories are also directly applicable to outdoor recreation situations. While reviewing these we will try to keep in mind our deprecia-

tive behavior categories (Harrison's result analysis) since this seems the best way to keep a grasp on the elusive subject, and, because results, or *consequences*, are what the manager must deal with, no matter what he or she may be able to discover about motivation.

Motivational Analysis

Acquisitive Vandalism. Acquisitive vandalism consists of destroying property in the process of illegally obtaining money or other desired objects. Examples include looting jukebox coin boxes, metered gas stoves, soft drink and candy machines, fee collection boxes, electricity meters, and telephone coin boxes. Also included are thefts of park equipment, such as park signs and nameplates (for souvenirs), valuable metals (such as brass, copper, or lead, usually for resale), athletic equipment, swing seats, garbage cans, picnic tables, and vehicle parts and supplies, including gasoline, tires, batteries, and tools. (To adhere to our original definition, these would come under the category of legal violations.)

Tactical Vandalism. Tactical vandalism, like acquisitive vandalism, is premeditated, but is not done for the purpose of acquiring money or property. Nor is it an expression of anger; tactical vandalism serves rather as a means of attracting attention or gaining publicity for a special cause. Such attention-getting vandalism may stem from psychological problems, often manifested by excreting in sinks or on toilet floors, or by setting incendiary fires. These must be distinguished from "spite" fires. Publicity-oriented vandalism, as contrasted to attention-getting vandalism, most often takes the form of names or slogans written on park buildings. (Some authors feel this is a form of territoriality.) Smashing windows in order to be arrested and thus obtain food and shelter is another example of tactical vandalism. In addition, employees might purposely jam or break a machine in order to obtain a rest period; this also falls into the category of tactical vandalism.

Most of these actions would fall under nuisance acts and legal violations; perhaps only incendiary fires would result in the willful destruction required for Harrison's definition of vandalism.

Vindictive Vandalism.

Vindictive vandalism is motivated by a desire for revenge on an individual, an organization, or simply the "system." Here vandalism seems to be an outlet or release of emotions for someone smarting under actual or imagined unfair treatment. It may also represent a chance to settle a grudge without resorting to personal violence. Being fired from a job, being discriminated against in job selection, receiving a traffic ticket, or being expelled from the park are frequently cited reasons for vindictive vandalism. The person being victimized is usually an authority figure, such as the manager, a park ranger, or a youth leader, and the active aggression is against property belonging to that individual or to the agency which he or she represents.

Fig. 13-2. The heavy log loading machine used to destroy three picnic shelters, the park restroom, trees, and barrier posts. The machine still holds the rock (lifted from the ground) which supports the park's dedication plaque. The park's facilities were totally demolished. Bingen Marina Park, Washington. (Photo by Daniel Spatz.)

Vindictive vandalism includes such acts as spilling paint over a privately owned automobile or placing bottles under the tires of park vehicles. Smashing park office windows or destroying office equipment are other means of obtaining revenge. Sometimes parks are damaged even when they are not involved in the employee-employer situation, such as in the display of displacement aggression shown when an employee dismissed from an adjacent sawmill later stole a log loading machine and used it to demolish this park's facilities (Fig. 13-2).

Many vindictive acts could be classified as nuisance acts or legal violations. Destruction of office equipment might be costly enough to qualify for the vandalism category, and certainly the destruction pictured in Figure 13-3 would be classified as classic vandalism in Harrison's scale.

Playful Vandalism.

Playful vandalism is the outgrowth of a group play situation, and accounts for a relatively large percentage of the vandalism found in parks. The destructive act is not planned, but grows out of "interstimulation," where one individual excites the others, who in turn further encourage the first person's excitement. Members of the group feel a sense of security in numbers, and regard their vandalism as simply "mischievous fun." Peer pressure causes many individuals to participate in the acts of vandalism which they might not otherwise commit.

Playful vandalism may become a game of skill to see who can do the most damage, such as spray painting the windshield of a park vehicle (Fig. 13-4) or breaking windows in a park building, or insulators on utility poles. Such competition leads to considerable damage, yet participants are often genuinely surprised to learn that their actions are considered serious destruction of property. In many instances the actions are cumulative but not continuous, as successive groups contribute to the destruction of facilities.

The fact that these acts are not willfully done would preclude them from Harrison's definition of vandalism, yet if such acts resulted in exten-

Fig. 13-3. This rubble is all that remains of the park's restroom. The log loader, pictured in Figure 13.2, was stolen at night from the sawmill seen in the background. One of the vandals was thought to be a former employee of the mill who took out his vengeance for being fired on the adjacent park. Bingen Marina Park, Washington. (Photo by Larry Espey.)

sive or costly damages the distinction would be largely meaningless.

Malicious Vandalism.   The stereotypic image of a vandal is drawn from this category, including as it does those who seem to derive enjoyment and satisfaction from plundering, ransack-

Fig. 13-4. A vandalized park patrol truck. Although not serious, this playful behavior does cause inconvenience. Note also the flat tire. (Photo courtesy of Long Island State Park and Recreation Commission.)

ing, and annihilating. Malicious vandals appear to vandalize for the pure excitement of it; wanton destruction is the charge laid to them.

Examples of malicious damage to parks include smashing restroom facilities or office equipment, setting fire to maintenance equipment, running equipment over a cliff or into a lake, sabotaging construction equipment, blowing up pit toilets, plugging sinks then tying water valves open to cause flooding, and pulling up shrubs around park buildings.

Cohen cites several of the feelings that might precede malicious vandalism: "boredom, despair, exasperation, resentment, failure, and frustration."[8] The exasperation, resentment, and frustration would in this case be directed against life in general rather than against a particular agency or person. The violence seems almost cathartic in these cases, perhaps this is why some judges treat it lightly, at least if no individuals were hurt, nor private property damaged. As suggested in the opening paragraph of this chapter, drinking plays a part in this behavior in many ways.

These acts seem to qualify both in willfulness and damage for Harrison's vandalism category.

Erosive Vandalism. An individual act of erosive vandalism might not be damaging, but when repeated by large numbers of people, such acts cause substantial damage. Erosive vandalism may be the result of ignorance, but it may also result from neglect or from disregard for the values of the park. The individuals probably do not regard their actions as harmful, or may feel they

Fig. 13-5. A smooth-barked quaking aspen, a tree easily vandalized by axes and pocket knives. Roy Frank's humor (On my way to Greenland) makes an interesting point. Carvings dating from 1412 would be revered, not decried. Grand Canyon National Park. (Photo courtesy of National Park Service.)

are justified in breaking this rule. Examples of erosive vandalism include shortcutting trails, walking off paths through sensitive vegetation, collecting park objects for souvenirs, picking wild flowers, littering, writing on rocks or walls, and carving names on wood surfaces and tree trunks (Fig. 13-5). These seem to fall within those nuisance acts and legal violations occurring so commonly that permanent damage results.

SEQUENCE OF ACTS IN GROUP BEHAVIOR

Another way of examining depreciative behavior is through the psychology of the group, since certain types of vandalistic acts are rarely solitary and seldom happen spontaneously. Wade suggests that there are five general steps in group acts of vandalism.[29]

Waiting for Something to Turn Up. This is the free, unsupervised time when the group is waiting for an action-provoking suggestion from one of its members.

Removal of Uncertainty: The Exploratory Gesture. At this point a suggestion, either cautious or bold, stimulates action within the group. Boredom disappears as interest develops. Vandalism can be prevented if some group members are convincing enough in the advice to "let it alone" or are able to divert attention to a less destructive form of activity at this stage.

Mutual Conversion. This stage may be brief, assuming agreement is reached, or it may include the need for more persuasion. Here, resisting individuals are under pressure. Should they stay within the norms of society at large, or yield to the standards of this smaller social group? Their courage and "manliness" are being tested by their peers; a dare is usually enough to convince them to go along with the crowd. Any resistance at all is often met with the taunt "chicken." Once the decision is made in favor of the peer group, the stage of mutual conversion is complete.

Joint Elaboration of the Act.   Whether the vandalism will be simple or will develop into substantial destruction depends on how the group interacts. What Wade calls "mutual excitation," that is, competition to see who can do the most damage, contributes to the magnitude of the act. Fritz Redel's phase, "group psychological intoxication," has a similar meaning; such intoxication causes a group to go far beyond its original intentions. Instead of breaking a single window, for example, the group breaks all the windows in the building.[10]

Mutual excitation also reinforces the tendency for the vandalizing individuals to temporarily lose all fear of retribution, since they know it would be almost impossible for authorities to single out one as the culprit.

Once the vandalism begins, it is difficult for any member of the group to slow it down. Instead, vandalism gathers momentum until everything vulnerable is destroyed, or until the group is apprehended or chased from the scene.[29]

Aftermath and Retrospect.   The fact that nothing is stolen during most of these acts of vandalism reinforces the perpetrators' rationalizations that they are merely pranksters, not criminals. Even if apprehended, such persons are consoled by the knowledge that they have peer approval for their actions. Guilt is further lessened by thinking along the lines of "It's only park property," or "The crew wouldn't have anything to do if it wasn't for us."

Not all vandals try to justify their acts in retrospect, however. Some are sorry for the behavior, are glad no one was hurt, and regret not showing better judgment.[29]

While some of these steps may be present in many vandalistic acts, this sequence is most typical of "playful vandalism." In fitting this to the Depreciative Behavior model, it seems it could occur in any of the three categories.

Some Typical Acts

What sort of acts cause problems for managers in North American parks? The following list is representative of the sorts of depreciative behavior that have taken place in recreation areas in recent years.

Bark stripped from live trees.

Boards of nature trail tread ripped up.

Boating safety signs shot up.

Bottles smashed in picnic shelter.

Bulletin board chopped with an axe.

Cars and engine of miniature train overturned.

Cars driven repeatedly over newly planted turf.

Cylinder locks jammed with wood splinters.

Doors on restrooms ripped off.

Doors to pump house pried off with tire irons.

Drinking fountains plugged with sand.

Drinking fountains smashed with sledgehammer.

Electric lights shot out (outside lighting).

Electric meter glass cover broken.

Entrance gate rammed with truck.

Fire weather station shot up with rifle bullets.

Fires built in restrooms.

Fireworks shot off in outdoor exhibits breaking plate glass.

Garbage cans and picnic tables thrown over cliff.

Garbage from cans strewn around park.

Group camp building burned to ground.

Initials carved in smooth-barked trees.

Landscape shrubbery uprooted and left to die.

Lifeguard tower destroyed.

Lipstick smeared on restroom wall.

Locks shot off gates.

Logs and rocks rolled down on park road.

Mirrors smashed in restroom.

Names and dates spray-painted on boulders, trees, and statues.

New tabletop carved with knife.

Paint smeared on walls of historic buildings.

Paper towels stuffed in flush toilets resulting in flooding.

Park benches smashed.

Park interpretive signs damaged with chains.

Park trail directional signs stolen.

Petroglyphs defaced.

Picnic table chopped for firewood.

Pit toilet blown up with dynamite.

Pit toilet burned to ground.

Pit toilet walls riddled with bullet holes.

Protective railing of bridge removed and thrown into river.

Road signs defaced.

Seats in outdoor amphitheater destroyed.

Shower fixtures pulled out of wall.

Spray paint used on park building walls.

Stalagtites in cave smashed.

Sugar poured into gasoline tanks of park vehicles.

Toilet bowls and sinks smashed.

Toilets plugged with plastic bags containing pebbles.

Vegetation destroyed by vehicle leaving designated road.

Wildflowers picked.

Windows broken in comfort station.

Wood shingles ripped loose from shelter.

Wooden bumper rails smashed with automobile.

Wooden interpretative sign repeatedly smashed by cars of drunken teenagers.

This is only a partial listing of the sorts of damage faced annually by park managers. Reading it may be enough to discourage anyone from wanting to work in parks. It may, on the other hand, be viewed as an opportunity to match wits with that section of the public commonly known as vandals, accepting the problems it poses as a challenge. If the latter is the case, knowledge of psychology and sociology will help, as well as an understanding of parks and facility design, and an appreciation of the need for prompt maintenance. Personnel in heavily vandalized parks are often depressed about the situation and consider combating vandals a hopeless task, since more keep coming as others "grow up." Perhaps most important of all is keeping a sense of humor despite the incursions of lawless tribes into "our territory."

Where and When Vandalism Takes Place

Vandalism and other depreciative behavior can take place anywhere and at almost any time, but are most likely to occur at certain favorable times and places.

Where These Acts Occur. Public property is more likely to be vandalized than is private property, since it is depersonalized and more readily abused by persons who rationalize that it "belongs to everyone," including them. Parks that are heavily vandalized are frequently secluded, dark, and covered with trees; vandalism, of course, is greatest in areas that are infrequently patrolled, hidden from public view, or which the ranger or police patrol cannot see into. Areas with extensive facilities suffer more vandalism than do areas with few facilities, since there is more to vandalize. Flimsy facilities also encourage vandalism as do facilities inappropriately located. Placing a visitor information exhibit shelter in the middle of a space once used as an impromptu athletic field is asking for vandalism. Facilities in disrepair are often looked upon as fair game. Vandalism is also frequent in buildings that are nearing completion but are not yet occupied, as well as in closed or abandoned buildings.

When These Acts Occur. Vandalism increases during the spring and summer. In early spring, near the end of the school year, high school and college groups hold beer parties in parks, and some damage often results. As weather grows warmer and park attendance rises, the incidence of vandalism rises too. Vandalism is also to be expected before or on Halloween, since the tradition of disturbing both public and private property at that time still persists. The park manager should be on the lookout at all times of the year for announcements of festivals, initiations, parties, and sporting events, the aftermath of which may contain potential for vandalism. The superintendent of a Canadian city park in Halifax stated that vandalism happens mostly late at night, after 2 to 3 A.M., and when school terms are starting or finishing.[23] Finally, facilities left unprotected overnight or longer (such as over weekends) are most susceptible to vandalism. Even in the daytime, little-used areas or facilities are in danger of being damaged when there is no one in the vicinity to discourage or report such behavior.

THE PARK MANAGER'S OPTIONS

It is ultimately the responsibility of the park manager to prevent or reduce all depreciative behavior in parks. Yet what works in one situation may not in another, and reading the available literature on the subject will not necessarily provide a specific solution. In fact, popular articles on vandalism may give rise to false hopes of easy success, while after more extensive reading, the manager might be so confused as to not know what approach to take. Unfortunately, much of the writing on depreciative behavior and vandalism is based on wishful thinking rather than on facts.

The writers of design articles feel that better-designed park facilities are the solution. Equally strong arguments are presented by authors favoring maintenance, law enforcement, education, and other options. Clark urges caution in searching the literature for "an answer to vandalism,"

pointing out that there is no single solution to the problem. He suggests that the manager weigh each "solution" carefully in terms of the specific situation, identifying unsubstantiated claims and avoiding reliance on data that are the result of poorly conceived research.[7]

In any instance, the reasons for the more serious acts of vandalism in parks are usually beyond the purview of the manager. They range from students' resentment toward homework, conflicts between youth and parents or teachers, "practical jokes," energetic high spirits, sylvan rites of passage, drunkenness, and disregard for public property, to serious psychological problems. Perhaps the vandal comes from a transient family, lives in a deteriorating neighborhood, or is somehow alienated from school and community. On the other hand, the offenders may well come from middle- or upper-income homes, drive to your park in expensive cars, and go home to a loving family. Most apprehended vandals are not able to explain their actions, or provide us with any insight into their behavior. So, we have to draw our own conclusions from several sources.

It is often said that young people lack respect for people's property. Not all vandalism involves young people and property loss, but much of it does. Teenagers are surrounded by older people's property; they realize respectability and status rest on ownership of material goods. They, however, have few possessions and less status. Thus Scott feels that teenagers are faced with an untenable situation regarding property values. While waiting to become adults, they are expected to spend several years of their lives in a state of "suspended animation." Lacking property and status, and resenting this, they may lack respect for the property of others.[25] If this is extended to public property, it may suggest why certain types of vandalism take place in parks and other public places.

Faced with these problems, what can managers do? Identifying the major cause and then creating opportunities to communicate with people who visit parks just to let off steam, have a little fun, or show off in front of their peers is a start. Learning to recognize the potential vandal without suspecting every park visitor is also important. These are public relations goals toward which conscientious park managers must strive. Von Kronenberger tells us that bringing vandals back into society and keeping nonvandals from leaving it is a critically important venture that all of us should become involved in.[28]

The park manager is not in the youth guidance or juvenile counseling business. No doubt he or she feels as helpless as the rest of us to prevent the millions of dollars of damage caused annually by vandalism to public schools, libraries, museums, transportation devices, street trees, telephone booths, and other favorite targets on public and private lands. Managers must try to protect their parks, however.

Vandalism in parks not only causes great financial loss—some agencies report spending between 10 and 20 percent of their entire budget on vandalism repairs amounting to many millions of dollars annually—but also affects the visitor's experience in several ways. Repair or replacement costs must often be met by funds that have been diverted from visitor services or from expansion of park facilities. For example, $25,000 expended for vandalism repairs would build several new campsites, picnic sites, or contribute substantially to a park's interpretive program. Vandalism also increases park employees' workloads, taking them away from other maintenance chores and thus lessening the beauty and appeal of the park. The visitor also suffers when irreplaceable objects or unusual resources are destroyed. Disfigurement and scarring of park features is irritating and unsightly, and obscenities scrawled on walls detract from the enjoyment of many families visiting a park. Finally, visitors lose when facilities that can contribute to the understanding and enjoyment of an area are not installed because of vulnerability to vandalism.

Understanding and friendship toward youthful park visitors is always a wise policy. Christensen and Clark point out that managers' attitudes are often part of the problem.[4] Developing a good relationship with the local schools is another long-range approach. Sponsoring special events such as photo contests, park cleanup days, improvement projects, environmental education opportunities, and other means of attracting youth into the local park for constructive activities can help reinforce a sense of ownership and propriety. Some suggest hiring an identified and notorious vandal as a caretaker or maintenance helper.[1]

Young people want attention, recognition, and understanding not only from their peers but from adults as well. Discovering that the local ranger is human, a nice person who gives people a break, may help bring about some changes in attitudes. Vindictive vandalism at least, should decrease. Unfortunately, a new crop of potential vandals is growing up each year. However, those persons who have, through the manager's efforts, gained a wider understanding of intelligent park behavior may not vandalize later in life and may think about constraining others from doing so.

Suggestions for Reducing Vandalism

Although attempts to reduce vandalism are difficult and discouraging, a passive approach is even less satisfactory. Successful long-range reduction of vandalism may be possible on further research into its causes; in the meantime, programs to encourage citizen responsibility both in children and in adults should also help alleviate the problem. Some interesting possibilities now being considered include various curriculum changes in schools and well thought out television publicity campaigns.[26] Another approach is live-in host caretakers. The fact that someone is nearby to hear and report damage immediately seems to have a deterrent effect.

There is a strong possibility that we will always have to endure a certain level of vandalism, but perhaps it can be reduced. In the meantime, the following suggestions, both tested and untested, might have some bearing on the readers's situation. Further ideas on vandalism control are found in the references listed at the end of the chapter.

Design of Facilities. The list on pages 201 and 202 shows that facilities are the prime target for acts of vandalism in parks. An extreme solution would be to remove all facilities from park areas. However, since facilities are put in parks for the comfort and convenience of park visitors and for protection of the park environment, removing them would be a drastic solution, and one not possible under most agency public service mandates.

Better-designed facilities are often proposed as a solution to damage cause by vandalism (Fig. 13-6). Weinmayer, for example, feels that 90 percent of all vandalism could be prevented through design.[30] A new manager often inherits poorly designed facilities and soon becomes aware of their vulnerability to vandalism, but may feel that little can be done until they are replaced.

When facilities are replaced, the strongest materials available should be used. The higher initial cost that this entails is justified in the long run.[9,18] Architects should consult with seasoned

Fig. 13-6.   A restroom designed to deter vandalism. The posts, walls, floor, and roof are concrete. Discovery Park, Seattle. (Photo by Grant W. Sharpe.)

park managers about facilities and vandalism. Both the architect and the manager should also be aware of new materials that offer some degree of protection from vandalistic assault.

Buildings. Buildings and their interiors are common objects of careless or depreciative behavior, or outright vandalistic attack. Making buildings visually pleasing yet physically strong enough to withstand vandalism is difficult, and probably not the manager's responsibility. None-the-less, the manager must often approve design plans, and should become acquainted with recent advances in vandalism prevention. For example, building design and location should make it impossible to gain access to the roof by climbing fences, walls, trees, or the outside of the building itself (Fig. 13-6). This precludes footholds on outside walls and strong shrubs or trees near buildings.[31]

Buildings themselves, particularly wooden pit toilets, are vulnerable. Where possible, these should be replaced with concrete block toilets; however, wooden pit toilets will probably remain part of the park scene in small campgrounds and as a winter toilet facility when flush systems must be closed because of freezing weather. Tipping over pit toilets is the classic act of vandalism, and park managers probably should resign themselves to it, possibly classifying it as nostalgic vandalism.

Building walls are often defaced with graffiti applied with lipstick, felt marker pens, crayons, pencils, and pens. Preventive measures include using wall material with textured rather than smooth surfaces. Outside walls must be able to withstand weathering and yet be inexpensive to maintain. Suggested outdoor materials include brick, concrete blocks, and rock. Inside, a smooth, nonporous material such as tile is preferred, since it is easy to clean and requires no painting. Glazed brick with a smooth surface is difficult to write on and is also easy to wash.

Spray paint represents another problem. Special coatings protect against some sprays, as they will wipe clean. The use of commercial paint-removers of the water-washable type is recommended. Frequently, a supply of the various types of solvents is needed to deal with different types of sprays.*

Restrooms. Restrooms are the favorite target of many vandals. Grosvenor gives an interesting history of the response of Forest Service architects to these assaults, emphasizing design and materials.[14] Suggestions for safeguarding these facilities include hiding all sink drain pipes from view, removing glass mirrors and paper towel holders (use metal mirrors and electric driers), and using push-button faucets and bathroom and shower fixtures which protrude as little as possible. Glass windows should be covered with heavy wire (hardware cloth) screens, or replaced by heavy plastic or thick glass brick windows. Windows with shutters or fiberglass skylights might also be used. Sinks and bowls made of reinforced thermo-setting polyester resins are comparable to steel in strength and weight.[2] Stall doors have been removed in many toilet facilities, on the premise that the privacy afforded fosters depreciative behavior.

Tables and Benches. Wooden tables and benches are attractive, inexpensive, and comfortable to picnic or sit on but are tempting to carve. Using wood planks for seats and tops in combination with precast concrete or pipe bases makes refinishing or replacement of wood parts easier and less expensive. New materials of polyvinyl chloride plastics, which resist carving, may also be used for seats and tops. One park director found that pastel picnic tables were better taken care of, more often washed after use, and less subject to carving than were unpainted tables,[24] but how many park managers could tolerate pastel-painted picnic tables?

---

*Information may be obtained by writing the National Paint and Coatings Association, 1500 Rhode Island Avenue, N.W., Washington, DC 20005.

Drinking Fountains. Survival of the drinking fountain depends on both construction and location. There is probably no fountain that is completely vandal proof, since the vertical shape, the spout, and the necessity for a drain makes it particularly vulnerable. Masonry and rock structures have always been popular, but are more expensive than the commercial porcelain type. All types present some people with irresistible challenges.

Location can deter vandalism to some extent. A fountain out in the open with paved paths leading to it is less subject to damage than is a secluded one near sand or rocks, which might be used as ammunition to demolish it, or to plug up the drain. Although not the most handsome model, a pipe attached to a wooden post is the least expensive water fixture to install or replace.

Fireplaces and Grills. These are usually waist-level charcoal stoves mounted on a standpipe, or ground-level forms of various descriptions. The waist-level types need to be theftproof, since the stove could be used at home in the backyard. The ground-level fireplace must be of material that can withstand sudden heat changes such as dousing with cold water to put out the fire. A simple grate set in concrete works best. The British Columbia Provincial Parks Branch is using an elegantly simple concrete ring for its amphitheater fireplace to confine the fire and the toxic effect of the ashes.

Signs. Signs are necessary for welcoming visitors and informing them about park facilities and features. They point out hazards and scenic areas and carry regulations and interpretive messages. Signs are vital to park management; unfortunately, they are also easily vandalized. Signs with negative messages such as ''Don't walk on the grass'' (as opposed to ''Please use paved paths'') are most frequently vandalized. Briefly explaining the reason for the regulation may lessen vandalism as well as obtain a greater degree of compliance. For example: ''Please wash dishes at your camp. Washing dishes here eventually causes the gravel drain to plug with grease'' is better than "No Dishwashing!" This strategy will probably do nothing to deter the malicious vandal but should decrease the ignorance or resentment that results in depreciative behavior.

Construction material should be considered carefully. Hand-routed wooden signs are pleasingly rustic, but are expensive to replace. Wooden and metal signs can be mass-produced at low cost using a silk screening process. Metal signs are good if their surface is scratch resistant, but they make a satisfying noise when shot at, and are therefore less desirable where hunting is permitted.

Sign location and the lighting of signs could reduce vandalism. They should be well anchored in concrete and protected from vehicles by barrier posts.

Park Lighting.   In cities, floodlights set atop tall poles provide security for public property. Lighting has also been found to be an effective deterrent to vandalism and theft in parks. High-intensity discharge lighting systems (HID) provide a light source covering a very large area. The presence of such lights in a building compound helps protect visitors as well as park property.[13] As Donahue puts it, "One light is worth five watchmen, because lighting discourages vandals and encourages full day use."[9] Letting lights burn all night in restrooms also acts as a deterrent to vandalism. Of course lights are a favorite target of vandals. Bulbs can be protected by screens or high-impact plastic.

Plantings.   Trees and shrubbery are often damaged by the "playful" vandal and are frequently stolen for use elsewhere or for resale. Where the planting of exotic species is not forbidden, thorny trees and shrubs such as thornapple, honeylocust, wild rose, bayberry, prickly ash, cat brier, and pyrocanthus are discouraging to these vandalistic acts. Such plantings also eliminate what Knudson calls "involuntary vandalism" (i.e., erosive vandalism or nuisance acts) by keeping people on trails as much as possible.[17]

Maintenance.   There is circumstantial evidence that good maintenance practices discourage depreciative behavior and help combat vandalism. The manager certainly hears about it from park visitors when an area is not clean and well maintained, but whether or not good maintenance actually prevents vandalism is unknown since no controlled research has yet been conducted. It can't be denied that clean and recently installed facilities do get vandalized, but vandalism seems to be reduced by keeping an area clean and immediately repairing or replacing vandalized objects. And it often happens that carvings on picnic tables or signs and writing on restroom walls inspire imitation. Once the first mark or remark is there, others follow in short order. While the influence which prompt maintenance has on controlling vandalism needs more study, it should certainly be practiced as a matter of policy, along with other preventive methods. Maintenance is discussed at length in Chapter 11.

Removing Temptation.   Managers should see to it that their employees do not tempt vandals and thieves by leaving doors unlocked, tools at job sites, or keys in vehicles or construction machinery. Vending machines with their tempting coin boxes should be placed in hallways or other areas open to public view, so that visitor traffic can help discourage theft. If theft from vending machines continues unabated, managers may have to remove them completely. Some success has been achieved by labeling vending machines with such signs as "This machine emptied of all cash each evening" or "This machine equipped with a silent alarm."

Closing little-used areas as the season draws to an end is another way to remove temptation from the paths of some potential vandals but, on the other hand, users who find a favorite camping spot blocked off may vandalize gates and vegetation in their attempt to get to it.[4]

Valuable artifacts must not be placed where theft is possible. Replicas should be exhibited and should be so identified in order to discourage the would-be thief.

User Fees. Some managers have reported less vandalism in areas where a user fee is imposed, but others believe that fees cause increased vandalism by making users feel they have the right to do as they wish. Fees are usually imposed on sites that are more developed (i.e., areas which have more facilities), such as traffic counters, fee collection stations, traffic barriers, a water supply, and flush toilet buildings. In contrast, free areas may have only tables, pit toilets, and a water source.

There are no reliable data to support the opinion that fees reduce vandalism or that they increase it. It is difficult to attribute reductions in vandalism to the fee system alone. The fact that a fee is collected means that park personnel are present at least periodically and their mere presence may act as a deterrent (Fig. 13-7). On the other hand, some managers are convinced that even minimal user fees have a positive effect on the type of visitors an area receives. The collec-

tion of fees is usually a policy matter, differing with each agency. Rather than being conceived of primarily as a method of vandalism control, the imposition of a fee usually aims at several objectives, including the recovery of some operational costs. Fees are considered at greater length in Chapter 6.

Surveillance. Surveillance is nothing more than keeping watch over facilities and people in parks, and is no doubt the greatest deterrent the park manager has against any form of depreciative behavior. A vigilant manager and staff could prevent all acts of this sort if they could be everywhere in the park at once. Since this is not possible, specific areas must be visited frequently, with increased patrolling during known problem periods. The schedule of a patrol in easily identifiable cars is quickly learned by the clever vandal or thief. Thus a varied schedule and travel pattern and occasional use of unidentified vehicles is recommended to throw the potential vandal off guard. Special patrols with well-trained personnel are necessary in troublesome areas.

The astute park manager will maintain a good liaison between park staff and local police, who might be more willing to help if kept informed of park vandalism problems. Caretakers, night watchmen, and citizen patrols are good supplements to the regular park staff in reducing vandalism. Park employees should have training in surveillance, and should know how to recognize potential vandals, and how to spot thieves on a "shopping tour" of the park.

Special equipment is sometimes useful in park areas where the incidence of vandalism is high. Two-way radio hookup between key employees and ranger patrol cars is helpful. Monitoring areas or buildings with closed-circuit TV is also useful. Larger parks or those near cities may have access to helicopter surveillance during critical periods.

Another useful tool, described by Reeves, in use in the Ravenswood Children's Center in East Palo Alto, California, is the intrusion detection

Fig. 13-7. The presence of uniformed personnel at park and campground entrances serves in some measure to deter vandalism. Mactaquac Provincial Park, New Brunswick. (Photo courtesy of New Brunswick Department of Tourism.)

and alarm system, which includes two basic protection systems.[22] These are (1) *perimeter protection*, where every entrance point—window, door, louver, or vent—is mechanically equipped with a device to signal movement, and (2) *space protection*, where the movement of an intruder within a area under surveillance is detected by either microwave or infrared detectors. Both security systems are compact, tamperproof, and low in cost compared to their effectiveness in protecting buildings containing valuable artifacts and equipment.[21] Any alarm system, either a noise alarm or a silent, monitored alarm system should be given extensive publicity since knowledge of the existence of such systems tends to discourage vandalism.

The campground host program has had favorable results in several ways, according to reports. Here a retired couple lives in the campground, and acts *in loco parentis* for the campers and potential vandals. Apparently an increase in voluntary compliance with the campground fee system was noted, as well as improved protection of the area.[4]

Law Enforcement. One key to reducing vandalism in its various forms is law enforcement. It is important that park employees know the laws pertaining to vandalism and that they operate within them. In order to be in any way effective as a deterrent to vandalism and other crimes in parks, law enforcement must end in punishment, so that potential vandals know that if caught they will face punishment.[16]

The chances of capturing the culprits are enhanced if surveillance is strong, but unfortunately, capture does not always guarantee a conviction. In prosecuting a case of vandalism, two things must always be demonstrated—first, that the damaged property had a value, and second, that the act was willfully committed with the intent to harm or destroy.[27] In minor acts of vandalism the elements necessary for prosecution do not exist.

Many prosecutors and judges are unfamiliar with the extent of serious vandalism problems in parks. Some courts might regard vandalism as a form of recreation: "After all, isn't that what parks are for?" After a mild rap on the knuckles, the offender goes free and the judge goes on to more serious matters. Perhaps the park managers will have to make their problems known to the court and general public and secure cooperation from the judiciary, including, if necessary, heavier penalties for vandalism. The news media can be very helpful in preparing the climate necessary to achieve these goals. (See Chapter 5, Politics).

The prosecutor also has considerable discretion as to whether or not to prosecute. In some instances there are offenses that a district attorney (prosecutor) will not press because of political consequences.

The park manager must have a working arrangement with local police in order for park employees, often not trained in police work, to know how to handle the apprehended individual suspected of a crime in the park. The park manager must understand that if he or she decides to drop charges on a person apprehended for vandalism, these former charges cannot be taken into consideration if the vandal is apprehended again.

There is much to know in making an arrest, holding persons once they are arrested, making a search, collecting evidence, and testifying in court. These topics are covered in Chapter 15, Law Enforcement.

Another important point is the visibility of the conviction. If a vandal is convicted and punished, potential vandals must know about it if law enforcement is to succeed in deterring further vandalism. "Where laws are enforced, crime goes down."[27] The cooperation of the news media is helpful here also.

The manager might be reluctant to prosecute an individual apprehended for vandalism. Matthews suggests several significant reasons for this: (1) fear of reprisal against the organization or individual, (2) uncertainty and lack of confidence in initiating action against violators, and (3) reluctance to make a "fuss" over rather insignificant acts. Such vacillation may well encourage depreciative behavior of all kinds. Law enforcement officials, for example, are reluctant to give full cooperation to organizations that have consistently failed to prosecute apprehended violators.[20]

Education and Public Involvement.   Education and public involvement are long-range methods that try to reach the public with messages that will presumably lessen vandalism. The intent is to instill a positive attitude toward parks and other public areas. Park environments have an advantage over other public areas in that they

Fig. 13-8.   Humor and practicality make this an arresting poster. (Courtesy of National Park Service and California Department of Parks and Recreation.)

offer natural settings that can be appreciated in many different ways. Managers and interpretive staff can encourage positive attitudes toward park values, particularly natural and cultural history offerings, through a well-planned series of slide programs and show-me tours of the park. If signs are used, the wording should tell the visitor *why* he or she can't do something, rather than simply listing negative imperatives. The public, including potential vandals, can better appreciate parks and other natural areas if they are informed as to the correct attitude and behavior in these settings (Fig. 13-8).

Involve Teenagers.   Youth programs aimed at park improvement are worthwhile, and include, as mentioned above, park cleanup days and other improvement projects that develop a sense of pride and identification with the goals of the park. The likelihood of youngsters vandalizing something they have helped create seems quite remote. Another possibility is sponsoring a vandalism prevention poster contest in the elementary grades at the local schools, thus involving the preteenagers in publicity, judging, and presenting prizes. Schoolchildren welcome a slide show about park animals, and if they come to your area later on a class field trip, you've made some friends. While this may not deter vandals, it might make noninvolved youths less tolerant of such activities, and perhaps more willing to speak out against them.

Managers sometimes invite vandalism. A manager who is unnecessarily hostile to teenagers can expect retaliation. As has already been noted, much vandalism is committed by males about 15 years old who live nearby (less than 30 miles from) a park. Without guidance and given the opportunity, youths of this age group can cause problems. Young people must be helped to realize their responsibilities and recognize the temptations that come with their growing freedom. They too must obey the law or suffer the consequences. Providing projects for teenagers, as suggested above, can help them develop a sense of responsibility and duty. For those who cannot be contacted in this way, surveillance and friendly patrols are probably the best that can be done.

The following suggestion has worked in some city parks, but might not be appropriate in more remote recreation areas: managers have permitted certain walls in parks to be used for self-expressive and decorative graffiti, where teenagers can vote for their favorite musical group or express various shades of feeling for their peers and the world in general.

As mentioned previously, some successes have been reported in involving the culprits in prevention of vandalism. This presumes a degree of control over the apprehended vandals that is not always possible, but where feasible, certainly it is worth trying. Perhaps the courts could be presented with information on this kind of restitution and prevention program, so that sentencing judges could consider it.

Involve Parents. When parents ask what they can do, the manager can suggest that parents know where their children are at all times when not in school. The manager should also put together a set of slides on vandalism in the park to inform the local community. Discussing records of annual repair costs, and showing how they have prevented the park from constructing facilities or have forced early closure could also be effective. It is the people's park, so the manager should share the problems with them.

The manager can also work for the enactment of parental responsibility laws, which make parents directly responsible for the actions of their children and permits suit to be brought against parents for recovery of damages incurred by their offspring. Parents faced with the costs and embarrassment of a court case will presumably make a greater effort to keep their teenagers out of trouble.[12]

Involve the Visitor. Researchers have found that recreational visitors prefer not to get involved in stopping vandalism and other acts of depreciative behavior that they may witness.[3,5,6] Indifference, fear of personal threat, or not knowing how to report an incident are among the reasons for this noninvolvement, as is the attitude "That's what rangers get paid for." Clark suggests people be shown how to handle the situation themselves, and be encouraged to report suspicious activity to park rangers so that rangers can take action. This is done by telling the visitor in advance "we have a problem here with violations of park rules. If you see any violations please report them to a ranger." Some visitors will report observed violations when questioned about an incident. CB radio operators will report observed violations when asked. This may be because they can do so without being noticed. Offering a reward for information about vandals has also been suggested.[7] In any case, the knowledge that their concern will be courteously heard and investigated might well encourage people to be more cooperative (Fig. 13-8). Visitors should be encouraged to think of parks as well-ordered places of beauty and relaxation, which should be defended against immature rowdies or malcontents wishing to give vent to their frustrations. In situations involving erosive vandalism, pointing out the result of certain behaviors to other visitors, as well as personally setting a good example can be helpful, if visitors will undertake to do this.

CONCLUSION

Park environments lend themselves to certain types of behavior, some of which may be depreciative or lead to vandalism. Some damage to park property is unavoidable, often accidental, and must be regarded as part of the cost of running an outdoor recreation area. On the other hand, much depreciative behavior is preventable; even costly deliberate vandalism can sometimes be circumvented. Park managers need to exert their best efforts to curb this drain on their budgets and time. If a manager has success in dealing with a problem he or she should let other managers know about it. Although solutions may not always be exportable, beleaguered managers need all the help they can get.

There is research being done on these problems; managers would be well advised to seek out and read some of the many reports available. Perhaps cooperating with researchers can provide an antidote to vandalism frustration.

REFERENCES

General References

Alfano, Sam S. and Arthur W. Magill. 1976. Technical coordinators of *Vandalism and Outdoor Recreation: Symposium Proceedings*. Includes 24 papers giving an overview of vandalism in outdoor recreation areas. USDA Forest Service General Technical Report PSW-17. Pacific Southwest Forest and Range Exp. Stn., Berkeley, CA.

Butler, James R. 1980. "The Role of Interpretation as a Motivating Agent Toward Park Resource Protection," unpublished doctoral dissertation, College of Forest Resources, University of Washington, Seattle.

Clinard, Marshal B. and Richard Quinney. 1973. *Criminal Behavior Systems: A Typology*, (rev. ed.). Holt, Rinehart and Winston, Inc., New York.

Clinard, Marshal B. 1974. *The Sociology of Deviant Behavior* (4th ed.). Holt, Rinehart and Winston, Inc., New York.

Dopkeen, Jonathan C. 1978. *Managing Vandalism*. Parkman Center for Urban Affairs. Boston, MA.

Schaffer, E. B. 1975. "The Roots of Vandalism," *Royal Society of Health Journal*, 95(2):79–82.

Stanley, Edwin J., Robert E. Meyers, and Anthony Gomez. 1972. *Guiding the Development of Youth Behavior in Recreational Settings*. A Handbook. Recreational and Youth Services Planning Council. Los Angeles, CA.

Ward, Colin (ed.). 1973. *Vandalism*, Van Nostrand Reinhold Company, New York.

Williams, Lance E. 1977. "Vandalism to Cultural Resources of the Rocky Mountain West," unpublished master's thesis, Department of Recreation Resources, Colorado State University, Fort Collins.

Wilson, George T. 1961. *Vandalism—How to Stop It*, American Institute of Park Executives, Management Aids, Bulletin No. 7.

References Cited

1. Alfano, Sam S. and Arthur W. Magill. 1976. "Recommendations," *Vandalism and Outdoor Recreation: Symposium Proceedings*. USDA Forest Service General Technical Report PSW-17. Pacific Southwest Forest and Range Exp. Stn., Berkeley, CA.

2. Anonymous. 1974. *California Parks and Recreation*. Aug./Sept. 30(4):14.

3. Campbell, Frederick L., John C. Hendee, and Roger N. Clark. 1968. "Law and Order in Public Parks," *Parks and Recreation*, 3(12):28–31, 51–55.

4. Christensen, Harriet H. and Roger N. Clark. 1978. "Understanding and Controlling Vandalism and Other Rule Violations in Urban Recreation Areas," *Proceedings of the National Urban Forestry Conference*, Washington, DC.

5. Clark, Roger N., John C. Hendee, and Frederick L. Campbell. 1971. *Depreciative Behavior in Forest Campgrounds: An Exploratory Study*. Bulletin PNW-161. USDA Forest Service, Pacific Northwest Forest and Range Exp. Stn., Portland, OR.

6. Clark, Roger N., John C. Hendee, and Frederick Campbell. 1971. "Values, Behavior, and Conflict in Modern Camping Culture." *Journal of Leisure Research*, 3(3):143–159.

7. Clark, Roger N. 1976. "Control of Vandalism in Recreation Areas—Fact, Fiction, or Folklore?" *Vandalism and Outdoor Recreation: Symposium Proceedings*. USDA For-

est Service General Technical Report PSW-17. Pacific Southwest Forest and Range Exp. Stn., Berkeley, CA.

8. Cohen, Stanley. 1973. "Property Destruction: Motives and Meanings," *Vandalism*, Colin Ward (ed.). Van Nostrand Company. New York.

9. Donahue, Ron. 1968. "How to Handle Vandalism," *Camping Magazine*, 40 (May): 24–25.

10. Eliot, Martha M. 1954. "What is Vandalism," *Federal Probation*, 18(1):3–5.

11. Encyclopedia Britannica, Inc. The University of Chicago.

12. Furno, O. F. and L. B. Wallace. 1972. "Vandalism: Recovery and Prevention," *American School & University*, 44(11): 19–20, 22.

13. Gaines, Dan M. 1973. "Lighting up the Parks," *Parks & Recreation*, 7(5):34, 49–50.

14. Grosvenor, John. 1976. "Control of Vandalism—An Architectural Design Approach," *Vandalism and Outdoor Recreation: Symposium Proceedings*. USDA Forest Service General Technical Report PSW-17. Pacific Southwest Forest and Range Exp. Stn., Berkeley, CA.

15. Harrison, Anne. 1982. "Problems: Vandalism and Depreciative Behavior," *Interpreting the Environment* (2nd ed.), Grant W. Sharpe (ed.). Wiley. New York.

16. Jeffery, C. Ray. 1971 *Crime Prevention Through Environmental Design*. Sage Publications. Beverly Hills, CA.

17. Knudsen, George J. 1967. *Techniques to Reduce Vandalism on Nature Trails*. Annual Workshop of the Association of Interpretive Naturalists, Oglebay Park, Wheeling, WV.

18. McCrea, Edward J. 1972. "Vandalism on Private Campgrounds," unpublished master's thesis, Pennsylvania State University, University Park.

19. Madison, Arnold. 1970 *Vandalism The Not-So-Senseless Crime*. The Seabury Press. New York.

20. Matthews, Robert P. 1970. "Theft and Vandalism in Western Washington Forests," J. For., 68(7):415–416.

21. Petty, Paul. 1966. "Vandalism in Natural Forests and Parks," unpublished master's thesis, Colorado State University, Fort Collins.

22. Reeves, David E. 1972. "Protecting Against Fire and Vandalism," *American School & University*, 44(9):62–66.

23. Reitelman, Michael. 1979. Personal communications with Jim Nickerson, Superintendent, Point Pleasant Park, Halifax, Nova Scotia.

24. Reynolds, Jesse A. 1967. "Public Disregard, Vandalism, Littering, Increase Workload," *Parks & Recreation*, 2(10):39, 40, 50.

25. Scott, Chester C. 1954. "Vandalism and Our Present-day Pattern of Living," *Federal Probation*, 18(1):10–11.

26. Sissons, Ron. 1976. "Can We Stop Vandalism in Our Parks?" *California Parks & Recreation*, Feb./Mar., 32(1):33–34.

27. Skellenger, Robert. 1967. "Vandalism—What We Can Do About It," unpublished paper. Presented at University of Michigan, Ann Arbor.

28. von Kronenberger, G. R. 1976. "Vandalism: A National Dilemma," *The Elks Magazine*, 54(9):12–14, 20, 36, 55.

29. Wade, Andrew L. 1967. "Social Process in the Act of Juvenile Vandalism," *Criminal Behavior Systems: A Typology*, Marshall B. Clinard and Richard Quinney, eds. Holt Rinehart and Winston, Inc. New York.

30. Weinmayer, V. Michael. 1969. "Vandalism by Design—A Critique," *Landscape Architecture*, 59(4):286.

31. Zeisel, John. 1974. *Planning Facilities to Discourage Vandalism*. Presentation made to American Association of School Administrators, Atlantic City, NJ.

CHAPTER FOURTEEN

CONFLICTS

Conflicts over land rights—or territories—have been with us since the beginning of time. They will continue so long as life exists on the face of this earth or in space. The recreation area manager will be primarily concerned with three different types: (1) the conflicts between recreational and nonrecreational users of the land, (2) the conflicts among recreation users themselves, and (3) the conflicts between recreation users and management agencies and their personnel.

To get a perspective let us take a look at the past. An understanding of their historical aspects should assist in seeing these conflicts calmly as part of an ongoing adjustment in land use. As pointed out in Chapter 1, the use and abuse of public lands is not a new issue.

A BRIEF HISTORY OF LAND-USE ATTITUDES

The following quote from Ernie Swift in the National Wildlife Federation's book, *The Glory Trail*, outlines the early conflicts.

Shortly after the Colonial Revolution, lands having naval stores and ship timbers were set aside. But with an embryo republic being ceded land from the original colonies and later acquiring the Louisiana Purchase, California and the southwest from Mexico, the young nation was much like a lumberjack with a quart of liquor under his belt and $2 in his pocket. It

owned the world and insisted on giving it away. Land was a drug on the market.

Land was given to the states, to the veterans of successive wars; sections were set aside for the development of school systems; it was purchased or fraudulently acquired by speculators; it was made available to settlers through various devices of purchase and homestead; it was given away to canal companies; and, millions of acres of the most fertile land together with additional millions of acres of the finest timber that looked up to the heavens were ceded to the freshly blossoming industry—the railroads.

The creation of the Forest Service did not end the fight—no indeed. But it marked the high tide of exploitation and the meager beginning of resource management and some restraints. [13]

Public and political interest was stimulated during the 1860s and 1870s as a result of two trips west. In 1859 Horace Greeley not only went west but publicized his trip to Yosemite. The portentous exploration of Yellowstone Country by the Washburne-Langford-Doane expedition took place in 1870. Citizen interest in the West increased. Political pressure to arrest exploitation grew, mainly through the efforts of conservationists and publishers. One manifestation of this interest and pressure was the effort to establish national reserve lands.

In 1864, administration of the Yosemite Grant was transferred to California in order to better protect it. It became part of the national park in 1906. Yellowstone (Chapter 1) was set aside in 1872, but without any funds to operate it. In 1891 the Forest Reserves, later called National Forests, were established. The Antiquities Act of 1906 gave the executive branch a method of protecting choice lands until such time as Congress might be persuaded to mandate protection.

Each time regulations and restrictions were proposed or enacted, conflicts were generated. Timber, mining, grazing, and railroad fortunes were involved, huge payrolls were affected, homesteaders were shut out, taxpayers were concerned with new demands on the budget, and the esthetic conservationists began to organize.

In the early twentieth century recreation on public lands was typified by automobile and tent campers (Fig. 14-1) as well as by hunters, fishermen, and hikers. However, it was limited by the Great Depression in the 1930s. At the same time, the federal government assisted outdoor recreation through the work of the Civilian Conservation Corps and the Works Progress Administration.

In the aftermath of World War II the stimulated economy brought a higher standard of living and a wider range of travel. Increased mobility within our society as well as economic and social trends helped to create a desire for outdoor recreational opportunities. Leisure ceased to be defined in negatives, and vacations became mandatory. The idea of "getting away from it all" somehow became entangled with the admonition "Be prepared!" and recreational vehicles were

Fig. 14-1. North Americans are heirs of a well-established tradition of camping out, starting with the native peoples, and continuing through the pioneers. The advent of the model-T Ford strongly revived the practice. A recreation vehicle, 1924 style. (Photo courtesy of Yellowstone National Park.)

hatched. These were soon followed by off road vehicles (ORVs), trail bikes, and snowmobiles.

During the 1960s there was a sharp increase in the recreational use of public lands. This increased use was not always taken into account in federal or state agency budgeting or by management and other personnel, who were often slow to adjust attitudes and methods in order to cope with this influx. As mentioned in Chapter 3, the Outdoor Recreation Resources Review Commission (ORRRC) outlined what resources were available and how people would want to use them. From this, and from a growing body of research, an understanding of the North American situation has finally emerged. Land and water must be managed to protect the resource, park visitors must be educated and regulated to provide for their understanding and safety, and the ensuing conflicts must be researched and met in a manner reasonably acceptable to all. Budgets must reflect these needs at all levels—a most formidable challenge!

In many ways the development of land-use attitudes in Canada paralleled those of the United States. Historians of the conservation movement have observed two streams of thought in the early days of the park movement in both the United States and Canada. One group argued for a "usefulness" type of conservation—the "rational" use of natural resources. The second group called for strict control of natural resource exploitation, and the preservation of unique environments. In the United States, the national parks adhered more closely to the "preservation" theme, whereas the national parks of Canada followed the "usefulness" stream of conservationist thought, at least in the early years. The first national park in Canada was established at Banff Springs in 1885, just 14 years after the establishment of Yellowstone National Park in the United States.[10] The creation of Algonquin Provincial Park in Ontario, which occurred in 1893, stressed the desirability of "government regulated logging, wildlife protection, and the potential for hotel- and cottage-style vacationing."[9]

Camping out and all its related activities—hiking, skiing, swimming, boating, running, biking, even the use of recreational vehicles in park settings—are now perceived as necessities by millions of North Americans as well as by visitors from other continents who come here to partake of these outdoor amenities. Some enthusiasts want space, quiet, solitude, pure air, trails through vast tracts unmarred by human endeavor; others expect well-groomed interlocking trail systems leading off from conveniently located facilities with hot water and electrical outlets. These groups will be in conflict with one another at times. Motorized groups bother hikers and horses, and on occasion, even each other. It seems that one person's recreation can be another person's annoyance.

The struggle over recreational lands is not limited to user groups but affects administration too. New agencies dealing with these lands have been created. Established agencies have awakened to the extent of their involvement. From *Reality and the Middle Ground*, we read the following.

Conflicts also develop between various entities of government and between existing resource uses contesting for the available capital. Higher levels of government are frequently able to establish higher priorities and exercise authorities over lesser levels of government. Such priorities and authorities have on more than one occasion been exercised to the detriment of recreation. Additionally, the resource allocations are nearly always made in favor of the use for which identifiable and quantifiable benefits can be calculated. Here again, recreation is virtually assured of being relegated to a secondary role."[11]

The above paragraph was written in 1948, but the problem of intragovernmental wrangling is still with us. Even though there is now more land set aside and, relatively speaking, more money available for recreation, the skirmishing continues between agencies and user groups and among the agencies themselves, with constantly shifting alliances. In all probability these conflicts will continue although their intensity and scope will no doubt vary with changing economic, social and political conditions.

We now discuss the manager's three main areas of concern, as mentioned in the beginning of this chapter.

CONFLICTS BETWEEN RECREATION USERS AND NONRECREATION USERS

Timber Management

Some hikers, backpackers and other recreationists are disturbed by timber harvesting and silvicultural methods that severely alter the ground cover. Many fishermen are irritated by the effects of logging practices and road construction on fish habitat. Swimmers complain about manufacturing wastes that adversely affect the appearance and quality of the beach, as well as the water. The recent concern for air quality and fuel conservation has brought about increased criticism of slash burning, while debate continues about the practice of clearcutting.

However, as with all conflicts, there is another side to the story. Many forest fires are started by thoughtless campers or sparks from ORVs. Snowmobiles damage the terminal buds of snow-buried evergreens, causing tree regeneration problems similar to those caused by deer or elk. Vandalism continues to plague landowners; broken gates and locks, stolen or damaged logging equipment and damaged signs are common problems. And if clearcutting bothers the environmentalists, tree theft angers timber growers.

Logging has been practiced in several Canadian parks and is very controversial. In the past, timber harvesting has taken place in Strathcona Provincial Park (B.C.) and in Quetico Provincial Park (Ontario), but current management policies have eliminated logging activities. Logging is still practiced in Algonquin Provincial Park (Ontario)

and some adverse impacts have been recorded.[3] Selective cutting of hardwoods has resulted in very poor browse for large ungulates, such as the deer. Since one of the main reasons tourists have come to Algonquin Park is to view deer, it is apparent that logging practices, although perhaps well intended, have been counterproductive for recreation objectives.

The issue of forest fire management is contentious, at least in the Ontario Park System. While many people realize that timber management practices such as controlled burns approximate natural processes, this practice has not been adopted by the Ontario Park System; instead, natural fires are suppressed. Fire suppression in the past has led to the growth of overmature forests in which natural forest fire hazards are severe. To allow natural forest fires to run their course in overmature forests would be catastrophic.

Minimizing Conflicts. Certainly it is true that wood and paper users—and this includes all of us—have to recognize that the accustomed comforts of civilization require raw materials, and that a clear-cut hillside has a very direct connection with our comfortable, even luxurious, North American standard of living. Also, certain recreational activities are in part dependent upon clear cuts or are facilitated by logging roads. Fortunately, there are the following ways to minimize the undesirable effects, both real and perceived, of timber harvesting.

1. Interpretation of timber practices to provide understanding of management methods and goals. Those groups most concerned about timber management should be approached with carefully chosen methods. A slick color film is not going to convince knowledgeable backpackers. They need show-me trips, short slide presentations by on-the-spot personnel, and a chance to pose hard questions and get honest answers.

2. Provision of buffer zones to screen the more

unsightly stages of timber regeneration, especially from major highways, and where possible, from trails.

3. Use of irregularly shaped cutting units that more nearly conform to natural clearings.

4. Greater care in transport of logs and disposal of debris near fish-breeding waters.

5. More imaginative efforts to make use of logging slash. No matter how convincing the economic argument, burning huge amounts of air polluting fuel simply to get rid of it cannot be unquestioningly accepted in today's fuel-conscious and environmentally aware society.

Watershed Management

As with timber management, there are also conflicts among people of sincere convictions over watershed management. What is a watershed? Miller, in *Our Native Land* tells us that:

> A watershed is a land area through which water flows on its way to a larger body of water. Watersheds include the original small streams of rainwater or melted snow that feed into larger bodies of water, such as rivers and lakes. Watersheds vary greatly in size and shape. Everyone lives in a watershed of some kind.[8]

Watershed management programs usually benefit the whole of society in one way or another. Yet the very magnitude of watersheds cause most people to identify benefits and drawbacks from the same project. For example, dams provide irrigation and power, control floods and create a reservoir for water-based recreational activities. These same dams also destroy stream fishing, some forms of hunting, and the beauty of the free-flowing rivers, although they replace the latter with their own form of beauty.

Watersheds for municipal drinking water are sometimes placed off limits to recreation users, and this often causes confusion, as in some areas (where tertiary treatment of water is undertaken) watersheds are open to recreation. Conflict not only exists between the watershed managers and the potential users but also involves medical people and other public health specialists who are concerned with over use, contamination, and litter.

The impacts of watershed management on recreation environments is an emerging issue in Canada. The development of the James Bay Power Project in northern Quebec altered several major river systems and their environments. Although not designated as a wilderness area or park, this type of ecosystem is currently underrepresented in the Parks Canada systems planning strategy, and so there is controversy over its development.

In Ontario, the Madawoska, Spanish, and Missinaibi are outstanding recreational rivers, but their future is constantly debated in terms of their potential to supply hydroelectric power. In British Columbia, the Stikine River faces similar pressure.[3] Also in British Columbia, the Campbell River on Vancouver Island was dammed in the past to provide hydroelectricity on Vancouver Island. When this dam was constructed the watershed was logged according to specifications of the time. The reservoir, known as Buttle Lake, is a significant feature of Strathcona Provincial Park. Unfortunately, when water levels are low, the stumps of this logged-off watershed are clearly visible, and detract from the spectacular landscape.

This same problem exists in many reservoirs in the United States, where at the time of logging, specifications for stump height were not as stringent as they are now.

Minimizing Conflicts. Some of the conflicts over dams of various kinds can be minimized by stressing the contributions of the project to the residents of the area through interpretation. This should be both on site (for visitors to the project) and off site (through slide programs made available to clubs and other groups) and by means of publications and articles in newspapers.

Various remedies for specific problems relating

to dams and reservoirs are available, such as trapping and trucking anadromous fish around dams, and creating shallow impoundments in reservoirs to provide natural plant feed for birds.

In the case of watersheds containing municipal water reservoirs, limiting the type of recreation equipment and the type and amount of use allowed, as well as providing suitable sanitation facilities should be considered. Managers of recreation areas involving dams and reservoirs should not be insensitive to the controversial nature of these projects, even though the necessity of the project might seem undeniable. Present-day visitors may be sophisticated consumers but are frequently disinterested in, if not downright hostile to, the mechanics of civilization such as irrigation or power generation. Managers must seek to identify the nature of conflicts and misunderstandings with an eye to alleviating them, as well as trying to interest the public in the way such utilities function.

Wildlife

Where park rules preclude hunting or allowing natural fires to burn, changes have taken place in the faunal composition that negate the policy of leaving the area unchanged. Large populations of elk have created overgrazing problems, for example, in Yellowstone National Park and the Canadian Rocky Mountain parks. Exotic animals such as the mountain goat in Olympic National Park and burros in Grand Canyon have caused problems for visitors, as well as for native fauna and flora.

Some animals, such as bears and poisonous snakes, can be dangerous to people and destructive of their belongings, although the amenity values of these animals seem greatly to outweigh the safety hazards. There is a history of this sort of conflict in the Rocky Mountain parks of North America, and the issue is hotly debated by managers, biologists, the legal profession, users, and nearby residents. On a less urgent level, insects such as mosquitoes and deerflies are often a nui-

sance to recreationists, and the matter of spraying or not spraying is controversial.

Minimizing Conflicts.   Park managers need to be abreast of agency policy as well as public sentiment in these matters, and act with discretion. Where the large herbivores and carnivores move beyond park boundaries, it may be necessary to establish buffer zones to prevent conflicts with adjacent ranchers. In some instances it may be necessary to fence certain areas. In addition resource managers should (1) listen and converse with people on both sides of these issues, (2) seek and study the technical advice of scientists, (3) consult with other groups who are involved in the same situation, and (4) develop carefully worked-out policies and seek to make them intelligible to the communications media and to the general public. It is of the greatest importance that visitors to parks with dangerous species be adequately forewarned and instructed in safety procedures.

Livestock

Cattle grazing is occurring with greater frequency on recreation lands. Areas having profuse growth of grasses are vulnerable to range fires in the dry season and grazing can reduce the accumulation of fuel. Having become accustomed to the cowboy mythology, we may take cattle grazing on the open range for granted, but there are those who believe that grazing causes undesirable changes and perhaps unacceptable damage to the range ecosystem. Certainly it subjects the range plants to the selective pressure of cattle grazing in addition to that already exerted by native species such as deer, antelope, and elk.

The desire of sheep ranchers to exterminate predators (especially coyotes) has resulted in confrontations with environmentalists, nature enthusiasts, and recreationists. Exploding "coyote getters" are dangerous to hikers, campers, and anyone else using public lands. Poisoned carcasses create esthetic as well as contamination problems, especially near fishing streams and streams popular with campers. Poisons kill non-target species of birds and mammals. Predator control programs upset recreationists who consider their outdoor experience enhanced by the presence of any and all wildlife. Recreationists and conservationists anger sheep ranchers who consider their livelihood threatened by these species and by what they consider to be the environmentalists' selfish and ill-informed meddling.

Competition for food between livestock and big-game animals results in conflicts between hunters and ranchers. Species such as deer, elk, and bighorn sheep sometimes compete for the same foods as domestic sheep and cattle.

Minimizing Conflicts. The resource manager will have little influence on the management of livestock that is grazed on private lands. Those resource managers who manage open or range lands will be exposed to the difficulties, but will also have some channels for minimizing conflicts, including (1) being certain that all such lands have established animal month units (AMU), which estimate the number of animals that can graze in a given period of time without damage to the vegetation, (2) careful posting of these lands so the general public will be aware of the presence of the livestock, and (3) interpretive programs aimed at targeted conservationists and rancher organizations and presented at their meetings. This task must be handled by open-minded, well-informed personnel who can stand firm amidst the crossfire of outraged animal lovers and furious ranchers.

Mining

Mining and recreation activities conflict in several ways, although usually not as dramatically as in previously mentioned conflicts.

Today we find many abandoned mines and accompanying mine shafts in wilderness areas. It must first be noted that mining is a congressionally approved activity within most wilderness areas under the Wilderness Act, and is also al-

lowed in certain classes of Canadian national parks. Where mines are still active they bring criticism for pollution and visual disruption, but such mines must operate under certain restrictions, and a climate of mutual tolerance should be fostered.

Abandoned shafts create serious safety hazards to hikers and ORV users and many constitute "attractive nuisances" to youthful explorers. To some, old mining machinery is an eyesore, while to others it is a reminder of a moment in history. The results of strip mining continue to offend the traveling public, not to mention the local environmentalists.

Another conflict is caused by water passing through shaft mines and running over and out of open-pit mines. Depending on the type of mine, adjacent streams may be found to have quantities of metals lethal to waterfowl.

Minimizing Conflicts. There are very few if any practical ways to minimize the adverse effects of mine-caused water pollution except to post the area. However, there are ways of alleviating the safety and esthetic problems of mines. Boarding up mine shafts will usually be short lived in effectiveness as enterprising explorers will soon open the most entrance-proof of barriers. High barbed fencing is one of the best deterrents, especially when accompanied by explanatory signing.

Historical interpretation gives recreationists a better understanding of the importance of mining today, as well as in the past. Proper screening of open-pit mines and strip-mined areas, along with planned landscaping, can mitigate the visual impact.

Highways and Roads

Environmentalist movements and inflationary pressures have brought new superhighway building to a virtual halt. Some highways and access roads are still being constructed, however, and logging roads remain an issue generating lively controversy.

Minimizing Conflicts. Certainly park managers need to be alert to point out the potential impact of any new roads or highways on their areas and to be ready to try to mitigate harmful effects if construction of these is unavoidable.

Ways are being found to convey visitors about the parks by jitney buses and aerial trams. Federal funds have been provided for highway beautification and abutting bicycle routes. Scenic and recreational highway systems are being created in some jurisdictions. Roadside rests in some areas are not only stops, but places of beauty and enjoyment with interpretive and directional materials available (Fig. 14-2).

The era of unthinking acceptance of new highways is probably over in much of North America. The situation calls for intelligent long-range policy decisions, as indeed, do all of the conflicts dealt with in this chapter. A political climate that fosters professional expertise and allows for wide public input will serve the resource and the recreationists best in the long run. In North America we can hope for this ideal, although it will not always be realized.

Native Rights

In Canada many provincial and national parks have been established in areas where native groups live or continue to hold some form of tenure or land-use privileges. In these parks, and also in the new national parks and monuments in Alaska, native peoples retain the right to hunt, fish, or trap for subsistence foods or materials (Fig. 14-3). While at first glance this may appear to contravene the conservation principle of wilderness management, it must be remembered that native people have interracted with these environments for thousands of years. Their subsistence activities for the most part have not jeopardized wildlife or natural features, and so, it can be argued, the continued subsistence activities of native people is a part of this natural environment. Conflicts, of course, are bound to occur from time to time between park managers and native groups over resource extraction within parks.

Nonconforming Uses

All of the foregoing topics involve conflicts between recreational and nonrecreational use of the land. There is another type of conflict brought about when the resource agency receives a request for a nonconforming use, often to erect a structure that is not related to recreational pursuits. Such structures might well include television or radio station antennae, civil defense buildings, or housing for personnel not employed by the park agency.

To handle such problems, most agencies adopt policies that assert that the agency is firmly opposed to the placement of any facilities that will adversely affect public recreation or despoil the natural environment. While such policies declare that public recreational needs and park values are paramount to any other use, they usually

Fig. 14-2. Roadside rests contain more than toilet facilities. Most are equipped with large parking lots, picnic tables, pet runs, and many have groves of trees screening adjacent land uses. Some also have interpretive and informational exhibits. Interstate 5 near Wilsonville, Oregon. (Photo courtesy of Oregon State Highway Department.)

Fig. 14-3. Eskimo people harvesting seal in the newly designated Cape Krusenstern National Monument in Alaska. Subsistence fishing and hunting by traditional means will continue in this and other newly established federal parks and monuments in Alaska. (National Park Service photo by Robert Belous.)

contain some statement that might allow exceptions. For instance, it might state that conflicting uses shall be considered only when no feasible alternative exists, and public welfare, safety, or necessity clearly requires the use of the site.

Given good legal counsel and the sensitivity of the public to encroachment on park areas, the integrity of parklands should be defensible.

CONFLICTS AMONG RECREATION USERS

Even though there are and always will be conflicts between recreational users and nonrecreational users of the lands under management, by far the greatest clash of personalities and the most vigorous forwarding of mutually exclusive objectives occurs among the users themselves. There is even conflict among devotees of the same sport, since levels of expertise and degrees of specialization exist within all activities. These problems can only increase, as in the future there will be less land on which to recreate and, presumably, there will be more people desiring to do

so. Further complications will arise from the fact that people will probably have even more time and more money to spend in recreational pursuits. Less gasoline at higher prices will also increase the intensity of the conflict by narrowing the choice of areas available for recreation.

The following examples of conflicts among user groups relate to specific uses, types of development, and areas. The list is not meant to be all inclusive, but rather, to provide examples of a variety of conflicts.

Hunting

There are basic conflicts between those who hunt and those who don't hunt as well as conflicts among the hunters themselves. There are nonhunters who are not necessarily against hunting but who do view hunting as a single-use activity and are critical of the large amount of land it requires. There are other nonhunters who object to hunting itself. These people generally lodge their complaints in one of the following three sweeping indictments.

1. The animals need to be saved from hunters. The balance of nature will keep the animal population in check without interference from the hunters.
2. Hunters lose their sense of judgment when pursuing wildlife and endanger other land users, as well as themselves.
3. Hunters trespass, vandalize signs and buildings, strew litter, start uncontrolled fires, harm livestock, and illegally cut trees for firewood, camp furniture, and tent poles.

On the other hand, the hunters feel strongly about their rights, and point out the following:

1. They pay their own way by purchase of expensive licenses.
2. They also help pay the way of nonconsumptive users such as birders, photographers, and backpackers.
3. They provide food for their families through their own efforts.
4. They help control excess numbers of animals.

The hunters themselves have conflicts concerning such items as length of hunting season, the best methods of conservation, and how to instill outdoor manners in those careless hunters who give the rest a bad name.

Minimizing Conflicts. Hunters, nonhunters, and resource management personnel must continue to strive to reduce these conflicts. Some ways include (1) increased enforcement to protect private property from trespass and vandalism, (2) separate seasons or zones for various types of hunters, (3) hunter information, training and safety programs, and (4) more widespread information for the general public on the place of hunting in wildlife management.

Off-Road Vehicles

Off-road vehicles include dune buggies, motorcycles and snowmobiles, and any other motorized land vehicle capable of travel in areas without roads. Nearly all of the conflict related to ORVs is between those who ride them and those who don't. There is very little disharmony among the ORV users themselves, except perhaps between the two wheelers and four wheelers.

As previously noted in this chapter, ORV users are accused of many illegal and irresponsible acts. Complaints against these riders include frightening wildlife, stampeding cattle, making too much noise, creating of hazardous situations for horseback riders, destroying vegetation, damaging roads, dropping litter, and invading the privacy of hikers, campers, canoeists, cross-country skiers, and snowshoers.[4] Although some of the accusations made against them are not substantiated, there can be little doubt they cause serious management problems and that most other recreationists have a difficult time accepting ORVs as a harmonious part of the backwoods scene.

Underaged motorcycle riders may sometimes be observed operating their machines dangerously on public roads in wooded areas. The problem is further complicated by the fact that some of the benefits to ORV operators stem from the risk of operating their machines in a challenging environment.[1] Thus, managers' responses to safety hazards may reduce the value of the experience.

Minimizing Conflicts. ORVs are often used in areas not designed to accommodate them. Managers often lack sufficient enforcement authority, funds, and personnel to cope with the problems presented. As Bury suggests, ORV policy should be directed by management objectives that will determine the amount of ecological change that could be tolerated and the types of outdoor experiences to be provided.[1]

Ideally, ORV areas and trails should be located and designed in such a way that minimum disturbance occurs to the natural environment, to other recreationists, and to local residents (Fig. 14-4). The location, size, and design of such areas should be planned in close cooperation with various ORV user groups, foot and horseback

Fig. 14-4. Trailbikers assemble on national forest land in South Carolina in an area set aside specifically for their use. The trail system includes separate trails for different levels of skill. (USDA Forest Service photo by Dave Devet.)

trail users, environmental experts, and affected public and private landowners. A park manager opening a section of an existing park to ORVs should carefully study all of the potential ramifications of such use.

ORV users should be reached by off-season interpretive programs tailored for their group. Acquainting ORV users with agency problems and stressing the need for self-regulation, while informing them on subjects of interest will often result in excellent cooperation. Resource managers will usually find these people eager to use their equipment in cooperative and helpful ways such as cleanup or rescue work.

Horseback Recreation

ORVs conflict with horseback recreation through the creation of noise, which can spook horses. Backpackers carrying sleeping bags high on their packs and thus masking the human silhouette, or wearing raingear over their packs and themselves, also scare horses. On the other hand, few hikers who have traveled a trail also used by horses have not complained about mud, manure, and the startling effect of a horse and rider suddenly looming up as one rounds a turn.

Overgrazing of meadows and damage to tree roots and trunks where horses have been tied, as well as damage to wet trails early in the season are chronic problems for managers. Rider groups complain of inexperienced park personnel and improperly planned facilities (Fig. 14-5).

Parks and recreation areas close to cities are experiencing problems of overuse. As areas urbanize there usually is an increase in riders with a corresponding decrease in available land.

Minimizing Conflicts. In some areas it may be necessary to prohibit early season use of trails until they dry out. Careful construction of horse trails might help reduce this sort of erosion also.

These conflicts, like so many others, can be minimized by better education of the user groups

Fig. 14-5 User groups should be consulted before specialized facilities are built. This tie stall shows little evidence of use. Most riding horses are kept in pastures and are not used to such confinement. Riders avoid the resultant problems by not using the tie stall. (Photo by Grant W. Sharpe.)

themselves to the problems of the resource and the needs of other users. Most organizations have a newsletter, and these can be an effective means of communication for the resource managers involved. The horse group can improve their image by practicing minimum impact, offering help with backcountry projects, and appealing to the trail ride leaders to police their own groups when traveling in the backcountry.

The manager can, in consultation with the horse groups, provide properly constructed trailer turnarounds, campgrounds, trails, and hitching racks; can limit party size; and perhaps require that feed be carried for all stock. When possible, off-season use should also be encouraged. Other users of these areas must learn tolerance and realize that horseback groups have a right to use most public lands, as indeed, do motorized groups. Mutual forbearance must be fostered in every possible way.

Primitive versus Developed Recreation

Conflicts between primitive and developed recreation exist in issues of land allocation and in the management of areas already set aside for nature preservation or dispersed recreation. These con-

flicts are evidenced both in philosophy and in actual practices, and manifest themselves in consideration of new areas, as well as in any changes proposed in the development, use of, or access to existing areas. Often the struggle centers around whether to improve public access to an area or leave it undeveloped for those willing and able to travel by primitive means. Easy access means loss of solitude and contact with primitive natural conditions. Dispersed recreation advocates want to exclude mass recreation.[7]

Everhart points out that psychologists feel the love of wilderness can be traced to a longing to get away from other human beings as much as to an urge to find some private scenery. He further notes an interesting phenomenon "that those who speak with disdain of the 'hordes' of park visitors somehow are able to use the same facilities without being a part of the horde," and comments that few who argue for restricting park use volunteer to be among those excluded.[2]

Minimizing Conflicts. One obvious method is to locate the developed campgrounds on forest or park fringes and the primitive recreation sites in the interior, providing a range of opportunities for campers. These areas would be in addition to designated wilderness areas, which should try to preserve natural conditions by avoiding any development. Separation of the two sorts of uses should help reduce conflicts in management philosophies and reduce recreation pressures on designated wilderness areas. Some of these more remote areas should contain no facilities, some should contain trail systems with shelters, and others should have trail systems with hostels. Access should be provided also to important scenic areas and natural attractions through controlled public transportation such as aerial trams, cog railways, and buses. These would provide a window on primitive areas without impacting them, and allow the general public some sense of participation in, and enjoyment of, these reserves.

All this presupposes new areas with enough funds to carry out such a logical plan. In reality, managers are faced with areas already laced with conflicting use patterns and a dearth of funds to effect any remedies. The same solutions must be tried here as in other conflict resolution—good communication with user groups—perhaps even asking them for input on problem solving. Skillful use of volunteers (see Chapter 8) might help provide control of some situations. Observation of other areas with similar problems often generates fresh thinking and might lead to some regional solutions. Professional workshops on these conflicts are also helpful.

Water-based Recreation

Problems here consist primarily of water-skiers and other motorboaters conflicting with activities such as canoeing, river floating, fishing, or swimming. Adverse effects of motorboats, with or without water-skiers, include noise, wave action eroding banks, oil film left on the water, disturbance to fishermen, and the safety hazard to other boaters as well as to swimmers.

Swimmers, including snorklers and scuba divers, need a safe environment and do not want to

Fig. 14-6 A water skiing regulation sign showing hours, season, speed limit and course location, and four basic rules. Flowing Lake County Park, Snohomish County, Washington. (Photo by Grant W. Sharpe.)

be threatened by fishermen, ski boats, or other motorboat use. They are especially vulnerable to injury from propellers of motor boats, as well as from gas and oil film resulting from operation of these boats.

Many problems associated with waterskiing are simply those of motorboats. These problems are magnified due to the larger motor size needed to pull a skier, the surface area requirements of waterskiing, and the problems of driving the boat with sufficient caution when concentrating on a skier's needs.

A relatively new source of conflict in water-based recreation is river traffic, including hand-propelled craft, jet boats with short-run sightseers, and river floaters on rubber rafts. The people in hand-propelled craft may well resent the noise and numbers of users associated with rafts and motorboats of all types, while bank and boat fishermen may be disturbed by any intrusion into their fishing areas.

Minimizing Conflicts. Probably there will be continuing conflict among water-based recreationists. The interface between land and water naturally attracts large numbers of users, so this area must be zoned where several uses coincide. Zoning can be by size of boat, horsepower, or by space or time (Fig. 14-6). Fishing and waterskiing could be allowed in the same waters by alternating days of use, or by *time zoning*, which permits the different activities at different times of day.[6] Waterskiing and boats with large motors could be kept off small lakes and ponds simply by excluding ramp facilities. On small ponds, limiting use to electric motors would eliminate problems of noise, excessive speeds, and fuel pollution. The use of booms and buoys, signing, and educational approaches also help to alleviate problems, particularly those of safety.

The sanitation problems associated with river floating can be overcome by portable toilet devices. Zoning on rivers can assist the different user groups in finding a space to enjoy their particular form of boating with minimal distraction. Interpretation aimed at making peace among the users and protecting the resource has proven to be helpful in some areas.[12]

Bicyclists, Roller Skaters, Skateboarders, Joggers, and Pedestrians

People in these five categories, plus automobile drivers, all travel at different speeds. When they use the same route there is bound to be conflict. In the city, neighborhood streets and sidewalks were designed originally to separate pedestrians and vehicular traffic for safety reasons. Joggers or runners—newcomers on the scene—frequently must make do with streets or sidewalks, even though these hard surfaces are not desirable, and here they must compete with established uses. Some use school or gymnasium tracks, but park settings with soft running surfaces and more pleasing surroundings are preferred.

Bicyclists, too, frequently have to use streets and sidewalks not designed to accomodate them. Special bicycling, jogging, and walking paths are being set aside in many areas. Unfortunately, removing the car from the scene does not solve all the problems, for these three uses are sometimes in conflict with each other.

Minimizing Conflicts. Green Lake Park in Seattle, Washington, contains a paved, circular path that accomodates pedestrians, joggers, and cyclists. This path is a heavily used facility, 5 km (3 mi) long and approximately 3 m (10 ft) wide, circling Green Lake. The asphalt path has a white stripe down the middle, and stenciled signs designating the inside for foot traffic and the outside for nonmotorized cycle or skating use. Cycle use is restricted to counterclockwise, one-way traffic with a speed limit of 16 km/h (10 mph). Joggers and walkers are permitted to go in either direction and may use the surfaced path or the jogger-beaten strip adjacent to the paved surface.

Even with this separation of users, conflicts persist. According to Wilder these include (1) bi-

cyclists, pedestrians, and joggers riding, walking, and running in the wrong lanes, (2) bicyclists riding in the wrong direction, (3) bicyclists exceeding the speed limit, (4) groups of users occupying the entire width of the path, blocking movement by others, (5) dogs, on or off leashes, running back and forth across the path without warning, (6) park users, especially small children, stepping into or across the path without looking first, (7) inexperienced bicycle riders weaving and making abrupt stops and, (8) bicyclists and joggers weaving in and out around slower traffic (Fig. 14-7). These problems result in numerous collisions and bad feelings, and the present overcrowded situation reduces enjoyment of the path for all participants.[14]

This so-called "solution" to bicyclists, joggers, and pedestrian problems might seem to have produced chaotic results but according to Mary Koch, a senior supervisor at Green Lake Community Center, there has been a pattern of accidents and complaints for a time after each new use is added. This is followed by a decrease in conflict, implying an adjustment on the part of the users.

Originally the path around the lake was used by strollers, and they objected when bicyclists invaded their quiet paths. These uses adjusted, only to be complicated by joggers. More recently,

Fig. 14-7. Skaters, walkers and bikers on a paved multiple use circular trail. Note the two users skating to stereo music. Green Lake Park, Seattle, Washington. (Photo by Grant W. Sharpe.)

roller skaters caused a new flurry of accidents and complaints. Koch states that these too have leveled off. She attributes this to the customary subsidence pattern, in this case augmented by the following factors.

1. Better signage.
2. Brochures on regulations distributed throughout the community.
3. Other areas for roller skating having opened up.
4. Level of skill among the roller skaters rising appreciably.[5]

Whether or not the adjustment also means that former strollers and other less aggressive users have simply given up is not known. Certainly some senior citizens might find the risks of walking there unacceptable now.

To assure proper use and control of a 10-mi-long bikepath on the island of Longboat Key in Florida, the town commissioners adopted the following set of rules.

1. Bikers should exercise caution, courtesy and common sense.
2. The path may be used only by cyclists, pedestrians, joggers, and baby carriages.
3. Motorcycles, mopeds, golf carts, or any other type of motorized vehicles are prohibited from the bikepath.
4. Cyclists should observe a 15-mph speed limit.
5. Bicycles must have a horn or bell and rearview mirror.
6. At night, bicycles are required to have a front light and rear reflectors.
7. Bicycles shall not tow other vehicles on the path.
8. Pedestrians should use caution when crossing the path.
9. Users of the path should slow down at intersections.
10. Bicycles should be walked across business parking lots.
11. No part of any vehicle may be parked on the path.
12. No more than one person may be carried on a bike unless it is equipped properly for an extra rider.

CONCLUSION

The most important point for the park manager to remember is that most conflicts can be minimized if park users can be educated to recognize the needs of nonrecreational users as well as those of other recreationists, and if all parties recognize the legitimacy of each other's views on the best way to relax and recreate. Managers too must put aside personal preferences and help to identify the uses and abuses that generate conflicts and then act to prevent these, or lessen their effects.

Separation by time or space, and regulation through limiting access and facilities often helps resolve conflicting uses. Education through interpretation should also be provided by signs and brochures, as well as by off-season, off-site presentations and special on-site programs designed to befriend and educate user groups. This is particularly important because recreationists are likely to ignore even the most imaginatively designed solutions to recreation conflicts if they don't understand their purposes.

Careful records of complaints and accidents should be kept, so that patterns of use and conflict can be delineated. These should prove useful for researchers as well as managers, and, researchers may be able to suggest new ways to circumvent conflicts. To keep informed of new developments managers should attend workshops, and read professional publications. They could also try to come up with some ingenious ideas of their own to help abate these conflicts.

REFERENCES

General References

Baldwin, Malcolm F. and Dan H. Stoddard, Jr. 1973. *The Off-road Vehicle and Environmental Quality* (2nd ed.). The Conservation Foundation. Washington, DC.

Bellrose, Frank C., Jr. 1964. "Spent Shot and Lead Poisoning," *Waterfowl Tomorrow*, Joseph P. Linduska (ed.). USDI Bureau Sport Fisheries and Wildlife. U.S. Government Printing Office, Washington, DC.

Brewer, James E. and David L. Fulton. 1974. *A Review of Recreation Land Allocation on the Mark Twain National Forest. Outdoor Recreational Research: Applying the Results.* USDA Forest Service General Technical Report NC-9.

Bryan, Hobson. 1979. Conflict in the Great Outdoors. Sociological Studies No. 4. Bureau of Public Administration. The University of Alabama, University, AL.

Butler, Richard W. 1974. "How to Control 1,000,000 Snowmobiles," *Canadian Geogr. J.*, 88(3):4–13.

Cain, Stanley A. 1965. "What Is the Place of Fish and Wildlife In Outdoor Recreation Programs?," *Proceedings 45th Conference Western Association State Game and Fish Commission*, 45:4–9.

Chubb, Michael (ed.). 1971. *Proceedings of the 1971 Snowmobile and Off-road Vehicle Research Symposium.* Michigan State University Technical Report No. 8, East Lansing, MI.

Dailey, Tom and Dave Redman. 1975. *Guidelines for Roadless Area Campsite Spacing to Minimize Impact of Human-related Noises.* USDA General Technical Report PNW-35. Portland, OR.

Ditton, Robert B. and Thomas C. Goodale. 1973. "Water Quality Perception and the Recreational Uses of Green Bay, Lake Michigan," *Water Resour. Res.*, 9(3):569–579.

Gibbons, Dave R. and Ernest O. Salo. 1973. *An Annotated Bibliography of the Effects of Logging on Fish of the Western United States and Canada.* USDA Forest Service General Technical Report NW-10.

Hendee, John C. 1972. "Management of Wildlife for Human Benefit," *Western Proceedings*, 52nd Annual Conference, Western Association State Game and Fish Commission, Portland, OR, pp. 175–181. Reproduced by USDA Forest Service.

Hendee, John C. and Dale R. Potter. 1975.

"Hunters and Hunting: Management Implications of Research," *Proceedings of the Southern States Recreation Research*, Applications Workshop, Asheville, NC., Sept. 15–18. Reproduced by USDA Forest Service General Technical Report SE-9.

Lindsay, John J. 1974. *Outdoor Recreation Conflict in Vermont, 1973.* School of Natural Resources, University of Vermont, Burlington. Research Report SNR-RM2.

McCallum, Gordon E. 1964. "Clean Water, and Enough of It," *Waterfowl Tomorrow*, Joseph L. Linduska (ed.). USDI Bureau Sport Fisheries and Wildlife. U.S. Government Printing Office, Washington, DC.

Milliken, J. Gordon and H.E. Mew, Jr. 1969. "Recreational Impact of Reclamation Reservoirs," USDI Bureau of Reclamation, Denver Research Institute, University of Denver, CO.

Penny, J.R. 1971. "Off-road Vehicles of the Public Lands in California." *Proceedings, 1971 Snowmobile and Off-road Vehicle Research Symposium*, Michael Chubb (ed.). Michigan State University Technical Report No. 8. East Lansing, MI.

Rasor, Robert. 1977. *Five State Approaches to Trailbike Recreation Facilities and Their Management.* American Motorcyclist Association. Westerville, OH.

Sincock, John L., Morton M. Smith, and John F. Lynch. 1974. "Ducks in Dixie," *Waterfowl Tomorrow*, Joseph P. Linduska (ed.). USDI Bureau Sport Fisheries and Wildlife. U.S. Government Printing Office, Washington, DC.

Stankey, George H. 1973. *Visitor Perception of Wilderness Recreation Carrying Capacity.* USDA Forest Service Res. Pap. INT-142.

Wagar, J. Alan. 1974. *Recreational and Aesthetic Considerations. Environmental Effects of Forest Residues Management in the Pacific Northwest: A State-of-knowledge Compendium*, Owen P. Gramer (ed.). USDA Forest Service General Technical Report PNW-24.

Wood, Samuel E. and Daryl Lembke. 1967. *The Federal Threats to the California Landscape.* California Tomorrow. Sacramento, CA.

References Cited

1. Bury, Richard L., Robert C. Wendling, and Stephen F. McCool. 1976. *Off-road Recreational Vehicles: A Research Summary, 1969–1975*. Texas Agric. Exp. Stn., Texas A & M University, College Station.
2. Everhart, William C. 1972. *The National Park Service*. Praeger Publishers. New York.
3. Hegens, Leo E. 1979–1980. From a series of articles in *Park News*. National and Provincial Park Association of Canada, Toronto.
4. Hope, Jack. 1972. "The Invasion of the Awful ORVs," *Audubon* (Jan.):37–43.
5. Koch, Mary. 1979. Personal communication. Senior Supervisor, Green Lake Community Center, Seattle, WA.
6. Lime, David W. and George H. Stankey. 1971. "Carrying Capacity: Maintaining Outdoor Recreation Quality," *Recreation Symposium Proceedings*, Warren T. Doolittle (ed.). USDA Forest Service Northeast Forest Exp. Stn., Upper Darby, PA.
7. Lloyd, R. Duane and Virlis L. Fischer. 1972. *Dispersed Versus Concentrated Recreation as Forest Policy*. Presented at the Seventh World Forestry Congress, Buenos Aires, Argentina, Oct. 4–18.
8. Miller, Kenneth. 1961. *Our Native Land*. Publication by Education Department, National Association of Manufacturers. New York.
9. Morrison, Ken. 1979. "The Evolution of the Ontario Provincial Park System," *Park News*. National and Provincial Park Association of Canada, Toronto.
10. Nicol, Jack I. 1968. "The National Parks Movement in Canada," *The Canadian National Parks: Today and Tomorrow*, J. G. Nelson (ed.). University of Calgary.
11. Ramsey, Maxwell D. and Kerry P. Schell (ed.). 1970. *Reality and the Middle Ground*. A Report on Outlook 70—Knoxville Institute of Agriculture, The University of Tennessee and Tennessee Valley Authority.
12. Roth, Carol. 1979. Personal communication. Bureau of Land Management. Medford District Office, OR.
13. Swift, Ernie. 1958 *The Glory Trail*. The National Wildlife Federation. Washington, DC.
14. Wilder, Robert L. 1976. Woodland Park-Green Lake Planning Study. An Inter-office memorandum from Robert L. Wilder to Robert E. Kildall, May 20, 1976. Seattle Parks Dept., Seattle, WA.

CHAPTER FIFTEEN

LAW ENFORCEMENT

One of the most challenging aspects of park management is assuring the protection of visitors, lands, and facilities. Enforcement of park regulations, as well as general statutory laws, poses unique problems for rangers and managers, who, until recently, seldom have been trained in police science prior to career employment. Additionally, certain goals sought by managers regarding employee morale and the visitors' recreation experiences can be adversely affected by misused law enforcement procedures.[19]

A basic understanding of park management must include an overview of law enforcement philosophy and procedures, as well as the peculiar difficulties of operating in the park setting. The ability to achieve desired management goals in diverse situations depends on properly used management tools. Law enforcement is merely one of the necessary tools available to assure visitors pleasant recreation experiences, and its importance must be weighed in that balance.[31]

Public recreation areas have attracted large numbers of recreationists on an increasing scale in the past several decades. Campgrounds and public facilities, during heavy-use periods, resemble small communities and experience many of the same problems. Among these problems are behaviors that depreciate the recreational experience and, violate the rights of others.[6]

Depreciative behavior is a serious problem, and one that increases in scope and cost annually. The term "depreciative behavior" may refer to a wide variety of activities ranging from simple nuisance acts like improper waste water disposal to serious legal violations, such as theft, vandalism or assault (see Chapter 13, Depreciative Behavior and Vandalism). The crime rate throughout National Park Service areas has increased at a greater rate than the crime rate for the United States in general. Other recreational land managing agencies have also reported an increase in crimes.[2,8]

Not every park experiences significant amounts of nuisance behavior, rule violation, or serious crimes, but very few public agencies are completely free from these problems. Most state and federal agencies manage a broad range of outdoor areas and experience problems in at least some of their areas.

Two nationwide surveys conducted by PRC/ Public Management Services, Inc., for the U.S. Army Corps of Engineers and the American Parks and Recreation Society, indicate several factors that may explain why certain areas experience more problems than others. The studies show that crimes are more likely to occur:

1. In a developed area as opposed to an undeveloped area.
2. Near an urban atmosphere or a simulated urban environment.
3. At a well-attended facility.
4. On weekends.
5. Between the hours of 8 P.M. and midnight.
6. During the summer months.[22]

Most outdoor recreation agencies have at least some facilities where one or more of these factors are operating.

LAW ENFORCEMENT: PAST AND PRESENT

Offenses against park and forest regulations and violations such as the illegal taking of wildlife are not new. However, increased visitation and an increasing proportion of urban visitors has brought a corresponding need to protect park values and visitors.[16] Organizations assigned to provide for public safety and protect park values have been in existence since the earliest days of park holdings. Having employees working in an ''enforcement posture'' dates back to when the military was the custodian of parks such as Yellowstone and Yosemite. Rangers commissioned as peace officers, however, are a more modern phenomenon.

The recreational employee's authority to enforce law varies a great deal from state to state, from federal agency to state agency, and even within a particular agency. Some state park agencies make no provision for official enforcement authority. On the other hand some have a special employee classification called *Park Police*. These rangers are commissioned as peace officers, have the authority to make arrests within the parks, and carry weapons.

General statues, which originally created many park systems and established agencies to manage those lands, often used very broad language. General charges such as ''protection of visitors and lands'' were common, but charges specifically delegating police authority were rare. In some instances, all agency employees were charged with the duty of protecting park and forest facilities without any of these employees being specifically commissioned to exercise law enforcement powers. In some agencies this general charge still holds true.

Historically the National Park Service has enforced all laws applicable to the parks where they exercised exclusive or partial legislative jurisdiction. The more serious cases, however, have usually been turned over to the FBI after initial investigation. In areas of proprietary jurisdiction, law enforcement is restricted to the rules set forth in Title 36—Code of Federal Regulations, which requires law enforcement to be shared with local authorities.[13,31] The National Park Service has acquired the legislative mandate to commission its rangers with full law enforcement authority. The enforcement capabilities of many other federal agencies have historically been low key or nonexistent, with the agencies relying almost exclusively on local assistance.

Though state and federal agencies have had a similar history of law enforcement noninvolvement, increased use of facilities has focused attention on visitor safety and park protection services. The capability of county and state police agencies to provide these services has come under question, according to the General Accounting Office (GAO).[11,22] Investigations of several state parks' policies identifies an increased interest in their own law enforcement capabilities, although many still have no program direction. Several state park systems, however, are currently revising their law enforcement policies.

Law enforcement policies in all outdoor recreation areas are a product of legislation, the judicial process, and individual agency administration. Law enforcement practices will continue to need review and revision—no present policies appear to have the perfect solution. Participation in some type of law enforcement program seems to be a common management practice and is now viewed as simply another aspect of providing professional services to the public. Law enforcement philosophy, programs, and practices that are utilized by traditional law enforcement bodies will no doubt be borrowed in some instances, but the wholesale adoption of any program without careful evaluation and application to the particular situation will probably be a serious mistake.

Enforcement Philosophy

The enforcement philosophy of park agencies is necessarily very closely related to the agencies' legislative authority. Law enforcement in public recreation areas can be handled in four different ways.

1. Recreation area employees carry out all law enforcement duties.
2. A separate police force is created by the agency to enforce laws.
3. Law enforcement is left up to traditional law enforcement agencies.
4. Recreation area employees and traditional law enforcement agencies share duties.

The agency objective expressed most often is to achieve compliance with all park regulations with the minimum necessary procedures. Some agencies state that enforcement of all laws and park regulations is desirable, although few agencies actually achieve full enforcement. An agency's policy may be to enforce all laws but this may mean in fact to merely cooperate with traditional police agencies in the enforcement of all laws. In an address at Shenandoah National Park, a National Park Service officer stated that "all law enforcement actions must be handled with judgment, dignity and intelligence, and applied uniformly as is practicable with regard for the particular circumstances in each violation."[20]

In an interview, a Washington State Park Ranger pointed out that law enforcement in a park is not an end in itself, but rather a tool that is used to achieve park objectives. He stated further an agency employee has two enforcement alternatives: first, reactive or negative contacts or second, preactive or positive contacts.[32] Flickinger found that in Ohio State parks, the majority of contacts were reactive as opposed to preactive and he found that sufficient emphasis on a preventive program for both serious crimes and park rule violation was lacking. He points out that *law enforcement can and should be "a constructive means of education and protection and must not be equated with repression and vengeance."*[10]

The enforcement philosophy or policy an agency adheres to sets the policy guidelines concerning who participates in enforcement activities, what measures will be used, when they will be used, and ultimately, how they will be executed.

Individuals involved with enforcing laws and regulations must maintain a positive, courteous, and objective attitude toward enforcement. This of course, is not an easy task when faced with repeated violation of park regulations.

Clark et al. point out that managers and recreation visitors often have considerably different sets of values. Managers and rangers with an orientation toward environmental preservation may view depreciative acts such as littering much more seriously than may a visitor.[7]

The individual employee must keep in mind that as an employee of the agency he or she has given up the *right to act spontaneously.* The agency philosophy must be the guide to all contacts no matter how difficult this may be at times.

The following suggestions come from the *Task Force Report on Law Enforcement in the National Park Service.*

1. An officer's private attitudes should not be permitted to influence official decisions.
2. An officer should not become *personally* involved when making an arrest. He or she must not look on a violation as a personal affront. It is a wrong against the state, the people, and not against him or her personally.
3. There is nothing in the rules that requires an officer to *like* the people he or she deals with. Similarly, and more important, nobody and nothing in the rules says he or she must *dislike* them. Bear in mind that if people either see or believe that you dislike them, your contact will always be more difficult and less effective.
4. The role of the law enforcement officer is not exclusively an authoritarian one. Officers are not the "parents of the community" in a disciplinary sense. Their control powers are limited by the law and they are not, beyond that, guardians of the peoples' morals and regulators of their conduct. If we put more emphasis on protection of public safety and

prevention of crime we can gradually enlist the cooperative good will of more and more people for the accomplishment of the mission they have given us.[19]

Enforcement Psychology

Psychology is the study of human behavior—of people and how and why they do what they do. Enforcement psychology is simply the using of findings from psychology in the performance of law enforcement activities. The chief problems of law enforcement revolve around handling people.

Public relations are a very important factor in a successful program. Even park employees who have little or no enforcement duty are often in uniform, and soon realize that the public regards them as persons in authority. A ranger in uniform may be regarded as a positive or a negative presence (Fig. 15-1). Two studies indicated that uniformed rangers are held in high public regard. Moeller et al. interviewed 157 campers and 281 boaters at a national forest reservoir and found that 80 percent felt regular patrols by uniformed officers were desirable.[17] Other writers indicate a concern that the ranger image is deteriorating to that of a "cop."[3,23] Bowman points out that "much depends . . . on the attitude and approach of the ranger to law enforcement."[3]

Fig. 15-1. A park ranger meets a park visitor. The ranger's approach has much to do with how he or she is accepted by the park visitor. (Photo courtesy of Ohio State Parks.)

Avoiding the "Cop" Image. As was pointed out above, the park ranger is not in the park to reform the public. The ranger must realize that people are less than perfect and most will at some time violate regulations. Every effort should be made to remain objective and impartial in dealing with park visitors.[28]

Effective and efficient enforcement does not require the ranger to be outfitted for battle complete with crash helmet, sidearm, flashy uniform, sunglasses, and the latest leatherware. Similarly, patrol vehicles do not have to be adorned with an intimidating double light system.[3] The National Park Service Task Force team concluded that defensive equipment should be as inconspicuous as possible. They recommend wearing a firearm only for special situations, either when authorized by the superintendent or when on night patrols. The task force team also recommended less visibility for patrol vehicles as well as hidden defensive equipment and maintenance of the traditional park uniform.[19]

Bowman points out that the ranger does not need to appear or act like a movie sheriff to be an effective enforcement officer. The ranger has several roles to play, with enforcement being only one. While an extremely visible law enforcement presence may better deter crime while the officer is present, other roles that the ranger must fill may be adversely affected. A public image that allows for diverse job roles, while supporting the ranger in enforcement duties, is the desired goal.[3]

The National Park Service is testing a Ranger Service Dog program, and reports a favorable response from visitors as well as from employees (Fig. 15-2). Not only are such dogs efficient partners in law enforcement and search and rescue, but they also foster good public relations. Bryson reports that "even persons in the act of being cited by a ranger have, with few exceptions, wanted to pet the dog." Some state parks are also using this combination of master-handler and dog.[4]

It is also interesting to note the increased use of horses in some park areas. Several reasons are advanced for this, including cost effectiveness in

Fig. 15-2. A park ranger and her German Shepherd partner in Yosemite National Park. The master-handler and dog team work well in both law enforcement and search and rescue. (Photo by J. Blackburn.)

crowd control, and the ability to command respect while at the same time fostering good public relations. The public reacts to horses somewhat the same way as to dogs. People often want to pet them and also are not reluctant to approach someone patrolling on horseback to ask questions or simply pass the time of day. This goes a long way toward replacing the "cop" image with a friendly association.

Enforcement Jurisdiction

Jurisdiction refers to the authority of a body of government to deal with a particular matter. German et al., in *Introduction to Law Enforcement*, defined jurisdiction as follows.

> *The jurisdiction of a police agency may apply to the specific laws it is responsible to enforce or to the geographical area in which it oper-*

ates. Thus police jurisdiction deals with the right to enforce certain laws or to operate in certain areas.[12]

A particular state or federal body may or may not have the legal right to enforce laws and regulations within a specified geographical area. In California, for example, a ranger is a state peace officer and technically has the authority to enforce all state laws. In most instances, however, these activities are restricted to the park system. Police powers are exercised independently of other agencies only with respect to minor violations.[16]

There are basically four types of jurisdictions: exclusive, concurrent, proprietary, and partial. All state bodies operate under concurrent jurisdiction, while federal bodies may operate under exclusive, concurrent, proprietary, partial or a combination of two or more jurisdictions.

Exclusive Jurisdiction. Exclusive jurisdiction occurs when one body of government maintains *sovereign* authority to enforce the laws. Several national parks operate under this type of jurisdiction and where it occurs the federal government authority displaces that of the state. Only federal law applies and only federal enforcement officers may act on violations.[27]

Concurrent Jurisdiction. Concurrent jurisdiction means more than one agency shares the legal right to participate in law enforcement activities. This type of jurisdiction applied to federal recreation areas implies that state as well as federal laws apply. Federal employees and traditional state enforcement officers share authority.[27]

Concurrent jurisdiction as applied to state areas such as a state park system refers to the sharing of enforcement activities between commissioned park officers and other state law enforcement bodies. Generally only state laws and regulations are applicable.[5]

Proprietary Jurisdiction. Proprietary jurisdiction refers to lands that the federal government has acquired but over which the state retains authority. Having proprietary jurisdiction is much like having no jurisdiction at all. Lands that are held in proprietary jurisdiction may be compared to lands held by a private landowner. Law enforcement duties are primarily the responsibility of traditional state and local law enforcement departments. The state's laws and regulations are operable in proprietary jurisdictions. All U.S. Forest Service, U.S. Army Corps of Engineers, and approximately 70 percent of all National Park Service areas operate under proprietary jurisdiction. These agencies have the authority to enforce regulations promulgated by their various departmental secretaries and codified in the Code of Federal Regulations sections pertaining to their agencies. They also generally have the authority to enforce other laws pertaining to federally owned land, such as specific federal fire and wildlife laws.[31]

Partial Jurisdiction.   Partial jurisdiction exists where a federally administered recreation area has been granted certain portions of the state's authority to enforce laws. State law enforcement agencies, depending on the particular situation, may exercise, by themselves or concurrently with the federal government, certain kinds of authorities.[27]

Origins of Jurisdiction

The jurisdiction that a state has over lands within its boundaries has its origin with the U.S. Constitution. Once sovereignty is established over a body of land, that sovereignty will remain. In the instance of state parks, authority is vested in the state, and since state park agencies are administrative arms of the state they operate entirely under its authority. The state can delegate its authority to state park agencies, local county sheriffs, state police, and wildlife protection officers, as well as other special bodies. These various agencies then operate concurrently under the sovereign authority of the state.

The authority that the federal government possesses over its lands within the states depends on the means by which the federal government *acquired* the land. As mentioned, the state is granted sovereign authority by the U.S. Constitution. That authority remains there unless the state relinquishes all or portions of its authority. When the federal government acquires a body of land, unless the state specifically releases certain parts of its authority that body of land will be held in proprietary jurisdiction. Exclusive, concurrent, and partial jurisdictions exist where the state has relinquished or shared its sovereign authority.[27]

Assistance from Other Agencies

Most park agencies rely heavily on assistance from outside law enforcement departments. While certain park agencies have the legal right to enforce all laws and regulations, the norm is definitely to rely on assistance. An individual manager or ranger must become familiar with the jurisdiction the agency has over its lands and with the policies to which it subscribes concerning enforcement assistance. The services that the agency can provide vary a great deal depending on the jurisdiction. Familiarity with a particular recreation agency's practices, combined with an understanding of traditional law enforcement departments, is the key to proper coordination.

Park managers must assess what their agency's role is in relation to assistance available from outside agencies. Local managers must assess who has primary responsibility and the most adequate capabilities to deal with a particular problem. A wildlife protection officer could be called for an offense concerning wildlife while the state police or the county sheriff would be summoned for a theft or vandalism. Also, with the exception of a very few national parks, such as Yosemite, Yellowstone, Mount Rainier, and Glacier Park most areas do not normally maintain detention facilities. Provision must be made with other agencies for this type of assistance.

In cases involving exclusive federal jurisdiction, federal law enforcement units (i.e., U.S. Marshals Service, Federal Bureau of Investigation) must be called for assistance.

Park managers and their respective agencies

have sometimes entered into more formal agreements. National park rangers have been deputized by local sheriff's departments or state wildlife agencies, for instance, to exercise broader authority.[29] In 1971 Congress passed the Cooperative Law Enforcement Program Act (P.L. 92-82), which allowed the U.S. Forest Service to appropriate money for local sheriff's departments to provide additional visitor protection services for forested lands. This type of agreement can be thought of as a contract with local law enforcement departments. In a study for the Corps of Engineers, entitled *A Study of the Law Enforcement Needs and Means of Providing Visitor Protection at Corps of Engineers Lakes*, the investigators recommend extending law enforcement contracting capabilities to other federal agencies such as the Corps of Engineers.[22]

Federal Law Enforcement Agencies. Federal law enforcement departments or law enforcement capabilities within a given agency exist on a specifically mandated basis. The United States is one of the few countries that does not have a national police force. When Congress creates a law enforcement body, the legislation also establishes specific jurisdictions and authority. The Federal Bureau of Investigation, for example, deals with 180 specified crimes and no others. Law enforcement duties are shared by special departments, as well as by units within major agencies including the following:

1. Federal Drug Enforcement Administration.
2. Federal Bureau of Investigation.
3. Border Patrol.
4. Secret Service.
5. U.S. Coast Guard.
6. U.S. Marshal.
7. U.S. Park Police.
8. Various units within Departments of Agriculture, Interior, Commerce, Labor, etc.[25]

State Law Enforcement Agencies. Unlike the federal government, states can maintain law enforcement agencies that have general police powers within the state. These types of depart-

ments are provided for in state constitutions and then mandated by the legislative body. State police forces operate under various names such as State Police, State Patrol, or Highway Patrol.

The state may also provide for various delegations of "restricted" law enforcement duties to a number of other departments. These law enforcement units may be utilized by the park manager in various situations including the following.

1. Fish and Game Protection Division.
2. Environmental Protection Division.
3. State Fire Warden.
4. State Drug Enforcement Department.[25]

Local Law Enforcement Agencies. Law enforcement at the local level consists of either county or municipal agencies. County law enforcement is usually by either a sheriff's department or county police department. County police departments are usually based on a consolidation of a county sheriff's department and a municipal police department in an urban area. The sheriff's position is enabled through the state constitution. Since the sheriff's position is an elected one, however, quality of professional services can vary a great deal from department to department. Park managers should be aware of the capabilities of their local sheriff's department.

County police and municipal police may be considered almost synonymous. While municipal police departments make up 37,000 out of 40,000 nationwide law enforcement departments, their services are seldom available to parklands in rural areas.[25] Although assistance from various agencies is available in theory, extraordinary circumstances, local law enforcement budgets, and rural locations can make prompt assistance very difficult.

LAW ENFORCEMENT TOOLS

The means by which law enforcement objectives are accomplished may be referred to as law enforcement tools. Tools that may be used for enforcing laws and regulations in park areas include preventive measures, compliance and education, citations, and arrests. To use the improper tool in a given situation may severely damage rapport with the public and may result in failure to achieve desired goals.

Preventive Measures

Eldefonso et al. in *Introduction to Law Enforcement*, point out three factors necessary for a violation or crime to occur.

1. The desire to commit an act.
2. The will to commit the act.
3. The opportunity.[9]

Preventive measures in parks deal with eliminating one of these three factors. Examples of such measures are preventive ranger patrols, park access control, design control, increased lighting, posting of regulations, immediate repairs to vandalized areas, alarms, installation of barriers, and visitor education (Fig. 15-3). The McCalls point out that preventive measures should be "low-key, such as disseminating information about campground rules and regulations." They also indicate that campground regulations should be handled in positive fashion, in contrast to a list of negations.[16]

Compliance and Education

An initial positive contact with a visitor can be very effective in stopping participation in a violation. Contact concerning nuisance behavior is most frequently an attempt to effect compliance through education. There are basically two types of contacts—verbal warnings and written warnings. The written warning is a somewhat more formal reprimand but can be handled in a positive fashion (Fig. 15-4). A written warning may or may not be recorded in office files.[15]

Another tool or technical form commonly used by patrol officers is the field interrogation card (Fig. 15-5). This is an interview record filled out on anyone encountered near the scene of a possible crime who might be either a potential witness

Crime Prevention in Your Parks

MARK YOUR GEAR
Mark your cloth gear with indelible ink, using your driver's license number and state abbreviation. Mark metal gear with an engraving pencil. Record serial numbers from camera gear, radios, etc. Check at ranger stations and visitor centers for marking kits and Operation ID stickers.

DON'T MAKE IT EASY
Keep gear out of sight, especially at night, during interpretive programs, and while you're away from camp. Get to know your neighbors. Watch their camp. Ask them to watch yours.

REDUCE THE OPPORTUNITIES
Reduce the opportunities for would-be thieves. Locked cars and trunks are not completely safe. Leave valuables and unnecessary equipment at home.

DON'T BROADCAST YOUR PLANS
Leave your expected return date with friends or a ranger, not on your car.

CALIFORNIA DEPARTMENT OF PARKS AND RECREATION

PRODUCED COURTESY OF THE NATIONAL PARK SERVICE, PACIFIC NORTHWEST REGIONAL OFFICE

Fig. 15-3. This crime prevention poster, designed for visitor education, is displayed on park bulletin boards. (Courtesy of National Park Service and California Department of Parks and Recreation.)

or suspect. The officer uses the triplicate form as a guide and a record so that such witnesses or suspects can later be identified or located. In the course of such a contact, he or she may ask the interviewee for identification, such as a driver's license, state alcoholic beverage I.D. card, Selective Service registration card, etc., and record the information on the form. Such recordings of information also have a deterrent effect on *potential* violators. They know that the "heat" knows who they are and how to find them.[31]

The Patrol

The patrol, although primarily a preventive measure, is the main tool of law enforcement used by park agencies as well as by traditional law en-

WARNING OF VIOLATION

No. 55007

CALIFORNIA DEPARTMENT OF PARKS AND RECREATION

1 Date Mo. Day Year	2 Time 24 hour clock	3 Day of Week Su-1 We-4 Sa-7 Mo-2 Th-5 Unknown-8 Tu-3 Fr-6
4 Name First Middle Last		5 P - Personal A- Absentee
6 Address City		State
7 Identification (Driver's Lic., S.S. No., Etc.)	8 Sex M F	9 Birthdate
10 Vehicle/Boat License No.		11 State
12 Make	13 Model/Year	14 Color
15 Violation Sec.(s)/Code(s)		16 Leave Blank
17 Description of Violation(s)		
18 Location of Violation(s)		
19 Area	20 Unit	
21 Issued By:		22 Badge No.

THIS IS A COURTESY WARNING
NO COURT APPEARANCE REQUIRED

DEPARTMENT OF PARKS AND RECREATION
CALIFORNIA STATE PARK SYSTEM

PARKS ARE FOREVER WITH YOUR HELP

DISTRICT COPY

DPR 420 (REV. 8-74)

26151-768 8-74 30M TRIP ④Z OSP

Fig. 15-4. The written warning form of reprimand, presented for minor rule violations. (Courtesy California Department of Parks and Recreation.)

TIME		DATE	

LAST NAME   FIRST   MIDDLE

ADDRESS

DATE OF BIRTH		HEIGHT
RACE	SEX	AGE	WEIGHT

LOCATION OF INTERROGATION   MAKE OF CAR   LICENSE   COLOR

IN COMPANY OF (NAME AND AGE)

REMARKS

FORM PD-587 SDPD FIELD INTERROGATION   ℗f   OFFICERS BADGE NOS.

Fig. 15-5. The field interrogation card, used to record names and addresses of anyone encountered near the scene of a crime. Such persons might be either witnesses or suspects. (Courtesy of San Diego Police Department.)

Fig. 15-6. A park ranger and his specialized patrol vehicle. Lake Ozark State Park, Missouri. (Missouri Department of Natural Resources photo by Nick Decker.)

forcement agencies. One of the important purposes of the patrol is the *presence* and *visibility* of the employee. Much does *not* happen because of this presence, even though it is a friendly and helpful presence. Besides its deterrent function, patrol is the means by which availability is assured for compliance and education, detection of violations, and visitor assistance.[9]

The patrol is carried out in many ways depending on the terrain to be covered, the focus of the patrol, and the agency policy. Patrol may be on foot, bicycle, horse, canoe, or by motor vehicle transportation (Fig. 15-6). Motorized transportation may include pickups, sedans, 4-wheel drives, power boats, helicopters, or airplanes.[16]

The utility of patrol operations has not gone unquestioned. Very little research exists comparing hours spent at patrol and types of patrols used with actual number of crimes. Nevertheless, three recent studies conclude that length of patrol and the amount of times at patrol both need to be significantly increased in the areas examined. The studies also recommended that patrolling techniques be improved.[10,15,22]

The Complaint

A complaint is a formal written charge, made under oath by an officer or private citizen, that a particular person has committed an offense. The officer or private citizen must show that *probable cause* exists to justify an arrest.[12] In the instance of a citation, the information gathered plus the officer's testimony can become the basis for a formal complaint if the citation is not answered by the violator. The court issues the warrant to an officer of the court to make the arrest. (This officer is the marshal in the federal system or the sheriff in the state.) In the federal system it can also be an FBI agent, and now under the Authorities Act (P.L. 94-458) it can be a properly trained and certified National Park Ranger.[31]

Citations

A citation is an order issued by a park employee to a violator. It includes a signed promise to appear before a magistrate, or in lieu of appearing,

the posting of bond that will be forfeited if the recipient chooses not to appear (Fig. 15-7). For the citation to be enforced by the court, however, the officer is required to appear sometime and attest to the facts and sign a formal complaint. Generally a scheduled time is set by the magistrate, and the officer appears and signs a whole list of complaints for citations issued over the previous week or month.

Citations may be issued for a violation when a written warning has previously been issued, or for first-time serious violations. A citation is usually a multicopied form with copies normally going to the violator, the courts, the citing officer, and the agency.[26] A citation may sometimes be served when the recipient is not present, such as in the instance of a parking violation. When a recipient is present, information must be provided concerning the exact nature of the offense.[16]

Search and Seizure

Stop and Frisk.   Under specific circumstances, a law enforcement officer may stop and search a person who he or she reasonably suspects has been involved in or is contemplating a criminal offense. The officer must suspect that person is armed and that his or her own personal safety is in danger.[26] Only a "pat down" for weapons is allowed when the officer has reason to conclude that the suspect may be armed and dangerous. Reasonable force not likely to cause death or bodily injury to stop such a person is all that is permitted.

Searches.   Just as an officer is limited in the authority to arrest a private citizen, he or she is also limited in the authority to conduct searches and seize products of that search. Searches are legal in the following instances.

1.   After obtaining a search warrant.
2.   Incident to a lawful arrest.
3.   When a private citizen consents to a search.[26]

CALIFORNIA DEPARTMENT OF PARKS AND RECREATION

NOTICE TO APPEAR

No. 103255

1. Mo.	Day	Year	2. Time - 24 Hr. Clock	3. Day of Week
				Su-1 Tu-3 Th-5 Sa-7
				Mo-2 We-4 Fr-6 Unkn-8

4. Name (First, Middle, Last)

5. P-Personal
   A-Absentee

6. Residence Address   City   State

7. Business Address   City   State

8. Drivers License No.   State   Birthdate

9. Sex	10. Hair	11. Eyes	12. Height	13. Weight	14. Other Des.
M F					

15. Vehicle License No.   State   16. Passengers
                                                        M   F

17. Yr. of Vehicle	18. Make	19. Model	20. Body Style	21. Color

22. Registered Owner or Lessee

23. Address of Owner or Lessee

24. Violation Code(s)/Sec.(s) & Desc. - Misdemeanor/Infraction   25. Leave Blank

26. App. Spd.	27. PF/Max. Spd.	28. Veh. Spd. Lmt.	29. Weather	30. Booking ☐ Req.

31. Location of Violation(s)   32. Area   33. Unit

34. Evidence Seized

35. ☐ Offense(s) not committed in my presence. Certified on information and belief.

36. I certify under penalty of perjury that the foregoing is true and correct.
    Executed on the date shown above at   Cal.

37. Citing Officer   38. Badge No.

39. Arresting Officer - If Different from Above   40. Badge No.

41. Without admitting guilt, I promise to appear at the time and place checked below.

X Signature

Before a judge or clerk of the municipal or justice court

Juvenile court traffic div. — juvenile probation officer

Date	Time		☐ Within 11 days
		M	☐ Court will notify within 11 days

FORM APPROVED BY THE JUDICIAL COUNCIL OF CALIFORNIA,
REV. 11-10-69 V.C. 40513(b) P.C. 853.9

DPR 319 (Rev. 2/75)

AREA COPY

Fig. 15-7. The citation is a notice for the violator to appear in court. The signature of the violator acknowledging the serving of the citation should be obtained on the citation form. (Courtesy California Department of Parks and Recreation.)

A search in criminal law is defined as "an exploratory investigation with a view to discovery of contraband, illicit or stolen property, or some evidence of guilt to be used in prosecution for a crime."

Search Warrant. A search may be authorized by a magistrate on receiving a written complaint under oath describing the particular property to be searched. Reasonable grounds must be shown for issuing the warrant. A warrant must describe the items sought, the premises to be searched, and who is to carry out the search.[26]

Search Incident to Arrest. When persons are legally arrested for an offense, a search may be made of those persons, their personal belongings, their automobiles, or the area within their immediate control. Items may be seized that are unlawful for a person to have whether or not that was the initial intent of the search (i.e., illegal game, drugs, etc.).

The Arrest

An arrest is the taking of a person into legal custody for the purpose of holding or delaying that person to answer to a court of law for an offense charged, or for preventing a person from committing an offense.[26] Ordinarily the arrest should be accomplished only by properly trained persons in sufficient numbers to reduce the likelihood of resistance and injury. The arrest is generally used for serious incidents, but is also commonly used for drunkenness or drug stupor in order to protect the public and the subject until the subject no longer is under the influence (Fig. 15-8). Even in such cases it is important to take the arrested person before a magistrate as soon as possible and have this person formally released *by the magistrate*—if he or she is to be released. Release by the magistrate reduces the potential for false arrest charges. Females should be arrested only by two or more officers, preferably one of them a female officer. Assistance from outside agencies is common when arrest is necessary in a public recreation area.

Fig. 15-8. A park ranger demonstrating the process of making an arrest at a law enforcement training session. (Photo courtesy of California Department of Parks and Recreation.)

A valid criminal arrest requires all of the following.

1. An intent to arrest.
2. The authority to arrest.
3. An actual or constructive seizure of the person.
4. A realization by the person of his or her arrest.[26]

In making an arrest, the officer should inform the person of his or her authority, of the intention to arrest, and of the specific offense for which the arrest is being made. The officer is justified in using only that force necessary to make the arrest. Even then the seriousness of the offense indicates the amount of force that may be used. The use of injurious force, for instance, is not acceptable in making arrests for misdemeanors.[26] Officers must be extremely careful since the use of excessive force may result in the officers themselves facing civil and criminal liability.

Arrest without a Warrant. A commissioned officer may make an arrest without a warrant when he or she has *probable cause* to believe a suspect has committed an offense.[24] Probable cause to justify an arrest must be based on two factors.

1. An honest belief that the person committed a crime.
2. Reasonable grounds for that belief.

When arresting without a warrant for a misdemeanor, the offense must have occurred in the officer's *presence*. In the case of a felony the crime need not have been committed in the officer's presence. Probable cause may be based on a witness's report and the officer's subsequent investigation.[26]

Arrest with a Warrant.   When an arrest is made with a valid warrant, the arresting officer need not satisfy the probable cause stipulation because in fact the magistrate, the superior court clerk, or the court that issued the warrant was required to substantiate reasonable grounds for its issuance. All warrants are initiated by a formal written *complaint*. The officer is responsible for the warrant's face validity only.[26]

Arrest by a Private Citizen.   A citizen's arrest is an arrest by a private person; it is allowed for by the statutes of the United States.

A ranger may be called on in certain situations either to make a citizen's arrest or to receive a person arrested by another citizen. A commissioned officer is required to receive a violator who has been taken into custody by a private party if the officer is satisfied that the arrest is legal. The McCalls point out that in California, the ranger is also required to assist a citizen in attempting a lawful arrest. If a ranger takes a suspect into custody on behalf of a private citizen, the citizen must sign a statement that he or she will appear to sign a complaint.[16] Since they must meet the same arrest requirements as an officer, it is important for private citizens to remember that they are not as well protected against the civil and criminal liability of an illegal arrest as is a law officer.

Rights of an Arrested Person

Certain rights, guaranteed by the U.S. Constitution and interpreted by judicial review over the years, have evolved into a solid procedure for the treatment of arrested persons. These rules are referred to as the *Miranda warning*. Arrested persons must be informed of the following rights.

1. They have the right to remain silent.
2. Anything they say can and will be used against them in a court of law.
3. They have the right to talk to a lawyer and have him or her present while being questioned.
4. If they cannot afford to have a lawyer, one will be appointed to represent them before any questioning, if they wish one.

Officers must also ask the defendants if they understand their rights. Also, even if the defendants waive their rights to remain silent or to counsel, they may change their minds at any time, in which case all questioning must cease.[25]

CLASSIFICATION OF OFFENSES

Crimes are typically classified as felonies or misdemeanors. Crimes are also classified by the punishment levied.

Felonies.   Felonies generally represent a group of criminal offenses that are punishable by one year or more in a penal institution, a $1,000 fine, or both. Felonies may include homicide, forcible rape, robbery, assault, burglary, larceny, and motor vehicle theft.[25]

Misdemeanors.   Misdemeanors usually refer to all other offenses and are less serious in nature than felonies. Misdemeanors are punishable by a $500 fine or six months in a penal institution, or both for a maximum penalty; for high misdemeanors, a $1,000 fine or one year, or both for maximum penalty.[31]

The actual classification of a crime may vary from state to state.[25] Federal law categorizes offenses, other than felonies, in terms of *misdemeanors*; *minor offenses*, and *petty offenses*. Minor offenses may involve such offenses as vandalism, petty larceny, and public drunkenness, while petty offenses cover many lesser offenses, such as park regulation violations and traffic violations. Most park regulation violations are petty offenses under federal law and are punishable by not more than six months in jail and $500 fine.

INVESTIGATIONS

An investigation is an inquiry for the discovery and collection of facts concerning the matter involved.[24] Investigations are, however, a complex process and often require specialized assistance. Some park agencies maintain regional law enforcement specialists who are fully trained in complex investigative techniques, but specialized outside assistance is usually necessary.

Eldefonso et al. break down the investigative process into two primary purposes.

1. The gathering of facts and other information for examination to determine whether a violation has occurred.
2. The collection, preservation and preparation of evidence that will be admissible and effective in a later judicial inquiry.[9]

Crime Scene Protection

A park employee may often be the first official person to arrive at the scene of an incident. Although a specialist may be needed, the employee can make a significant contribution to the investigation, making note of who was present, what happened, when and where the incident took place, and how it took place.

Except where an injury has occurred, the actual scene of an incident must be preserved for the ultimate collection and examination of all evidence. Preserving the scene of an incident means keeping the site in the same physical condition as it was left by the perpetrator. The official in charge must apply needed safeguards to bar all forms of disturbance until photographs, sketches, and final collection of information are made. Unauthorized persons, even other park employees and officials, must be excluded. All articles which are, or may be, of value as evidence must be collected. Articles that need documentation or collection may include finger prints, tool impressions, foot and tire marks, weapons, glass fragments, stains, or clothing.[14]

Collection of Evidence

In collecting possible evidence, investigators usually follow the following procedures.

1. Photographs or sketches are made of the scene.
2. Searches are made to locate all pertinent objects.
3. Possible evidence is placed in some type of protective container and labeled. Labels include date, name of collector, and place of origin.
4. Careful record is kept (in a notebook) of the items collected as well as other miscellaneous information.[9]

Location of Witnesses

Investigations are not only concerned with collection and preservation of physical items but are also concerned with people. Few incidents actually take place in an officer's presence, but in many instances other individuals may have been present. Witnesses at the scene of an incident may be readily available, but often may be just a face among many others present. A potential witness may be a passing motorist, a victim of the crime, or a person talking to another observer, describing what happened. Although a private citizen may be willing to share information with another bystander, he or she may be reluctant to make an official statement or talk to an official. Keen observation and effective public relations skills may be needed to locate and secure information.[14]

On-the-Scene Interviews

Excitement, confusion, and poor weather are just a few of the problems that typify the scene of an incident or serious crime. The purpose of an initial interview is to obtain information as quickly as possible, as this is crucial for optimum accuracy. Careful records should be kept of the exact information volunteered by the interviewee, including the person's verified name, the location while staying at the park, home address, home phone, and all statements concerning the incident.[14]

Evidence

Evidence is any means of mind or matter by which an alleged matter of fact is established or disproved. It may include testimony, records, documents, objects, and inferences therefrom, which can legally be presented later in a court of law. Evidence is classified in three general ways—direct, circumstantial, and real.

1. *Direct evidence* is evidence that can show the existence of facts through direct observation by a witness. Observation can be made by one of the five senses: seeing, hearing, feeling, smelling, or tasting.
2. *Circumstantial evidence* or indirect evidence is that evidence established by fact or a group of facts that tends to prove or disprove a case (i.e., suspect seen in vicinity of a crime).
3. *Real evidence* is evidence that is in a tangible form and is related to a specific case (i.e., any object or physical item).[18]

Rules of Evidence. The rules governing the admissibility of evidence were established as a means of testing evidence to be presented in court. The question of admissibility is based on two features. First, does it deal with circumstances surrounding the subject in question? Second, does it tend, logically, naturally, and with reasonable inference, to establish a fact concerning the case? Evidence to be presented must be the following.

1. Relevant (bears directly on the point).
2. Material (relevant evidence that proves a substantial matter in question).

3. Competent (witness must be capable and competent).

Technical Reports

An agency with law enforcement responsibilities participates in several types of activities such as accident investigations, patrols, criminal investigations, minor incident reporting, and sometimes, in making arrests. In order to complete each of these functions and evaluate field programs, an agency must be properly administered. Proper administration is accomplished by accurate reports fed into a good record system. Reports not only help with program evaluations, but also provide the necessary information for solution of a case.[26]

Flickinger pointed out, in his study of Ohio's state parks, that park managers did not know if crime was a serious problem in their own park system. Poor field reporting procedures and administrative handling of field reports were major reasons given for this lack of management information. Flickinger recommended that the parks improve their technical reports as well as their agency's record keeping systems.[10]

Report Writing

"Good writing depends on clear thinking. Think first, then write, is a basic simple rule for good reports."[26] Officers should avoid the use of slang, big or fancy words, and exaggeration. The report should have clarity of thought and have short, concise sentences and paragraphs.

Principles of technical report writing are universal whether the subject is an interoffice memo, a traffic report, or a complex investigative report. A law enforcement report ". . . should be clear, pertinent, brief, complete, current, accurate, fair, properly classified, informative, and objective".[26]

Technical report writing, although often a difficult task, is an essential link between actual field operations, park management, and outside organizations. On an individual basis, rangers and managers can contribute a great deal to overall operations by taking a positive attitude towards good report writing.

THE PROSECUTOR

A prosecutor has many duties in the U.S. criminal justice system including the following.

1. Reviewing evidence prior to an arrest and recommending the appropriate action.
2. Reviewing evidence and circumstances after an arrest without a warrant, to determine if it was justified.
3. Determining if a specific charge will be filed against an accused person and initiating formal charges.
4. Terminating the case when appropriate.
5. Representing the state in various pretrial hearings and examinations.
6. Recommending to the court the bail for the defendant.
7. Representing the state in the trial of the case. [25]

THE RANGER IN COURT

A park ranger involved in testifying before a court will normally be dealing with the U.S. magistrate or the local justice of the peace, depending on the jurisdiction involved. A federal ranger would primarily have exposure to federal lower courts and a state park ranger would have dealings with the state court system. On occasion, a park peace officer may be involved with proceedings at the trial court level. This would normally take place when a defendant for a lesser offense has requested a jury trial. However, a trial court appearance may also take place in the event of a more serious incident.

Pretrial Preparation

A ranger's basic link to the judicial process is the public prosecutor. The prosecutor is the officer's advisor both before and after an arrest, as well as during the court hearing.

When a particular case is to come before a magistrate's court or district court the prosecuting attorney will offer necessary advice concerning testimony preparation, court appearance, and case strategy. Before the trial the ranger should review all personal notes and technical reports concerning the incident. The officer should also be prepared to identify all witnesses interviewed during the hearing. [24]

Legal Advice

In certain instances the state park ranger may need advice on some legal matter, and could call the State Attorney General's office for this. The Attorney General would defend the state park ranger should he or she be civilly sued for actions that were taken as an official representative of the state. In cases that involve federal jurisdiction the U.S. Attorney's office would be the place to seek counsel.

Another source of legal advice may be agency attorneys. Within the Department of the Interior, for example, regional solicitors are available for counsel. [29] In some situations, however, the agency may not provide legal staff, in which instance private counsel may have to be sought.

TESTIFYING IN COURT

Manner

Good courtroom technique requires that evidence be presented logically and in a concise manner. All statements should be made in a conversational tone and presented in an impartial manner. The purpose of a court inquiry is to review potential evidence, not personal opinion. Testimony should not be memorized. Having personal notes available during testimony is acceptable, but they may rightfully be requested for the court records. Information should not be volunteered unless asked for by the examining attorney.

Cross examination by an attorney is probably the most difficult feature of a court appearance.

The ranger should maintain a professional manner and consider each question deliberately. Difficult questions may be forthcoming but the ranger should not allow himself or herself to be misquoted. An individual, while testifying, should not be afraid to admit that he or she does not know the answer to a question.

Appearance

An individual's appearance while in court may affect the court case. Traditional law enforcement literature recommends an especially crisp appearance when in court; however, an appearance that is normally acceptable while involved in regular duties seems adequate. Rangers should wear the same sort of uniform they had on at the time of the incident.[21]

A sincere, courteous, and unassuming manner is desirable. The ranger should not appear to be friendly with the prosecuting attorney, even though they may have worked together on several occasions.

In some instances the ranger may have some responsibility toward the witnesses. The ranger may want to meet them at the door, seat them, and if necessary, help put them at ease.

TRAINING FOR PARK PEACE OFFICERS

Law enforcement training provided for rangers and managers working for different agencies varies just as significantly as do the agencies' enforcement policies. Training programs range from a cursory review to 500 or more hours of formal instruction. The Michigan Department of Natural Resources, for example, commissions permanent park employees only after completion of an in-service training session. In the state of California, new state park rangers must receive formalized training at a state training center. Florida Division of Parks also sends rangers through a standard program.

Formal Training

The National Park Service has perhaps been the agency most extensively involved in formalized law enforcement training. It has upgraded its police science training to the level of many local sheriff's departments. In recent years the National Park Service has utilized the Federal Law Enforcement Training Center (FLETC), ordinarily used by traditional law enforcement departments. Training has included such technical subjects as constitutional law and civil liberties, firearms training, search and seizure, traffic accident investigations, human relations, and juvenile procedures. Rangers participating in law enforcement duties have also been required to update skills annually with 40 additional hours of training.

Formal law enforcement training academies exist in all regions of the country. Most state police departments, larger municipalities, and some federal agencies maintain training facilities (Fig. 15-9). Several major universities, colleges, and junior colleges also offer police science course work.

Fig. 15-9. California state park rangers are instructed on the use of hand guns at a firing range as part of their extensive law enforcement training. The photo represents one stage in a series of several firing distances. (Photo courtesy of California Department of Parks and Recreation.)

Utilization of established training centers has certain advantages over sometimes limited in-service programs. There is, moreover, a need to integrate the prescription-type program that an agency might conduct on its own, with broader professional law enforcement orientation.

The National Park Service's 200-hour course is an attempt by a park agency to offer a comprehensive law enforcement orientation while keeping the length and content of training in proper perspective. The list of recommended subjects as well as the required hours of training are seen in Figure 15-10.

Although this list represents a single agency's

SUBJECT	REQUIRED TRAINING HOURS
1. Accident Investigation	20
2. Bombs and Explosives	2
3. Constitutional Law & Civil Liberties	6
4. Courtroom Testimony & Procedures	2
5. Criminalistics	2
6. Defensive Driving (Basic Driver Training)	24
7. Defensive Tactics	2
8. Descriptions & Identifications	3
9. Detention & Arrest	10
10. Deviant Behavior/Abnormal Behavior	6
11. Ethics and Conduct	2
12. Firearms Training	24
13. Human Relations	8
14. Interviewing	4
15. Jurisdiction	2
16. Juvenile Procedures	6
17. Law Enforcement Techniques	3
18. Marksmanship/Moral/Legal Aspects of Firearms	8
19. Narcotics	2
20. Organization & Function of Law Enforcement Agency	1
21. Practical Exercises	22
22. Principles of Evidence	4
23. Philosophy & Objectives of NPS Law Enforcement	4
24. Radio Communications	1
25. Report Writing	4
26. Search and Seizure	10
27. Security of Buildings	2
28. U.S. Code & CFR—Federal Law	16
	200

Fig. 15-10. A list of recommended subjects and required training hours for the National Park Service's 200-hour course in Law Inforcement Orientation.

effort, other federal and state agencies could utilize a similar format. Specific park codes and the agency's philosophies could be substituted for those of the National Park Service.[19]

In-Service Programs

In-service law enforcement training programs are those training sessions that are conducted entirely within the agency. Arrangements can be made to utilize local resources as well as expertise from within the agency. In-service programs are much less expensive and can be more convenient than outside training programs. While in-service training may not be a substitute for a comprehensive introduction to law enforcement, it can provide necessary updates and supplement skills. An annual in-service training program conducted by the Forest Service within Region Six covered such broad topics as constitutional law, crime scene photography, evidence marking and collection, and note taking.[30] Other topics that have been covered by agencies utilizing guest instructors, as well as agency specialists, are as follows.

1. Emergency services.
2. Communication systems.
3. Park security.
4. Equipment use.
5. Patrol procedures.
6. Crime scene protection.
7. Updates on violation-prevention techniques.
8. Report writing.
9. Courtroom testimony.
10. Various defensive tactics.

CHALLENGES AND PROBLEMS

Resource Manager versus Policeman

There are many difficulties, and subsequently, challenges, for park managers who have serious law enforcement problems. Lack of positive action in certain situations can be detrimental to park values, while inappropriate actions may cause more problems. Incorporation of professional law enforcement skills in employee training seems to be a trend in outdoor recreation areas faced with increased usage and limited resources. Several of the most recent studies concerning law enforcement in outdoor recreation areas find most present programs inadequate and recommend increased emphasis. Other investigators express concern about the park employee's new image in areas like the national parks that have upgraded their programs.

Bernard Shanks, in "Guns in the Parks," expresses concern that new emphasis for law enforcement programs is creating a "new breed of ranger" trained in negative kinds of contacts instead of positive contacts and educational skills.[23] Traditional law enforcement consultants counter by saying that many park employees already spend a good deal of their time in an enforcement role, but have no professional training. They imply that resource-oriented managers untrained in proper law enforcement procedures can be more vengeful and repressive than a carefully recruited and professionally trained force. Shanks also indicates that increased expenditures for law enforcement in the national parks have come at the expense of environmental education, trail maintenance, and various other park management programs. One of the major justifications for increased law enforcement emphasis is visitor protection safety, but Shanks noted that very few injuries or fatalities are caused by crime. His implication is that rangers who should be involved in warning inexperienced visitors about natural hazards are now remaining "locked in their high-powered police cruisers," establishing primarily negative contacts.[23]

While not concurring with the findings of many recent studies, Shanks does represent one side of the debate that has surfaced among many park professionals. In the *Task Force Report on Law Enforcement in the National Park Service*, the investigators acknowledged dissatisfaction expressed by some field rangers concerning overly emphasized law enforcement programs. The report recommends several changes to help put field law enforcement programs in step with other park goals. While problems in many parks are significant, the reaction to one park management problem must not be allowed to disrupt ongoing programs, erode employee morale, or run counter to the guiding philosophy of that organization.

Patrol vehicles were also mentioned as a source of possible problems. It was pointed out that the style of park vehicles as well as the type of emergency lighting system used in recent years were too imposing.[19] The implication is that differing styles of patrol vehicles broadcast contrasting impressions to members of the public (Figs. 15-1 and 15-6). Patrol vehicle style and use of emergency light and siren systems must be compatible with park management objectives. Overall equipment acquisition and policies for equipment use must reflect the desired direction for an individual park, as well as the managing agency's goals.

The challenge developing for park managers is to effectively control crime and depreciative behavior in their areas without creating a negative public image or sacrificing their original mission.

Firearms

Whether or not park employees involved with law enforcement duties should be allowed to have available, or carry firearms is the subject of much debate (Fig. 15-11). The study completed by the GAO recommends that specific legislation be enacted that authorizes designated officials of all federal recreation areas *to carry firearms*, though in certain instances firearms have been worn and available to rangers in the past.

In Flickinger's study of Ohio state parks he found that the majority of state park managers and rangers, as well as visitors, thought park employees should be allowed to carry firearms for park security, to deter crime, and for self-protection. Many Ohio state park managers and rangers seemed to think that having weapons available was a panacea for solving the problems of increasing crime. Flickinger, in concluding his study, recommended that limited access to firearms be allowed, but only on an experimental ba-

Fig. 15-11. Should park rangers carry firearms? Some park agencies say "yes," some "no." Because more and more crimes are being committed with weapons, the trend in the United States is for commissioned peace officers to be armed while on duty in certain problem parks. (Photo courtesy of California Department of Parks and Recreation.)

sis, expressing concern about allowing all employees who were involved in law enforcement patrol duties access to firearms. He recommended that firearms should be used only by commissioned peace officers within problem parks and then only for night patrol and emergencies.[10]

Access to firearms by park employees has in the past been almost nonexistent, but isolated incidents of assaults on park employees, increased law enforcement duties, and recommendations of several studies have increased their use. Allowing access to firearms poses many challenges and additional responsibilities for agencies and managers. Specific policies must be formulated concerning what type of firearms will be allowed, who should be allowed access, and under what conditions. The possibility of adverse reaction to rangers carrying firearms may also develop in a particular area, or from a particular group of visitors. (The National Park Service for instance, has reduced the size and type of revolver issued to commissioned rangers, in order to present a lower profile to visitors.) In any situation, to allow law enforcement employees to have firearms available is a major decision, and must be made only after careful consideration.

Liability

Commissioned peace officers, field employees, and administering departments can be held responsible for their actions while engaging in law enforcement practices. A commissioned officer has somewhat more protection than a ranger who is not commissioned. An individual employee may be held liable by criminal law as well as civil law. In other words a park officer making an illegal arrest may be sued by the private party, as well as arrested and charged for the deed.

Peace officers may, in unusual instances, be held liable both by criminal law and civil law for arbitrarily arresting someone, detaining a person without filing charges, assaulting a private person, unreasonable searches, failure to promptly arraign a suspect, and several other abuses against private citizens. The complexities involved in law enforcement leave untrained and inexperienced employees vulnerable to committing illegal or wrongful acts against members of the public. In the International Association of Chiefs of Police report prepared for the National Park Service, the investigators found that several rangers on occasion had illegally detained park visitors—a practice that could have resulted in legal action by a private party. They also found that makeshift detention facilities were unsafe in several parks.

An administrative officer may also be held liable for improper supervision of a ranger committing an illegal act. The hearings may show that an administrator failed to adequately supervise an employee who committed the act.

In the IACP report it was pointed out that many seasonal rangers were participating in law enforcement activities with no background checks, no previous law enforcement experience, and without adequate on-the-job training.[15] Although the National Park Service now requires seasonal rangers to participate in preseason training, many agencies do not. Field employees acting in a potential law enforcement posture are many times seasonal employees who assume duties immediately on arrival or after short in-service training programs.

Civil liability may also be imposed on an agency for failure to properly train commissioned peace officers and field employees. "The law relating to insufficient training generally falls into four subjects: firearms, brutality, traffic control, and medical aid. Lack of exposure is also evident in cases involving arrests and searches, high speed pursuits, and character defamation."[1] An agency may be held liable, for example, if an employee has an accident while operating an emergency vheicle and it can be shown that adequate training was not provided.

The Canadian Approach

For the most part this chapter deals with law enforcement in the United States. The Canadian approach differs somewhat, and is not uniform from province to province. However, for the most part, park rangers and supervisors in Canada can concentrate on park management while keeping a relatively low profile on hard-core law enforcement. A professional police organization, the Royal Canadian Mounted Police (RCMP), is authorized to enforce all that country's laws and serve as the provincial police force, as well as the municipal police force, in many areas.

The RCMP is regarded as *ex officio* park staff

and as such, it routinely patrols parks. The federal government charges the individual provinces for this police service through a fee structure based on a per capita assessment, so there is no direct expense to the individual park. The RCMP serves both provincial and national parks.

To a greater or lesser extent, depending on the provincial situation, park rangers or wardens still have many of the same duties that their U.S. counterparts have. These include enforcing checkout time, leash laws, litter laws, and traffic laws; evicting drunks and rowdies, seizing illegal firearms, drugs, and alcohol, and enforcing dozens of other regulations listed in their agencies' respective Park Acts. The park officer is also responsible for detaining violators, protecting evidence, and providing other assistance to the RCMP staff, as well as pinpointing troublesome times and places so that RCMP patrols may be stepped up.

In some provincial park systems there are park rangers who possess special constable appointments and are authorized to enforce statutes beyond those cited in the Park Act. In such instances they take initial action on all unlawful acts committed in the parks, calling in members of the local RCMP detachment only when backup is needed.

CONCLUSION

Proper and adequate procedures in law enforcement depend on professional training, adequate supervision, and irreproachable employeee conduct. Professional handling of operations, especially those involving law enforcement is not only necessary for maintenance of good visitor-agency relations, it is also required by law. Agencies involved in law enforcement that provide less than adequate training and supervision of field employees leave themselves, their field employees, and the visiting public unnecessarily vulnerable.

Park rangers are diplomats and public relations officers in uniform. Even if they do not have a peace officer's commission, carry no weapons, and lack the power of arrest, they still have a challenging variety of tasks related to keeping the peace and assuring good order. The ranger in uniform is a symbol of security.

REFERENCES

General References

Adams, Thomas F. 1971. *Police Patrol; Tactics and Techniques.* Prentice-Hall, Inc. Englewood Cliffs, NJ.

Baker, J. Standard. 1975. *Traffic Accident Investigation.* The Traffic Institute, Northwestern University. Evanston, IL.

Clark, Roger N. 1976. "Control of Vandalism in Recreation Areas—Fact, Fiction, or Folklore?" *Vandalism and Outdoor Recreation: Symposium Proceedings.* USDA Forest Service PSW-17 Pacific Southwest Forest and Range Exp. Stn., Berkeley, CA.

Code of Federal Regulations, Title 36, Parks, Forests and Public Property, Revised July 1, 1976. Republished by Department of the Federal Register. Washington, DC.

Coffey, Alan R., Edward Eldefonso, and Walter Hartinger. 1971. *Police-Community Relations.* Prentice-Hall, Inc. Englewood Cliffs, NJ.

Crockett, Thompson S. 1968. *Law Enforcement Education.* International Association of Chiefs of Police, Inc., Professional Standards Division. Washington, DC.

Eldefonso, Edward. 1967. *Law Enforcement and the Youthful Offenders: Juvenile Procedures,* Wiley. New York.

Peel, John Donald. 1970. *Fundamentals of Training for Security Officers.* Charles C. Thomas. Springfield, Il.

Public Law 94-458, October 7, 1976, 94th Congress, "General Authorities Bill."

Public Law 92-82, August 10, 1971, 92nd Congress, "Cooperative Law Enforcement Program."

Schwartz, Eugene. 1973. "Police Services in the Parks," *Parks and Recreation,* 8(4):38, 72–74.

Shanks, Bernard, 1977. "U.S. Park Rangers Trade In Guidebooks for Guns," *University of Washington Daily*, January 4.

Watson, Nelson A. 1969. "Issues in Human Relations," *Guides for Police Practice*. International Association of Chiefs of Police. Washington, DC.

Whisenand, Paul M. 1971. *Police Supervision: Theory and Practice*. Prentice-Hall, Inc. Englewood Cliffs, NJ.

References Cited

1. Americans for Effective Law Enforcement Inc. 1974. "Liability for Insufficient Supervision and Training of Police Officers," Brief 74-1, February.

2. American Park and Recreation Society. 1974. *National Survey of Crime, Violence and Vandalism in Park, and Recreation Areas.* (PRC/Public Management Services, Inc., assisted in compilation of data and analysis). National Recreation and Park Association, Arlington, VA.

3. Bowman, Elton G. 1971. "The Cop Image," *Parks and Recreation*, 6(1):35–36.

4. Bryson, Sandy. 1978. "Ranger's Four-Pawed Partner," *Trends*. Park Practice Program. NRPA. 15(3):18–20.

5. California Department of Parks and Recreation. 1975. "Public Protection and Law Enforcement," *Operations Manual*.

6. Campbell, Frederick L., John C. Hendee, and Roger N. Clark. 1968. "Law and Order in Public Parks," *Parks and Recreation*, 3(12):28–31, 51–55.

7. Clark, Roger N., John C. Hendee, and Frederick L. Campbell. 1969. "Values, Behavior and Conflict in Modern Camping Culture," *J. of Leisure Research*, 1(4).

8. Dowell, C. D. 1973. "Panic in the Parks," *Parks and Recreation*, 8(1).

9. Eldefonso, Edward, Alan Coffey, and Richard C. Grace. 1968. *Principles of Law Enforcement*. Wiley. New York.

10. Flickinger, Theodore Blair. 1976. "Crime and Law Enforcement in Ohio's State Parks," unpublished doctoral dissertation, Ohio State University, Columbus.

11. General Accounting Office. 1977. *Crime is a Serious Problem in Federal Recreational Areas* (draft). Washington, DC.

12. German, A. C., Frank D. Day, and Robert R. Gallati. 1966. *Introduction to Law Enforcement*. Charles C. Thomas. Springfield, Il.

13. Hadley, Lawrence C. 1971. "Perspectives on Law Enforcement in Recreation Areas," *Recreation Symposium Proceedings*, USDA Forest Service Northeast Forest Exp. Stn., Upper Darby, PA.

14. International Association of Chiefs of Police. 1965. *The Patrol Operation*. Gaithersburg, MD.

15. International Association of Chiefs of Police. 1970. *A Staff Study of Law Enforcement and Public Safety Resources in the National Park Service*. Washington, DC.

16. McCall, Joseph R. and Virginia M. McCall. 1977. "Through Appreciation Protection," *Outdoor Recreation, Forest, Park, and Wilderness*. Benziger Bruce & Glencoe, Inc. Beverly Hills, CA.

17. Moeller, George H., Rodney G. Larson, and Douglas A. Morrison. 1974. *Opinions of Campers and Boaters at the Allegheny Reservoir*, USDA Forest Service Research Paper NE-307. Northeast Forest Exp. Stn., Upper Darby, PA.

18. National Park Service. *Seasonal Law Enforcement Training Material*. Pacific Northwest Region. Seattle, WA.

19. National Park Service Law Enforcement Task Force. 1977. *Task Force Report on Law Enforcement in the National Park Service*. Washington, DC.

20. National Park Service. 1966. *National Park Service Policy Changes Affecting Law Enforcement*. Statements on Law Enforcement by Chief of Management and Visitor

Protection Training Program, Shenandoah National Park. Luray, VA.

21. Pantaleoni, C. A. 1971. *Handbook of Courtroom Demeanor and Testimony.* Prentice-Hall, Inc. Englewood Cliffs, NJ.

22. PRC/Public Management Services, Inc., U.S. Army Corps of Engineers. 1974. *A Study of Law Enforcement Needs and Means of Providing Visitor Protection at Corps of Engineers Lakes.* Washington, DC.

23. Shanks, Bernard. 1976. ''Guns in the Parks,'' *The Progressive*, 40:21–23.

24. Sigler, William F. 1972. *Wildlife Law Enforcement.* William C. Brown Co. Dubuque, IA.

25. Vetter, Harold J. and Clifford E. Simonsen. 1976. *Criminal Justice in America, The System, The Process, The People.* W. B. Saunders Co. Philadelphia, PA.

26. Washington State Parks and Recreation Commission. (Updated periodically.) *Enforcement Manual.* Olympia, WA.

27. Watts, James F. 1976–1977. ''The Criminal Law Enforcement Authority of Park Rangers in Proprietary Jurisdiction Natural Parks—Where Is It? *California Western Law Review*, 13(1).

Personal Contacts

28. Greig, John. (Telephone interview, personal interview and correspondence.) Washington State Parks and Recreation Commission, Olympia.

29. Finks, Larry. (Personal interview.) U.S. Park Police, PNW Regional Law Enforcement Specialist, National Park Service, Seattle, WA.

30. Hull, Ben. (Personal interview.) USDA Forest Service, Law Enforcement Specialist Region 6, Portland, OR.

31. Twight, Ben. (Correspondence.) The Pennsylvania State University, University Park.

32. Washington State Parks and Recreation Commission. 1977. (Personal interview and correspondence.) Deception Pass State Park and Regional Office, Burlington, WA.

CHAPTER SIXTEEN

FIRE MANAGEMENT

Prehistoric fires probably burned most of North America at one time or another. The primeval conifer forests that were found here, with their associated deciduous components, were largely fire-dependent ecosystems. In more recent times the native Americans were known to use fire to improve the range where lightning fires were not keeping the vegetation down. With the arrival of the Europeans, Asians, and Africans, more burning took place to open up the forests for agricultural lands and homesites as well as for mineral exploration. In the wake of severe damage and loss by human-caused fires, strong fire suppression organizations and anti-fire campaigns were established by federal, state, and provincial governments. But fire exclusion has tended to produce an unnatural forest, at least in those areas of North America where fire was once a relatively frequent natural event. In discussing fire control remember that fire is not an unnatural disturbance, and that whole ecosystems have evolved in response to it.[4]

Although fire is now acknowledged as being natural and useful under certain conditions, the fact still remains that fire burning *out of control* (wildfire) can be a park manager's biggest nightmare (Fig. 16-1). Parks are generally characterized by large continuous areas of mixed vegetation with a few buildings interspersed. Most of the vegetation, at least during some part of the year, is flammable. Most park managers have some other organization, such as the state or pro-

vincial forestry agency, which serves as the park's first line of defense. However, should a wildfire occur, the protection of human lives, public property, and natural resources is still the responsibility of the park manager, even though help may be on the way. For this reason a chapter on fire management has been included in this book.

Several terms must be defined in order to understand this chapter. A distinction must be made at the outset between controlled burns and wildfires. *Fire management* includes fire prevention, fire suppression, and the use of fire for specific purposes such as *controlled* fires or *prescribed burning*—the use of fire as a management tool. *Wildfires* are fires burning out of control. They are commonly called *forest fires*, or *grass fires* in areas devoid of trees or brush.

FIRE MANAGEMENT AND PRESCRIBED FIRE

The term *fire management* implies that fires in the forest may be both good and bad. For example, the same fire may be good for some parts of a forest ecosystem, but be bad for forest industry or the safety of the public.[8] Fire management is designed to deal with such conflicts by recognizing that the factors of time, location, fuel flammability, ecology, and economics make fires in the forest either tolerable or intolerable.[1]

The prescribed fire is widely used today, not

Fig. 16-1.   A fire out of control can be a park manager's biggest nightmare. Human lives, public property, and natural resources are involved. This fire is burning in Mesa Verde National Park, Colorado. (National Park Service photo by Fred E. Mang, Jr.)

only in North America but on other continents as well. In Australia large areas are burned annually by igniting the fuels from aircraft. In Kruger National Park, in South Africa, areas up to 100 sq mi (258 km²) are burned at one time.

Land managers use fire to prepare a favorable site before planting tree seedlings, to provide more suitable habitat for wildlife, to control weeds, to eliminate disease and insects, and to remove logging slash. Fire is also used under controlled conditions to eliminate accumulations of forest fuels (living and dead underbrush) before these assume hazardous proportions as *flash fuels*. Such fires are known in land management practices as *prescribed fire*. They may also be called *controlled burns*, or *management fires*.

The objectives of prescribed fire in land management generally are as follows.

Hazard reduction (presuppression).

Nutrient release.

The control of undesirable species.

Cover type conversion.

Improved grazing.

Planting site preparation.

Sanitation (eliminating diseased or insect-infested trees).

Wildlife habitat improvement.

Each burning situation requires special consideration of the safety, cost, fuel type, weather conditions, available manpower, topography, and the objectives of the burn prescription.

Park managers should study the use of the prescribed or controlled burn, and determine if such land management practices might have application in their parks. Although many of the above objectives may not be relevant to park management, hazard reduction and cover type conversion usually is. Burning of undergrowth and dead trees under controlled conditions is preferable to an uncontrolled wildfire, and this limited slower burning gives wildlife a chance to escape the area. Controlled burning may also stimulate germination and growth of species favorable for wildlife. This practice may be a matter dealt with by agency policy, so the manager must be familiar with the latitude allowed in these matters. Campgrounds and other parts of the park with high human values should not be burned. Because of esthetic values only small parts of a park should be burned by prescription at any one time.[5]

Since large sections of the public have been conditioned to believe that all fires are bad, it may be necessary for the managers to launch a public education program if they wish to practice fire management. The interpretive staff can assist by disseminating information on its objectives, techniques, and advantages.

Smoke from fires would normally be considered a nuisance. It limits visibility, smells unpleasant to some, spoils photographs, and thus may reduce visitation. This, however, depends on the location of the park and how long it takes visitors to get there. If the park is difficult to reach, and reservations must be made well in advance and funds committed long before the trip, visitors may not cancel. This happened in Denali National Park (formerly Mount McKinley) during a season when wildfires were burning in much of interior Alaska. Although the mountain was not visible during most of the summer, visitation actually increased but length of stay was reduced.[7]

An example of a fire management program is the California State Park System, which has over 200 park units in a great variety of vegetative types. Many of these have a high potential for destruction by wildfire because of the large accumulations of fuel. Because of the placement of campgrounds, picnic areas, residences, trails,

roads, and other developments within areas of high fire potential, the state has adopted a policy to do the following.

1. Protecting state park units and visitors from major wildfires sweeping in from outside.
2. Preventing damage from wildfires originating within park lands.
3. Accomplishing well-defined environmental management objectives involving vegetation, soils, wildlife, scenic, and esthetic considerations.

The fuels of certain parks are modified or broken up into smaller manageable units by a system of narrow 10-ft-wide (3 m) firebreaks, or wider 100 to 300 ft (30 to 90 m) shaded fuelbreaks. Fire management in California state parks, then, is essentially a fuel management program.[3]

Fire management also encompasses the concept of permitting some lightning-caused wildfires to burn without direct suppression. This "natural fire" policy has gained acceptance in the larger western national parks and forests as well as in national wildlife refuge wilderness areas. This idea is relatively new to land management agencies in the United States but has been practiced in Canada for many years. As stated above, fire has always been an important element in maintaining natural ecosystems. In areas such as these, which are managed to maintain natural conditions, fires started by lightning may be allowed to burn as long as human life, public developments, or other agencies' lands are not being threatened.[9] However, before the decision is made to control or not control a fire, the manager must be in a position to be able to predict what will be the result of a given course of action.[6]

Many large parks today possess fine stands of trees that no one would wish to see destroyed, yet these trees are extremely vulnerable. Because of careful protection in the years since the parks were established, the understory fuel has built up to the point where these stands would be destroyed should a major fire break out.

Controlled burning under appropriate conditions of temperature, relative humidity, and wind, as well as proper moisture content of fuel, has long been a standard practice in some commercial forests. Now it is being practiced in parks and other areas where tree protection, not timber production, is the major consideration.

As the knowledge of fire management increases through practice and research, more information will be available to the park manager. The references at the end of this chapter, particularly the one by Peter Gaidula, will provide the reader with more details.

WILDFIRES

A wildfire is a freely burning conflagration. This sort of fire consumes millions of acres of forests annually in North America. Attempts are made to limit and extinguish most of these fires, especially those that are human–caused and that are located in areas where damage to human life, property, and perhaps even recreational values exceed long-term ecological considerations.

Causes of Wildfires

Because fires may either start outside park boundaries and spread into the park, or vice versa, it is important for the park manager to have some knowledge of the causes of fires. Uncontrolled fires are quite a different matter from controlled burns, and nearly always come at a time when any conflagration in the park would be dangerous. Although statistics specifically related to parks are not available, in the United States generally, the causes of wildfires have been classified under nine headings. Lightning accounts for 10 percent, the other 90 percent are human caused. Each cause is considered here.

Incendiary. This is the largest category of human-caused fires in the United States, and it accounts for approximately 28 percent of the wildfires. An incendiary fire is one set purposely on someone else's land without the owner's permis-

Fig. 16-2. An incendiary fire at Fort Macon State Park, North Carolina. This bathhouse, valued at $250,000, was ignited by an arsonist on a Labor Day weekend. (Photo courtesy of North Carolina Department of Natural Resources and Community Development.)

sion. The reasons for setting such fires include gaining employment as a firefighter, improving hunting conditions, killing insects or snakes, paying back a personal grudge against the landowner, diverting attention from other illicit activities, or as an unprovoked act of vandalism (Fig. 16-2).

Debris Burning. This is the second ranking cause of wildfires, responsible for 22 percent of human-caused fires. This is a traditional and widespread land management practice that many landowners are loathe to give up. No doubt their forebears also burned dead leaves in the spring or dead grass in the fall. Unwillingness on the part of the burner to obtain the necessary labor force to contain debris fires, or misjudgment as to weather and wind conditions when burning, results in the fire escaping to adjoining land. Sometimes this may be parkland, and thus managers must be aware of adjoining owner's practices in this regard. Legislation regulating air pollution may reduce this percentage in the future.

Smoker.   Fires of this origin average about 11 percent of each year's total (the number three cause today). Smokers include all types of people using tobacco, including hunters and fishermen, berry pickers, truck drivers, picnickers, and any of dozens of other park- or forest-user designations. Perhaps the total number of smoker-caused fires may also decline in the future as health awareness and the protests of nonsmokers discourage this habit.

Children.   Accounting for about 9 percent of the designated total are wildfires caused by children less than 12 years old. Playing with matches is still one of the major risks in children-caused fires.

Railroad.   Railroad operations account for about 6 percent of all these wildfires. Sparks from overheated brake shoes and smokestacks, burning rights-of-way, and any other activity causing fires related to railroads are included in railroad fires. Where railroad tracks skirt the boundaries of a park area the park manager must be aware of this potential hazard.

Camper.   This category, responsible for about 3 percent of all human-caused wildfires, includes campfires for cooking, warmth, and light. Very few such fires, of course, start in developed campgrounds with standard fireplaces or stoves. Most camper fires are caused by hikers, hunters, fishermen, and other backcountry users.

Equipment Use.   These wildfires, some 4 percent of the designated total, are caused by any mechanical equipment other than that used in railroad operations. Power saws, bulldozers, and other construction and logging equipment are included.

Miscellaneous.   These wildfires, which account for about 9 percent of the total of human-caused fires, cannot be classified under the other categories of wildfires. Cabin fires, autos leaving the highway and burning, sparks from a chimney—all these are grouped under miscellaneous causes.

Lightning.   Approximately 10 percent of all wildfires start from lightning strikes. Most occur in the Rocky Mountain and Pacific Coast states. Unlike the fires mentioned in the eight preceding groups, these are not preventable.

There are regional variations in these totals. For example, incendiary fires account for 39 percent in the southern states, 10 percent in the Pacific states, but only 2 percent in the Rocky Mountain states. On the other hand, lightning fires account for 61 percent in the Rocky Mountain states, 31 percent in the Pacific states, and only 2 percent in the southern states.[2]

WILDFIRE PREVENTION

Two national fire prevention programs in the United States continuously bring fire prevention information to the public. One is the National Cooperative Forest Fire Prevention Program, also known as the federal- and state-sponsored *Smokey Bear Program*. The second is the *Keep Green Program* sponsored by forest industries. Both programs, through radio, TV, and newspapers, constantly keep the public aware of the need to be careful of fire when in a forest or range environment. The Smokey Bear Program is also used in most parts of the Dominion of Canada. In the Northwest Territories, however, the fire prevention symbol is Taktu, a Friendly Caribou. Considering the fact that nearly 9 out of 10 wildfires are caused by people, it appears there is still a great need for the cautionary role of these programs.

Most state and provincial forest land is under some type of organized fire protection. Thus when a fire occurs and is detected, it is attacked by a fire control agency. In most areas the state or provincial forestry agency is ultimately responsible for wildfire control unless the fire is on federal land. In either case, in park areas the initial attack may be the duty of the park staff.

As noted earlier many fires are started by people camping or smoking in the backcountry. Park managers with trail systems, fishing streams, or boat-access forested sites should attempt to warn user groups before they leave the front country. Posting signs at trailheads reading ''No Smoking While Traveling'' and reminding users to ''Drown Your Campfire'' at backcountry sites must be counted as minimum endeavors. During the critical seasons the park personnel at entrance stations and information desks, as well as those conducting interpretive activities, should be stressing fire danger. Fire permits for backcountry users detailing fire regulations and emphasizing fire hazard conditions can be helpful. Signs displaying the fire danger, located along the road to or just inside park entrances, are another means of keeping the public informed at critical times (Fig. 16-3). Off-site, off-season

programs targeted to reach specific user groups are often effective in reducing backcountry fires in the following season.

In the developed campground, with its permanent fireplaces and stoves, fire danger is not great (except under extreme conditions and human error), as these management devices are designed primarily to prevent wildfires. Campfires are sometimes prohibited outside of developed campsites. Carry-in stoves are permitted along some backcountry trails or in designated sites in certain areas.

The park manager may have to curtail backcountry use during critical fire danger periods. Keeping hikers out of the woods during extremely severe fire conditions by posting the area *closed due to extreme fire hazard* not only reduces the fire risk but also protects the hikers themselves, who might be trapped should fire break out. On

Fig. 16-3. A Forest Fire Danger Board located along routes leading to parks informs visitors of the fire danger for that day. The four-color sequence with bright red for extreme danger dramatizes the message. (Photo courtesy of British Columbia Ministry of Forests.)

the other hand, backcountry users can be effective fire detection agents.

Fire Risk. Wildfire prevention deals with the reduction of both fire risk and fire hazard. *Fire risk* is the *means* by which forest fuels catch fire. It refers to the causative agent such as a lightning strike, cigarette or match, or an abandoned campfire. Although nothing can be done to control the lightning strike, there are ways to lessen other forms of risk, such as the area closure example above.

Fire Hazard. Dead leaves along a trail, dry grass along a roadside, or snags and slash in a forest constitute fuel that can be easily ignited. This fuel and its condition with respect to ignition and flammability is called the *fire hazard*. Fire hazard reduction is a part of fire prevention, and it can be accomplished by removing fuels from areas exposed to high fire risk. The park manager can reduce fire hazard by removing fuel from a plowed strip along the park boundary, especially where the boundary runs next to a road where smoker fires could start. This firebreak might also guard the park from adjacent farmland or urban land where debris burning is practiced. Some park managers remove light ground fuels through periodic prescribed burns. Fire hazard reduction can be effected by type conversion, such as annuals to perennials, or brush to grass. This may require approval from higher authorities, and presupposes an informed visitor clientele. Another way to reduce fire hazard, where permissible, is to permit livestock grazing.

The cost of hazard reduction is often high and should be considered carefully. When both risk and hazard are high, it follows that such an area should receive attention whereas one of limited risk and high hazard might be better placed in a lower priority.[8]

Fire Behavior

Before discussing presuppression and suppression activities, there should be some understanding of how a fire can be expected to behave once

it is started. No two fires are alike of course, but generally speaking, an experienced fire fighter can predict what a fire will do.

Basically, fires tend to burn in the direction the wind is blowing, and uphill. They move slowly in heavy fuels such as logs and large limbs, but often burn more intensely here. Fires burn faster in light fuels such as grass, leaves, and fine brush (Fig. 16-4). In the absence of wind, and on flat topography, a fire will spread out uniformly, assuming the fuels it encounters are similar.

A fire that burns slowly through the forest organic matter below the surface is termed a *ground fire*. A fire that consumes the loose debris and smaller vegetation on top of the ground is termed a *surface fire*. When a fire burns between the surface and crown it is referred to as an *understory fire*. If the fire rises to the branches and foliage of the forest and moves forward through the treetops, it is called a *crown fire*.

Most wildfires start as surface or ground fires and may eventually become crown fires. Embers from the crown may fall to the forest floor and start new surface or ground fires. All three may occur at the same time. A fire whose heat is lifting and blowing embers ahead of itself, generat-

Fig. 16-4. Fire behavior is affected by several factors. This fire is burning uphill in light fuels of grass, leaves, and fine brush. Note radios in firefighter's pockets. (Photo courtesy of USDA Forest Service.)

ing new separate fires, is said to be developing *spot fires*.

When a fire is crowning and burning several hundred acres at once it creates tremendous heat, and often generates its own weather, including small tornadoes. In such a situation the course of the fire becomes unpredictable, and the danger to firefighting personnel is great. This kind of fire is sometimes called a *blowup*. Fire behavior is affected by topography, temperature, relative humidity, wind speed and direction, and a host of other factors, including fuels.

Fuel and Its Effects on Fire Behavior. Fuel includes all burnable material in the forest such as duff, roots, rotting wood, stumps, leaves and needles, bark, branches, and standing trunks. Included also are the many forms of grasses and other herbs, as well as shrubs and small trees. The rate of spread through fuels varies with such factors as moisture content, fuel quantity, size and arrangement; fuel continuity, pitch and resin content, season of the year, and whether the fuel is alive or dead. Therefore, a knowledge of fuels is important in predicting fire behavior. Even more to the point, fuels are one component of the fire triangle (see page 268) that can be manipulated. This can be done through the construction of firebreaks, by reducing fuel volume, or by converting vegetation from one type to another through prescribed burning.

Wind and Its Effects on Fire Behavior. Wind is also an important factor in fire behavior, for it supplies oxygen to the fire, dries out fuels, and increases the rate of spread exponentially proportionate to the wind speed. Fire-created whirlwinds lift burning embers aloft, then drop them, producing spot fires up to a half mile ahead of the fire.

Winds associated with frontal systems can quickly change the direction of a fire. With the passing of a cold front, the wind may become turbulent, changing its direction about 90° to the right. This can create havoc with established fire lines.

Local winds may determine fire direction and rate of spread. Local winds known as "mountain winds" tend to flow downslope at night after the sun goes down, and upslope in the morning after the sun warms the valley.[2] Additionally, winds blow off bodies of water (sea breezes) toward land in daytime, and toward the water from the land surface at night.

Topography and Its Effects on Fire Behavior. Topography affects fire behavior in several ways. Fire moves upslope in a manner similar to a fire moving before a strong wind. The steeper the slope, the closer the flames to the fuel. Preheating is accelerated and the fire spreads faster (Fig. 16-4).

Slope affects fuels in another way also. Compass direction of slope, or aspect, can influence fuel moisture. North and northwest slopes tend to be more moist than the sun-facing south and southeast slopes. Thus fuels on the southern exposures usually burn faster than those on wetter, northern slopes.

Elevation, another aspect of topography, also influences fire. Most fuels at lower elevations dry out first and may be ready to burn, while those at high elevations may still be covered with snow. Also, fuel quantity tends to be less at higher elevations. Topography may also influence wind patterns in that wind moves faster in valleys oriented parallel to the direction of the prevailing wind than it does in valleys that lie at right angles to it.

Presuppression Activities

The Organization and Fire Control Plan. A park with a small staff often must rely on another agency to handle major fire control activities. A cooperative agreement should be established between the park and that agency. In most instances, however, park personnel are responsible for the initial attack on park fires and then must cooperate with the fire control forces of other agencies when they arrive.

One of the most important presuppression ac-

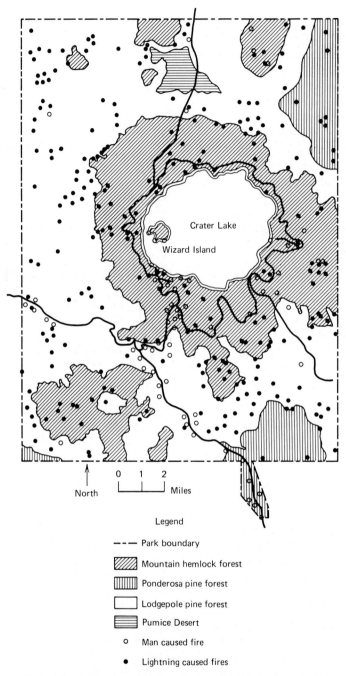

Legend

--- Park boundary

▨ Mountain hemlock forest

▥ Ponderosa pine forest

☐ Lodgepole pine forest

▤ Pumice Desert

○ Man caused fire

● Lightning caused fires

Fig. 16-5. A fire location map showing both human-caused fires (circles) and lightning-caused fires (dots) for a 50-year period between 1931 and 1981, in Crater Lake National Park, Oregon. Note the higher incidence of human-caused fires along the park roads. (Courtesy of Crater Lake National Park.)

tivities is preparing a *fire control plan*. The fire control plan should state who is responsible for detection, when the fire lookout personnel are to be on duty, what the priorities are for crews in fire dispatch, mutual aid agreements with neighboring agencies, and include evacuation plans for residences, campgrounds, and backcountry. The fire plan should cover training, who gets it and how much, and what qualifications are needed for various firefighting positions.

Data must be gathered for the fire plan on park topography, vegetative cover types, risk and hazard, weather patterns, equipment and labor availability, tool cache location, transportation routes by road and trail, communication facilities, and visitor-use patterns. A history of past human-caused and lightning-caused wildfires, including their behavior, should be compiled for risk analysis and other purposes (Fig. 16-5).

The plan should include instructions for each employee in the park in the event of a fire, as well as contingency plans for weekends or times when staffing may be reduced. These data must be kept up to date or they will be worse than useless: they will cause confusion and delay when speed of reaction is important.

Fire control duties are not separate from other employee duties. They should be integrated into the organization plan so that not only the maintenance division but the entire park staff can quickly assume a readiness or standby posture. When the alarm sounds, people with fire plan assignments leave what they are doing and become the fire control force. Regularly scheduled fire drills should become a standard procedure in order to achieve and maintain efficiency.

Fire Training.   Seasonal help must be given preseason instructions on safely handling flammable liquids, fire tools, and the proper use of pumper and hose equipment. Other fire school training should include map interpretation, compass reading, use of weather instruments, radio and telephone procedures, and general fire-control techniques (Fig. 16-6). The training course should also include general familiarity with park

Fig. 16-6.   A firefighter demonstrating the safe use of hand tools, radio equipment, and other firefighting equipment. Prospect Ranger District, Rogue River National Forest, Oregon. (Photo by Grant W. Sharpe.)

features such as road and trail location, sources of water, topography of the park, location of fire tool caches, and areas of high risk and hazard.

Fire line duty is extremely demanding physically. A crew may be in the field long hours working as hard as they have ever worked in their lives. The physical fitness of members of the initial attack crew must be taken into consideration by the dispatcher.

It is vital that personnel be thoroughly checked out on the operation and maintenance of specialized equipment such as hand pumpers, small engine pumps (Fig. 16-7), hose connections, and pumper trucks. The very nature of fire presumes emergencies, therefore training and practice sessions must be conducted by persons who can imbue the employees with that degree of interest

Fig. 16-7. A group of park management students is shown the use of a portable pump at Strathcona Provincial Park, British Columbia. (Photo by Grant W. Sharpe.)

and urgency required to facilitate learning. As with other safety practice sessions, boredom and a false sense of security must be overcome by skillful teaching techniques.

Permanent park personnel in any park with a fire threat should attend local or regional interagency fire suppression training courses. These courses are available through both federal and state fire control agencies.

Detection. "Hit the fire when it's small" is sound advice, but nothing happens until the fire is reported, so an efficient detection system is essential to a fire plan. Small parks can and do depend on visitors as detectors, asking them to report the fire at ranger or warden stations, or by telephone. Larger parks may have a fixed-point detection system—the lookout cabin or tower—where a fire watch is posted during critical fire periods. A mobile ground detector may also be used. This person patrols on foot, bicycle, motorcycle, or truck, in areas of high risk and hazard.

Larger parks, or those in a cooperative pact with other landowners, may rely on aerial detection during periods of high fire danger. Smoke spotted from aircraft can be scouted at close range and access to the fire, as well as fuel types, natural barriers, and other data can be reported. In some areas a combination of ground and air detection is used.[8]

Communication. Communication between the person who spots the fire and those concerned with suppressing the fire is a vital link. A fire spotter, such as a fire lookout or airplane spotter, should have a two-way radio connection to park headquarters. Commercial telephone and CB radios are used also, particularly when a park is dependent on visitors to report fires. Information on where to report fires should be posted. Park personnel must be notified by the dispatcher; this too requires a communication network. Usually it is done by two-way radio and telephone.

The Dispatcher. Someone in the park organization must serve as the fire dispatcher. It is this person who determines the location of the fire by plotting received information on park maps. The dispatcher also asks questions about the size of the fire, the fuel type it is in, the topography, wind direction and speed, nearness of water, and anything else that will be useful in determining the size of crew necessary to attack the fire.

Transportation. The *getaway time* is the time it takes for a crew to leave once it is notified of a fire by the dispatcher. The fire fighting equipment must be ready and available so there is a minimum of delay. The time between leaving and arrival at the fire is called *travel time*. To minimize this the dispatcher must have travel maps prepared. These maps show the road and trail system, and cross-country routes necessary to reach the fire. Vehicles must be available to avoid unnecessary delay. For this reason it should be standard practice to fill pumper trucks with water and to fill all gas tanks before trucks are parked for the night. By the same reasoning, personnel must make periodic radio contact with headquarters when working away from vehicles in more remote areas.

Equipment. The presuppression plan must list the kinds and numbers of tools, radios, provisions, and other pieces of equipment needed for fires of various sizes. Caches of tools should be located in strategic points around the park. Often these are sealed in red-painted boxes. On days of high fire danger, certain equipment must be kept in readiness for immediate use in fire suppression.

Small parks may need only a modest cache of hand tools and pump cans. A large park may require power saws, pumper trucks, and bulldozers to fight its building or forest fires, yet it too must have caches of hand tools in certain areas. Frequent inspection is necessary to guarantee that the tools are instantly available. Tools set aside for fire suppression should not be used for any other purposes. They must be kept sharp and in good condition.

Fighting fire by hand is unpopular and crews prefer to have the bulldozer do their work for them. Certainly the bulldozer is a versatile piece of equipment. It can construct fire lines quickly,

Fig. 16-8. The bulldozer is a versatile piece of firefighting equipment. It should be used with discretion on parklands, however, because of its potential for leaving long-lasting scars. (Photo courtesy of U.S. Bureau of Land Management.)

save property and sometimes human lives. In parks, however, compared with the more precise hand tools, a bulldozer is a blunt weapon and necessity, not convenience, should dictate its employment on the fire line (Fig. 16-8). The wide path a bulldozer carves may result in serious soil slippage at a later date, as well as leaving an unsightly scar for many seasons to come.

Interpreting Fire Danger. Another presuppression activity is the measurement of conditions that affect *fire danger*. A park manager wishing to keep track of fire danger must keep records of such environmental factors as temperature, relative humidity, wind direction and velocity, fuel moisture content, conditions of vegetation, the sky condition (clear or overcast), number of days since the last precipitation, and amount of precipitation. All these factors affect the ability of a fire to start, the rate of its spread, and the difficulty of control. A small weather instrument shelter containing minimum-maximum thermometers, rain gauge, sling psychrometer (or fuel moisture sticks), barometer, and wind vane and anemometer can be very helpful. Even though there is a National Fire-Danger Rating System available from the Forest Service, park managers must know how to gather and interpret local data in order to apply this to their particular area. They should obtain the daily fire weather forecasts for their area, and during critical periods, know how to interpret this information in terms of local fire danger.

Cooperative Protection. As mentioned above, the park manager will usually find neighboring agencies and local fire districts whose interest in fire control coincides with that of the park. Agreements can be made on use of roads, personnel, water, and equipment, as well as landing strips and helipads, since the use of aircraft is extensive now, in larger fires. Aircraft are used in all phases: detection, air drop of smoke jumpers and supplies, retardant and water application, and mop-up patrol. Cooperation is most effective when agreed on and coordinated long before the need arises. Information on these agreements must be incorporated in the fire-control plan.

The park manager should become acquainted with fire personnel, review the plans of neighboring agencies and local landowners, arrange for joint employee fire training sessions, and keep in close touch during periods of high fire danger. Friendly communications with neighbors may prevent some fires and will lead to greater efficiency in suppression of those wildfires that do occur.

Suppression Activities

A wildfire has been detected and reported, and a crew has been dispatched to suppress it. On arrival at the scene, the fire boss or crew chief must assess the fire with respect to the character of the fuel, the slope, wind direction and speed, volume of heat, and anything else that characterizes this particular fire. Is it a ground fire, surface fire, or crown fire? Is it small enough for this crew to contain or will additional help and equipment be needed? Are people or buildings in danger?

Methods of bringing wildfires under control are based on the theory that removing any one of the sides of the *fire triangle*—fuel, temperature, or oxygen—will cause the fire to go out. The fuel is removed by raking or digging a cleared line across the path of the fire, thus breaking the continuity of the fuel supply. The fire is also deprived of its fuel when this side of the triangle is made nonflammable by applying chemicals, water, or dirt. The temperature, or third side of the triangle, is also reduced through the cooling effect of applying chemicals, water, or dirt. Oxygen is eliminated by smothering the fire with any of these same materials.[8]

The attack on the fire is usually made frontally. If there is danger of the fire running or crowning, and thus endangering firefighters, it must be approached from the flanks. This strategy envisions the opportunity to pinch it off at the head when the fire reaches a natural barrier or when the wind changes direction.

Some fires may be attacked directly at their advancing edge by throwing dirt or water on the flames, or by beating them out with wet burlap bags or specially designed beaters. When it is unsafe to be so close to the flames, a line must be constructed ahead of, and parallel to, the advancing edge of the fire.

The crew must construct the fireline by clearing brush and grass down to mineral soil, thus forming a break wide enough to prevent the fire from reaching the other side. On fires that are advancing rapidly, the fireline must be constructed well in advance of the fire, and when possible, tied in with natural breaks such as ridges, streams, rockslides, or a roadway, if one exists. Trees along the fire side of the break must be felled if overhanging limbs could permit sparks to fly across the line. In some instances the fuel inside the fire break is ignited or *backfired* to rob the advancing fire of its sustenance, thus removing a side of the fire triangle.

After the fire is contained, *mopping up* begins. A reduced crew must remain to patrol the lines in order to take care of any sparks that may jump the fire break. When the burned area has cooled sufficiently, the mop-up crew must reenter the site and make sure that all burning materials within the boundaries of the fire are extinguished. Snags must be felled, logs rolled over, partially burned wood chunks dispersed to safe sites, and all smoke smothered with dirt or water. Many fires have been "contained" only to break out again because of inadequate mop-up in conjunction with an unexpected wind. Undetected "hot spots" often become active during the hottest time of the day.

Reports

Fire records must be carefully kept. As soon as a fire is suppressed a report should be filled out. This contains a detailed record of tools and equipment used, and number of members in the crew. It should also include such information as location, size of area burned, estimated damage, cost of suppression, probable cause of the fire, and any problems or weak spots noted in the execution of the fire plan.

CONCLUSION

Fire still maintains its dual role of friend and enemy. For the most part park managers will be involved in preventing fires and standing ready to suppress those that might start on or nearby their lands. Research and new equipment cause changes in methods and emphasis. Since fire management is a dynamic subject park managers must make an effort to keep up with the new ideas by reading and attending workshops.

REFERENCES

General References

Agee, James K. 1977. "Fire Management in the National Parks," *Western Wildlands*, 4(1): 79–85.

Despain, Don G. and Robert E. Sellers. 1977. "Natural Fire in Yellowstone National Park," *Western Wildlands*, 4(1):20–24.

Gaylor, Harry P. 1974. *Wildfires: Prevention and Control*. Robert J. Brady Co. of Prentice-Hall, Inc, Bowie, MD.

Kerr, Ed. 1981 "Update: Forest Arson in the South," *Amer. Forests*, 87(6):30–35, 62–63.

Kilgore, Bruce M. 1975. "Restoring Fire to National Park Wilderness," *Amer. Forests*, 81(3):16–19, 57–59.

Kozlowski, Theodore and C. E. Ahlgren. 1974. *Fire and Ecosystems*. Academic Press. New York.

Mutch, Robert W. 1977. "Fire Management and Land Use Planning Today: Tradition and Change in the Forest Service," *Western Wildlands*, 4(1):37–52.

Nelson, Thomas B. 1979. "Fire Management Policy in the National Forests—A New Era," *J. Forestry*, 77(11):723–725.

Parsons, D. J. and S. H. DeBenedetti. 1979. "Impact of Fire Suppression on a Mixed-Conifer Forest," *Forest Ecology and Management*, 2(2):21–23.

Pyne, Stephen J. 1982. *Fire In America: A Cultural History of Wildland and Rural Fire*. Princeton University Press. Princeton, NJ.

Sando, Rodney W. 1978. "Natural Fire Regimes and Fire Management—Foundations for Direction," *Western Wildlands*, 4(4):34–44.

Stankey, George H. 1976. *Wilderness Fire Policy, An Investigation of Visitor Knowledge and Beliefs*. USDA Forest Service Research Paper INT-180. Intermt. Forest and Range Exp. Stn., Ogden, UT.

Wood, Donald B. 1982. "Fuel Management's Potential for Reducing Frequency of Large Fires in the Northern Rockies," *J. Forestry*, 80(2):96, 105–107.

Wright, Henry A. and Arthur W. Bailey. 1982. *Fire Ecology: United States and Southern Canada*. Wiley. New York.

References Cited

1. Barrows, Jack S. 1973. "Forest Fire Management: For Ecology and People," *Fire Management*, 39(3), U.S. Department of Agriculture.

2. Brown, Arthur A., and Kenneth P. Davis. 1973. *Forest Fire: Control and Use* (2nd ed.). McGraw-Hill Book Company, New York.

3. Gaidula, Peter. 1976. *Wildland Fuel Management Guidelines for the California State Park System*. State of California Department of Parks and Recreation. Sacramento, CA.

4. Heinselman, Miron L. 1970. "The Natural Role of Fire in Northern Conifer Forests," *Proceedings—The Role of Fire in the Intermountain West—A Symposium*. Intermountain Fire Research Council. Missoula, MT.

5. Hoffman, Joseph E. 1971. "Fire in Park Management," *Proceedings—Fire in the Northern Environment—A Symposium*.

USDA Forest Service Pacific Northwest Forest and Range Exp. Stn., Portland, OR.

6. Lotspeich, Frederick B. and Ernst W. Mueller. 1971. "Effects of Fire in the Taiga on the Environment," *Proceedings—Fire in the Northern Environment—A Symposium*. USDA Forest Service Pacific Northwest Forest and Range Exp. Stn., Portland, OR.

7. Miller, Ivan D. 1971. "Effects of Forest Fire Smoke on Tourism in Mount McKinley National Park, Alaska," *Proceedings—Fire in the Northern Environment—A Symposium*.

USDA Forest Service Pacific Northwest Forest and Range Exp. Stn., Portland, OR.

8. Sharpe, Grant W., Clare W. Hendee, and Wenonah F. Sharpe. 1984. *Introduction to Forestry*. (5th ed.). McGraw-Hill Book Company. New York.

9. Prasil, Richard G. 1971. "National Park Service Fire Policy in National Parks and Monuments," *Proceedings—Fire in the Northern Environment—A Symposium*. USDA Forest Service Pacific Northwest Forest and Range Exp. Stn., Portland, OR.

CHAPTER SEVENTEEN

INTERPRETATION

Interpretation is a park function and therefore falls within the purview of the park manager. Unfortunately, not all managers understand its role in park management. Most park managers have not had interpretive experience, and fail to realize what interpretation can do to help them with their problems.

This lack of understanding is not necessarily the park manager's fault, it may be the result of agency policy. In some instances, the merits of interpretation have yet to be discovered. The attitude is "We don't have time for it," or, "Any interpretation attempted must on the employee's own time." In other agencies a high quality interpretive program is an agency directive. Certainly interpretation is an integral part of a mature and sophisticated park operation. Another reason for managers not realizing what interpretation can offer is that some interpreters themselves do not understand its possibilities as a management tool. This aspect has only recently been stressed. Before proceeding we should define interpretation.

INTERPRETATION—WHAT IS IT?

Interpretation is a service for visitors to parks, forests, refuges, and similar recreation areas. Visitors to these areas come for relaxation and inspiration, yet many also wish to learn about the area's natural and cultural resources. These resources are the area's geological features, animals, plants, ecological communities, and human history.[16]

Interpretation is an educational service that explains the park's varied resources to visitors in terms they can understand. Interpretation has three objectives.

1. To assist visitors in developing a keener awareness, appreciation, and understanding of the area they are visiting. Interpretation should help to make the visit a rich and enjoyable experience (Fig. 17-1).
2. To accomplish management goals. This is done in two ways. First, interpretation encourages thoughtful use of the recreation resources by the visitor, helping reinforce the idea that parks are special places requiring special behavior. Second, interpretation can be used to minimize human impact on the resource.
3. To promote public understanding of an agency's goals and objectives. Every agency, organization, or corporation has a message to convey. Well-done interpretation enhances the image of the sponsoring agency. If overdone, however, the message will be labeled propaganda rather than interpretation or public information.[16]

Interpretation, of sorts, has been going on for centuries through writers passing on their impressions of the natural environment to readers.

Fig. 17-1. Interpretation's first objective is to assist visitors in developing a keener awareness, appreciation, and understanding of the area they are visiting. Here the interpreter explains an object of interest along the shoreline at Fort Point National Historic Site, San Francisco Bay. (National Park Service photo by Richard Frear.)

Often the reader was removed from the resource. Today, in contrast, those who interpret are usually able to work more closely with the feature itself, or in direct contact with the recipient, and have a greater variety of media to work with.[16]

The overall interpretive effort is called the *interpretive program*. In larger parks it is usually under the direction of a permanent interpretive specialist or naturalist. This person answers directly to the park manager and usually employs other permanent and seasonal staff. In smaller parks, managers may be personally involved in the interpretive program even though they may not be trained in this work.

Careful planning of the interpretive program is important, and there are people who specialize in this aspect of interpretation. The interpretive planner, with the assistance of other resource management specialists, follows a series of seven logical steps: determining objectives, taking inventory, analyzing the data, synthesizing alternatives, developing the plan, implementing the plan, and evaluating and revising the plan (Fig. 17-2). This planning approach seeks to ensure that the natural and cultural amenities important to the area's interpretive study are identified and located before any development takes place that might destroy or modify these features, and that the appropriate interpretive media are used to reveal the story. The planning sequence also considers visitor needs and alternative choices of action before the final plan is selected.[1]

Park visitors are the reason for developing the interpretive program. These visitors vary greatly in their age, education, culture, and experience. Because of this diversity, the interpretive program should be varied, and this presents a challenge to the person considering interpretation.

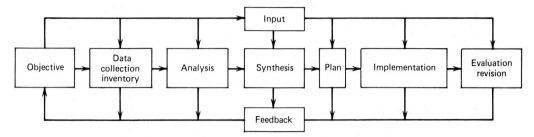

Fig. 17-2. The seven logical steps of Interpretive Planning. Note the opportunity for input and feed-back at every step. (From Bradley, Chapter 4 of *Interpreting the Environment*.)

Interpretation is an educational process, but not in the formal sense. Participation is voluntary, and visitors may leave the presentation at any time should the program not meet their expectations. To hold the visitors' attention, the interpretive experience must be inspiring and of high quality, and must strike the right balance between instruction and entertainment.

Seasonal interpretive employees, persons who work only during the heavy visitor-use season, do much of the day-to-day interpretation. Generally, these seasonal people form the direct link between the park phenomena and the park visitor. The interpretive staff also works directly with other park personnel in matters related to park protection and maintenance, as well as in public relations.[16]

WHO UTILIZES INTERPRETATION?

Interpretation is not limited to park agencies, but may be utilized by any organization that deals with the public. This would include public and private museums, nature centers, timber harvesting companies, public and private utilities, historical buildings and forts, wildlife refuges, fish hatcheries, restored villages and towns, and large engineering works such as hydroelectric power dams or nuclear plants. Although our main concern here is park interpretation, these other locations often have elaborate interpretive programs and are excellent areas to visit in order to obtain information and exchange ideas with the interpretive personnel working there. Also, because

those locations often receive large numbers of visitors, they are excellent places for off-site park interpretation.

THE ROLE OF INTERPRETATION AS A MANAGEMENT TOOL

Traditionally interpreters have envisioned their role as *helping people enjoy the park*. Certainly in the past most naturalists or interpreters have been oriented toward natural and human history. Earlier interpreters were for most part college graduates holding degrees in some aspect of natural history, and often lacked understanding of the fundamentals of park management. Managers look at parks from a different perspective than does the interpretive specialist. The manager has a resource to guard, visitors to protect, and contending pressure groups to placate. The manager is responsible for all park activities, including administration, planning, development, protection, budget preparation, interpretation, public relations, maintenance, and operations. Interpretation can contribute to the proper functioning of the organization, and interpreters must ask themselves: How do we fit into this organization? How do we become team members? How can we assist the manager in achieving management objectives? If interpreters don't understand this role it may become necessary for the manager to tactfully remind them of the park goals.

Interpreters are part of the park organization and must accept and define their role in the administrative affairs of the park. This is partly a survival action, for interpretive programs are often the first to have budgets reduced when funding is tight. To maintain their program, interpreters must prove their services are not only useful, but necessary. They cannot remain aloof from the business of park management.[18]

While Chief of Interpretation for the NPS, William Dunmire addressed this topic:

Interpretation should be employed by park management as a primary means of achieving all management objectives affecting the public. Interpreters should think of themselves as an integral part of the management team and should actively participate in developing and reviewing park-wide objectives and programs.[4]

Let us briefly review the objectives of interpretation as cited earlier: (1) to assist the visitor in appreciating the area, (2) to accomplish management goals, and (3) to provide visitor understanding of the agency. The second objective is the one that we will concentrate on. How can interpretation assist the park manager to solve problems related to visitor use of an area?

Park visits increase yearly, and this higher visitation brings more vandalism, theft, fire, and safety problems. Park managers should encourage their interpretive staff to assist in reducing these problems.

For example:

Suppose your park contains a high mountain area with fragile flower meadows. The visitors are ruining these meadows with a network of impromptu "social trails."

Perhaps there is an unacceptably high rate of death and injury each year in your park, among both concession employees and visitors.

Your park has a problem of visitors collecting sea shells, arrowheads, rare plants or animals, fossils, or unusual rocks.

You wish to close off an area or phase out a popular activity. You know there will be a pub-

lic outcry, yet protection of the site is your responsibility.

You have a poaching problem or perhaps a conflict between visitors and park animals.

All these problems are susceptible to interpretive solutions. As yet, little has been written on the topic of interpretation as a management tool and even less research has been conducted on the topic. However, interpretive researchers are turning their attention to this area of concern, so publications will be forthcoming. Let us now look at how some managers have used interpretation to assist in park management.

APPLICATION OF INTERPRETATION TO PARK MANAGEMENT

This section examines the potential of interpretation in four distinct areas of park management: natural resource management, historical and cultural site management, visitor protection and law enforcement, and maintenance.

Natural Resource Management

Meadow Rehabilitation. In recent years increased visitor use severely damaged the high mountain meadows of Mount Rainier National Park. Hikers crisscrossed the meadows with social trails, some of which ran straight up and down the slopes. The soil layer is thin, and plant regeneration is a long and laborious process. The problem: How could the meadows be saved while still providing visitor access?

Initially TRAIL CLOSED signs were placed at either end of the social trails. Jute matting was laid over the trails to hold down the soil and encourage regeneration.

People continued to walk on the trails. When visitors were asked why they were not obeying the signs, they replied that they did not understand why the signs were there. Other visitors thought the jute matting was provided for better traction, and was actually part of the trail system. These visitors were confused by the signs, and contin-

WHAT IS IT?

...Jute matting,
like a giant bandage,
provides first aid
for eroded meadows.

Please walk only on
paved or rock-lined trails.

High Mountain Meadows
Are Fragile Places

Give Them a Chance
PLEASE
STAY ON CONSTRUCTED TRAILS

Fig. 17-3.   An outside bulletin board that appeals to visitors in a positive way by using a friendly, explanatory approach. Mount Rainier National Park. (Photo by David C. Martin.)

ued to use the closed trails. Their use set an example for others, and the problem remained unresolved.[18]

After some consideration, the signs were changed to read CLOSED FOR MEADOW REHABILITATION. Brochures were printed to explain the delicate nature of the meadows. A self-guiding trail was constructed to simultaneously draw impact away from the meadows and educate the visitors. According to one ranger, who was with the project for six years, the new interpretive approach reduced use of the closed trails by 95 percent.[3] The park scored several pluses by using an interpretive approach. First, the resource management problem was solved; impact on the meadows was sharply reduced. Second, use of signs and brochures to convey the management message reduced ranger time on meadow patrol, thus freeing this personnel for other duties. Finally, the friendly and explanatory tone of the outdoor exhibits and brochures gave visitors a feeling of cooperation in a joint enterprise, rather than of being preemptorily ordered around on public land (Fig. 17-3).

Many people visit parks to escape the city with its traffic lights and NO TRESSPASSING signs. Perhaps the less of this tone they encounter in parks the more cooperative they will be. Some writers believe that the less threatened visitors are, the more likely they are to comply with rules.[2]

The ranger in the above Mount Rainier project believes that management should always use the "least impacting" technique. Accordingly, education and interpretation should be the first techniques used because they are the least restrictive. Interpretation means using reason rather than regulation. It tries to show relationships rather than give orders, such as DO NOT or KEEP OFF, even though this is really the message.[3]

Proper Backcountry Use. A study of backcountry management at Rocky Mountain National Park demonstrated the effectiveness of using selected educational interpretive methods, combined with a permit system, to alleviate problems of improper backcountry use.[6] According to one reviewer, the results showed that backpackers who had seen one of several interpretive exhibits or programs explaining the reasons for regulations had a significantly higher inclination to observe the rules than those who had not been exposed to an interpretive contact before their trip. A further finding was that this group had a more positive attitude toward the park's various backcountry restrictions and had acquired a greater sensitivity to wilderness values.[5]

Littering. State parks in northern California were having a problem with littering. It seems seasonal personnel were spending 60 percent of their time picking up after visitors. Signs and ranger contacts were not getting the message across. The solution was to start a concentrated litter-getter program in each park. An individualized award patch was created for each park, and visitors of all ages were challenged to take a stand against litter. The program was very successful. The visitors, both young and old, have fun earning the awards, and the park managers can employ the seasonal staff in more constructive ways.[15]

Off-Road Vehicles. Another California state park was having a problem keeping four-wheel drive vehicles on the park roadways. Ranger contact, enforcement, and signs did little good. The area manager, working with the interpretive specialist, tried to find some way to get the four-wheel groups to take a more positive interest in the park. The staff worked up a series of conservation projects, such as cleaning the beach, closing off short-cut roads, brushing out park roads and interpretive trails, and assisting with new signing. The program was presented to the local four-wheelers at a regular club meeting, and the membership took on all the projects. Off-road vehicle vandalism went down almost immediately and it was found that club members were warning nonmembers about staying on roadways and

Fig. 17-4. The conservation award patch presented to four-wheel drive club members who participated in several work projects on state park lands in northern California.

using marked access routes only. To reward each club member that participated in a number of work projects, a certificate was prepared, as well as a conservation award patch that could be worn on the club jacket (Fig. 17-4).[15]

Fire Management. For many years the policy of most government agencies regarding wildfire was simply "put it out." To help gain public assistance on this program, elaborate fire prevention campaigns, including the successful *Smokey Bear* project, were launched.

More recently, the National Park Service and other public agencies have accepted prescribed fire to accomplish certain management objectives, such as maintaining natural conditions in wilderness areas, helping to prevent large uncontrolled fires, improving soil conditions for the entrance of desired species, and fighting insect and disease problems.[21]

Not surprisingly, the National Park Service encountered considerable public resistance to its fire management policy. Citizens, taught for years to help prevent fires, did not understand why some fires were allowed to burn.

The park service turned to interpretation to

help solve its problem. Controlled burning of 10- to 40-acre blocks of Sequoia and Kings Canyon National Parks was prescribed to rejuvenate the stagnant sequoia stands. To avoid public outcry and sell their program, the park service developed an interpretive approach. Evening campfire talks, regular media releases, and publications described the "why" of this prescribed burning before it occurred. Interpreters were later stationed at the site of the fire to explain prescribed burning while it was occurring. As a result of this approach, the program met with a minimum of public resistance.[14]

Fossil Protection.   Visitors to Dinosaur Provincial Park in Alberta and Driftwood Canyon Provincial Park in British Columbia are encouraged to report significant sightings of fossilized materials in return for a certificate acknowledging

their help (Fig. 17-5). Use of the certificate has been largely responsible for altering the "take it home" tendency of earlier park visitors. The reporting also enables the park staff to systematically record and map these fossil finds.[11]

Wildlife Protection.   In Yellowstone National Park, heavy fishing pressure at Fishing Bridge on the Yellowstone River disrupted the ecological balance of the river system. As a result, many animals dependent on the fish for their existence left the area. To make matters worse, fish catches were often discarded.

The park first reduced the take limit. Still the problems continued. Management decided it was necessary to stop all fishing at the bridge. The bridge was closed and signed "No Fishing From Bridge." Interpretation was chosen as the method of enforcement, and two automatic vide-

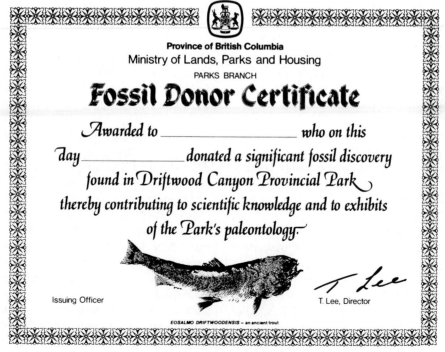

Fig. 17-5.   The certificate awarded by the park manager to visitors reporting significant finds of fossils. The certificate has now replaced the fossil as a take-home souvenir. This example is from Driftwood Canyon Provincial Park, British Columbia.

otape machines were placed on the bridge. The taped program described the life history of the fish, and their important role in the area's food chain. The hope was that visitors would comply with the closure rule if they understood the reasoning behind it. The program was successful; fishing at the bridge dropped, and no complaints were made.[14]

At Garrison Bay on San Juan Island, Washington, visitors to the National Historical Park disrupted the ecological processes of the beach by overdigging clams. An interpretive brochure was prepared for dispersal at information stations. The brochure described the life history of the clams, identified common species, and gave tips on safety and good clamming procedures. It was low keyed, positive, and easy to read. In addition to the brochure, a researcher working on a scientific study of the area's clam catch made information contact with the visitors on the beach. The researcher was not a park service interpreter, but she did perform an interpretive contact function.

The program was successful. Once clammers became engaged in conversation with a researcher, they were cooperative. Those visitors receiving the brochure also learned interesting and useful information during their stay at the park.[7]

Salmon poaching was becoming a problem during the early and late hours of the day in Terra Nova National Park in Newfoundland. The interpretive staff scheduled a guided walk during these same hours to watch beavers. Introducing people into the area kept poachers away.[20]

Similarly, deer poaching was becoming a problem in Fundy National Park in New Brunswick. The problem was reduced by scheduling deer watching at the lakes frequently used by poachers. These events were held at dawn and dusk and averaged 40 people each trip.[20]

Cultural Site Management

Many recreation systems contain areas where the resource managed is of cultural significance. In these archeological and historical areas outdoor recreation pursuits, such as overnight camping, are usually not permitted. Those permitted may be concentrated in a small area. The problem of how best to tell the story of the site, without endangering the site or structure itself, must be addressed in the management objectives.

The National Park Service has long used interpretive methods to bring alive the story of its cultural history. Traditional interpretive techniques include exhibits, movies, living interpretation, and guided tours. Guided tours provide access to sensitive sites normally closed to the public.[17] Living interpretation portrays the persons and events associated with the site or structure in an unforgettable way.

Living interpretation can also stimulate public interest and support for historical site preservation. This example comes from Fort Washington, a once-dilapidated National Park Service structure located on the Potomac River. A cannon-firing demonstration utilizing local volunteers was organized, which eventually generated enough public interest, funds, and services to restore and preserve the fort.[8]

Interpretive demonstrations can encourage protection of existing sites. At Stones River National Battlefield and Cemetery in Tennessee, the park gained local support for its presence by employing young townspeople in living interpretation demonstrations. When urban and industrial encroachment later threatened the park, the townspeople rallied to the cause and lent their support by stating, both verbally and in writing, that they were in favor of saving the park.[8]

Interpretive techniques can be applied to specific problems of site preservation. In 1975 a large (250 to 300 unit) private recreational vehicle campground opened just outside of Anza-Borrego Desert State Park in California. In the nearby area there were over a dozen native American rock-art sites, many of which were within walking distance of the campground. Park personnel, fearing vandalism and souvenir taking but lacking funds for adequate physical protection of the sites, devised an exclusively interpretive method of protection.

A sign was posted inside the private camp-

Fig. 17-6. Access to the native writings on these cliffs is not permitted unless one is on a conducted walk. Since this policy was initiated, vandalism to the pictographs and petroglyphs has virtually ceased. (Alberta Recreation and Parks photo by David McIntyre.)

ground clubhouse, where visitors would be likely to see it. Mounted on a papier-maché mock-up of an Indian pictograph, the sign explained the sites, and described the ongoing archeological efforts to record their story. The sign enlisted visitor assistance with these efforts, and directed hikers to obtain a special field brochure for use in recording their discoveries. The hope was to offer visitors an alternative to vandalism or souvenir collecting.[10]

Unfortunately, the program had only a short test period. Nine months after its inception the campground was destroyed by a tropical storm. Nonetheless, the program appeared successful. During this period, two-thirds of which included the primary visitor-use season, there was *no* vandalism at the sites.[12]

Another example of cultural resource protection comes from Writing-on-Stone Provincial Park, in southern Alberta. Vandalism of the native writings, for which the park was established and named, has virtually ceased since conducted walks were utilized as the sole means of visitor access (Fig. 17-6).[11]

Visitor Protection and Law Enforcement

Visitor protection encompasses not only protection of the visitor from injury but also protection of the park from the depreciative behavior of the visitors. Protection against bears, proper signing regarding other dangerous animals, roadway and trail signing, and display of safety tips, are examples of the first type of protection (Fig. 17-7). Apprehension of persons involved in theft, vandalism and other unsuitable behavior, as well as prevention of this sort of conduct, are examples of the second type.

Park managers in Los Angeles's Griffith Park are trained in interpretive nature study, handling of emergencies, and public relations. These rangers combine the activities of interpreter, first aider, temporary firefighter, and law enforce-

Fig. 17-7. This simple, easy-to-read, interpretive sign in Yosemite National Park gets the protection message across to park visitors. (Photo by Gunnar Fagerlund.)

ment assistant, "persuading disruptive individuals or groups to cooperate in protecting the rights of all users of the park, and offering guidance and help whenever sought or needed."[22] Mounted rangers alert for safety hazards patrol the bridle trails, and, by their presence, encourage proper equestrian behavior. Two-way radios allow the rangers to call for help from the city police department since they themselves carry neither guns nor batons. Widespread public acceptance of the ranger program has led to its expansion in other major Los Angeles parks.[23]

Bear Management. The recent deaths of several visitors by grizzly bear attack have intensified concern for visitors' safety at Glacier National Park in Montana. Park management has shifted personnel and dollars to the grizzly management problem at the expense of other services. The use of interpretation in solving this problem has won the support of the park superintendent. In a request for emergency finding for the bear management program, superintendent Phillip R. Iverson stated the following.

In 1976 interpreters issued approximately 85 percent of all back-country permits through Glacier's three main visitor centers. These personal contacts were critical due to the need to better inform visitors, especially hikers and campers, about bears and safety.

Iverson requested increased funding to expand hours of operation of the visitor centers, to provide increased staffing of the centers, and to extend the training time of interpreters in order to add safety, bear management, and other management concerns to their program.[9]

Campground Law Enforcement. The following example illustrates the use of interpretive techniques in solving a campground problem. Several years ago, overenthusiastic visitor use of motorbikes led to disturbances at a popular campground in Eldorado National Forest, in California. Lacking enforcement surveillance, the district decided to use an interpretive approach. A short interpretive brochure, with a motorbike on the cover, was printed and in plain, unofficial language it firmly stated use regulations. These were distributed to all patrol personnel, visitor centers, and administrative sites. Brochures were given to all cyclists, and placed on all parked motorbikes. At the same time, campground programs began to include a message on campground behavior and proper use of motorbikes.

According to the district ranger, the change in use of the campground was startling.[14] Once cyclists understood the rules, they complied with them. The success of Eldorado confirms the findings of a study by Ross and Moeller, which suggests that campers are generally not well informed about rules. Use of brochures will increase knowledge of rules, possibly bringing a change in visitor behavior.[13]

Maintenance

As we saw in Chapter 11, maintenance chores are an integral part of park life. Maintenance concerns include road and trail upkeep, maintaining safe and pleasant conditions within buildings, and the cleaning of restrooms, campgrounds, and other public-use areas. A properly maintained park offers a more enjoyable experience, contributes to good public relations, and reduces operational costs. Prevention of vandalism avoids costly repairs as well as presenting a more serene and restful milieu. Skellinger expressed this belief as follows.

I believe there are three areas we must explore in combating vandalism—education, maintenance, and enforcement. I cannot give priority to any one of these three as they all must be used and are, to some extent, dependent on each other for a successful program.

Skellinger listed two pressing needs. The first was for competent public relations.

Unless we let the public know that the object was broken by vandals, visitors think that it is just poor maintenance and wonder why they are paying taxes for this type of service.

The second was for education.

. . . Over the period of the last ten years I have noticed a continuing drop in the really malicious damage done in our nature centers. Another thing that I notice is that the older teenage kids will come to us and report acts of destruction that they observe. When this happens, they usually remark that because of the things they learn from the naturalist when they were in the lower grades they want to help keep the area in good condition and don't like kids that destroy the area for others.[19]

Public relations, education, and personalizing the park experience are jobs ideally suited to interpretation, and the foregoing has illustrated ways in which interpretation may assist the manager with certain problems. Since managers are responsible for the total park operation, including interpretation, they should have some knowledge of interpretive techniques. A brief survey of these follows.

THE TECHNIQUES OF INTERPRETATION

The manager, as well as the interpretive planner or other interpretive specialist, must have some understanding of the various media used in interpretation in order to choose the most appropriate means to communicate with visitors. Both the visitor and the resource should be considered when media are being selected.

The Visitor

1. Visitors need orientation on arrival at your park. What medium would make them feel more welcome? What facilities does your park offer and how can interpretive media provide answers to the visitor's questions?
2. Visitors in great numbers have a certain impact on a park area. What interpretive media can lessen this impact?
3. Visitors in unfamiliar areas need some warn-

ing of the dangers involved. What media can best inform the visitors of these dangers?

4. Visitors' length of stay varies greatly, so there needs to be a variety of media available in order to reach both the three-day and the three-hour visitor.

5. Are many of your visitors from another language group? Do your signs and brochures speak to them too?

6. Are many of your visitors urban dwellers with little information on appropriate behavior in parks? How will you reach these people?

The Resource

1. Each park has at least one interpretive theme. The essential feature may be geological, ecological, or historical. Some large areas may have several themes. The inventory phase of the interpretive plan will reveal these themes.

2. Some features are more vulnerable to visitor impact than others and certain media have greater resource protection potential than others. On the other hand, some media have greater environmental impact than others. For instance, a conducted walk, with 150 people, will have greater impact than a self-guided walk over the same trail. In another example, such as a fragile cave or historic building, a conducted walk with 20 people in attendance would be the wiser choice if one were to choose between it and a self-guided activity.

4. Permanent facilities must be carefully planned. Even small facilities that require such developments as water, a waste disposal system, electricity, and a parking lot will have an impact on a fragile environment.

Other considerations in media selection include the cost of the original investment, maintenance and replacement cost, durability under local weather conditions, and appropriateness to an agency. Every situation presents different problems; some media, as we have noted, have advantages over others.

MEDIA CHOICES

The interpretive program consists of both personal or attended services and nonpersonal or unattended services.[17]

Personal Services

In personal services, the visitor comes into direct contact with the interpretive specialist, and a two-way conversation may be entered into. The activity may be kept flexible in order to accommodate different groups. Personal services include the following.

Fig. 17-8. This truck-mounted mobile theater is equipped with an audio system, screen, and a sound-dampened electric generator. Illustrated messages dealing with interpretive management and informative demonstrations are thus brought to the more remote areas that do not have an amphitheater, or perhaps not even electricity. (Alberta Recreation and Parks photo by Dave McIntyre.)

Information Duty. This takes place in a park entrance station, campground office, visitor center, roadside information booth, trailhead, or overlook. Here the visitor seeks out the person on information duty.

Talks to Groups. In this activity, the interpreter makes a formal or informal presentation at announced times and in such places as amphitheaters, campfires, or auditoriums (Fig. 17-8). The topic matter is normally related to the natural and cultural history of the local area and is usually illustrated with slides. Visitors are also interested in such management-related problems as fire control, mountain rescue, bear control problems, police protection, and other behind-

Fig. 17-9. Park interpreters rehearse a clown skit aimed at solving park management problems such as drinking, picking wildflowers, and making excessive noise, at Cypress Hills Provincial Park. (Alberta Recreation and Parks photo by David McIntyre.)

the-scenes activities. Management problems such as vandalism, feeding wildlife, playing music loudly, allowing pets to run loose, or drinking in the park can also be dealt with during these talks (Fig. 17-9).

Living Interpretation. This is a form of historical interpretation in which some cultural activity such as wood carving, preparing food, making candles, firing old guns, bow and arrow making and use, or playing early musical instruments is demonstrated. These activities may be a part of a vignette depicting the past. The wearing of costumes and use of dialect are often part of the performance, which may be presented by one or more interpreters or local people familiar with the activity.

Nonpersonal Services

Here the interpreter relies on various devices to present the interpretive story. Communication flows one way only. Although nonpersonal services are a means of expanding the interpretive program beyond the capabilities of individual interpreters, they should not totally replace personal services.

In most instances the nonpersonal services are unscheduled, and may be participated in at the convenience of the visitor. Nonpersonal services include the following.

Audio Devices. These machines, which utilize human voices, music, and sound effects, include tape recorders and playback units, speakers and handphones, induction loops, and radio transmitters. Audio equipment is frequently used in conjunction with other devices, such as slide programs and exhibits.

Written Material. Included here are signs, labels, and a variety of publications, including everything from simple checklists to elaborate books on flora, fauna, geology, and history. Publications are used where detailed presentations are needed; they also have a souvenir value which is missing in other media.

Self-guided Activities. These include both self-guided trails (SGT) and self-guided auto tours (SGAT) and are particularly useful where visitor numbers are large and the interpretive staff is limited. Both activities are available to visitors at their convenience and at their own pace. Trails are specially built for the SGT but existing roads are used for the SGAT.

Exhibits. These are found both indoors and outdoors and are a very popular medium. Used properly, exhibits are highly effective. The main difficulty is in poor design, where too much detail is attempted.

Visitor Centers. These usually serve as the interpretive headquarters for the park. As they are major installations, their expense is relatively high. Such buildings are commonly equipped with an information desk, exhibit room, auditorium, staff offices and working space, restrooms, and drinking fountains.

CONCLUSION

The foregoing material has briefly outlined some interpretive responses to management problems. Although funds for interpretation may be difficult to obtain, the principles and techniques found in this chapter can often be put into practice with the help of interested staff, whether or not they have had interpretive training. Help is usually available from agency sources and from nearby universities or high schools. Volunteers can also recruit and organize interpretive help for your management problems.

REFERENCES

General References

Aldridge, Don. 1975. *Principles of Countryside Interpretation*. Part One: Guide to Countryside Interpretation. Her Majesty's Stationery Office, Edinburgh. Countryside Commission, Scotland.

Brown, William E. 1971. *Islands of Hope*. National Recreation and Park Association. Washington, DC.

Freed, Mike and Broc Stenman. 1980. Interpretation For Resource Management, *The Interpreter*, 11(4):27–30.

Lewis, William J. 1980. *Interpreting for Park Visitors*. Eastern National Park and Monument Association. Eastern Acorn Press. Philadelphia, PA.

Pennyfather, Keith. 1975. *Interpretive Media and Facilities*. Part Two: Guide to Countryside Interpretation. Her Majesty's Stationery Office, Edinburgh. Countryside Commission, Scotland.

Robinson, Alan H. 1975. Marine Parks: Planning For Recreation Interpretation and Environmental Education. *Trends*. Park Practice Program. NRPA.

Sharpe, Grant W. (ed.). 1982. *Interpreting the Environment* (2nd ed.). Wiley. New York.

Tildon, Freeman. 1967. *Interpreting Our Heritage*. The University of North Carolina Press. Chapel Hill.

Veverka, John A. and Sandra A. Poneleit. 1981. "Interpretation As a Management Tool for Underwater Parks," *J. of Interpretation*, 6(2):10–14.

Womble, Peter, Gordon Bultena, and Donald Field. 1981. "Interpretation and Backcountry Management," *J. of Interpretation*, 6(2): 21–23.

References Cited

1. Bradley, Gordon A. 1982. "The Interpretive Plan," Chapter 4 of *Interpreting the Environment* (2nd ed.), Grant W. Sharpe (ed.). Wiley. New York.

2. Castro, Nash. 1972. "Humanizing Park Signs," *Parks and Recreation*, 7(9):39, 74–76.

3. Dalle-Molle, John. 1976. Personal Communication. Mount Rainier National Park. Longmire, WA.

4.   Dunmire, William W. 1976. "Servicewide Goals for Interpretation," *In Touch*, 1(12):2–3, National Park Service, Washington, DC.

5.   Dunmire, William W. 1976. *Stretching Recreation Dollars Through Interpretation*. John S. Wright Forestry Conference, Purdue University. Lafayette, IN.

6.   Fazio, James R. 1974. "A Mandatory Permit System and Interpretation for Backcountry User Control in Rocky Mountain National Park: An Evaluative Study," unpublished Ph.D. thesis, Colorado State University, Fort Collins.

7.   Gallucci, Vincent F. 1976. *Clams of Garrison Bay*. Phamphlet prepared for the National Park Service, Washington, DC, and personal communication.

8.   Gibbs, Ron. 1977. "Living History and Historic Preservation: Incompatible?" *In Touch*, 1(18):11. National Park Service, Washington, DC.

9.   Iverson, Phillip R. 1976. Memo from Superintendent of Glacier National Park, Montana to Regional Director of the Rocky Mountain Regional Office.

10.   Johnson, Paul R. 1975. "Protective Interpretation," *The Interpreter*, 7(3):17–19. Western Interpreters Association.

11.   McIntyre, David. 1980. Regional Annual Report. Alberta Provincial Parks, Vulcan, Alberta.

12.   Patton, Ray. 1977. Anza-Borrego Desert State Park. Personal communication. Borrego Springs, CA.

13.   Ross, Terence L. and George H. Moeller. 1974. *Communicating Rules in Recreation Areas*, USDA Forest Service Research Paper NE-297.

14.   Schlamp, Phil G. 1976. *Interpretation as a Management Tool*. Presentation to Eastern Region. USDA Forest Service. VIS Workshop. Milwaukee, WI.

15.   Schlotter, Jack W. 1979. Personal communication. District Interpretive Specialist, Eureka, CA.

16.   Sharpe, Grant W. 1982. "An Overview of Interpretation," Chapter 1 of *Interpreting the Environment* (2nd ed.), Grant W. Sharpe (ed.). Wiley. New York.

17.   Sharpe, Grant W. 1982. "Selecting the Interpretive Media," Chapter 5 of *Interpreting the Environment* (2nd ed.), Grant W. Sharpe (ed.). Wiley. New York.

18.   Sharpe, Grant W. and Gail Gensler. 1978. "Interpretation as a Management Tool," *Proceedings, Association of Interpreters of Canadian Heritage*, Banff, Alberta. Also *Journal of Interpretation*, November 1978, Association of Interpretive Naturalists.

19.   Skellenger, Robert. 1967. *Vandalism—What We Can Do About It*. Presentation, University of Michigan, Ann Arbor.

20.   Stevens, Blair. 1977. Personal communication. Interpretive Services, Parks Canada, Ottawa.

21.   USDA Forest Service. 1976. *Forest Interpreter's Primer on Fire Management*. U.S. Government Printing Office, Washington, DC.

22.   Weeks, Glen. 1971 "Park Ranger Plan Proves Valuable," *California Parks and Recreation*, 13(2):4–5.

23.   Wilson, Atoy. 1977. Personal communication. Los Angeles Recreation and Parks, Ranger Division, Los Angeles, CA.

Interpretive Journals

Interpretive journals are obtained through membership in the following organizations.

Interpretation Canada. Association of Canadian Interpreters. Box 160, Aylmer, P.Q. Canada. J9H 5E5.

The Journal of Interpretation. Association of Interpretive Naturalists, Inc. 6700 Needwood Road, Derwood, MD 20855.

The Interpreter. Western Interpreters Association. P.O. Box 28366, Sacramento, CA 95828.

CHAPTER EIGHTEEN

CARE OF VISITORS

There may be times when the park manager will be the only official of the sponsoring agency present in the "city by the stream." In that case he or she will serve as mayor, sheriff, doctor, firefighter, maintenance superintendent, accountant, counselor, arbitrator, and host. The manager will be seen by some as one who protects rights and by others as one who interferes, by some as one who is concerned about the foliage, and by others as a damned environmentalist. Managers must occasionally try to be all things to all people. In other words, they are responsible for the care of the visitors.

VISITOR CHARACTERISTICS

There is, of course, no *average visitor*. Park visitors come from all types of cultural backgrounds, life-styles, age classes, interests, occupations, incomes, educational levels, beliefs, mental and physical capabilities, and from all geographical areas. There is at least one commonality, however: people seldom go to parks alone; they go in social groups, usually families or friendship groups.

Parks are places where informality prevails, and it is considered appropriate for strangers to interact with one another.[2] This is an interesting feature of parks—the fact that although people seldom communicate with their neighbors at home, they will smile and speak to strangers when in park settings. In fact, in parks, interac-

tion among strangers is expected, enjoyed, and even sought.[1]

The length of time that visitors stay in a park can be influenced by a park's size, the attractions in and near the park, kinds of facilities and accommodations, interpretive opportunities, location in reference to major travel routes, the length-of-stay policy, and the cost of the overnight fees.

VISITOR EXPECTATIONS

Visitors are usually looking for a particular experience when they arrive at a park. These anticipations will be influenced by their background, previous experience with parks, and motivations for visiting a park. The name of the park arouses certain expectations. For example, the words *fort*, *village*, or *homestead* indicate the possibility of it being a culturally oriented park. A park with the words *recreation area* may be seen as simply a place to have fun. One named after a person doesn't give any clues, but one with the name of a lake, mountain, wilderness or other natural feature, or one incorporating an agency designation gives a hint of what to expect.

Not every activity can or should be provided in each park. Certain parks can better offer specific activities than can other parks. It must be made clear to potential visitors which parks offer which activities and where in the park they are available. There are various ways to accomplish this, including off-site presentations, radio, TV, newspapers, agency maps or brochures, and a centralized phone information system providing prearrival information.

Prearrival Information

This is not a static body of information; some changes occur seasonally and some from day to day; for example, a popular park camping area may be filled to capacity by noon on the Thursday preceding a long holiday weekend, whereas in early autumn camping sites in the same park will be available all weekend. Agencies generally endorse dissemination of prearrival information because the users who plan ahead are more likely to have an enjoyable experience.

Response to this need, while possible on an individual park basis, really requires a central and widely available information center to fully serve the public. Such a center needs to include a means of receiving and dispensing information, information that may change rapidly. It also needs a means of storing statistical data concerning a large variety of recreational activities and facilities that might only occasionally be sought by patrons, but that, when sought, are needed quickly.

One tool of a central information center is the toll-free telephone line. This system, which must not be confused with the reservation system discussed earlier, nor the on-site information that follows, provides toll-free access to information specialists or trained volunteers. If personnel costs exceed budget resources the same lines can be answered by a recording device, which allows the calling party to leave a message on tape. A staff person can then answer periodically. It is important that this telephone number be widely publicized so the public is aware of the service.

In the United States, at least, any state-owned recreational land is a "park" in the mind of most patrons. Many generalize even further and believe that any recreational area in a given state is a state park—whether it is part of the National Park Service, the U.S. Forest Service, or a county

or a city park. Some patrons even lump all private resorts and recreational areas into their definition of a "state park." Whatever the reason for this lack of discrimination on the part of users, it suggests the need for coordinated information dispersal. An effort to establish a moderately comprehensive data system is sometimes undertaken at the state or provincial levels. In local jurisdictions, such as at the regional, county, municipal, or city level, the job is less imposing. Basic contact lists for current information about related facilities can be maintained. Updates can be made on a periodic basis through the use of mail-out questionnaires. Public agencies can be requested to volunteer information on changes for which they are responsible, and most of them will cooperate.

REGULATING NUMBERS

Regulating the number and placement of visitors is becoming more common. Regrettable though this interference might be, it is necessary to protect the resource. The numbers of people using parks need to be controlled as well as limited in certain time periods and situations.

How Many?

In the chapters on facilities and environmental impact the subject of use limits has been discussed. Most agencies establish a capacity limit and require managers to enforce it by refusing admittance to the park once that capacity has been reached. In situations where this has not been done, the maintenance of good order and fairness make it important that the agency formally adopt a capacity policy and convey to the agency head the authority to administer the policy. It is also important that the agency head provide the park manager with the needed authority and flexibility for determining when the park should be open and when it must be closed because of overcrowding.

A park currently maintaining its optimum capacity might be in trouble if visitation should dramatically increase for some reason. An improved road system leading to the park, a local population increase due to a contract awarded to a manufacturer, close proximity to a population center during an energy shortage or even a natural catastrophe such as a huge rock or snow slide, or the eruption of a volcano—all may cause visitation to increase suddenly.

Once it has been established that use limits are necessary, it is important that notice be posted at each park so that visitors are aware of the rules. It is also important for the park manager to have the posting as evidence of a rule violation if it is needed in a dispute or arrest.

Permits

There will be many circumstances when the agency will want to control the place of use, the amount of use, and the time it will take place. These controls will seek to protect people, areas and facilities. The issuance of special permits is the usual method of control. The following are some common examples: *climbing permits* to regulate the number of climbers on a mountain face and the hours when the climb may be undertaken; *trail permits* to regulate the number of people on trails (usually to control erosion); *backcountry permits* to disperse use, to ensure safety, and to register people so they can be traced should they not reach their destination on time; *fire permits* for campfires out of designated fire pits; *facility permits* to ensure the availability of ball fields or kitchen shelters for family outings and to control group use; and *research permits* for the collecting of specimens or to record and monitor authorized archeological digs.

Reservation Systems

The major factor in the establishment of reservation systems has been that of rapidly increasing park use. This use is often focused on a relatively small number of parks within a given state or province during peak usage periods such as summer months (June through September), weekends (Friday through Sunday), and holidays. At these parks prospective campers are turned away in large numbers, often after a long delay caused by traffic buildup on park entrance roads. The resulting complaints have encouraged park officials to consider instituting reservation systems (Fig. 18-1). Some popular state and national parks in the United States have had to go to a computerized or write-in reservation system, since campgrounds in these parks are often filled to capacity throughout the summer.

A related problem is the overuse of certain parks that are well known coupled with the underutilization of others. An important asset of a reservation system is the inventory of currently available sites that allows campers to switch from one park to another thus assuring distribution of use among all areas.

There are four basic reasons for reservation systems: (1) to alleviate park overuse by redistribution of campers, (2) to reduce campers' anxiety and frustrations by assuring them a place to sleep that night, (3) to reduce fuel consumption and costs by allowing campers to proceed directly to an assured campsite, and (4) to assist management and planners in serving the users.

Since the irritations and consequences of reservation systems fall rather directly on managers, it is worthwhile for them to understand the ramifications of trying to set up such a system. If and when a decision is made to develop and implement a reservation system within an agency, the following questions must be considered.

1. Should the reservation system be centralized or decentralized at individual parks? (Centralized control is essential if the system is to have the ability to redistribute campers to other parks.)
2. Should the reservation system be a manual or a computerized system? For a state-generated system, the initial cost and annual personnel cost for operations and equipment must be carefully calculated, although one can assume the computer costs and telephone charges will far exceed projections.

EAST BAY REGIONAL PARK DISTRICT
11500 SKYLINE BLVD. • OAKLAND, CALIFORNIA 94619
RESERVATION PERMIT

PARK ________ ACTIVITY ________ DATE __/__/__ 17895

AREA ________

DATE NEEDED ________ TIME: ____ A.M., TO: ____ P.M.

ORGANIZATION ________ DAY PHONE: ________

NUMBER IN PARTY ________ RENTAL FEE $ ________

CATERER INFORMATION ________ PHONE ________

ADDRESS ________

NAME ________

ADDRESS ________

CITY, STATE, ZIP CODE ________

FOR OFFICE USE ONLY
RECEIPT NO. ________
DATE OF RECEIPT __/__/__
AMOUNT OF RECEIPT $ ________

NOTE: USE OF PARK FACILITIES ARE SUBJECT TO RULES AND REGULATIONS AS DEFINED ON BACK OF THIS FORM. PERSON SIGNING THIS FORM HEREBY ACKNOWLEDGES RULES AND REGULATIONS AND ASSUMES RESPONSIBILITY FOR THEIR ADHERENCE.

X ________
SIGNATURE OF RESPONSIBLE PERSON

BY ________
EAST BAY REGIONAL PARK DISTRICT

SEE REVERSE SIDE FOR EAST BAY REGIONAL PARK DISTRICT RULES AND REGULATIONS

RESERVATION PHONE: 531-9043 FOR 24 HOUR EMERGENCY SERVICE, PHONE: 531-9300

RULES AND REGULATIONS

THE FOLLOWING RULES AND REGULATIONS ARE ENFORCED THROUGH ORDINANCES OF THE EAST BAY REGIONAL PARK DISTRICT:

RESERVATION RULES

1. RESERVATION PERMITS MAY NOT BE GUARANTEED AND FEE MAY BE FORFEITED IF OCCUPANCY DOES NOT OCCUR WITHIN 30 MINUTES AFTER DESIGNATED TIME OF ARRIVAL. THE RESERVATION CLERK MUST BE NOTIFIED WITHIN 10 DAYS IN ADVANCE OF ANY CHANGE IN ARRIVAL TIME.
2. CANCELLATIONS - NO REFUND WITHOUT PRIOR NOTICE: 30 DAYS NOTICE ON PICNICKING & CAMPING. 60 DAYS ON CLUBROOM.

ORDINANCES & REGULATIONS

A. PARK HOURS ARE FROM 8A.M. TO 10 P.M. WITH THE EXCEPTION THAT CLUBROOMS MAY BE USED UNTIL MIDNIGHT.
B. GAMBLING IS STRICTLY PROHIBITED.
C. ALCOHOLIC BEVERAGES ARE PROHIBITED WITH THE EXCEPTION THAT BEER MAY BE SERVED AT PICNICS.
D. DOGS MUST BE ON LEASH AND UNDER CONTROL AT ALL TIMES.
E. WEAPONS, FIREARMS, BOWS AND ARROWS, B - B GUNS, AND OTHER WEAPONS ARE PROHIBITED.
F. REMOVAL OF PLANTS, TREES, BIRDS, ANIMALS, OR ANY OBJECT FROM PARK LANDS IS PROHIBITED.
G. ALL MOTOR VEHICLES MUST STAY ON PAVED PARK ROADS.
H. SELLING OR DISTRIBUTING OF MERCHANDISE, PROPERTY, TICKETS IS PROHIBITED ON PARK PROPERTY.
I. FIRES ARE RESTRICTED TO CONSTRUCTED FIRE CIRCLES, BARBECUE PITS, OR BRAZIERS.

Fig. 18-1. (Upper) A reservation permit used for picnic shelters, group camps, and clubroom meeting space. (Lower) The reverse side of the visitor's copy lists both reservation rules, and park ordinances and regulations. The permit comes in triplicate. (Courtesy of East Bay Regional Park District, Oakland, California.)

3. What percentage of the sites in each park, or in the total system, should be reserved? To allow for possible error and to consider special circumstances, a small number of sites—two to six—should be withheld from inventory to act as a cushion.
4. Should the sites be assigned by drawing lots or "first ask, first receive"?
5. Should the system be self-supporting (fee charged pays for cost of system) or subsidized?
6. Should campsites be assigned by specific site number before campers arrive in a park or after they arrive?
7. Should there be year-round or just busy-season reservation coverage?
8. Should there be a toll-free or a toll telephone system? Should there be a mail request system in conjunction with the phone system, or should this be the only method used?
9. Should payment be required in advance or on the campers' arrival at the park? If there is a mail-in reservation deposit, should all

CAMPING PERMIT

SITE NO _____   NAME_____

PARK_____   NO. 723776   STREET_____

CITY_____ STATE_____

CAR LICENSE(S)_____

STATE		PET?	

NO. IN PARTY_____ NO. VEHICLES_____

			SENIOR CITIZEN		REGULAR		ELECTRICITY		INITIALS
DAYS PREREGISTERED	IN	OUT	DAYS	RATE	DAYS	RATE	DAYS	RATE	
	M D	M D							
			SUBTOTAL		SUBTOTAL		SUBTOTAL		TOTAL
RENEWAL?				+		+		=	
TOTAL DAYS TO DATE		OVERNIGHT VEHICLE PERMIT			REFUND NUMBER			REFUND AMT.	

MINNESOTA DEPARTMENT OF NATURAL RESOURCES - DIVISION OF PARKS & RECREATION

WASHINGTON STATE
PARKS AND RECREATION COMMISSION
CAMPING PERMIT
(PLACE IN HOLDER AT CAMP SITE)

NAME LAST	FIRST	M.I.
DATE	SITE NO	
VEHICLE LICENSE NO	STATE	

	FEE	NIGHTS	TOTAL
HOOK UP SITE			
TE TR MH PC O			
1·2·3·4·5·6·7·8·9·10	$4.50 X	=	
NON·HOOK UP SITE			
TE TR MH PC O			
1·2·3·4·5·6·7·8·9·10	3.50 X	=	
ORANGE PASSPORT HOOK UP SITE			
TE TR MH PC O			
1·2·3·4·5·6·7·8·9·10	2.25 X	=	
ORANGE PASSPORT NON HOOK UP SITE			
TE TR MH PC O			
1·2·3·4·5·6·7·8·9·10	1.75 X	=	
GREEN PASSPORT			$10.00
TE TR MH PC O	FREE		ANNUAL
1·2·3·4·5·6·7·8·9·10			FEE
GROUP CAMPING AREA			
TE TR MH PC O			
NUMBER OF PEOPLE	X	X	=

GROUP DAY USE RESERVATION $5.00

CHECK OUT TIME IS 3:00 PM

RANGER   CIRCLE FEE(S) COLLECTED, NUMBER OF PEOPLE, AND TYPE OF CAMPING UNIT, ENTER NUMBER OF NIGHTS AND TOTAL

CAMPER   PLEASE SEE REVERSE SIDE OF THIS FORM

629751

P & R FORM 0 220 (10 77)

Gouvernement du Québec
Ministère du Tourisme,
de la Chasse et de la Pêche
Service des parcs et du plein air   684993
DROIT D'ACCÈS AU CAMPING

NUMÉRO D'EMPLACEMENT	DATE DE SORTIE

R.A.M.Q.   NOM/PRÉNOM

SPECIMEN

N°   RUE

MUNICIPALITÉ

COMTÉ   PROVINCE

NON-RÉSIDENT: PAYS – PROVINCE OU ÉTAT

PARC OU RÉSERVE		TERRAIN DE CAMPING	NOMBRE DE PERSONNES
PLAQUE MINÉRALOGIQUE	ANNÉE DATE D'ÉMISE MOIS JOUR		
DURÉE DU SÉJOUR	NUMÉRO DU PERMIS PRÉCÉDENT	DURÉE DE PROLONGATION	DURÉE TOTALE DU SÉJOUR

PLAQUE MINÉRALOGIQUE

ÉQUIPEMENT

TENTE ☐   TENTE-ROULOTTE   ROULOTTE

CAMION-CAMPING   ROULOTTE-MOTORISÉE

TARIF

TAUX JOURNALIER	NOMBRE DE JOURS	MONTANT TOTAL
$	X	= $

SERVICES: EAU ☐   ÉGOÛT ☐   ÉLECTRICITÉ

SIGNATURE DE L'ÉMETTEUR

SIGNATURE DU DÉTENTEUR

TCP 494 Rev. (78-12)
COPIE - BUREAU D'ÉMISSION

Fig. 18-2. These examples of camper registration forms from Minnesota, Washington, and Quebec, are written in triplicate. Such permits provide a means of accounting for fees paid, give proof of payment at the campsite, and supply the agency with registration data.

or part or any of it apply toward the camping fee?

10. If a camper cancels, does the camper get a refund, rain check, or nothing?

The first season or two after converting to a reservation system park personnel must be prepared for confusion and resentment among visitors who, despite notice by media and signs, arrive without reservations.

Camper Registration

The primary purpose of camper registration is to have an acceptable means of accounting for the fees charged for an overnight stay. This is done through camper registration forms, which provide a triplicate accounting of the transactions,

one copy going to the agency fiscal officer in charge of fees, one copy remaining with the park, and the third going to the user. There are other benefits or opportunities inherent in registration, but all are secondary to the fiscal aspect. The additional benefits include a means for campers to prove a given site is theirs by right of payment, a way to locate a visitor if the need arises, and, provision of statistical data for agency or other use. Figure 18-2 illustrates three common types of camper registration forms.

Self-registration. An alternative method, *self-registration*, has been used by some agencies for many years. Policy on this matter changes as availability of personnel and other factors influence decisions. The overnight self-registration system is used in the Province of British Colum-

Fig. 18-3. The self-registration system frees staff to perform other duties. In this example visitors receive instructions from the panels (boaters at left, hikers at right). The visitor removes the registration envelope from the box at left, then fills out the requested information (see Fig. 18-4), removes the receipt portions, encloses the fee, licks the seal, and deposits the envelope in the locked deposit vault (between the signs). (Photo by Grant W. Sharpe.)

bia for both auto campgrounds and marine parks. The example illustrated here comes from Newcastle Island Provincial Park.

Newcastle Island, a marine park near Nanaimo, British Columbia, can be reached only by private boat and foot-passenger ferry. There is a resident manager, but the island is large, and the workload requires that visitors register themselves.

On arrival by private boat or ferry the visitor is notified of the self-registration system by a sign on the dock. On walking ashore the visitor is greeted by a second and more conspicuous entrance sign (see Fig. 10-10). Just beyond this, adjacent to the footpath, is the self-registration fee station, designed in this instance for both boaters and walk-in campers. The station includes two signs, a small registration box containing fee envelopes, and a locked deposit vault (Fig. 18-3). The two panels are brown-painted marine plywood. White silk-screen lettering is used, except for the fee amount, which is made of press-on

Province of
British Columbia

Minstry of Lands,
Parks and Housing

Parks & Outdoor
Recreation

SELF-REGISTRATION CAMPING PERMIT

TO VALIDATE, COMPLETE THE FOLLOWING:

PURCHASE DATE: ____________ No. OF NIGHTS: ________ AMOUNT PAID: $________

VEHICLE LICENCE No: ____________ PROV. OR STATE. ____________ ____________
CAMPSITE NUMBER

B.C. SENIOR CITIZEN EXEMPT BUT PERMIT MUST BE COMPLETED SIGNED AND DEPOSITED IN VAULT.

B.C. SENIOR CITIZEN: ____________
SIGNATURE

THANK YOU

Nº 27553

TEAR HERE

CAMPING PERMIT RECEIPT

DETACH THIS STUB AND DISPLAY AS INSTRUCTED

OCCUPIED

NO REFUNDS

Nº 27553

CAMPSITE NUMBER

PURCHASE DATE: ____________

No. OF NIGHTS ____________

AMOUNT PAID: ____________

B.C. SENIOR CITIZEN ( )
MAXIMUM STAY - 14 NIGHTS
CHECK-OUT TIME 12 NOON

Please keep this portion of receipt for your records.

Nº 27553

CAMPSITE NUMBER

PURCHASE DATE: ____________

Fig. 18-4. The province of British Columbia's self-registration camping permit. (Top) the front of the envelope, which is used to record information. (Lower) The reverse side, showing the numbered receipt and campsite display portion (left); and the smaller personal record receipt (right). When these receipts are removed from the envelope, a clear window space reveals the envelope contents.

plastic material so it can be changed if the fee changes. The envelope containing the fee and registration information (Fig. 18-4) is slipped through a slot into the double-locked deposit vault.

With minor adjustment to the wording, either of these signs could be used for vehicle registration in other types of parks. Neither vandalism nor theft has been a problem here yet, perhaps in part because the self-registration station is within easy view of the manager's residence.

It is still necessary to visit each campsite and moorage slip to see if the registration stub is displayed. If the ranger or park aide carries the forms people will not bother to register, but will wait for the park employee to arrive. This must be avoided, and delinquent users should be asked to go to the box to register. Of course it is possible to cheat under this system. Some areas state a fine will be levied or campers will be evicted if self-registration is not properly carried out.

ACCOMMODATION OF GROUPS

The basic camping unit used to be the family; however, camping today is frequently a group activity. There are several ways to provide for people who wish to camp as a group.

Group Camping Areas

These are areas in the park apart from the regularly designated overnight family–camping area. Such areas may or may not have full restroom facilities, but should at least have pit toilets and water.

A group can be any formal organization, such as Scouts, trailer clubs, special interest clubs, church members, or school groups, or it can be an organized collection of families who wish to camp together. The group must have identifiable leadership such as a president, chairman, or wagon master, or, if a youth group, at least one adult who is responsible for the minors. This leader should be able to control the group as well as represent them.

Groups in Regularly Designated Areas

Areas used by individual families may also be used for groups, provided regulations about the number of campers per site are enforced. There are campground designs suitable for groups that avoid undue burden on facilities or inconvenience for other campers. One of these is the "wheel" or "daisy," illustrated in Figure 18-5. This design provides the opportunity to use the area entirely for groups (one to six), or for a mixture of single families and groups. If the park manager chooses to mix individuals and groups or even different groups, advance planning is advisable. Groups should be separated by a greater distance than even the wheel design allows if noise level potential seems high. The wheel also provides the opportunity for the manager to close a different unit for rehabilitation every six years while the base facilities (toilets, showers, and roads) continue to meet the needs of campers.

Reservations for Groups

Advanced notice of group camping is usually encouraged so that group campers can be separated from regular campers, if possible. Reservations are usually taken by the park manager rather than through a central office.

Group Fees

Those groups camping in regular camp areas and sites used by individual campers should pay the regular fee charged the individual family unit. Those groups using designated group-camping areas should also pay a fee, but a lesser one, computed on a different basis. This is usually a fee per person with a minimum and maximum limit, based on the services and facilities provided. The purpose of this system is to encourage groups to reserve and use these areas by offering privacy and group rates while also discouraging use by one or two people, rather than an actual group. Consideration should also be given to a per-car charge as an incentive to fuel conservation.

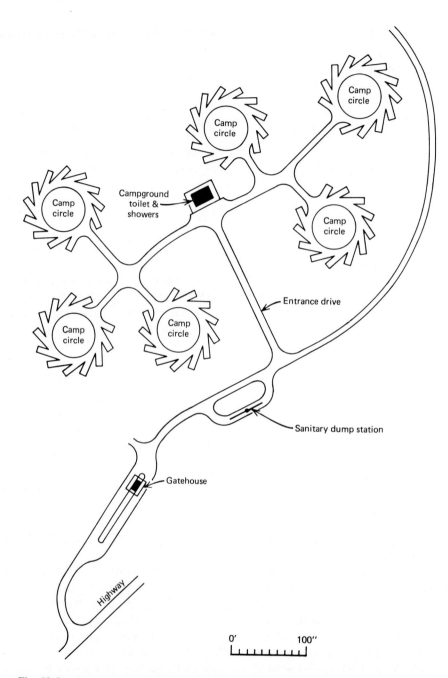

Fig. 18-5. The *daisy* or *wheel* general campground layout, consisting of a series of clusters, each of which may be used for single family campsites or reserved for groups, when needed. From Indian Lake State Park, Michigan. (Courtesy the Park Practice Program.)

Environmental Learning Camps

In many states and provinces there are special camps, either strategically located within a given park or comprising a total park within themselves, devoted to environmental learning. These camps contain sleeping and living quarters for enrollees and staff, a nurse's station, food preparation and dining areas, environmental education facilities, and recreational facilities. They are often called ELC (Environmental Learning Camps or Centers).

The objective of ELCs is to provide an opportunity for groups to participate in educational, social, intellectual, spiritual, and physical development programs in a group living situation within an outdoor environment.

These resident camping facilities are made available to school and other interested groups to provide the opportunity to live, work, study, and play in the outdoor environment. The agency provides the *facilities* and the *environment*. The *program* of utilization can be provided either by the agency or the users. It is the combination of facilities, environment, and program of utilization that makes a complete ELC.

Hostels

Hosteling is a very old, time-tested method of providing safe, pleasant accommodations for an overnight stay. Hosteling has not been as common in the United States as in Europe or Canada. Agencies engaged in hosteling try to provide a structure where the traveling public (usually youths hiking, biking, or hitchhiking) can stay overnight at minimal cost. The structure will contain basic sleeping and cooking accommodations and have a person or couple to serve as house parents.

Park managers interested in providing this sort of opportunity should determine if there are suitable unused facilities available. Those facilities might include bunkers, barracks, lighthouses, Civilian Conservation Corps buildings, construction camps, or surplus trailers. Hostels should be located away from the park campground or heavy use areas, if possible.

American Youth Hostels or Canadian Youth Hostels should be contacted to determine if the structure is suitable. At this point, if not sooner, the manager should contact supervisory personnel to obtain permission.

Group Use of Day-Use Areas

Frequently park managers will be asked to provide a picnic shelter or other place in the day-use area for groups to gather for reunions, annual picnics, or farewell parties. Meeting these requests may cause scheduling problems and increased costs. There will be a need for additional cleanup, and, these groups may annoy or inconvenience families using the facilities. Conspicuous consumption of alcohol, whether tolerated or not, sometimes complicates the situation. For these reasons, park managers might want to develop a group-use policy and also utilize a permit process. These steps, plus providing a separate area where possible, should help meet the needs of such users with minimum disruption. For the handling of more serious problems, see Group Disturbances, page 301.

PROVIDING FOR NEEDS

The users have arrived. They are in the campsites, on the diving boards, sitzmarking the slopes, exploring the caves, climbing the mountains, and snowmobiling the woods. They also are hungry and thirsty, and having emergencies—losing kids, getting hurt, awaiting an important phone call, getting bitten by animals, or becoming lost or stranded themselves. Let's look at how managers can handle these emergencies, and perhaps even prevent some of them.

Safety

Each park organization has responsibility for the safety of park visitors and park personnel. Every reasonable precaution should be taken to reduce or eliminate existing and potentially hazardous or defective conditions that might be sources of injury to persons and property. Operating procedures should provide for the detection and reduction of these conditions through an adequate program of inspection (see Chapter 11, Maintenance and Safety). When accidents or disturbances do occur, the manager must be ready.

First Aid.   First aid is defined as the immediate and temporary care given the victim of an accident or sudden illness until the services of a physician can be obtained. Visitors expect park personnel to assist them in personal injury emergencies and for this reason employees *must* be qualified to practice first aid, and should keep their training up to date (Fig. 18-6). Even seasonal employees should be qualified first aiders. If there are sufficient employees needing them, first aid classes should be conducted in the park, during working hours, if necessary. Often first aid classes are available on a regular basis in nearby communities. First aid supplies should be available in park vehicles, ranger stations, visitor centers, and elsewhere and should be checked frequently to see that they are adequate. The storage place should be well marked and highly visible.

Injuries to park visitors must be reported on appropriate forms. It is important that the necessary information on the injury be obtained as soon as possible after the treatment so that the data are accurate. Accurate information is also needed about any treatment so the manager will be able to properly represent the agency or self in a lawsuit. The park employee must not prescribe treatment or medicine unless trained to do so, nor recommend a physician. Provide the victim with a list of local doctors and let him or her make the choice of which one to go to. A respirator should be purchased if the park has water resources and employees, particularly lifeguards, should be trained in its use.

Public Telephone

Park visitors often need to make phone calls during their stay, to check on family or friends left behind, to see if there are any messages waiting at home, to conduct business, or to make plans for the rest of the trip. Phones should be outside, lighted, sheltered, and available 24 hours a day.

Fig. 18-6.   An interpreter administering first aid to a visitor. Visitors expect park personnel to assist them in personal injury emergencies. Dinosaur Provincial Park, Alberta. (Photo by David McIntyre.)

Phone books and coin boxes, as well as the booth and phone itself, are frequently targets of vandals, so booths should be placed in an area where surveillance is possible and frequently checked to make sure they are in working order, and to remove graffiti and repair minor damage. Some people seem susceptible to suggestion, so upkeep may reduce these problems.

Emergency Procedures

Regardless of how well the park is planned, constructed, and operated, there are certain situations that cannot be circumvented. Emergencies, by their very nature, are unexpected, yet demand an immediate coordinated response on the part of park personnel. These emergencies will include fires, accidents, lost persons, group disturbances, and evacuation in the event of fire, flood, severe storm threat, or other catastrophes. Emergency routes should be clearly identified and kept clear of obstacles.

Whatever the emergency, there are five basic rules common to the correct method of handling it.

1. Get *complete* information.
2. Think it through. Plan first, then act. Don't turn an emergency into a disaster by precipitous action.
3. Act to prevent compounding of the emergency.
4. Ask for assistance. Better too much than too little.
5. Alert your supervisor.

Equipment. Emergency equipment must be stored in working condition, ready to go instantly when certain emergencies arise, particularly in parks in remote areas. Such emergencies include auto accidents, trees across a roadway or fallen in a campground, and rock climbing accidents. These emergency equipment kits usually contain blankets, lanterns, floodlights, winch, ropes and other materials that the particular park has found to be essential to the handling of

their situations. Figures 18-7, 18-8, 18-9 and 18-10 show three excellent examples.

The park may have emergency equipment which is carried where needed in an ordinary park vehicle, or there may be a vehicle completely dedicated to this purpose. *Emergency medical services vehicles* and the operating personnel may be carefully regulated by the state or provincial department of social and health services. The intent is to see that all emergency vehicles, both private and public, meet acceptable standards where the transportation and treatment of prehospital victims is concerned (Fig. 18-11). Even the mechanical condition of the vehicle and its radio communications, as well as its seating space, medical equipment, and supplies must meet minimum requirements and be subject to periodic inspection. Basic medical equipment and supplies should include resuscitation equipment, litters, splints, linen supplies, dressings, and supplies for poison control, emergency childbirth, and equipment for extricating the injured from autos and other trapped conditions. The extent of these supplies and equipment differs on whether the vehicle is rated an ambulance or a first aid vehicle.

Finally, the liability insurance coverage of the operators, and their medical technician and first aid training must be certified and licensed before they can be authorized to render emergency medical care.

The need for this type of service would be indicated by the distance to regular medical facilities and by the number of visitors a park receives. If the decision be made to equip and staff such a vehicle, state or provincial standards must be met, except in federal areas, where federal standards prevail.

Lost Persons

In any survival situation the majority of hazards result from the victim's lack of preparation, inability to navigate, and ignorance of survival techniques. Survival depends on protecting one's energy from being dissipated by exertion and exposure. Anyone can become disoriented, a situa-

Fig. 18-7. Three portable wooden boxes containing emergency equipment. When checked and packed each box is secured with a metal seal. The contents are listed on the lids. Strathcona Provincial Park, British Columbia. (Photos by Grant W. Sharpe.)

Fig. 18-8. The contents of Box No. 1. At top: three wool blankets; at right one pillow in a plastic cover and two hand lanterns; the metal suitcase at left contains #3 first aid kit, as recommended by B.C. Workmen's Compensation Board and Emergency Measures Manual.

Fig. 18-9. The contents of Box No. 2. From left to right: one long and two short padded splints, chain with hooks, nylon tow rope with hooks, shovel, peevee, single bit axe, come-along (hand winch—2 ton), 30 m (100 ft) nylon rope, pinch bar, and stretcher.

Fig. 18-10. The contents of Box No. 3. From left to right: file set and saw wrench, funnel, gas and oil containers, small power saw, portable generator, spare bulb, and tripod stakes with floodlight bar and three bulbs at top. The foam rubber pad in the lid cushions the floodlights when packed.

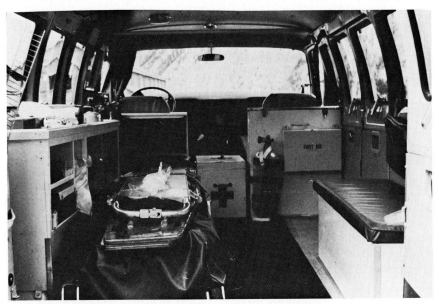

Fig. 18-11.   The interior of an emergency medical services vehicle. Yellowstone National Park. (Photo by Jeff Cobb.)

tion that can become disastrous if the individual is mentally unprepared to handle the situation. A lost person often fails to recognize the trouble signs of exhaustion, or worse yet, of incipient hypothermia, when the body cools off at a faster rate than it can produce heat to keep warm. Agencies should offer workshops and literature to train employees in the handling of this condition, as immediate action is vital where hypothermia complicates a search and rescue situation.

Excessive heat can also affect one's body and behavior. Heat will often affect older people more quickly than younger people. Temperatures that produce heat cramps in a younger person could produce heat stroke or exhaustion in an older person. Dehydration, hunger, and injury all diminish a person's ability to survive. Fear and despair may contribute to reckless behavior, perhaps ending in panic and injury.

Eliciting Information.   The most critical point of any search is securing complete detailed information *before* the search is started. Generally, this information will, in the long run, speed up

the actual finding of the person, thereby decreasing exposure time and rescue hours.

Questioning of the informant should be the responsibility of the most experienced person available, because considerable persuasion and tact is sometimes necessary to get the essential information from distraught relatives or friends. A form should be used, so that all necessary information is elicited and available for future reference. When you have the details, alert your immediate superior at once, and ask for more help than you think you need.

If the lost person is a child, immediate action is often crucial and sometimes someone should be sent to the area even before questioning of the informant is completed. This is especially vital if the area is on a river, lake, busy highway, or other location where danger to children is immediate. These danger areas should be checked first and the search designed so as to intercept the child before he or she can reach the high-danger areas. Insist that someone, preferably a parent, remain at the campsite and impress on the parent the need to notify you immediately if the child returns.

The Search. Children in the woods seldom follow an obvious route. They may go through a patch of brush rather than around it. They may actually cross a trail and go right back into the brush. Do not expect logic from them. Do not count on a reply to your calls, even if you call by name, since they frequently panic at the sound of strangers calling their name.

In contrast, adults will generally follow the line of least resistance—that is, go around brush, avoid heavy cover, and often go downhill. (Occasionally, however, an adult will climb a hill or peak for a better view.) Therefore, if the general vicinity of the person is known, search such places as natural paths, stream drainages, game trails, clearings, and approaches to logs across streams for signs of passage. An adult will generally respond to signals and behave logically but may panic and run to the point of helpless exhaustion in a very short time.

Search and rescue procedures should be set up with local law enforcement agencies, usually the county sheriff, and volunteer search and rescue groups in order to facilitate swift action. Few emergencies are so urgent that a manager can afford to tie up manpower and drastically lower response capability overall, so the services of volunteer groups are to be welcomed.

Group Disturbances

The surveillance, reporting, and containment of unruly groups is one of the most difficult jobs a park manager has. Human life and public property must be protected, taxpaying campers must be protected from each other, and yet the manager must attempt to keep community goodwill both personally and for the agency he or she represents.

Disturbances come from a variety of sources and manifest themselves in many ways. In some instances, the people involved are simply a group of young people out for a good time, but it could be people who are drunk or on drugs and people who have knives and guns. Some of these people care what others think, while others have no regard for their reputations. Some will respond to the warden's or ranger's warning promptly, almost with appreciation for being stopped before they make fools of themselves. Others will challenge authority instantly, perhaps viciously.

The appearance on the scene of vehicles marked with identifying authority and uniformed personnel with badges in evidence will sometimes be sufficient to control such situations, and should be used before more severe measures are contemplated.

Generally speaking, the role of the park ranger will be one of planning: observing, collecting data, reporting, coordinating, and helping local law enforcement officials, rather than actually quelling the disturbance with physical force.

Groups with Special Needs

We need to recognize that neither "the handicapped," nor "the elderly" are very accurate designations. The range of abilities, disabilities, needs, and desires encompassed by these catchall titles is wide. Managers should cultivate an awareness of these differences. Beechel's *Handbook*, cited in the General References, is useful in this respect. The facility and service needs of the disabled and elderly must be considered in the planning process. This is a legal responsibility in most instances where federal, state, or provincial funds are used for public buildings. It is also a moral commitment now recognized after many years of ignoring the problem. Today there are approximately 36 million physically or mentally disabled people in the United States alone. It's no wonder many of these people regard the rest of the population as temporarily able bodied.

Another good reason for accepting the responsibility lies in the fact that the elderly comprise an ever-increasing percentage of the population. The number of disabled venturing out to public recreation areas also seems to be increasing.

Disabled Visitors. Disability is a handicap. There now is considerable thought being given, in Canada and the United States, to assisting the handicapped in enjoying the outdoors. To provide for wheelchairs, trails are being hard surfaced, railings placed at fishing decks, and ramps and special toilet facilities installed in recreational buildings. While it is recognized that all special provisions cannot be installed in all facilities immediately, agencies still have the responsibility of incorporating all possible adaptations to provide barrier-free access.

The needs of the blind are also being recognized. Interpretive labels are made with routed or raised letters, audio stations are used, and activities are being scheduled that include and subtly assist these and other visitors who need special consideration. Some interpreters are learning sign language to communicate with the deaf and hard of hearing.

Retired and Elderly Visitors. Sometimes the concerns of the disabled and the elderly merge as age imposes its limitations, but generally speaking, those visitors to recreation areas who have reached retirement age and beyond have different potentials, problems, and needs than do the disabled; indeed, they vary greatly among themselves. Some will be out hiking your backcountry, others will be eyeing your interpretive exhibits for historical accuracy, while still others will be interested mostly in your restrooms. Fixed incomes are sometimes a problem, but these visitors also have the advantage of plentiful free time. Special programs are now designed to suit their social needs and rich store of experiences. Where possible these programs should be conducted by a person of mature years and scheduled for the off season when the crowds have lessened.

Many park agencies offer reduced rates for single admission, or a seasonal or year-round passport that senior citizens can obtain for a reasonable amount. This passport also encourages camping in the off season, thus easing the crunch during the summer and holiday season. In federal areas in the United States the Golden Eagle Passport is the best known and most widely used example of special consideration for visitors of and beyond retirement age. Note, in Figures 18-3

and 18-4, that British Columbia senior citizens are exempt from overnight camping fees.

Accessibility

As a service to disabled persons each park should have a handout stating the access problems and opportunities for people requesting such information. A suggested title is *General Information for Disabled Visitors*. This handout should provide a brief description of those services and facilities that have disabled persons access. A map of the park, noting access areas, could accompany the handout. The International Symbol of Access should be displayed at primary public

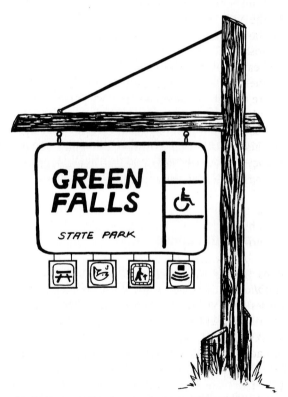

Fig. 18-12. The International Symbol of Access displayed at a park entrance. As new activity areas become accessible, the symbol sign is added to the main sign. The symbols here indicate a picnic area, fishing site, interpretive trail, and amphitheater as having total access. (Courtesy of Kathryn Sharpe.)

contact points, such as entrance gates, fee collection booths, and visitor centers. As individual activity areas become accessible, symbol signs indicating accessibility could be suspended from the main sign (Fig. 18-12).

Food and Water

If food service is adequately provided in close proximity to the park, there is no need for the service to be provided by the park. However, if food service is not being provided, the park should do so. These provisions might range from a "Mom and Pop" short-order stand to a full-fledged restaurant or grocery store. Again, the park manager should be concerned for the health of the park patron and assure that the proper sanitary conditions exist for the preparation and disposal of food.

Clean, potable water is a most precious but frequently taken-for-granted commodity. Even where there is an adequate supply of good water, samples should be taken regularly in order to detect contamination. Any failure of responsibility in this matter might lead to serious consequences. Streams, lakes, and rivers also need testing at regular intervals. Backcountry water supplies present a problem. Drinking from remote mountain streams was once considered safe, but as park use has increased many streams are now contaminated. Hikers and backpackers must be warned through brochures or on-site signs to boil their water. The disease, *Giardia lamblia*, results from a protozoan parasite that causes stomach pains and diarrhea. The disease usually infects streams through the feces of muskrats and beaver. Infected humans can spread it in the same way, and should therefore be encouraged to void their body wastes well away from any water source.

Where there is a scarcity of water not only must the public be warned of that scarcity in advance, but they should be informed as to *why* there is a lack of water, and the *need* for water conservation should be emphasized and its use regulated.

Toilet Facilities

One of the most crucial services in any park is the provision of toilet facilities. Visitors who notice nothing else will comment on this aspect of their park experience. The park employees and the agency will be criticized for everything from the odor in pit toilets to the cost of the construction of flush pumper stations.

Managers should give careful attention to maintenance of floor, mirrors, waste paper receptacles, toilets, and urinals, and be sure adequate supplies are available. Out-of-order or vandalized facilities must be repaired as soon as possible, both for the visitors' convenience, and to prevent further damage. Chapter 11 (Maintenance and Safety) covers this topic in more detail.

Firewood

Providing free firewood for campers has mixed results. Some people appreciate it and use it wisely, but many waste it or carry it home.

A supply of wood should reduce the impact on the forest floor near campgrounds and certainly it is good for public relations. Parks where wood is not provided are often compared unfavorably to parks where wood is available. What isn't mentioned is the tendency of campers to build larger-than-necessary fires when the supply is free, or to carry wood off with them when they leave, in case the next park doesn't supply it, or, as noted, to take it home. Local people also may drive into the park and load up the trunk of their cars with firewood. In spite of these problems, some parks supply wood for their campers, especially if a good supply is conveniently located.

Having a central wood bin makes hauling in wood easier for the park staff. Sometimes mill ends are available from a nearby lumber mill or box factory, often at no charge to the park.

In heavily used campgrounds, where the demand is great enough, firewood may be sold either by the park staff or a park concessioner (Fig. 18-13). Two advantages stem from this

Fig. 18-13. Here the wood supply is handled through a concession. The shed is open during specified hours of the day. The employee is seen stacking the wood into a pipe frame. This device assures that "arm loads" are of similar size. Cougar Rock Campground, Mount Rainier National Park. (Photo by Grant W. Sharpe.)

practice: campers conserve wood and keep fires smaller, and if they haul wood away with them it's wood they have paid for. It is also possible that a modest profit may be made in the transaction. Agency policy may allow these monies to be used within the park.

INFORMATION

Once visitors have decided which park they want to stay in, and have arrived in the area, the need for information does not lessen. It changes, however. There will be a need for a different sort of information from that offered by the reservation and central information services. It will be more detailed and site specific, yet will be wide ranging, as these visitors seek to satisfy individual needs and interests.

Outside the Park

Since parks and other recreational lands are prime tourist attractions, entities other than the land managing agencies themselves may well have information available. Sometimes merchants will offer this as an incentive to sales. Automobile service stations may have maps and information about what is available in the area. Retail stores dealing in camping and recreational supplies often have similar information and may even hire clerks who have specialized knowledge about park features or popular local recreation activities.

Libraries may have special exhibits on natural or historical areas and certainly should be sources of information and publications about recreation land in the area and elsewhere, as should bookstores. Local radio and television stations may also have features or announcements that publicize such areas. Newspapers are a good source of information, and in some areas publish special editions seasonally, specifically dealing with regional tourist attractions. Motels and hotels often distribute these and other material on nearby areas.

Grocery stores sometimes have posters or free handouts, and stores in remote areas, such as on islands or in the backwoods, often serve as combined bookstores, bulletin boards, guide service contacts, and local knowledge repositories.

Billboards erected by chambers of commerce, highway signage, and tourist information centers are all important checkpoints as visitors near their goal, the park itself.

Managers should be aware of these sources as they represent an advance guard, giving out information and regulatory data and also present an opportunity to create an atmosphere that can help in achieving management goals. Try to ensure that the facts given are correct and that the relationship with these sources is friendly. Certainly these local entrepreneurs will appreciate knowing about any important changes in regulations or other pertinent matters such as road conditions or hazards. If there is no time to maintain such a liaison, volunteers might be found who will handle this for the park.

Within the Park

Once visitors reach the park, everyone with whom they speak should be able to supply information, even if all this person can do is direct the questioner to the place where answers may be obtained. This applies to all employees, from the maintenance worker mowing the lawn to the manager walking from the truck or car into the office at headquarters. A continuous effort must be made to assure that all personnel are informed about current activities, and they should be well aware of the location of information centers in their park.

Interpretive Services. Increasing visitors' enjoyment of the park, contributing to resource protection, and forwarding understanding of the managing agency's objectives: these are the goals of interpretive services. In Chapter 17, the many personal and nonpersonal approaches to interpretation available to park managers are discussed. Four of these are also mentioned here, because of their roles in information dispersal.

Information Duty. In the larger parks certain people are employed specifically to answer visitors' questions. Often they are located at an entrance station, at a visitor center, or placed on roving or point duty in order to effectively cover areas of visitor concentration.

The person on information duty not only greets and informs the new arrivals but is a tangible representative of the agency and, as such, is performing in the area of public relations perhaps more definitively than anyone else the visitor will meet during the park stay. For this reason, appearance and politeness must be stressed. A pleasant, mature personality is indispensible as the information post will also be a magnet for complaints. Employees must be instructed in the proper way to handle these. An-

other useful adjunct to information services is a checklist of nearby services and supplies.

Publications. Some areas have a map and informational handout to give to visitors when they enter the park or make contact at an information station. This may be as elaborate as a broadside with color or as simple as a single-folded sheet. It can carry informational, educational, and regulatory messages and will help orient and direct the visitors both geographically and behaviorally.

Limited Range Broadcasting. This means of transmitting information might be available to managers of certain areas. Most automobiles today have AM radio, and visitors can be advised by roadside signs to tune in to a certain frequency to obtain park information. In Canada's Rocky Mountain national parks limited range broadcasts are used to warn of avalanche danger, as well as to provide information and interpretation. In some areas in the United States they are used to disseminate information on accommodations.

Bulletin Boards. Nearly every park unit has a bulletin board that serves as an information center 24 hours a day. Display of park information

Fig. 18-14. An example of a modular system of displaying information. Each category is laid out separately with clear titles and boundaries. The board looks clean and neat. (Courtesy of Gary and Sally Machlis.)

Fig. 18-15. A typical bulletin board with its paper plates and outdated personal messages. Provision of blank note cards would help reduce this clutter. Official messages could be placed on a separate board, as in Fig. 18-14. (Courtesy of Gary and Sally Machlis.)

should be given careful thought. It must be kept to an essential minimum and must look fresh to be accepted as up to date (Fig. 18-14). Regulatory messages are often found here, as well as an orientation map.

That portion of the board devoted to personal messages should have blank cards available, and users should be instructed to date their messages so that they can be removed after a reasonable length of time. Bulletin boards present an image of the park and of your management style, so it is well worthwhile to take the time to keep them in good order (Fig. 18-15).

Administrative Signs. Several kinds of administrative signs may be distinguished, each with its informational message. Besides entrance and directional signs, these are as follows.

Regulatory Signs. The preservation of park values requires regulation. The messages in each park informing the public of these essential rules should be firm but friendly and, where space and subject permit, contain an explanation of the regulation. A positive approach should be employed wherever possible. Long lists of "do nots" might be largely ignored, or might serve as a primer for beginning vandals. It is also important to avoid proliferation of signs, as this reduces effectiveness, and certainly the resultant clutter is unattractive.

An increasing number of park agencies are utilizing international graphic signs that not only avoid the use of the words "NO" and "DO NOT," but also carry the message to park guests not speaking the official language.

Construction Signs. Where construction work is in progress or imminent, signs should be prominently placed informing the public about the new facility, the approximate date of completion and any other matters germane to good public relations. Warnings of danger to passersby or trespassers in the work area are also essential for safety and liability reasons. Frequently these signs will be the property or responsibility of the construction company; however, the agency, through the manager, must monitor .placement and clarity of the signs throughout the duration of the construction period.

Recognition Signs. As the title implies, these are for public relations purposes and usually recognize cooperating agencies or call public attention to donors or officials. They are important. The three most common uses are as follows.

1. *Acquisition.* Today most parks are acquired via funds from more than one source. This may be noted on the entrance sign, and perhaps elsewhere on a separate sign.
2. *Construction.* Construction too may be funded by more than one source, and these will probably be designated on the facility.
3. *Dedication.* These provide the opportunity to recognize the governing political officials as well as those who are cooperating in the program.

Placement and care of all types of recognition signs reflects your attitude toward your agency, and sets an example of respect, or lack of it, for park visitors to observe.

CONCLUSION

The composite annual total of visitor days to federal, state, provincial, and local park areas in North America is in the billions. During whatever time of the 24-hour period that these visitors are in the parks, their care is of prime concern to the park staff.

All too frequently, park professionals secretly or openly express the sentiment that visitors are a necessary evil and the land itself is all important. This attitude must be replaced with one of balanced concern: care for the visitors and care for the resource. The main reason a park agency exists is to provide places where the visitors can recreate. Preservation is paramount, conservation is crucial—but both are for naught if we do not care for our visitor-guests in such a way that they enjoy and appreciate their park experience.

REFERENCES

General References

Beechel, Jacque. 1975. *Interpretation for Handicapped Persons: A Handbook for Outdoor Recreational Personnel*. National Park Service, Cooperative Park Studies Unit, College of Forest Resources, University of Washington. Seattle.

Brockman, C. Frank and Laurence C. Merriam, Jr. 1979. *Recreational Use of Wild Lands* (3rd ed.). McGraw-Hill Book Company. New York.

Christiansen, Monty I. 1977. *Park Planning Handbook*. Wiley. New York.

Machlis, Gary and Sally Machlis. 1974. *Creative Design for Bulletin Boards*. National Park Service, Cooperative Park Studies Unit, College of Forest Resources, University of Washington. Seattle.

Magill, Arthur W. 1976. *Campsite reservation systems . . . the campers viewpoint*. USDA Forest Service Research Paper PSW-121. Pacific Southwest Forest and Range Exp. Stn., Berkeley, CA.

Sharpe, Grant W. (ed.). 1982 *Interpreting the Environment* (2nd ed.). Wiley. New York.

Stanford Research Institute. 1972. "The Need for and the Implementation of a Fee, Charge, and Reservation System for the Washington State Parks and Recreation Commission." Menlo Park, CA.

Sternloff, Robert E. and Roger Warren. 1977. *Park and Recreation Maintenance Management*. Hollbrook Press, Inc. Boston, MA.

References Cited

1. Cheek, Neil H., Jr. 1970. "Today's Park Visitor, Who Is He and What Facilities Does He Need?," *Proceedings of Recreation Management Institute*. Texas A&M University, College Station.
2. Field, Donald R. and J. Alan Wagar. 1982. "People and Interpretation," Chapter 3 of *Interpreting the Environment* (2nd ed.), Grant W. Sharpe (ed.). Wiley. New York.

PART FIVE

ON THE JOB

CHAPTER NINETEEN

THE PARK MANAGER

It is time now to consider park managers—the agency's representatives, the people on the front line in park management. To many observers, the work of the park manager seems romantic and ideal for a person interested in the outdoors. To others it is a chance to be of service to humanity, while to some, of course, it is "just a job." Many people do not realize that dealing with *people* (rather than *land and water resources*) takes up a large part of a manager's time. For this reason, persons wishing to be in the outdoors and away from humanity would do well to consider the full range of skills and talents needed to be happy and successful as a park manager.

A Day in the Life of a Park Manager

To help illustrate the diversity of the manager's experiences, examples of a typical day's activities were obtained from practicing managers. From a large, multistaffed state park came this response about a day in July.

6:00 A.M.	Meet with morning shift seasonal park aide crew. Assign work for the day.
6:30	Patrol park. Check for vandalism.
7:00	Go to the park office. Prepare money for day's camper registration and prepare money transmittal of previous night's receipts.
8:30	Receive complaint from camper that

people in site next to them were partying, cursing, and playing the radio at 3:00 A.M.

8:40	Investigate camper complaint.
9:15	Park aide informs me the muffler on the park truck is disconnected or has a hole in it. Very noisy! I tell him I'll be right up to fix it.
9:25	Another park aide says the urinal in the restroom is stopped up and the floor flooded. She cannot get it unplugged.
9:30	Unplug urinal. Have park aide mop floor.
10:15	Patron finds me at restroom and wants to make arrangements for a family reunion in our day-use reservation area.
10:35	Go back to office with patron and give her forms for a day-use reservation.
10:50	Phone rings. "I been tryin' to get ahold of you guys all morning! Doesn't anyone work around there? What I called about is renting a cabin." I give him the private resort's phone number to rent a cabin.
2:50 P.M.	Meet with night shift rangers coming on duty. Discuss days happenings and status of ongoing work in park.
3:10	Go to park interpretive center and

ask interpretive assistant if he has any concerns or operational problems. All is well.

3:45 Back to office to open mail and take care of any immediate correspondence requirements.

4:30 Check beach area again and check in with lifeguards.

4:45 Decide to go home for the day. Have worked almost 10 hours. (Many things did not get done, but there never seems to be enough time.)

4:55 Administer first aid to park patron for an abrasion on his foot.

5:05 Get information from victim and complete accident report.

5:20 Leaving office when phone rings. Private resort down the road two miles informs me an adult was just in and purchased two cases of beer for four minors (informant saw him give it to the minors) in a gray Pontiac and he thinks they're heading for the state park to camp.

5:25 Locate night duty ranger in the camp area and inform him about the phone call and to be on the lookout.

5:35 Go home for the day . . . Darn! Forgot about that muffler!

The next example comes from the manager of a small state park having only one permanent employee (himself) and several seasonal park aides. His log recounts a day in August.

2:02 A.M. Awakened by telephone. It's a park visitor who drove back to town to call the park to find out why he's been locked out of the park.

5:45 Awakened by telephone. Where are the fish biting?

6:00 Awakened by park aide starting truck. Stayed up.

7:50 Arrive at contact station to find a line of 11 vehicles at entrance to see about getting a campsite. We are completely full.

8:00 Put all employees on job assignments and routine duties.

8:15 First patrol of park.

8:40 Help park aide repair malfunctioning mower.

9:06 Irrigation system turned on.

9:30 Asked four campers to put dogs on leash. Told three campers to put extra vehicle in extra-vehicle parking lot.

10:15 Discovered break in irrigation line. Shut down system. Drove to town for replacement part.

11:30 Installed part and turned on system.

11:50 Break up keg party just starting.

12:15 P.M. Lunch break.

1:00 Park patrol resumed. Issued citation to vehicle blocking boat launch.

2:13 Motorcycle gang enters park and heads for the day use area.

3:00 Check lifeguards at the beach.

3:20 Break up confrontation between visitors over campsite mixup.

4:00 Patrol day use area. Evict motorcycle gang for drinking.

4:35 Turned over money and registration books to night shift park aide. Check mail. Add to pile of correspondence and paper work waiting to be done.

5:00 Dinner break.

5:45 Camper stops at house instead of park office to ask questions about fishing on the lake.

7:00 Patrol park.

10:00 Close park entrance gate.

10:15 Patrol campground. Ask campers in two campsites to turn off loud music.

10:30 Escort campers to vacant campsite and register them.

11:00 Finish patrolling park. Turn over duties to night park aide.

11:15 Camper stops at house and asks how he can get into the park since the gates are closed.

For most parks in North America summer is the busy season. What does the park manager do in the winter? Here is a typical day in December.

8:00 A.M.	Opened up park entrance gate, raised flags; noted deer tracks at entrance.
8:30	Phoned in weather data. Two inches of new snow overnight.
8:40	Patrolled park. No evidence of poaching. Told a family where the sledding hill is located. Removed small windfall from the road.
10:00	Opened mail; answered inquiries.
10:30	Worked on park slide-tape program. Needs some winter use slides.
12:00 P.M.	Lunch break.
1:00	Worked on equipment maintenance.
3:00	Took 2 hours adjusted time off.

Are these unusual days? Not really, although most agencies encourage their managers to try to limit their duty hours to the regulation eight.

This is particularly important for those with law enforcement responsibilities. Knowing how to handle people seems paramount. Knowing how to repair various facility and equipment problems runs a close second. Let's take a look at the skills and abilities that are demanded of park managers.

PERSONAL QUALIFICATIONS

Presumably persons interested in park management are personally interested in outdoor recreation activities as participants, perhaps as fishermen, hunters, hikers, mountain climbers, or skiers. They may have a desire to share this enthusiasm and skill with others. Some may just wish to be closer to the recreation opportunity or away from the city scene. Perhaps it is an interest in natural resources that makes such a career seem desirable. Often working as a seasonal employee in a park sparks an interest in pursuing a career in park management (Fig. 19-1).

Fig. 19-1. Seasonals often become interested in permanent park work. For instance, driving a tour bus would acquaint a person with the situation and opportunities. LBJ State Historical Park, Texas. (National Park Service photo by Fred E. Mang, Jr.)

A student considering a career in park management will need more than a desire to participate in outdoor recreation or a concern for environmental protection, however. The park manager must *like people* and *be able to cope with visitors* and the strange behavior they sometimes exhibit when in the park setting.

A career in professional park management requires considerable preparation. Some of the skills and knowledge can be learned; some of the talents required to do a good job have to be inborn. Certain work may require physical strength and stamina. At other times the energy goes into being a diplomat while performing such tasks as directing and correcting park visitors, placating adjacent landowners, deferentially escorting elected officials, or conversing intelligently with other park professionals.

Successful park managers must get their ideas accepted by decisionmakers, must be arbitrators of conflicts, must create the conditions for obtaining favorable public support, and must get the necessary funding to manage their park. Managers must have the ability to supervise their employees, to understand their needs and desires, and to handle delicate personnel problems. Management tasks also include the handling of funds, therefore honesty and responsibility are essential.

Ideally, park managers should be good communicators. They are often called on to give talks to school groups, sportsmen's clubs, garden groups, local civic organizations, or environmental groups, so they must be familiar with the preparation of talks and slide presentations, including the use and care of audio-visual equipment. They have to write effectively, for their work requires more than just filling out accident reports. They must write news releases, letters of reprimand, letters of recommendation, letters of apology, and acknowledgments of critical or complimentary correspondence from the public.

Yearly, quarterly, monthly, weekly, and even daily reports will be required, and timeliness and thoroughness of their completion will be noted by superiors. The amount of paperwork and the time it demands will probably be greater than the beginning manager envisioned. Good record keeping and systematic filing procedures will help keep the paper jungle from closing in.

Park managers are usually public servants, and as such, are sometimes challenged and criticized by the public. When such criticism is a result of misunderstanding or is unjustified, they must be able to exhibit patience and tolerance, waiting for time and facts to vindicate them rather than speaking out hastily in self-defense. If they must comment on a situation they must make their points calmly, objectively, and succinctly.

The ability to remain calm while acting effectively when natural disasters or other emergencies occur is another requirement. As stressed in preceding chapters, managers need to be trained in law enforcement, search and rescue, and firefighting. Ability to do small motor repair and some basic knowledge of automobile and truck repair are very useful skills and should be diligently sought at every opportunity. Skills should also include some general maintenance and construction ability, since managers may need to up-

Fig. 19-2. An Alaska park ranger patrols his state park in a snowmobile. (Photo by Neil Johannsen.)

date exhibits, repair machinery, or determine what is wrong with a faulty water supply or a stopped-up sanitation system. They will have to order the parts, and, very possibly, fix the problem themselves. As pointed out in Chapter 10, Park Facilities, keeping these utilities functioning is of primary importance.

Skills such as marksmanship, scuba training, motor maintenance, mountaineering, horse riding and packing, medical technician, seamanship, navigation, and piloting may prove useful.

Park managers need to be in good physical condition. They must be able to travel on foot across country, handle a horse, paddle a canoe, or run a snowmobile ((Fig. 19-2). Map and compass skills are expected of such persons.

Even if it means taking some of their days off to visit remote areas, managers must know the park thoroughly. This means familiarity with its plants, animals, soils, watersheds, forest cover types, history, and geology.

Park managers must realize they are part of a bigger system. They do not own the parks they manage; they are only custodians. There must be responsiveness to the public concerns. Certainly managers must not attempt to operate the park independently of region and headquarter's directives.

A good disposition, a well-groomed appearance, a mature philosophical outlook, and a pleasant, friendly personality completes our list of assets and accomplishments that experience has proven desirable for park managers to have (Fig. 19-3).

EDUCATIONAL REQUIREMENTS

Those who specifically study for resource-oriented park management follow a four-year curriculum in forest or wildland recreation, outdoor recreation, park management, or a closely related field. Because of the way civil service specifications are written, however, people with degrees in other professions are often qualified for these same positions.[1] Examples would be graduates in wildlife sciences, forest management, wa-

Fig. 19-3. A well-groomed appearance and friendly personality are assets that have proven to be useful in park work. Here a park ranger checks with a biker at Lake Meridith National Recreation Area, Texas. (National Park Service photo by Fred E. Mang, Jr.)

tershed management, engineering, and other natural sciences. In some instances a two-year technician program may be sufficient. When competition is keen, the four-year degree usually means greater success in advancement. Some agencies prefer people with a police science background so they can readily assist in law enforcement and vandalism problems. Some management positions may be filled with people having business administration or political science backgrounds; these candidates must work up through the ranger ranks in order to gain the necessary experience for higher-level positions.[1]

Ideally, students in the field of park management obtain experience while still in college as seasonal park aides or recreation assistants. This practical experience complements their academic courses. After graduation and perhaps another season or more of field experience, the park management graduate should be able to pass the civil service entrance exam for park ranger, warden, or other entry-level position.

Another route to managerial positions is through the interpretive role. Specialists such as botanists, zoologists, geologists, historians, archeologists, and anthropologists, who work in the interpretive division, may feel their career advancement is limited. After several years work in their specialty they may apply for park manager positions. Many of these people have excelled as managers.

Whatever field the ranger comes from, the steps leading to a position as manager usually include an entrance-level position in a large park, followed by some upward movement in the same park prior to transferring to a more responsible position in a small park, then back to a larger park or even to another agency (Fig. 19-4). As rangers gain experience, develop confidence and become aware of their deficiencies, they seek new parks that will contribute to their educational experience. In some agencies the rise from ranger to upper-level manager may involve several steps or grades.

Education never stops. Ambitious men and women in park ranger positions looking toward management will take specialized courses or training sessions in a variety of topics. Anything that contributes to skills and qualifications for park work is suitable (Fig. 19-5). Such courses include in-depth training in aspects of law enforcement, mountain rescue, public and staff relations, public speaking, business techniques, interpretive methods, and writing skills as well as the other possibilities mentioned under Personal

Fig. 19-4. Park rangers often start out in small one-person parks before advancing to larger ones. The duties in a one-person park could encompass everything—including maintenance. Newcastle Island Provincial Park, British Columbia. (Photo by Grant W. Sharpe.)

Fig. 19-5. A park ranger practices mountain rescue techniques by rapelling down a rock face in a Maryland state park. (Photo courtesy Maryland Park Service.)

Qualifications. These can be obtained through interagency courses and workshops, correspondence courses, and extension and short courses at colleges and universities.

Administrators, when hiring or considering an employee for advancement, look to see if the person has taken advantage of learning opportunities in the form of transfers from one park to another. Has the person attended a reasonable number of training sessions? Has the person spent money out of his or her own pocket to take pertinent correspondence courses? Such actions show enthusiasm and interest in the job and deserve special recognition and reward through advancement. There is no reason why learning should stop after graduation from college.

AGENCY EXPECTATIONS

The park agency has a right to expect certain things from employees who aspire to become park managers. Employees must show a willingness to conform to reasonable and traditional standards of dress and personal grooming habits. Ignoring the suggestions of a supervisor, and thus of the agency, is not the way to advance a career.

The manager is expected to avoid any actions or behavior that would embarrass the agency, including any activity that might appear to be a conflict of interest. When in doubt the manager or ranger should seek counsel from supervisory personnel.

The agency expects the manager to be an exemplary citizen, who works with the community by becoming involved in school activities, contributing to charities, by joining service or business clubs, or perhaps by teaching some skill or craft.

A potential manager must be able to accept, as well as offer criticism, and to show respect to both those above and below in the chain of command. The employee should be willing to defend the agency position and to remain silent on matters of policy if his or her personal views conflict with the official stance. If this is not possible, and if suggestions submitted through the chain of command have not resulted in change, resignation may be the answer. Remember however, that change is often a gradual process.

Most agencies expect employees to move every few years in order to round out their experience and to enable them to move up the promotional ladder. For various reasons some park areas are more desirable than others, but a variety of situations is necessary, and the inevitability of such moves must be understood at the outset.

The manager is the agency's local representative. He or she should be aware of any potential or simmering conflicts that might need attention, either personally or from a higher authority. The manager should also be on the lookout for any land opportunities on the park boundaries, that may be added to the park through gift or purchase.

Anyone in a park uniform is a ranger as far as the public is concerned, and all employees, no matter what their position, must respond to visitors' requests promptly and politely. Managers and other supervisory personnel set a powerful example for employees by their manner and voice as they answer some routine query from a visitor.

PERSONAL AND PROFESSIONAL PROBLEMS

By their very nature, resource-oriented parks are often located in sparsely settled parts of the country that lack the amenities of urban living. Much of the joy of working in such parks, however, is the opportunity to live in a remote area, perhaps in a superlative setting. This is particularly true if, after specializing in the field of outdoor recreation in college, the years of hard work in a city are now climaxed with a professional position in a beautiful area. One is very happy, thinking of what a wonderful place this will be to live, particularly in the off season, when the pace is slower. Unfortunately, this joy is not always shared by a spouse, particularly if the husband or wife is city oriented and finds the long winters, scorching summers, or isolation a problem.

One might not be all that isolated. But living near small towns has drawbacks as well as rewards. The cultural activities of the city, such as concerts, plays, first-run movies, good radio stations, and fine restaurants are wanting. The library services are probably minimal, and employees sometimes feel the world is moving along without them. Then there are the local people who make the park employee's business their business, thus putting further strain on personal relationships and perhaps even on a marriage.

The employee and family living in and managing isolated parks ideally should have strong self-generating interests, perhaps in music or crafts, or areas of study that can be pursued without outside or community resources.

When both people in the marriage are rangers, new complications arise. In many instances policy prevents a married couple from working in the same park, which can cause duress. One may be able to work in a different division within the park, but that may require one spouse to sacrifice his or her career goals. Perhaps it will be necessary for the couple to set up two households, or for one to commute long distance—neither of which does much to enhance a marriage or career.

Another problem may come when it's time to send children to school. The park may be so isolated that transportation becomes a hardship because of winter road conditions. Some park families have to board their children out during the school year. This is expensive, and the separation may be difficult for all involved. More than one ranger or manager has had to either leave the job or ask for a transfer to a less remote park in order to solve the education problem.

The isolation has another drawback, sometimes called social in-breeding. Often the people one works with during the day are social companions at night, because there are simply no other people around. This constant exposure to the same personalities is usually rather wearing on the nerves and can take the freshness and challenge out of both relationships. It can also make objective supervision and discipline extremely difficult, if not impossible.

Isolation or small town living may not be the problem. As the emphasis in parkland acquisition shifts toward urban recreation sites, many prospective rangers find their first job far from their fantasy. Isolation is the *least* of their worries. Stresses associated with law enforcement, rescue operations, "graveyard" work shifts, constant radio traffic, vehicle operation on busy roads, vandalism, and city living can take their toll quickly.

Where housing is provided by the agency, an annoying paradox may exist. The manager and spouse are assigned the spacious quarters, even if their children have left home, while the rangers with young families probably live in cramped quarters. The perquisites of authority thus create a situation, which, while understandable, does nothing to promote community harmony.

Even worse, it can be a real shock to eventually

be moved to a location where no park housing is provided. Here the manager and family must rent at high prices, or try to buy. If they've always lived in park housing, they find they have no equity built up to provide the down payment. So unless they have savings, they must rent—at high prices—and with nothing to show for it when the next transfer comes. For these reasons it is important to invest or save an amount equivalent to rental during tenancy in agency housing.

In parks where there are very few employees, the office phone is often wired to the house. This means the employee's spouse must answer the phone when the manager is not in the office. Some spouses enjoy this involvement; some don't. Acceptance by the spouse of the conditions of employment is critical, as this person plays a very large role in determining the employee's attitude.

Other problems associated with living in the park include the fact that the public doesn't always respect the manager's privacy, and some visitors feel it their right to call any time of the day or night, often for trivial or mistaken reasons. Another drawback is constantly living under park rules, such as not being allowed to have pets in the park. Yet the park employee and family must "live with" park wildlife, and this can be a nuisance or even a threat. Another dampening edict is that personal goods cannot be displayed for sale.

Finally, there is the relationship between the manager and the local community. Resource-oriented parks are usually found in areas where the local population is politically conservative. The park, surrounded by forest, farm, or ranch lands, is often regarded as an irritating intrusion. Acceptance of the manager can be colored by the attitudes the local people have toward the agency, toward the former manager, and even by their attitudes toward authority figures generally. Resentment dies slowly. For example, if a local person was arrested a few years ago for hunting illegally in the park, or for speeding, it possibly resulted in a heavy fine. Resentment

over this may last a long time, lingering even after the previous manager has moved to a new location.

Usually the area newspaper aligns itself closely with the local population, and its staff may take pleasure in criticizing both the agency and manager. This newspaper will often prove to be a source of admonition and advice to managers through editorials, and in the tone and subject of feature articles. It will provide a forum for irate citizens via the letters to the editor.

Neighbors may well come from different educational and religious backgrounds, and have different values from park personnel. Hardworking, independent people, these neighbors will not be easy to get to know. Park personnel will have to work with them and live in their community awhile before they will be accepted. Some will remember the area before the park came. Some will tend to be suspicious, even hostile, to any government agency or its employees. However, although approval from all may never come, park personnel should be able to win respect.

If these attitudes annoy the manager, he or she may react by becoming isolated from the community. In some instances problems such as loss of perspective, hostility, depression, and perhaps even illness, alcoholism, or drug addiction may result. Under these circumstances the manager becomes less effective as an agency representative, to say the least.

Managers are most effective when they have the support of the local community, so they must expand social contacts beyond the park family. They should become involved in civic and community activities and intelligently seek ways to strengthen social relationships with the local population. This will mean occasionally giving evenings to meetings or entertaining when one might rather be pursuing personal interests.

But this involvement with local people may yield valuable historical information about the park. It can invite local people to share their feelings about the direction they think park management should go. When the public sees park employees out of uniform, they discover managers and rangers are more like themselves than not.

Special Problems of Women Rangers and Managers

As women rangers are still considered to be in a ''nontraditional role,'' they may have a few additional problems to contend with. In many instances, before she even speaks or acts, she is resented by the local community on three counts: (1) as a figure of authority, (2) as an employee of the park that once was their home or pasture or neighbor's land, (3) as a woman in a ''man's job'' (especially if she carries a weapon). Her smile, demeanor, and confidence level thus become very important. If she is prepared and perseveres she will gradually be accepted.

Additionally, it is often difficult for a woman park employee to be accepted by park families. There may be resentment by wives who feel insecure about the time the female ranger spends with her husband on patrol in isolated areas. Wives may feel jealous of her novel career especially if she is a manager. This requires additional sensitivity on the part of the woman employee.

Special Problems of Law Enforcement

Where law enforcement is a part of the park responsibility, additional personal problems can arise for men or women. Vigorous training is required along with frequent upgrading of qualifications. For some, law enforcement is the least desirable aspect of the job, yet there is little hope that this role will become any less important in the future. For the family, this adds a certain tension, as concern for the employee's welfare increases. In many instances, rangers or managers are also required to go out at night to deal with emergency accidents and law enforcement situations in the park and to act as assistants to the other peace officers.

THE REWARDS OF THE JOB

With a little care and foresight, park living can be very rewarding. It is a job that requires special skills and education, a job that is out of reach for many. The location will be the envy of most, for part of the salary comes in the form of scenery; living in a place people on vacations may visit, but where the park employees can live all year. It is a special kind of environment, close to the natural world. The income is usually sufficient to support a family. There is also the personal satisfaction of knowing park work is of service to society (Fig. 19-6). Increasingly, authority and respect are gained.

After a beginning employee completes the climb through the ranks from seasonal aide to ranger or warden to assistant manager, and fi-

Fig. 19-6.   There is personal satisfaction in knowing park work is of service to society. (Utah State Division of Parks and Recreation photo by Kay Boulter.)

nally, to manager, there are still opportunities. During the course of this rise, one accumulates a wealth of knowledge through exposure to day-to-day problems in a variety of parks. When the intricacies and challenges of the job, once exciting but now somewhat predictable, start to become annoying, it might be time to move on to a district or regional office where this experience can be put to good use. With the children gone or off at college the employee and spouse can move into the fine big house in the best park in the system and entertain visiting dignitaries.

For those who excel at politics and demonstrate superior management abilities, there is always the agency's headquarters office. One of the complaints often heard in the field is that the people at headquarters lack field experience. For the truly dedicated manager who may also have felt this way, here is another chance to be of service. Perhaps another agency or state will offer an administrative position. One might even end up in Washington DC or Ottawa—removed from the natural setting but with the chance to assist in long-range policy or planning.

CONCLUSION

A park is a great laboratory filled with endless surprises for those sensitive to the environment. The addition of visitors creates another dimension, one filled with challenge, frustrations, and laughter; the basic ingredients for great memories. Whichever is your strong desire—preservation and conservation of our natural and cultural resources or working with people—you will have the opportunity to give of yourself.

Albert Schweitzer perhaps said it best: "I don't know what your destiny will be, but one thing I know; the only ones among you who will be really happy are those who have sought and found how to serve."

REFERENCES

General References

Sutton, Ann and Myron Sutton. 1965. *Guarding the Treasured Lands. The Story of the National Park Service*. J.B. Lippincott Company. Philadelphia, PA.

References Cited

1. Sharpe, Grant W. 1979. "Outdoor Recreation," Chapter 5 of *Careers in Conservation: Opportunities in Natural Resource Management*, Henry Clepper (ed.), Natural Resources Council of America. Wiley. New York.

INDEX

Page numbers in **bold face** refer to photographs or other illustrations